W9-BGJ-712

The George W. Bush Presidency

WITHDRAWN

The George W. Bush Presidency

An Early Assessment

Edited by
Fred I. Greenstein

The Johns Hopkins University Press

Baltimore and London

The Johns Hopkins University Press
2715 North Charles Street
Baltimore, Maryland 21218-4363
www.press.jhu.edu

Library of Congress Cataloging-in-Publication Data

The George W. Bush presidency: an early assessment / edited by Fred I. Greenstein.
 p. cm.
 Includes bibliographical references and index.
 ISBN 0-8018-7845-4 (hardcover: alk. paper) — ISBN 0-8018-7846-2 (pbk. : alk. paper)
 1. United States—Politics and government—2001– . 2. Bush, George W. (George
Walker), 1946– . I. Greenstein, Fred I.
 E902.G46   2003
 973.931′092—dc22   2003017428

A catalog record for this book is available from the British Library.

The chapters in this book were originally presented at the conference "The Bush
Presidency: An Early Assessment," held at the Woodrow Wilson School, Princeton
University, April 25–26, 2003.

To Julie J. Kidd

with continuing appreciation

Contents

Contents

Preface

EVEN THE MOST committed proponent of the thesis that political outcomes are mainly the product of impersonal historical forces is bound to acknowledge that individuals can make a difference, particularly when they are as pivotally placed as the president of the United States. It was not a force of history that authorized the use of nuclear weapons against Japan or transformed the American advisory mission in South Vietnam into a full-scale military intervention; it was Harry S. Truman and Lyndon B. Johnson.

The historical record provides the basis of innumerable thought experiments about the impact of the occupant of the Oval Office. When President Johnson took the first steps in what was to become a half-million-troop commitment in Vietnam, for example, Vice President Hubert H. Humphrey unsuccessfully urged him to use his talents as a politician to avoid going to war in Southeast Asia. What if Johnson had passed from the scene and Humphrey had been thrust into his place? It cannot be proven that a President Humphrey would have steered clear of the Vietnamese quagmire, but it is likely that he would have.

A thought experiment that bears directly on this volume on the unexpectedly eventful presidency of George W. Bush is prompted by the razor-thin outcome of the election of 2000. What if it had been Al Gore who had been inaugurated as president on January 20, 2001? *Any* White House incumbent would surely have responded roughly as Bush did to the acts of terrorism of September 11, 2001. To remain passive would have been to court impeachment. But it is unlikely that a President Gore would have gone on to wage war in Iraq, and Gore almost certainly would not have sought to revive a flagging economy with a massive tax cut.

Given the multitude of ways in which a chief executive can shape events, it is not surprising that each new presidency is met by a deluge of reporting and commentary. Most of the outpouring is the work of journalists and members of the political community, but scholars have increasingly joined the chorus. In so doing they bring distinctive assets to bear, including analytic clarity, rigorous reasoning, sensitivity to complexity, and the ability to place new developments in a historical context.

Although analytic detachment is another desideratum of sound scholarship, the reader of this work will quickly learn that its contributors do not proceed in lockstep. Some of them are clinically neutral in their dissection of Bush's performance, but others advance distinct points of view, ranging from near awe at the skill and will with which Bush has advanced his purposes to deep concern about the merit of those purposes. On one matter, however, there is broad agreement—this is a president who (as he has put it) should not be "misunderestimated." Bush's first two and a half years in office are likely to assure him of more space in future history books than the eight years in the White House of the president who preceded him.

The first three chapters of this work examine Bush the man, his political methods, and his White House. My own chapter on Bush's political style reviews his early years, business and political careers, and early presidency, commenting on his emotional and cognitive qualities, communication ability, organizational capacity, political skill, and policy vision. Hugh Heclo's contribution also traces Bush's life and works, but with a view to identifying the "guiding beliefs" that underpin his presidential leadership—his political ethos. A principal element of that ethos is the Bush family's dedication to public service, a three-generation commitment that began with Connecticut Senator Prescott Bush and has continued from President George H. W. Bush to President George W. Bush.

In Chapter 3 Karen M. Hult examines how Bush has organized his White House. Hult's comparison of George W. Bush's White House with the White Houses of his recent predecessors provides a reminder of the extent to which the modern presidency has developed a generic organization, a little-noticed development in an institution that lacked a clearly articulated structure before the presidency of the organizationally astute Dwight D. Eisenhower in the 1950s.

Chapters 4 and 5 examine the two areas in which Bush's policies have departed most dramatically from Bill Clinton's: budgetary policy (Allen Schick) and foreign policy (Ivo H. Daalder and James M. Lindsay). The authors of both chapters are critical of the policies they examine. Schick argues that the tax cuts that have been the centerpiece of Bush's domestic program have had their intended effect of depriving government of the resources to advance ambitious domestic policies. But, Schick continues, the first wave of the post–World War II baby boom generation will be reaching retirement age before the decade is over, and future administrations will be left with inadequate resources to address its needs.

Daalder and Lindsay describe Bush as "a surprising foreign policy revolutionary" in that he spoke out against an expansive foreign policy in the 2000 presidential campaign, but has signed off not only on major military commitments in Afghanistan and Iraq, but also on ambitious peace-keeping and nation-building efforts in those nations. In the authors' view the Bush administration has taken a "hegemonist" approach to international relations, devoting its energies more to maintaining the overwhelming military supremacy of the United States than to building and nurturing alliances. The danger of such a focus, Daalder and Lindsay warn, is that other countries may "decide they have had enough," and America may become "a great power shackled in the pursuit of its most important goals."

Chapters 6 and 7 examine complementary facets of the Bush administration's relations with Congress. John C. Fortier and Norman J. Ornstein frame their analysis with an account of how Bush related to the state legislature during his time as governor of Texas. Adapting to that body's heavily Democratic majority, Bush practiced a flexible bipartisanship. But in Washington the Republicans were in control on Capitol Hill when Bush took office. In that context, his approach was to mobilize virtually every Republican lawmaker behind his policies and win over a handful of conservative Democrats. The common denominator between Texas and Washington appears to be Bush's own political style, which is flexible, but issue-driven and highly determined. He will compromise when he has to, but given the choice he will strive for results that are as close as possible to his policy aims.

Charles O. Jones's chapter focuses on the demanding partisan environment Bush faced in the first Congress of his presidency. Although the Republicans controlled both houses of Congress when Bush took office, their margin of control was very narrow. And in May 2001, control of the Senate shifted to the Democrats following the defection of Vermont Senator Jim Jeffords from the Republican Party. As Jones remarks, one might have expected Bush to be cautious in advancing his program, in view of both the even division in Congress and the closeness of the 2000 election. Instead, boldness was his watchword. He sought ambitious aims and advanced them by taking skilled advantage of his position as the nation's highest elected official. Jones concludes with a point-by-point elucidation of Bush's operating methods, a set of prescriptions from which any new chief executive would be bound to profit.

In Chapters 8 and 9 attention shifts from the political stage to its audience. Gary C. Jacobson and Richard A. Brody explore the links between the American public and the Bush presidency, including the public's shifting evaluations of Bush's job performance. As Jacobson notes, Bush has had "the longest stretch of approval ratings over 60 percent of any president in forty years," but as Brody shows, after each surge in crisis-induced public approval, "Bush's approval ratings have been subject to steady erosion."

As both authors make clear, public responses to Bush and his presidency have been highly dependent on events. In the first week of September 2001, Bush returned from a vacation at his Texas ranch with the lowest Gallup Poll rating of his fledgling presidency—51 percent. Then, in the wake of September 11, the nation rallied around its commander in chief, and Bush's approval level soared to 90 percent. But the senior Bush had also experienced record-high public approval in 1991, yet had gone down to defeat the following year. It is appropriate, therefore, to echo Yogi Berra: "It ain't over till it's over."

The volume's final contribution is a distinct novelty in a collection of essays by scholars—a view from within the presidency under consideration. As Hult notes in Chapter 3, presidents typically highlight some of their policy innovations by setting up special offices in the White House to advance them. George W. Bush did this in the case of his White House Office of Faith-Based and Community Initiatives, a body that was headed by University of Pennsylvania political scientist John J. DiIulio, Jr., during the early months of his presidency. Professor DiIulio concludes the volume with a report on what he observed about the workings of the Bush presidency and reflections on how his experience in the Bush White House has affected his scholarly perspective on the presidency.

The contributions to this volume are revisions of papers delivered at a conference on George W. Bush's presidency held on April 25 and 26, 2003, at Princeton University's Woodrow Wilson School of Public and International Affairs. It was to the advantage of the paper-writers that they had the comments of participants in two roundtables, one of political scientists and the other of journalists. The political scientists were Colin Campbell, University of British Columbia; Martha Joynt Kumar,

Towson University; Thomas Mann, Brookings Institution; and Bert A. Rockman, Ohio State University. The journalists were Dan Balz, *Washington Post;* Ken Bode, Medill School of Journalism, Northwestern University; Carl Cannon, *National Journal;* Jeanne Cummings, *Wall Street Journal;* and Todd Purdum, *New York Times.* Also included in the second group was the former press secretary for President Clinton, Mike McCurry.

Particular thanks are due to two dedicated members of the staff of Princeton's Woodrow Wilson School for their work on the conference and the conference volume: Diane Price and Helene Wood. This volume and the conference that preceded it were sponsored by three units of Princeton's Woodrow Wilson School: the Center for the Study of Democratic Politics, the Center for International Studies, and the Program in Leadership Studies. The conference was funded by the last of these units, drawing on the income from an endowment provided by the Christian Johnson Endeavor Foundation. It is a pleasure to dedicate this volume to Endeavor Foundation President Julie J. Kidd in appreciation of the foundation's continuing generosity to the Woodrow Wilson School.

The George W. Bush Presidency

Chapter 1

The Leadership Style of George W. Bush

Fred I. Greenstein

GEORGE W. BUSH is the twelfth in the sequence of White House incumbents of the period that began with the presidency of Franklin D. Roosevelt. In the course of F.D.R.'s three terms and one month in office, the United States became a nascent welfare state and global superpower, thus vastly increasing the responsibilities of its chief executive. Meanwhile, the presidency itself underwent a metamorphosis: the president began to take on much of the traditional congressional function of setting the nation's policy agenda, the presidency acquired major staff resources in the form of the Executive Office of the President, and the persona of the occupant of 1600 Pennsylvania Avenue became a ubiquitous presence in the nation and the world, a development that was made possible by advances in the technology of modern mass communication.

Such is the institution George W. Bush inherited from his eleven modern predecessors. What has he added to its legacy? What is his leadership style, and how has it evolved during his unexpectedly eventful presidency? How successful has it been? In what follows I provide a basis for exploring these questions by reviewing Bush's formative years, political ascent, and early presidency. I then characterize his political style in terms of the categories I have employed elsewhere for studying presidential leadership—emotional intelligence, cognitive style, effectiveness as a public communicator, organizational capacity, political skill, and policy vision. I conclude with a paradoxical observation about how the presidency of George W. Bush could come to resemble the otherwise strikingly different presidency of his father.[1]

Formative Years

George W. Bush was born on July 6, 1946, in New Haven, Connecticut, where his war hero father was a Yale undergraduate.[2] In contrast to George H. W. Bush, whose claim to be a Texan is belied by his Eastern accent and diffident manner, George W. Bush is very much a product of the Lone Star State. Whereas the elder Bush attended a private day school in the wealthy New York suburb of Greenwich, Connecticut, the younger Bush went to public school in the West Texas town of Midland, where oil was the dominant economic force and the ambience was that of tract houses, Little League baseball, and easy informality. Acknowledging the difference between his Connecticut-bred father and himself, Bush has commented that while his father is mild-mannered and avoids confrontation, he has the brashness and directness of a typical Texan.[3]

In 1953 the Bush family was devastated by the death of George's three-year-old sister, Robin, from leukemia. The seven-year-old George, who had no idea that his sister was gravely ill, was stunned when he was taken out of school and told that his sister was dead. His mother sank into a depression. His father was at a career stage in which he was frequently away from home on business, and the son sought to be his mother's consoler. He did so by playing the clown, developing the bantering manner that is one of his adult hallmarks.[4]

After completing elementary school in Texas, George followed in his father's footsteps, attending two intellectually rarified schools in the Northeast—Phillips Academy, in Andover, Massachusetts, and Yale University. He had unhappy experiences at both. At Andover he wrote a composition about the wrenching experience of learning of his sister's death, but used an inappropriate word to refer to the tears he shed. He was deeply hurt when the instructor ignored the content of the paper and criticized him for the way it was written. At Yale he was offended when the college chaplain commented that his father had been beaten by "a better man" in his 1964 run for the Senate. The ironic effect of Bush's exposure to Andover and Yale was to alienate him from what he came to think of as the "intellectual snobs" who set the tone of these institutions.

Bush was a lackluster student in prep school and college, but was conspicuous for his social skills and popularity. At Andover he became the football team's head cheerleader and "high commissioner" of a tongue-in-cheek stickball league. At Yale he won ready admission to a fraternity that was legendary for its parties and beer consumption after revealing that he could name all of his fifty-odd fellow applicants. (None of the others could name more than a half dozen.) Bush went on to become the fraternity's president and to win admission to Yale's most exclusive secret society, returning to Texas with friendships that served him well when he ran for public office.

Bush's freshman year at Yale saw the beginning of the American military intervention in Vietnam. By his senior year the campus was wracked with anti-war protest. The political ferment of the 1960s largely passed Bush by, but he was far from indifferent to politics. In 1964 the eighteen-year-old Bush took part in his father's race for the Senate, delighting in the camaraderie and ballyhoo of campaign politics. By his mid-thirties he had worked on the campaigns of two other senatorial aspirants and participated in his father's unsuccessful campaigns for the Senate in 1970 and for the Republican presidential nomination in 1980.

After Yale Bush spent two years in the Texas Air National Guard and went on to Harvard Business School, graduating in 1974 with an MBA. He then returned to Midland, first holding an entry-level position in the oil industry and then forming an oil exploration company with funds raised through family connections. In 1978 the congressman in the district that included Midland announced that he was retiring, and Bush entered the race to succeed him. He won the Republican nomination, but lost the general election to a conservative Democrat, who portrayed him as a carpetbagger from the Northeast and a representative of his party's moderate wing. Nevertheless, he received 47 percent of the vote in a traditionally Democratic congressional district and learned a lesson he took to heart when he reentered electoral politics—that of refusing to be outflanked from the right.

There is another theme in Bush's early adulthood. For most of the two decades after he graduated from college, he was conspicuous as the underachieving son of a superachieving father. He drank to excess and had a devil-may-care lifestyle that was marked by periodic alcohol-related scrapes. Gradually his life came together. In 1977 he married the level-headed librarian Laura Welch. In 1981 he became a father. During the next several years he experienced a spiritual awakening and became a regular reader of the Bible. Then, after waking up with a fierce hangover on the morning of his fortieth birthday, he swore off alcohol, anchoring his resolve in his Christian faith.

Pre-Presidential Political Career

Oil prices plunged in the 1980s, and Bush's oil exploration company went deeply in the red. Because of favorable provisions in the tax code, he was able to sell it for $2.2 million to a firm specializing in takeovers. The sale coincided with the initial stage of his father's efforts to become the 1988 Republican presidential nominee. Bush moved his family to Washington and became co-director, along with the veteran political consultant Lee Atwater, of his father's campaign. Bush's account of the part he played in the campaign provides insight into his managerial philosophy: "I was a loyalty enforcer and a listening ear. When someone wanted to talk to the candidate but couldn't, I was a good substitute; people felt that if they said something to me, it would probably get to my dad. It did only if I believed it as important for him to know. A candidate needs to focus on the big picture, his message and agenda, and let others worry about most of the details."[5]

After his father's election, Bush returned to Texas, where a promising business opportunity came his way. He was asked to organize an investment group to buy the Texas Rangers, a second-tier major league baseball team that had come on the market. Bush was an ideal fund-raiser. He had never struck it rich in the oil business, but he had been successful in raising capital, and it did not hurt that his father was president of the United States. He assembled a consortium of investors that purchased the team, naming him its managing general partner. With new leadership and greater resources, the team prospered, hiring star players and finally making its way to the play-offs. Bush proved to be an excellent front man. He became a popular speaker at meetings of Texas business, civic, and athletic groups, and was regularly seen on television, rooting for the team from the sidelines. Before long he was a state celebrity.

Baseball was Bush's political springboard. It publicized him, demonstrated that he could manage a complex organization, and gave him financial independence. After his father was defeated for reelection in 1992, Bush felt free to resume his own political career. The next year he entered the running to become the 1994 Republican opponent of Ann Richards, the state's feisty, popular Democratic governor. Assembling a highly professional campaign staff, he raised an impressive war chest and handily won his party's nomination.

Bush's next hurdle was the outspoken Richards, who had famously declared at the 1988 Democratic convention that the senior George Bush had been born "with a silver foot in his mouth." Richards derided the younger Bush, calling him "Shrub." Rather than replying in kind, Bush ran an issue-driven campaign. Taking as a warning his father's failure to enunciate a clear policy vision during his time as president, Bush ran on a small number of explicitly stated issues that already had a degree of support in the Democratically controlled legislature—greater local control of education, welfare reform, stiffer penalties for juvenile offenders, and limitations on the right to litigate against businesses. He campaigned vigorously, staying on message and ignoring Richards's provocations, and won with 53 percent of the two-party vote.

Bush conducted his governorship in a whirl of face-to-face communication and give-and-take. Even before the election results were in, he forged a bond with the legislature's most influential Democrat. Upon taking office, he formally proposed the program on which he had campaigned. By the end of the first legislative session he had advanced that program in over one hundred meetings with lawmakers of both parties. All four of his signature measures were enacted. Although he had gone along with compromises in their provisions, Bush declared victory and went on to run for a second term in 1998.[6] He was reelected with a record 69 percent of the vote, drawing strongly from such traditionally Democratic groups as women and minorities.

As governor Bush was sweeping in his acts of delegation. A study of his Texas schedule found that when he received a lengthy report on a tragedy in which a number of Texas A&M students had been killed in a bonfire, he read neither the report nor its executive summary, leaving it to his aides to highlight a few paragraphs of its conclusions. Even in the sensitive realm of capital punishment, Bush relied heavily on the recommendations of his aides, reducing the time he spent on reviews of death sentences from 30 to 15 minutes in the course of his governorship. There was a laid-back quality to his management of his time as governor, including an extended midday break during which he worked out and had lunch.[7] It was by no means obvious that he would seek higher office.

To the White House

As the 2000 presidential primary season approached, the Republican Party's kingmakers were acutely aware that their party needed a strong presidential candidate if it was not to go down to defeat as it had in 1992 and 1996. Bush's name recognition and electoral record in Texas made him an instant front-runner, a status that enabled him to raise a record $90 million in campaign funds. Bush suffered a stinging blow in the New Hampshire primary, where he was defeated by Arizona Senator John McCain, but he rebounded, clinching the nomination in March with victories in California, New York, and seven other states. Vice President Al Gore locked in the Democratic nomination the same week, and the candidates girded themselves for the longest presidential campaign in American history.

As he had in his quest for the Texas governorship, Bush campaigned on a small number of tirelessly reiterated issues, including proposals for lower taxes and reforms of education, health, and Social Security. His policies, he asserted, reflected his commitment to "compassionate conservatism." He was an economic conservative, he explained, holding that cutting taxes fosters economic growth, but he recognized that there was no assurance that the benefits of conservative economic policies could reach all groups in society. He therefore favored continuing such government welfare programs as Medicaid and instituting new programs designed to help the disadvantaged, for example, by enabling students in "failing schools" to attend good schools and making it possible for federal funds to be made available to church-based charities.[8]

Bush said nothing in the campaign that anticipated his administration's major military involvements in Afghanistan and Iraq, much less its commitment to rebuild those nations economically and politically. Indeed, he declared his opposition to a globally expansive foreign policy, criticizing the use of the American military in "nation building." The danger of an assertive foreign policy, he declared, was that the United States would be disliked for its arrogance, whereas "if we are a humble nation, they'll welcome us."[9]

Whatever the electoral appeal of Bush's policies, it was widely held that he was unlikely to defeat Gore. The vice president represented the incumbent administration in a period of prosperity, he had far more governmental experience than Bush, and he was a formidable debater. But the economy began to sag, Bush held his own in the presidential debates, and Gore ran an uninspiring campaign. As Election Day approached, the public opinion polls showed Bush and Gore to be running neck and neck. What resulted was one of the closest and most controversial election outcomes in the nation's history. Gore ran ahead in the popular vote by a fraction of 1 percent, and the all-important electoral vote was also a near tie.

The outcome of the election hinged on Florida, where Bush and Gore were in a dead heat and there was a bewildering array of controversies about the mechanics of the voting. There ensued a thirty-six-day impasse over the Florida vote count, which was broken by a five-to-four ruling of the United States Supreme Court that made Bush the winner. On the evening of December 13, Gore conceded. Within the hour, Bush made his victory speech, doing so in the chamber of the Texas House of Representatives. He had chosen that venue, he explained, "because it has been home to bipartisan cooperation," adding that "the spirit of cooperation we have seen in this hall is what is needed in Washington, D.C."[10]

A Bland Beginning

Given the intensely controversial conclusion of the 2000 presidential campaign, Bush might have been expected to assume the presidency in a firestorm of contention. In fact, the political system's healing processes had set in. The media coverage of Bush's inauguration focused on the dignified pomp of the occasion, not the legitimacy of the process that had led up to it. Bush seemed at ease as he took the oath of office, and his 14-minute inaugural address, the work of talented speechwriter Michael Gerson, was free of apologetics.

The address was widely praised for its eloquence. Taking its theme from Bush's frequent campaign references to "compassion," it declared that "the ambitions of many Americans are limited by failing schools and hidden prejudice and the circumstances of their birth," promising to "reclaim America's schools, before ignorance and apathy claim more young lives." The speech went on to enumerate the issues on which Bush had campaigned: Social Security and Medicare reform, tax reduction and strengthening of the nation's military defenses. Its final passage began with a rhetorical question asked of Thomas Jefferson by one of his contemporaries during the dark days of the American Revolution: "Do you not think an angel rides in the whirlwind and directs this storm?" It concluded with the questioner's assertion that "an angel still rides the whirlwind and directs this storm."

Despite the moving imagery of Bush's address, its effect left much to be desired. Bush's delivery lacked dramatic force and was weakened by his propensity to stumble over words and pause mid-phrase instead of at logical breaking points. By the time Bush arrived at the address's peroration, his halting presentation made it obvious that he was reading a script rather than speaking in his own voice. Bush was more fluent on unscripted occasions, but then there was the risk that his lack of national experience would lead him to misspeak, as he did three months later in an April 26 interview in which he stated that the United States was committed to do "whatever it takes" to defend Taiwan from attack by the People's Republic of China. In fact, it had long been American policy to remain vague about how it would respond to such a contingency, and Bush had not intended to signal a policy departure. The State Department was compelled to engage in damage control, saying that Bush had only meant to highlight the seriousness with which the United States took its relationship with Taiwan.[11]

There was another problem with Bush's early public communications —their infrequency. Bush never addressed the nation from the Oval Office until the night of September 11, 2001. He never convened a full-fledged, prime-time press conference until a month after that date. He periodically responded to questions from reporters, but did so in snap exchanges with the White House press pool, avoiding preannounced press conferences in which he would face the heavyweights of the media. Bush also took a minimalist approach to communicating with the public on occasions when presidents often speak out as the nation's symbolic leader. Thus he made no statement to the nation when the city of Cincinnati was wracked with racial unrest and did not join in the welcoming ceremony for the crew of a reconnaissance plane that had been held captive in China for eleven days. Three months into the Bush presidency, the *Washington Post*'s David Broder devoted a column to Bush's neglect of the bully pulpit, saying that it had left the American people without a "clear definition" of their new leader.[12]

Yet in other respects Bush exhibited impressive strengths—for example, in organizing his presidency and advancing his program. Bush made his most important organizational choice even before he became his party's official nominee, in choosing as his running mate the Washington-wise, strategically shrewd Dick Cheney, opting for someone who would compensate for his own lack of national experience rather than serving mainly to balance the ticket or share the burdens of campaigning.

With Cheney as a source of advice, Bush appointed an experienced White House staff and cabinet, not waiting until the resolution of the Florida electoral dispute to engage in transition planning. Bush's appointees included veterans of the Ford, Reagan, and first Bush presidencies, and two of Bush's longtime Texas aides, political strategist Karl Rove and communications adviser Karen Hughes. His national security team was particularly well seasoned: the secretary of state (Colin Powell) had been chairman of the Joint Chiefs of Staff and national security adviser, the secretary of defense (Donald Rumsfeld) had previously held the same position, and the national security adviser (Condoleezza Rice) had been a White House foreign policy adviser.

The political skill the Bush team displayed in promoting its legislative agenda is explored in this volume by the chapter of Charles O. Jones and that of John C. Fortier and Norman J. Ornstein. Suffice it to say that Bush and his associates had notable successes not only by practicing the bipartisanship that Bush lauded in his victory speech but also by dint of rigorous partisanship. On the bipartisan front, Bush began his presidency by launching what the media referred to as a "charm offensive," meeting with a wide range of Democrats. He put particular effort into wooing Massachusetts Senator Edward Kennedy, whose cooperation was necessary to pass Bush's education bill, inviting the Kennedy family to the

White House for a screening of a film on John F. Kennedy's handling of the Cuban Missile Crisis and naming the Justice Department building for Robert Kennedy. By the end of the year Congress enacted an education bill with provisions favored by legislators on both sides of the aisle. In praising the outcome, Kennedy declared, "President Bush was there every step of the way."[13]

But earlier in the year Bush had focused single-mindedly on mobilizing the congressional Republicans and a handful of Democrats to enact his proposed tax reduction. Here, too, he was open to compromise, first pushing for the $1.6 trillion cut he had requested and then settling for $1.35 trillion. Four months into the Bush presidency, however, the administration's hard-edged partisanship boomeranged. On May 24, Vermont Senator James Jeffords, a moderate Republican, announced that he was resigning from his party and becoming an independent, though he intended to vote with the Democrats. Bush and the Republican congressional leaders had sought to punish Jeffords for voting for a smaller tax reduction than Bush had called for by eliminating a dairy program that was vital to his state. Jeffords's defection placed the Democrats in control of the closely divided Senate.

On the eve of the fateful events of September 11, there was a widespread view in the political community that Bush was out of his depth in the presidency. Still, there were signs that he was growing into the job. In the April episode in which the American reconnaissance aircraft was forced down by China, for example, Bush's first response had been to issue a peremptory demand that the plane be returned and the crew released. He then backed off, remaining patient while negotiations went on to release the crew. And in August he gave a thoughtful address to the nation on the complexly controversial issue of funding embryonic stem cell research, making it evident that he had begun to recognize the importance of the teaching and preaching side of presidential leadership. Nevertheless, the second Bush presidency was not off to an auspicious start.

Terror and Transformation

Bush was visiting a Sarasota, Florida, elementary school to promote his administration's "No Child Left Behind" education bill on the morning of September 11 when he was informed that an airliner had crashed into the north tower of the World Trade Center. When a second airliner crashed into the south tower fifteen minutes later, it became evident that the first collision had been no accident. By mid-morning a third plane had crashed into the Pentagon and the twin towers of the World Trade

Center had collapsed. Before leaving the school, Bush read a statement declaring that "terrorism against our nation will not stand."

Because there was concern that he would be targeted by terrorists, Bush was flown to an Air Force base in Louisiana, where he made another public statement, and then to the control center of the Strategic Air Command in Nebraska, where he presided by electronic means over a meeting of the National Security Council (NSC). At the meeting the director of the Central Intelligence Agency reported that the attacks were almost certainly the work of Al Qaeda, an Afghanistan-based terrorist organization that had been behind other acts of terrorism directed at the United States. Bush then returned to the White House, where he addressed the nation from the Oval Office, declaring that the attacks were "acts of war," that there "would be a monumental struggle between good and evil" in which "good will prevail," and that the United States would "make no distinction between the terrorists who committed these acts and those who harbor them."

In the chaotic first day of the episode, Bush came across as less than fully self-assured. He read his statements from Florida and Louisiana mechanically and did not seem fully at ease as he delivered his September 11 address to the nation. But then he underwent a transformation. On September 14 he delivered a moving tribute to the victims of the terrorist attacks at a memorial service at Washington's National Cathedral. He then flew to New York City, where he inspected the wreckage of the World Trade Center, using a bullhorn to address the rescue workers. When members of the audience shouted that they could not hear him, Bush replied, "I can hear you. The rest of the world hears you, and the people who knocked these buildings down will hear all of us soon!"

In the weeks that followed, Bush became a compelling public presence. On September 20 he made a forceful presentation to Congress, giving the Taliban regime in Afghanistan an ultimatum to turn the Al Qaeda leadership over to the United States and close down its terrorist camps. Three weeks later he gave a similarly strong address to the United Nations. Most impressive was his October 11 prime-time news conference in the East Room of the White House. Responding in depth to questions, he radiated a sense of composure and made evident his detailed mastery of what his administration had come to call the war on terror.

Just as Bush's conduct of his responsibilities improved dramatically, so did the American public's response to him. There can be few more vivid graphic representations of quantitative data than Figure 9.1 of Richard A. Brody's chapter of this book, which shows a near perpendicular spike in the public's approval of Bush in the aftermath of September 11. In a Gallup Poll fielded the week before the attacks on the World

Trade Center and the Pentagon, Bush's approval level was at low ebb for his presidency—51 percent. Two weeks later, it had soared to 90 percent, the record high in Gallup-recorded presidential approval ratings.

Meanwhile, members of the political community formed markedly more positive views of Bush's leadership qualities. Before September 11 even a good number of his supporters had not been persuaded that he was up to his responsibilities. Thereafter, even many of his critics concluded that he had been underestimated, a view that extended to other nations. On October 20, for example, a columnist for the influential *Frankfurter Allgemeine* commented that Bush had grown into his job "before our eyes," comparing him to another president who had risen to meet the demands of his times after an unpromising start—Harry S. Truman.[14]

One reason Bush improved his mastery of policy in the weeks following September 11 was the depth of his immersion in policy deliberations. In the month between the bombings of the World Trade Center and the Pentagon and his bravura October 11 press conference, Bush met with his NSC twenty-four times.[15] These meetings, moreover, were far from pro forma. In the September 12 meeting, for example, there was a sharp debate that foreshadowed the 2003 war in Iraq. Vice President Cheney and Defense Secretary Rumsfeld advocated attacking not just Al Qaeda, but also states that sponsor terrorism, notably Iraq. Secretary of State Powell disagreed, arguing that the American people would readily back action against the terrorists linked to the September 11 attacks, but would be puzzled by a proposal to attack Iraq. Bush put a halt to the debate, indicating that that was not the time to resolve that issue.

In early October the Afghan regime let it be known that it would not surrender the Al Qaeda leadership, and the United States and its ally Great Britain began an extensive bombing campaign. Later in the month, U.S. Special Forces entered Afghanistan and began to provide support to the military forces of the anti-Taliban Northern Alliance. By November 13 the Northern Alliance had occupied the Afghan capital of Kabul, and in early December the last major Taliban stronghold surrendered. When the Gallup organization polled the U.S. public at the end of December, Bush's approval level was a towering 86 percent.

On to Iraq

Bush had postponed a decision on whether to target Iraq in the war on terror in the September 12, 2001, NSC meeting, but Iraq came into his crosshairs in his January 2002 State of the Union address. Anticipating the doctrine of preemption that his administration would formally promulgate later in the year, Bush declared that he would not "wait on events" while "the world's most dangerous weapons" were acquired by "the world's most dangerous regimes." One such regime, he specified, was Saddam Hussein's Iraq, which he grouped with Iran and North Korea in what he referred to as an "axis of evil."

Bush's address sent out shock waves. Whereas his rhetoric and actions in response to September 11 had been favorably received, there was widespread criticism at home and abroad of his "axis of evil" locution. Some of it was prompted by a belief that Bush had lumped together nations that were very different in terms of whether and to what extent they posed threats; some was directed at the usage of "evil," which led critics to worry about whether the president's private commitment to evangelical Christianity was leading him to advance an inappropriately moralistic public policy.

Despite the attention Bush's assertions about the global situation received, a good half of his address was devoted to his domestic program. "We have clear priorities," he declared, "and we must act at home with the same purpose and resolve we have shown abroad." The actions he proposed included giving the president authority to take initiatives to promote free trade, promoting policies designed to reduce the nation's reliance on foreign oil imports, and reforming Social Security, Medicare, and welfare. Above all, Bush promoted his signature policy for stimulating the economy—further tax reduction. Acknowledging that the economy was in recession, Bush declared that the "way out" was to provide "tax relief so people have more money to spend." In short, he invoked the controversial "supply-side" economic theory that had informed the huge tax cut of Ronald Reagan's first year in the White House, a doctrine that his father had once derided as "voodoo economics" for its premise that tax cuts pay for themselves by stimulating economic growth.

Bush's address presaged two major preoccupations of the second and third years of his presidency: his efforts to come to terms with Iraq and to stimulate the sluggish economy. These matters are dealt with in detail in the chapters of this volume on foreign policy, by Ivo H. Daalder and James M. Lindsay, and on budgetary policy, by Allen Schick, both of which are critical of the administration's performance. Bush himself was sufficiently dissatisfied on the economic front to accept the resignations of his secretary of the treasury and top economic adviser in December 2002. Any assessment of his administration's international performance with respect to Iraq would have to examine such questions as whether the administration gave diplomacy and inspections a fair shake before embarking on military action, whether it could have taken such action without antagonizing so much of the world, and whether the victory in Iraq will be negated by the turbulent conditions that have followed the war. But whatever the future has in store for George W. Bush, he has proved to have a highly distinctive, and often impressively effective, political style.

The Elements of a Political Style

The headings under which I examine Bush's political style are derived from the job requirements of the modern presidency. The terms *emotional intelligence* and *cognitive style* refer to the personal qualities that bear on the actions of any individual, but are especially important in the chief executive of a global superpower. *Public communication* and *organizational capacity* refer to the inner and outer faces of the president's leadership—to the president's proficiency in the bully pulpit and his effectiveness in selecting and managing the multitude of subordinates who are a defining characteristic of the modern presidency. *Political skill* is important in any leader, but it is of inordinate importance in the stalemate-prone American system of formal and informal checks and balances. But skill may be counterproductive if it is not wed to a viable *policy vision*.

Emotional intelligence. "Emotional intelligence" has come into currency as a summary term for the many ways in which emotional strengths or weaknesses can enhance or undermine the actions of even the most cognitively gifted individual.[16] No quality could be more important in the custodian of the most potentially lethal military force in human history. To be emotionally intelligent a president need not be a paragon of mental health. Franklin D. Roosevelt, for example, left much to be desired as a husband and father, but there was a superb fit between his emotions and the demands he faced as president. What is critical for a president's emotional intelligence is that his (and someday her) *public* actions not be distorted by uncontrolled passions.

By this litmus test, the heavy-drinking young George W. Bush was too volatile and unreliable to be a promising prospect for a responsible public position. It would not be surprising if a man who had abused alcohol until early middle age and had abruptly gone on the wagon proved to be an emotional tinderbox, but Bush's performance as a private sector executive and governor of Texas was not marred by emotional excesses; he weathered the 2000 presidential campaign, including his setback in New Hampshire, with seeming equanimity; and he held up well in the extended deadlock over the election outcome.

Bush also appears to have been unruffled by the April 2001 mini-crisis over the forcing down of the American reconnaissance plane by China, but the sterner test was his performance in the genuine national security crises of the period after September 11. Here again he appears to have had his emotions well in hand. There are no instances in which Bush is described as acting on uncontrolled impulse in Bob Woodward's in-depth account of his administration's decision making on Afghanistan. Indeed, Bush explained to Woodward that it was in his nature to be "fiery" in the sense of wanting to take an action before the conditions were ripe, but that he relied on National Security Adviser Rice to "take the edge off" such impulses, adding that "she's good at that."[17] Insight into how Bush's emotions figured in the war in Iraq is provided by a lengthy interview he granted to NBC News anchor Tom Brokaw just after the conclusion of the fighting. Whereas Bush might have been expected to have been defensive about the widespread criticism of his administration's actions or boastful about the rapidity of the military victor, he was neither. Instead he was good humored and reflective, expressing regret that the use of force had been necessary, but insisting that inaction would have been more costly. Whatever the merits of his actions, they appeared to be those of a man who was at peace with himself.[18]

Consider by way of contrast the needlessly confrontational actions of Richard Nixon in the course of his efforts to terminate the American military involvement in Vietnam in the early 1970s. At one point Nixon decided to buy time for South Vietnam by ordering an American military strike against a concentration of communist forces on the Cambodian side of the Ho Chi Minh Trail. Spurning advice that the action be reported by the Pentagon as a matter of military routine, Nixon announced it himself in a truculent speech from the Oval Office. In so doing, he triggered an intense nationwide wave of anti-war protest, creating a political climate that much complicated his effort to extricate the United States from Vietnam.

Cognitive style. Late-night television comedy notwithstanding, Bush has ample native intelligence. But he appears never to have been marked by intellectual curiosity or drawn to the play of ideas. Moreover, as the nation's first MBA chief executive, he favors a corporate leadership model in which he relies on his subordinates to structure his options. As we have seen, Bush was often remote from specifics as the governor of Texas and seemed ill informed in the early months of his presidency. After September 11, however, there was a dramatic increase in his mastery of the content of his administration's policies, a development that has been documented in interviews with members of Congress who are in regular contact with Bush. As one of them put it, "He's as smart as he wants to be."[19]

It is possible, however, to be well informed without being well equipped to reason clearly about the complex tradeoffs presidents typically have to make. Judging from his extemporaneous statements, Bush is better at enunciating the broad outlines of his administration's positions than at elucidating their subtleties. In this he contrasts with a statesman with whom he periodically shares a podium, British Prime Minister Tony Blair. At a March 25, 2003, joint "press availability," for example, Bush and Blair responded to questions about how long the fighting in Iraq would continue. Bush was laconic and uninformative, contenting himself with such assertions as "however long it takes," whereas Blair was expansive and analytic, reviewing the roots of the conflict, its global ramifications, and its likely aftermath. All told, Blair rather than Bush provided a model of the intellectual suppleness one might hope for in the American chief executive.[20]

Effectiveness as a public communicator. As we have seen, early in his presidency Bush was a flawed public speaker and seemed not to recognize the rhetorical potentialities of the presidency. Within days after September 11, however, he was presiding over a teaching and preaching presidency, addressing the public regularly and with force, effectiveness, and even eloquence. Thereafter he has sometimes slipped into the plodding mode of delivery that marked his inaugural address, especially when he reads routine prepared remarks. But now he is quite effective in prepared addresses for which he had rehearsed, and on unscripted occasions he has come to employ a punchy vernacular manner that has served him with most Americans, but is more effective at home than abroad.

Organizational capacity. Organizational leadership is one of the strengths of the nation's first MBA president. Bush has chosen strong associates, he is a natural when it comes to rallying his subordinates, and he encourages diversity of advice. Because avoiding public disagreement is a watchword of the Bush administration, the precise dynamics of its deliberative processes are not well documented, despite the only partially veiled conflict between Secretary of Defense Rumsfeld and Secretary of State Powell and their supporters.

Woodward's account of the administration's post–September 11 decision making points to two respects in which Bush's deliberative processes leave something to be desired. Woodward reports that Powell and Rumsfeld expressed their differences more sharply in the meetings from which Bush was absent than in those at which he was present, which suggests that Bush may sometimes be shielded from potentially valuable debate. Woodward also describes an instance in which Powell arranged to meet privately with Bush and National Security Adviser Rice in order to register his disagreement with the hawkish proposals of Rumsfeld and Vice President Cheney.[21] When subordinates advance policies by making end runs on their colleagues, the advice a president gets tends to be a function of his advisers' bureaucratic skills rather than the intrinsic merit of their recommendations.

Such practices would have been anathema to the modern president who was most gifted at organizational leadership, Dwight Eisenhower. "I know of only one way in which you can be sure you have done your best to make a wise decision," the former allied supreme commander once remarked. "That is to get all of the responsible policy makers with their different viewpoints in front of you, and listen to them debate. I do not believe in bringing them in one at a time, and therefore being more impressed by the most recent one you hear instead of earlier ones."[22]

Political skill. The congenitally gregarious George W. Bush resembles his fellow Texan Lyndon Johnson in his aptitude for personal politics. As he did in Texas, Bush sometimes has worked effectively on both sides of the aisle. However, there has been a hard edge to his administration's partisanship in Washington that was not evident in Texas, as is shown in the chapter of this volume by John C. Fortier and Norman J. Ornstein. Morever, Bush and his highly professional aides have sometimes been less surefooted in the international arena than in the domestic. This was particularly evident in the lead-up to the Iraq war, when the Bush administration failed to make a case for the urgency of immediate military action and wound up going to war in the face of the opposition of a number of the nation's traditional allies.

Policy vision. The topic of policy vision permits a concluding observation about an unlikely parallel between George W. Bush and George H. W. Bush. The senior Bush was famously indifferent to "the vision thing." The younger Bush has faulted his father for failing to enunciate clear goals for his presidency and not building on the momentum of victory in the 1991 Gulf War to rack up domestic accomplishments on which he could campaign for reelection. George W. Bush *does* have the "vision thing," not because he is an aficionado of policy, but because he holds that if a leader does not set his own goals, others will set them for him.

Therein lies a potential irony. The senior Bush suffered politically from the lack of vision. If the supply-side remedy of tax cuts fails to alleviate the nation's economic woes or there is a dire aftermath to victory in the Iraq war, the junior Bush may prove to suffer *because* of his policy vision.

Chapter 2

The Political Ethos of George W. Bush

Hugh Heclo

> I'm the commander—see, I don't need to explain—I do
> not need to explain why I say things. That's the interesting
> thing about being the president. Maybe somebody needs
> to explain to me why they say something, but I don't feel
> like I owe anybody an explanation.
> —President George W. Bush, 2002

TAKEN AT FACE VALUE, the preceding quotation[1] must rank as one of the most disturbing things an American president has ever said (at least on the record). If one chooses, it can be read as an assertion of democratic Caesarism: the tribune of the people has no need to justify his decisions to lesser beings.

However, that reading would misjudge both the statement and the man who made it. Put in context, they are the words of a plainspoken man who is telling an interviewer frankly about his situation and his thinking—in this case, his hidden intention to provoke his war cabinet into achieving a clearer sense of purpose and forward movement in the coming military confrontation with the Taliban. Bush was stating, with self-confident directness, what he judged to be the essence of a given situation, its personal nature, and the appropriate allocation of responsibilities between a president and his top advisers.

The fleeting incident represented by this quotation does not mean that George W. Bush is reluctant to explain his actions to the American people. However, at a deeper level it does offer some important hints about the way this president has learned to look at the political world. This chapter explores those hints about a man whose presidency is already destined for a remarkable place in the history books. With the narrowest of election mandates, George Bush brushed aside the conventional academic advice about proceeding with caution, building a broad consensus, and undertaking steps piecemeal. By the halfway mark of his first term, President Bush had announced a dramatic American doctrine of preemptive war. He had taken the United States from being an object of worldwide sympathy after September 11 to being the target of worldwide condemnation. While he claimed publicly that an American attack on Iraq would be "in the highest moral traditions of our country,"[2] a substantial body of opinion at home and abroad saw his leadership as a greater threat to world peace than were the terrorists he was fighting. In fact, in much of the world, including among U.S. allies, George W. Bush was even losing a popularity contest with Saddam Hussein, the delusional butcher he faced in Iraq. Bush then embarked on the most daring risk any president can take—one that even a master politician like Franklin D. Roosevelt would not venture despite the menace of Hitler—taking the United States into war amid national dissention rather than unity. And to repeat, all this was done with a virtually nonexistent electoral mandate from the 2000 election debacle. The only modern president with less of a mandate was Gerald Ford, who became president in August 1974 with zero popular votes (after Richard Nixon resigned from the presidency because of Watergate).

The events of September 11, 2001, were obviously important in emboldening the president, but they themselves explain little about Bush's approach to politics, which some have dismissed as arrogance or mental obtuseness. Intellectual critics have enjoyed ridiculing this president's mental and verbal abilities, but we would do well to recall that those who have fallen in George W. Bush's political crosshairs now include Ann Richards, John McCain, Al Gore, the Taliban, and Saddam Hussein. If anything, what Richard Nixon once said of Ronald Reagan is even truer of George W. Bush: "The political landscape is littered with those who underestimated [him]."[3]

The aim of this chapter is not to discuss Bush's particular acts of leadership or the merits of his administration's policies. Rather, its purpose is to achieve a better understanding of the distinguishing character of and guiding beliefs behind George W. Bush's approach to politics. This is what I am calling his "political ethos." We might think of any ethos as an inner schema for generating and applying personal energy. It produces and sends out energy along certain lines, but not others. It is also the grid through which feedback is returned and, if necessary, rationalized to protect the basic power supply. A "political" ethos is such a schema applied to public affairs.

Inquiring into an abstraction such as a political ethos is the sort of introspective analysis that George Bush personally has always considered useless. It suggests an inner wobbliness and therapeutic self-absorption he finds distasteful. That viewpoint is itself, as we shall see, an interesting datum. Regardless of how the man personally might feel about such an exercise, a Bush political ethos does exist even though it may never be directly articulated. It holds the promise of immense strengths and vulnerabilities over the long term. The following pages discuss Bush's political ethos in terms of four interrelated themes. These concern the ethic of responsibility associated with his family, his apprenticeship in modern politics, his strategy of decision making, and his growth in personal and political self-discipline. The points made in relation to these themes are at times admittedly speculative, but I hope they are something more than idle speculations. A fifth and final section discusses the opportunities and dangers of a political ethos, the central temptation of which is to lead without teaching, to sell without educating.

Family: The Ethic of Responsibility

The first and most fundamental theme related to the political ethos of George W. Bush is that of the Bush family ethos. It was the understanding (usually unspoken) of one's responsibility and station in life, exemplified in the legacy passed on from his grandfather to his father, that was foundational for the younger Bush's outlook on public affairs. Even into middle age, the younger Bush could seemingly cavort on the surface of life because the subsoil was rock solid.

George W. Bush grew up as the first son in a large, generationally extended family with substantial wealth on all sides. For both his mother and his father, the network of kinship ties to big business and New York finance were dense and extended back to the Gilded Age of the latter nineteenth century. Although his family's wealth was not as vast as that of the Rockefellers, the combined assets of his mother's side (her father, Marvin Pierce, was president of McCall Publishing and a descendant of President Franklin Pierce) and of his father's even wealthier side (the Bush-Walker marriage was a union at the top of the oldest and largest private investment house in New York, Brown Brothers Harriman) was imposing. It meant that George W. Bush was part of a sprawling family that was rich beyond the imaginings of ordinary American households. The family was East Coast rich, which meant his parents could move in a circuit of winter homes, summer residences, and social contacts that easily set them apart from the prominent but only middling-rich public families of middle America, such as the Tafts or the Stevensons.

At the same time, Bush's parents were a young couple—she a World War II debutante bride and George senior a returned combat vet—who yearned to establish their independence and escape some of the attention of this close family. It was this yearning that led George and Barbara Bush, who would remain infatuated with each other, to begin the move to Odessa, Texas, with their two-year-old son on the day after the young vet's graduation from Yale in 1948. Backstopped by the family resources in the East, George Bush took his shot at the booming Texas oil business, worked hard, seized opportunities, and soon succeeded. By the summer of 1959, when thirteen-year-old Bill Clinton (born August 19, 1946) was trying to protect his mother from the beatings of his alcoholic stepfather, thirteen-year-old George Walker Bush (born July 6, 1946) was moving with his millionaire father and family from a prominent civic position in Midland to an upscale Houston neighborhood.

The result of this family legacy was that the younger Bush grew up secure and with a foot solidly planted in two worlds. While the posh Eastern Walker-Bush clan was a constant and supportive presence, in Texas he lived mainly the roustabout life of a normal middle-class American schoolboy. By his teenage years, the common touch of Main Street, Texas, had been imprinted. Midland was a boomtown with a Western egalitarianism that hated pretense, enjoyed ribbing people, and valued speak-your-mind bluntness, the latter a trait that also characterized the matriarchs of the Bush-Walker family. Starting in 1959, a succession of more elite schools and his father's rising status in the Texas oil business and politics brought the younger Bush into more rarified circles, where he learned to play the social status game, but could see it was only a game. What was not a game were the understandings that bonded his parents' home with the ethos of the larger Bush-Walker family.

It was a family life of consistently high expectations but also quick deflation for anyone puffing up his or her accomplishments. The family wealth and ethos provided security, but not spoon-feeding. Though help was always available, each member of the family was expected to stand on his or her own two feet, yet no one was to behave in a prideful manner for doing so. In effect, amid their substantial and growing wealth, the Bush family was carrying a venerable New England Puritan tradition forward into the heart of the twentieth century. Survival and acceptance were ensured. But exertion and achievement were also expected. The

Bushes were a competitive, kinetic clan like the Kennedys, but without the dark underside of the duplicity and overweening ambition of the paterfamilias. Joe Kennedy senior lusted after recognition in America's upper crust; the WASPish Bushes were already there. Thus, unfortunately for later biographers and pundits, the Bushes were an essentially healthy, functional family, with the normal mixture of tragedies and joys that is the human lot. As part of this nurturing family, George W. Bush could grow up never doubting that he was part of an established order of things, that he was loved, and that it would be devastating to disappoint those who loved him. He was outgoing, enjoyed being popular, and relished the competitive sports atmosphere of the family, but he did not need popularity contests or election victories to confirm his own sense of worth.

At the center of all this was his father, his father's father, and the example of their lives. Grandfather Prescott Bush was an impressive, stern presence throughout the first twenty-five years of the younger Bush's life. The elder Bush presided over his extended family with both an attentive and a patrician manner, and like the other Bush children, George W. learned to show the proper deference. The visits of U.S. Senator Prescott Bush to the young family of George and Barbara in the Texas outback were times of excitement and pride that an authentic national-level businessman-statesman had come to town. Observations about personalities behind the affairs of state in Washington, not legislative or policy agendas, provided the substance of political talk during the continual decades-long round of family gatherings ranging from Kennebunkport, Maine, Greenwich, Connecticut, and New York to South Carolina and Florida. Steady, proper, and a preferred golfing partner of President Eisenhower, Prescott Bush symbolized the internationalist and pro-business mainstream Republicanism of his time. While the younger Bush was moving through the exclusive schooling of the Phillips Academy and Yale, Prescott Bush (having retired from the Senate in 1963) was serving as the leading alumnus overseeing both institutions. Not surprisingly, George W. Bush felt that the death of his grandfather in 1972 was the loss of a living legend.[4] Prescott's widow sat with the grandchildren at the funeral, and young George and the other boys served as his pallbearers. Their responsibility was to live the legacy.

The young George saw his father as an even more impressive embodiment of the family ethos of responsibility. George Herbert Walker Bush had inherited some of his father Prescott's courtly manner, but was also graced with considerable athletic ability and an outgoing, glad-handing decency that set him apart. Before a more cynical time would turn his values into the object of derision, Bush seemed genetically designed to live out "prep school" values, including the noblesse oblige implied by Andover's school motto (*Non Sibi,* not for oneself). At Andover he captained the varsity baseball and soccer teams to record victories, and he served as deacon at the chapel and president of the leading student club. Upon graduation in 1942 the eighteen-year-old George announced he was relinquishing the safe place prepared for him at Yale and going to war. The youngest commissioned officer in the navy, he flew eighty-eight missions as a fighter pilot, but was shot down southeast of Japan in 1944, was rescued miraculously at sea by a submarine, and returned home with the Distinguished Flying Cross. He then married the Manhattan debutante who had waited four years for him and charged through Yale, captaining and starring on its varsity baseball team as well as making Phi Beta Kappa with an economics major. Not least of all in his son's eyes, he then turned his back on the plush career prepared for him at Brown Brothers Harriman and set out for the hardscrabble Texas oil patch. There he made his own independent family fortune, served in every manner of civic good works, and proved himself an attentive if overscheduled father. As George H. W. Bush watched his boisterous, at times mouthy, first son grow up, he had no need to try to succeed through making demands on his offspring. His expectations of achievement were expressed sotto voce, always in the background and thus always present. His son, in turn, became committed to his father as "a beacon . . . by his actions not his words."[5] The most devastating words he might have imagined from his father—or his father might have imagined from Prescott—would have been: "Son, I'm disappointed in you."[6]

What achievements were expected to result from the family ethic of responsibility? In general, of course, there were the standard parental admonitions: "Try your best at whatever you do" and "Be responsible for your actions." The Bushes did not look down upon intellectual achievement, but they did not assume that achievement was about contemplation and books. It was about taking action and making one's mark in the world. What sort of action? As with other prominent families of the early twentieth century, what appears to have been at work was a hazy patrician image carried over from the lore of America's founding and the even older ideas of classic civic republicanism stressed at places like Andover. To be sure, the gentleman politician never became a strong feature of U.S. politics, despite the Founding Fathers' predemocratic hopes. Nevertheless, the lure of patrician images did surface from time to time, and we would do well to take it seriously. Especially after the late nineteenth century, this vision of leadership above partisanship took hold among some of the nation's leading families in an amalgamation with the typically American idea of public-spirited business leadership. And the Bush-

Walker family was clearly one of those families.[7] In this ethos, the important thing was not just to desire respect, public honor, or fame, but to deserve it. Thus at the end of the day the top rung of achievement among men in the Bush-Walker family was understood in terms of something vaguely called public service.

Public service, of course, can take many forms. Obviously in this family's case one was not talking about a career as a fireman, nurse, or public defender. At a minimum public service referred to taking a leadership role in civic activities, and the Bushes were always engaged in a whirlwind of leadership in various community causes. When the two Bush presidencies later promoted volunteerism, expressed as "a thousand points of light" and "faith-based initiatives," they were expressing long-standing ideals arising from the family's ethic of responsibility. That said, there is no doubt that Prescott Bush clearly modeled a more demanding ideal: for Bush men, public service meant political leadership. It was no doubt with this in mind that by 1952 the newly minted Texan, twenty-eight-year-old George H. W. Bush, was energetically embarked on the seemingly thankless job of organizing the first Republican precinct in the heart of this solidly Democratic state. Soon his eldest son was accompanying him on some of his political outings.

Given this family ethos, what is one to make of the much-publicized stories of young George W. Bush's rebellious drift as he sought to find himself through partying? It is certainly true that as the younger Bush passed into manhood through a succession of America's elite institutions, he typically played the role of cut-up, big man on campus, and good-time Charlie that came naturally to his extroverted personality. However, this was not so much a rebellion as a sort of backhanded affirmation of the immovable Bush-Walker foundations he was building upon. He could play around, assured that there was a path in life that was demonstrably true and worthy, a path exemplified in the persons of his father and his father's father. In time the alleged "nomadic years" he experienced after he left Yale essentially turned into a myth that journalists could embellish for public consumption (and that political candidate Bush himself later found useful for establishing his image as an ordinary guy).

The less dramatic facts are that after graduating from Yale in the tumultuous year of 1968, George W. Bush followed a respectable if uninspiring course in which he was "socially active" but hardly a rebellious free spirit leading a nomadic life. Helped by family connections, immediately after leaving Yale he entered the Texas Air National Guard and succeeded in a rigorous year-long pilot training program, becoming a respectable if noncombatant fighter pilot. After a year of reserve flying duty and rejection by the University of Texas Law School, he took himself to the nation's top business school to earn a master's degree. During this time he also worked in a succession of three business apprenticeship jobs his father arranged, busied himself in three Senate campaigns, dropped at least one girlfriend at his parents' insistence, and toyed with but abandoned the idea of running for the Texas state legislature. After getting his MBA from Harvard in 1975, the twenty-nine-year-old Bush returned to Midland to began his own family-subsidized gamble in the Texas oil business, and in 1976 he surprised many people by running for Congress. Through all this, the young Bush faithfully and happily attended the recurring family gatherings from Kennebunkport to Florida. In sum, George W. Bush, with an admittedly brash style, did what Bush men were supposed to do.

None of this could match the stellar performance of Bush's father from the preceding generation, but it was far from a rebellious or nomadic life. In effect, what the younger Bush was doing was not much different from what his parents had done in the 1940s as together they had both embraced their families' values and sought some measure of independence from their influential clans' powerful gaze. Young Bush's bombastic frothiness was integrated with a Bush family ethic whose foundation went deep and knew itself to be noble in intent. These were not overlays of his personality that could be peeled away to reveal vastly different levels or compartments. They were granular intermixes in a consistent whole. The cultural confusions and political turmoil of the 1960s and 1970s washed over but did not overturn this foundation. What George W. Bush thought about these times as a twenty-something representative of the Bush family at Yale College and Harvard Business School had not changed much when he spoke of them as a fifty-year-old man: not for him but for many others in the 1960s, "the sharp contrast between right and wrong became blurred. . . . [W]e went from accepting responsibility to assigning blame. We became a nation of victims."[8] The Bush family ethic was not about accepting victimhood or ducking responsibility. Bush's 1994 inaugural speech as governor of Texas would play up the theme not of a new Texas, but of a "responsible Texas."

Public Office: All Politics Is Personal

Having served less than six years as governor of a state in which that office lacks significant executive power, George W. Bush sought the nation's top job with the scantiest record in public office of any modern president. Even former governor Jimmy Carter had also spent at least a little time in the state legislature, and Ronald Reagan, after his two four-year terms in the powerful California governorship, had put in six years on the national stage before reaching the White House. However, it would be far off the mark to say that the younger George Bush lacked political experience. With two generations of businessmen-politicians in his life from birth and over two decades of apprenticeship as a kind of de facto political consultant, no other president in living memory has had such a lifelong, high-level exposure to the inner workings of modern American politics.

The point goes deeper. First watching, then helping, and finally advising his father, the younger Bush had been a participant-observer as the Bush family ethos ran up against the huge systemic changes in the American political system that took place during the last half of the twentieth century. George W. Bush had acquired his political education by sharing the journey as his father, with his patrician sensibilities, navigated the new era of smash-mouth politics. It was an education that no political scientists writing conference papers can hope to match.

The introductory lessons came from the old codes of a family that had spent several generations in the public eye. To say that they considered politics a game would be an understatement in a family for whom sporting competition was the preferred metaphor for almost every aspect of life.[9] Games, contests, and rankings were pervasive in the Walker-Bush households, and the same mentality translated into public affairs. Politics was essentially about people, not political ideas or policies, and what it spoke to most loudly concerning people was character, just as in sports contests. Politics was not a shadowy, Nixonian landscape of enemies, pretense, and intrigue. Neither was it Ronald Reagan's sunny upland, where America's calling and conservative values sanctified the nitty-gritty chores of everyday politics. For the Bush family politics was not an arena of dark forces or bright visions, but a sports field. To seek an unfair competitive advantage would mean that one did not understand why winning is valued—namely, as the sign of and reward for demonstrating qualities of worthiness to oneself and others. The tangible reward was the honor of public office, which deserved dignity and respect. Any further introspective analysis was beside the point. It is action that reveals character, and politics is the preeminent arena for this most important of all revelations about a person.

Of course no one could grow up in any political family and think that this high-minded view represented the full story of what happened in the rough-and-tumble world of American politics. It was, however, considered a model that mattered very much, the central tendency that decent people should be striving for in the rough sport of political competition. Thus rather than "running," Prescott Bush had almost literally "stood" for national office in the old-fashioned patrician sense, trying unsuccessfully in 1950 to ascend directly from a position as esteemed civic leader and town moderator of Greenwich, Connecticut, to one as a member of the U.S. Senate. Two years later he had won a special election to fill the seat of a deceased Democratic senator, arriving in Washington with the new Eisenhower administration.

However, as the teenage George W. Bush watched his own father launch himself toward public office in the late 1950s, American politics was also beginning to undergo profound changes. The political climb of father and son would turn into a sustained pilgrimage across the rapidly changing landscape of American politics. Step by step, they had to learn the new ways as they decided how to give Americans the respectable Bush leaders they "should" want but often did not. The new politics would be dominated by opinion polling, professional political consultants, television advertising, carefully crafted campaign images and messages, ideologically divided policy activists, and the huge fund-raising efforts needed to pay for this mass marketing of politics.[10]

The Bush family's lessons in the new school of politics began in the 1960s. By 1963 the thirty-nine-year-old George H. W. Bush had spent over a decade doing the unglamorous work of helping people like John Tower build a mainstream Republican Party in Democratic Texas. The next year he sought to repeat his father's leap, in this case trying to go from a position as a respected Houston businessman and civic leader to one as a member of the U.S. Senate. With his eighteen-year-old son at his side, the father rode in a bus caravan that wound its way across Texas. Bush good-naturedly laid out his issues as a Goldwater supporter (against Johnson's civil rights bill, the Nuclear Test Ban Treaty, and extravagant anti-poverty programs; for the Vietnam War, a Cuban exile government, and possible withdrawal from the United Nations) while trying to fend off but not totally alienate what the candidate privately called "nuts" on the radical right.

Probably no Republican could have prevailed in Lyndon B. Johnson's Texas during that year following John F. Kennedy's assassination. Even so, Bush suffered a crushing defeat when liberal incumbent Senator Ralph Yarborough unleashed a blistering populist attack against one he branded the "tool" of Connecticut investment bankers, "a carpetbagger . . . who is drilling oil for the Sheik of Kuwait." George W. Bush had the experience of putting up the returns that recorded his father's humiliating defeat to the election night crowd. When he resumed his freshman year at Yale, he also had to endure the condescending comments of the school's intellectual crowd and the observation of Yale's esteemed anti-war chaplain

William Sloan Coffin that a better man had beaten his father; it was an insult that would smolder in the son's mind for decades.[11]

In retrospect, the new lessons were quickly starting to accumulate for the Bushes. It had not been who George Bush really was or what he proposed that had mattered, but how he was portrayed. Politics was personal, but to run as a decent, accomplished man is not enough in this kind of world. George W. Bush saw the good character of his father misrepresented not simply by voters, but by people at Yale whom he thought should have known better.

The election in 1966 was another story. This time George Bush resigned his position as CEO in his oil business to run as a full-time candidate in a newly drawn congressional district in the booming Houston area. A vice president of the blue-ribbon New York ad agency J. Walter Thompson was brought on board to help design and implement a comprehensive campaign strategy to market Bush using the same PR skills the firm applied to other "products," such as those of Ford Motors and Pan American Airways. Media buys in the press, on radio, and above all on television blanketed the district for months before the Democratic opponent launched his general election campaign. The unfolding sequence of professionally produced television commercials shunned party identification and issues in the cause of selling the persona of George Bush as war hero, business leader, family man, doer, nice guy, and, not least of all, Texan. This time Bush's twenty-year-old son put up for a cheering crowd returns recording his father's landslide victory in the presumptively Democratic state.

Few races for Congress, for the House or the Senate, had ever been anything like Bush's campaign for the Senate. His political consultants wrote a history of the 1966 campaign as a model of the new way of doing politics.[12] Two years later a nationalized version of the new politics using the same ad agency was rolled out in Richard Nixon's march to the White House and described in Joe McGinnis's book *The Selling of the President*. By then it was not a book the Bushes needed to read in order to get an education. In the 1968 campaign season, George W. Bush spent several months after leaving Yale working as a paid aide in the Florida Senate campaign that one of his father's political consultants was helping manage. While shepherding the media along the candidate's campaign trail, young Bush watched another hero of World War II, Edward Gurney, use his powerful personality to pound away on three and only three conservative themes (fighting to win in Vietnam, cutting Johnson's domestic spending, and restoring law and order). California's new governor, Ronald Reagan, came to endorse the sharpening conservative message, and the younger Bush shared in the excitement of the upset victory that turned Gurney into Florida's first Republican Senator since the Reconstruction. Personality plus unswerving focus on a short list of issues suited to the times paid off. Another lesson learned. (Later Senator Gurney, Nixon's preeminent defender during the 1973–74 Watergate hearings, and facing charges arising from his own illegal campaign activities, would watched his political career dissolve before his first term was completed.)

In the 1970s there were lessons to be learned about loyalty and its misplacement. The new Congressman George Bush had already attracted the attention of President Nixon, not only for his skills in the new politics and his sense of loyalty, but particularly as a piece of a strategy for building a new Republican majority by breaking the Democratic Party's hold on the South. Bush was one of those whom Nixon courted and recruited to try to unseat vulnerable Democrats in the 1970 mid-term elections; Ralph Yarborough was near the top of Nixon's list, if not at the top. For Bush, personal ambition combined smoothly with respect for requests coming from the president's office, and at the beginning of 1970 the two-term congressman gave up his seat to launch a second run for Yarborough's Senate seat. In the background, Nixon had dangled the bait that a Bush win in 1970 would mean a place as his vice presidential running mate in 1972.

Unfortunately for Bush, the Texas Democrats also recognized the rightward political drift and dumped the liberal Yarborough in favor of the more conservative Houston businessman and decorated war hero Lloyd Bentsen. With Bentsen matching his own personal résumé, Bush ran a campaign brimming with positions on issues but no theme. George W. Bush threw himself into the Senate campaign as a surrogate candidate for his father and as an organizer of college interns during this volatile year of youth unrest. By all accounts the main point for the son and the young students he led was to work loyally for the man and not necessarily to agree with all the issues, which few people could keep track of anyway. For his part, President Nixon offered support with visits and money, but also let it be known that he did not think Bush was being "tough" enough on Bentsen and the Democrats. When Nixon's favorite Texan, former Democrat John Connally, appeared in damaging ads supporting Bush's opponent, there were no consequences except for Connally to be appointed Nixon's secretary of the treasury shortly afterward.

Once again, George W. Bush recorded the results as his father went down to a major electoral defeat. In fact, it seemed the final political defeat. Shortly after the election, George senior acquiesced to Nixon's request that he become ambassador to the United Nations (UN)—a certain career-ender for anyone interested in Texas politics. While this might also have been seen as an opportunity to build a national reputation, for Nixon it was a matter of choosing someone to perform a social and ceremonial role in New York. Behind the back of the UN ambassador (as well as that of the secretary of state), Nixon and his national security adviser, Henry Kissinger, made the real policies, typically undercutting Ambassador Bush's public statements and embarrassing him personally. As Watergate clouds gathered after the president's 1972 re-election, Nixon exploited Bush's reputation for decency, and Bush in turn loyally accepted the call to become chairman of the Republican National Committee, just as the scandals began exploding.

In the meantime, during 1972 son George was gaining more apprenticeship experience in the new profession of political consulting. Alabama businessman and U.S. Postmaster General Winton M. "Red" Blount was another of those persons Nixon recruited to undertake a Senate race to try to break the Democrats' hold on the south. The consultants and Bush family friends who had helped orchestrate the new media campaigns for George senior in 1966 and for Gurney in 1968 now had their own political consulting firm with ties to the Republican National Party. They offered the twenty-five-year-old George Bush the chance to go to Alabama as paid political director of Blount's Senate campaign, an offer the younger Bush eagerly accepted once he had decided not to make a quick run for the Texas state legislature.

The campaign young Bush directed hit hard on simplistic conservative issues—against coddling criminals and welfare freeloaders, against forced busing, and for Blount's philosophy of personal responsibility. But it was difficult to counter populist charges that Blount was an overprivileged business fat cat who had raised postal rates and was out of touch with ordinary people. Worse, the candidate really did lack the personal qualities necessary to connect with ordinary people, something that was clearly no problem for his opponent, the charming thirty-six-year veteran of Capitol Hill, John Sparkman. Realizing what was in the works, Nixon made a public display of mending fences with the Democrat Sparkman, and Blount went down to devastating defeat. Within a year, George W. Bush had gone on to Harvard Business School. There he experienced a steady dose of the disdain and glee with which Cambridge liberals observed the unfolding Watergate scandals that enveloped not only Nixon's White House, but also the Republican National Committee, which his father was manning like a good soldier in the midst of a mud fight. When Nixon finally resigned and it came time for President Ford to anoint a new vice president, George Bush was passed over for carrying too much Watergate baggage. The reward for his loyalty was an ambassadorial appointment to the distant reaches of China and then a brief stint as director of the CIA, which put him out of political reach of anything to do with the forthcoming 1976 election.

With his father politically sidelined after Jimmy Carter's 1976 victory, and perhaps recalling how his father's strategy of advancement by loyalty had not paid off, George W. Bush decided to plunge into his own campaign for Congress in 1977. In effect, he would return to the career mark at which his father had left off being his own man, though that thought certainly would not have been verbalized by either father or son. For his part, George senior was immensely pleased (as he put it) to see the family's competitiveness in the political game resumed and the "passing on of legacy."[13] In part, this was true, but the thirty-one-year-old first son was also breaking with tradition. In the new age of professionalized politics there was less need to build up a lengthy résumé as his grandfather and father had done before "allowing" their names to be brought forward for national office. What accomplishments a résumé lacked, campaigning skills might make up for. Having been back in Texas less than two years after graduating from Harvard Business School, and with the barest of returns from his one-room oil business, George W. Bush set out to run for Congress. A year before the 1978 election, the far-flung network of the Bush family's political advisers, donors, and friends began wheeling into action. This power base and the candidate's own political skills were enough for the younger Bush to win the Republican primary, despite his opponent's endorsement by Ronald Reagan and other anti-Bush GOP forces (the Reagan versus Bush presidential primaries were about to begin). In the 1978 general election, however, young George's network of outside support turned into an insurmountable liability. His Democratic opponent hammered away on the theme that a blue-blooded Easterner was using family resources to become a pretend Texan. And, as in 1964, the elitist-carpetbagger label stuck to a Bush. Once again the political was the personal, and George W. Bush lost fourteen out of seventeen counties in his first election contest, with less than 47 percent of the vote. Bush learned a lesson when he realized he had been beaten by an opponent who had defined him and had stayed on that simple message.[14] The younger Bush would have to show himself more of his own man and a Texan before making his next grab for the ring of power.

During his father's unsuccessful bid for the Republican presidential nomination in 1979–80 and continuing through George senior's campaigns as Reagan's running mate in 1980 and 1984, the first son periodically took on a range of political responsibilities. There was surrogate speech making, checking on staff performance, coordinating activities at all levels, schmoozing with donors, massaging journalists, and energizing the troops, among any number of other political chores. George W.

Bush's political efforts on his father's behalf culminated in the 1988 presidential race, for which the family began planning in early 1985. The younger Bush now became a senior, and eventually a full-time, adviser in his father's campaign to succeed Ronald Reagan.

In terms of substantive issues, the central problem was that Bush's candidacy needed to be perceived as something more than Ronald Reagan's third term. The phrase "compassionate conservative" put in its first appearance, intending to suggest an empathy for the vulnerable that was part of Bush's personal kindliness but not of Reagan's sunniness. More important, there was the issue of taxes, which President Reagan had actually raised on some occasions. Candidate Bush made his reckless pledge, "Read my lips, no new taxes," feeding the media craving for the dramatic sound bites that modern politics demanded. Bush seemed to promise that there would never, ever, be any new taxes under a Bush presidency, thereby volunteering himself as a campaign hostage to the necessities of governing.

However, as the younger Bush worked at the top of his father's presidential campaign it became clear that the essential point was not policy but the person voters were being asked to choose. Following years of long-suffering loyalty and decent intentions, George Bush had finally obtained his own shot at the presidency, but one already could hear all the old talk beginning about East Coast blue bloods, not being his own man. Those working for the Bush campaign could not predict the exact words, but they knew something was coming like Ann Richards's hated line at the 1988 Democratic convention: "Poor George, he couldn't help it that he was born with a silver foot in his mouth." So it was that George H. W. Bush, his first son, and the rest of his family felt no need to apologize for unleashing all the weaponry in the arsenal of the new politics on his behalf.

To do this unleashing, the family brought in the hardball star of Republican political consultants, Lee Atwater, as the campaign's field marshal and chief gunner. When he met Atwater in 1985 to begin planning the campaign, George W. Bush suspected Atwater of less than 100 percent loyalty to his father, a reasonable suspicion in the modern world of political consulting. At Atwater's invitation, the first son became his father's alter ego and loyalty checker, working side by side with the wunderkind of modern campaigning. It became an educational experience that soon developed into a close personal relationship between these generational peers. For Atwater politics was a ruthless, immensely fun calling to sell a candidate's persona to a wondering, hip public. Playing at the leading edge of modern national politics, George W. Bush became the human go-between responsible for meshing the campaign machinery and candidate George Bush's personal interests. He relished and thrived in the job and its high-stakes atmosphere. By now the elder Bush's media-savvy marketing approach of 1966 was a mere Wright Brothers version of the jet-propelled, smash-mouth politics of the professionally managed modern political campaign. The consensus after the election was that the 1988 campaign, stained in American political memory by the infamous Willie Horton television ads, had been the most vapid and ugly presidential race in modern history. But it all worked to sell a President George Bush to the voters and destroy the candidacy of Democrat Michael Dukakis. Afterward the younger Bush returned to building his business career in Texas.

In his father's 1992 reelection campaign, George W. Bush remained a senior political adviser and powerful agent for his father, but he did not repeat his 1988 move to Washington and took a less active part in the day-to-day running of the campaign. It was, after all, a campaign that presumably should be managed from the White House. The first son acted firmly to help his father deal with the disloyalty and infighting that plagued the White House staff, and then he was transferred into the campaign effort. Still, after Atwater died of a brain tumor in early 1991, the reelection effort drifted without a strategic focus and increasingly seemed to be playing pure defense against combined attacks from an energized Clinton campaign, dissidents on the Republican Right, and Ross Perot's wild-card independent movement. After the Gulf War the younger Bush saw his father caught in a kind of mission-accomplished lethargy, seemingly reluctant to focus on domestic issues central to the reelection effort. In another sense, however, there was too much focus. The "Read my lips" pledge was the one substantive thing people could latch on to about the 1988 Bush campaign. When President Bush did finally succumb to governing realities and agreed to tax increases as part of a deficit reduction package, the broken campaign pledge became an albatross that hung around his neck throughout the reelection effort.

As the 1992 election reached its climax, the younger Bush saw his father, hero, and president fighting valiantly not only against the character-challenged Bill Clinton, but also against the media's infuriating misrepresentations of his father's persona as a loser, a preppy wimp who was out of touch. This time his father's political career truly had come to an end. Now it would be the son's turn at the game.

Mainly through his father's career, George W. Bush had attended an elite school of politics, and its curriculum had been the new American political system. This new system was in many ways well suited to the Bushes and their view of politics as a competitive game. In 1966 Bush's father had broken new ground, entering the era of PR campaigns. As the hold of political parties weakened and the importance of fund-raising for media-driven campaigns grew, the ever-expanding personal network George Bush and his family cultivated—the FOBs (friends of the Bushes) —became a serious political asset. Likewise, in the personalizing of politics there was a peculiar kind of fit with the older family ethos. In both cases the working assumption was that the self presented in politics is a reflection. For patrician politics it is a reflection of the attributes of character. For smash-mouth politics it is a reflection of an image crafted by all the modern political techniques. Neither style of politics stressed any self-analysis of motives; neither cared about the insights that can be hidden in ambiguity, much less introspection. And while one might genuinely care about the country's problems, "policy issues" were to be chosen as campaign focal points, not for their intrinsic importance but as strategic instruments for (take your pick) revealing character or molding the desired image-response from the public.

Others might call this a cynical view, but to those willing to act in the public arena, all of it was simply a recognition and acceptance of the game to be played. As the family ethos required, one worked all-out to play the game well, but one also "got it" in the sense of not being taken in, realizing that politics is, after all, a show. George Bush senior had to learn this lesson in middle age and never became very good at the media image game, despite all his efforts. The younger Bush absorbed it from his youth and had a personality that could even wryly delight in lampooning the show and its pretensions from offstage. As something of a patrician carryover from an earlier age, the elder George Bush had played with a certain amount of trust in the good intentions of other players—even the media; frequently his reward had been to be left holding the bag for men of lesser character. The younger Bush learned the more practical lessons of playing hardball politics to win. In Washington, loyalty was one of the most prized personal qualities, so valuable that it was rarely displayed. George W. Bush would make loyalty one of the key features of his political ethos.

Within four months of his father's losing the presidency, in 1994 a refocused George W. Bush set out on his own run for major office, the Texas governorship. The next generation of Team Bush assembled in the spring of 1993, including a colleague and disciple of Atwater's approach to modern politics, Karl Rove. Bush and Rove had first met in 1974 while the young Rove was working for Bush's father at the Republican National Committee. During the younger Bush's failed congressional race in 1978, Rove had become a part-time volunteer adviser, on leave from the elder Bush's pre-presidential primary campaign. Later Rove had settled in Austin, Texas, and masterminded a series of party-building victories for

Republicans in the state. Less gonzo in style than Atwater, Rove was a historically acute practitioner of the same hardball approach to managing the professional public game of politics. For the more cerebral Rove, politics was a historical saga of personalities and issue-focused electoral strategies. But victory at the polls was still its own best apologetic for whatever one did in order to get elected. In an age when the management of personalities and issues determined election outcomes, the race was always on for a person in elective office. Public service was never-ending campaigning. Prescott Bush would not have understood.

By 1994, Rove and Bush were bonding. However, contrary to recently popular accounts, Rove was neither "Bush's mind" nor the utterly indispensable "boy genius" who made a hapless George Bush into a political winner. The fact is that Rove complemented Bush's own political mind and experience with his fuller range and depth of professional skills in the new politics. Having watched Atwater close up, Bush could recognize a brilliant political consultant when he saw one. Having seen what it took as his father played the game, he could enlist Rove in the Bush brand of full-time loyalty that few political consultants demonstrated. As Bush progressed through the governorship toward the presidency, he had the self-confidence to let such a man teach him more things he needed to know and do in order to be a better candidate in the permanent campaign that now characterized American politics. Bush could do these things because he had his own mind, a thoroughly political mind. In his 1994 debate with incumbent Texas Governor Ann Richards, George Bush intoned one of his thematic campaign lines: "If Texans want someone who has spent [an] entire life in politics, they should not be for me." The truth is, if that is what Texans wanted, George W. Bush was the perfect choice.

Vision: Do What You Know

The changing political game the Bush men experienced was one instance of a recurring theme in George W. Bush's encounters with postwar America. Again and again he seemed to arrive on the scene just when the old fixed order—the way things were supposed to work—was coming undone.

At Andover in the early 1960s, prep school norms were giving way to a knowing sarcasm.[15] This intellectualized, Mort Sahl–like ennui found targets for ridicule everywhere. It saw hypocrisy as the real motto of the older generation and noblesse oblige as a corny joke. Given his personality, George W. Bush took to this smart-mouthed sarcastic style, and he could certainly hold his own in the competition of cutting comments.

However, he found this new "hip" style no reason to disrespect the good men and women that were his elders. Captaining the cheerleading squad provided an excellent fit, part tongue-in-cheek mockery and part genuine school spirit.

As George Bush arrived at Yale in 1964, a much greater transformation was getting under way. Here, in the last of Yale's all-male classes, he found himself part of an establishment institution where the trend-setting students were dramatically turning against the establishment and its ways. In his first term there was the widely publicized Goldwater debacle and his father's defeat in his race for the Senate. From then on the pace of change quickened in step with the deepening war in Vietnam and the 1960s youth culture upheaval. Status on campus was going not to the big men of athletics, fraternities, and the secret societies, but to the articulate critics of American society and its political leadership. Elites like the Bushes were told that they should feel guilty about their privilege and that their power was part of a corrupt system. Self-criticism, not self-confidence, was held up as the authentic American patriotism. The old order was giving way, and by the younger Bush's graduation in 1968 it had given way. Seniors depended on freshmen for the latest trends in music, drugs, and social criticism. George Bush's reaction to all this was to resolutely occupy himself with the old Yale: fraternity leadership, pranks, initiations, boozy parties, such sports activities as his limited talent allowed, and other traditions of male social bonding.

Bush ended up attending Harvard Business School at a time when there was no honor to be gained by being the scion of a blue-blooded Republican business dynasty. On the contrary, when one's father was chairman of Richard Nixon's Republican National Committee the more likely reaction was a knowing condescension. Bush's first year in Cambridge was spent in an atmosphere of the ever-unfolding Watergate crisis, his father's futile efforts to defend Nixon and buoy Republican spirits, and the public humiliation of Nixon's resignation. Once his father had been deceived and embarrassed as the nation's top Republican official and passed over as Ford's vice president, his second year at Harvard was a time of enduring the gloating of Cambridge's liberal know-it-alls. Bush's response was to reassert his Texan demeanor, get his class work done, and escape whenever possible to family and friends. Disregarding the snobbish attitudes of Harvard Square, George W. Bush wore his flight jacket to classes, relaxed at the few country music beer joints in Boston, and was the only one in Harvard Business School's class photos not to wear a shirt and tie. In effect, he stayed with what he knew and stuck it out. After finishing all the requirements for his MBA, he figuratively got on the next plane to Texas.

The same pattern repeated itself when George Bush got back to what were supposed to be the booming oil fields of Texas. At first blush, the Organization of Petroleum Exporting Countries and the energy crisis made it appear that George W. might be able to reenact his father's adventure in the oil business. But by the late 1970s the oil business had greatly changed. In an ever-consolidating industry there was far less running room for the upstart would-be oil tycoon, and oil prices soon began to decline. By the end of 1985 world oil markets were collapsing, and so were George W. Bush's flimsy oil ventures. A combination of good personal connections and fortunate timing let Bush parlay his tanking oil interests into a stake in the investment group buying the Texas Rangers. The former cheerleader captain now became a managing partner and, much more important, the public spokesman and media handler for the team. It was here, in the sport that he had known and loved as a child and whose masses of statistics he had mastered for years, that Bush would make the personal mark he needed in order to take the long shot against the Democratic governor and insulter of his father, Ann Richards. The popular, wisecracking governor really had no idea of the force that was coming at her. She thought it was a pampered playboy. In fact, it was a seasoned survivalist.

As George Bush grew into manhood and repeatedly experienced a world out of joint, he developed a repertoire of coping mechanisms. These were basically reactive, but cumulatively effective. In a political culture that was confusing itself with therapeutic self-examination, ever-greater complexities, and heaviness of spirit, the First Son learned there was refuge in a kind of political essentialism.[16] One survives by focusing only on the big things one knows or needs to know. This was not a defensive crouch, but rather an inner resolve to move ahead doing what he knew how to do, the kind of full-speed-ahead golf game he, like his father, enjoyed playing. There is integrity in doing what one knows. One is not faking it. Bush prized that sort of direct stance toward the world. Later, White House reporters would find it difficult to believe that the forty-third president and his people generally said what they meant, that they were manipulative but sincere.

The remarkable fact is not simply that between 1964 and 1974 young George Bush passed through ten of the most politically frenzied years in American political history at two of the most ideologically charged educational institutions in the country. It is that he did so with scarcely a ripple of involvement in any of the teeming political organizations, campus movements, or public debates or, it seems, even private conversations with peers. For Bush this kind of politics about causes and movements was something alien and superficial. It was like watching people in a water fight who do not know how the plumbing works. Through his family legacy and his father's career, he had seen politics from the inside out. Politics was about people more than policies, about election know-how, not ideological programs. At its best, it was about traditional values of character, not new, irresponsible crusades. This was what George W. Bush knew and what he stuck to. Experience, not abstract ideas, had taught him to live with two faces of politics—the new professional smash-mouth version he had learned the hard way in the last half of the twentieth century and the patrician responsibility version he had inherited more naturally from the older legacy of his family. Politics was theater, but the play was about character. That was essentialism in politics.

Cultural essentialism in the turbulent 1960s and 1970s meant simple American patriotism; the nation did not need to apologize for being a great country, and one did not need to listen to people who doubted its good intentions in the world. Likewise, it meant seeing business not as a realm of oppression, but as a realm of worthy endeavor; the wealth resulting from that endeavor was not something for which one needed to be ashamed or apologetic. To see the key, simple things in life was to enlarge one's thinking, not shrink it. That was an unspoken insight of the political ethos the younger George Bush learned as he struggled and survived in a world out of joint.

In all this, George W. Bush was a conservative. But he was not a movement conservative any more than his father was. The essentialist approach he was learning discounted any real interest in ideas as such. Just as it dismissed the grandiose ideas on the Left, so too it brushed off the dialectic oppositions on the Right. The Bushes were equal opportunity disparagers of political ideology. This was something leaders of the growing Christian Right always sensed in these years and why they never provided enthusiastic help to the Bushes in achieving their political ambitions in the 1970s, 1980s or 1990s. Deep down, they sensed that the Bushes regarded them merely as a political constituency, not as the inspiration for a mission in politics. Broadly speaking, such suspicion of both father and son was correct.

George Bush senior had been comfortable and even in the forefront of the new politics and its professional marketing of personal campaigns. He had demonstrated far less comfort with that other development in the new American political system, its more ideologically divisive turn. In effect, the first Bush-Reagan debate occurred in 1964. Both men were promising new faces and were invited by the conservative *National Review* to offer their analyses of Lyndon Johnson's landslide defeat of Barry Goldwater.[17] Even though Bush had lost the Senate race in Texas as a

Goldwater supporter, his analysis was a call to hold on to the mainstream Republicanism of the Grand Old Party. In Ronald Reagan's analysis, 1964 had opened up the opportunity to bring ordinary working Americans to a new understanding of their interests. George Bush spoke of the need to "re-package our philosophy" and build up a Republican Party that welcomed "all who want to be Republicans." Ronald Reagan commended and identified himself with those who "cross party lines in our dedication to a philosophy."

As he grew up, George W. Bush had come to admire Ronald Reagan, but it was not because of Reagan's commitment to ideas or his sacramental vision of America's mission. It was *after* Reagan had defeated his father in the 1980 race for the White House that the younger Bush voiced his strongest admiration for Reagan, based on the man's personal skills and political toughness. Reagan, he said, was clearheaded, easygoing, decisive, not distracted by the trappings of things. George W. Bush especially liked that he was the crafty epitome of the outside-the-Beltway campaigner and liked even more that he had not hesitated to fire his campaign manager as soon as he won the New Hampshire primary.[18] In short, all politics was personal, and the essential thing for the first son was that Reagan played the game extremely well.

The younger Bush prospered politically as he learned to play the game very well himself. Skill at doing what he knew and sticking to essentials helped Bush squeeze out a national victory in 2000. However, instead of engaging the political debates of his times, he essentially turned aside from confronting the conflict of ideas. Without such conflict there was very little basis for growing his political vision. By the time of his first summer vacation from the White House, this second Bush presidency was on track to fulfill a place in political time that Professor Stephen Skowronek has called that of the "orthodox innovator."[19] George W. Bush, it seemed, would be a transactional leader, not a transformational one, doing deals around the table, not really changing the shape of things. On August 3, 2001, the president met with the media and his cabinet in the Rose Garden to tote up progress on the Bush agenda. In the first twenty months his presidency had scored success with a major tax cut, some educational reforms, better health protection, more emergency help for farmers. Also, in the leaden language of old-guard Republicanism, foreign policy had been put "on [a] sound footing."

Then, once again, it happened. George Bush's closing comments that August afternoon in 2001 proved only too true: "In September, the second stage of our work begins."[20] Just when Bush had achieved the ultimate prize in public life, the world he expected to inherit was thrown out of joint. For over two generations his predecessors had successfully contained the massed power of the Soviet Union, and with the end of the cold war something like a fog of peace had seemed to settle in. By repelling a dictator's military aggression against his neighbors, his father's 1991 Gulf War had replayed the familiar script of World War II, and George W. Bush was able to become president at a time when Americans were even less interested than usual in foreign affairs. Then on September 11 it became clear that Bush had become president as America faced an entirely new kind of enemy. This was a fanatical enemy whose power was dispersed outside the traditional bounds of any nation-state. It was not an enemy with whom one could negotiate or sign treaties or against whom one could deploy massed military power or exercise counter-vailing containment strategies. Here was a threat from that distant realm of foreign affairs about which Americans cared so little, and yet, given the amazing modern technologies of mass murder, it was a threat that almost effortlessly touched every detail of their domestic lives. In a sense it called for total war, but a kind of total war that did not require public sacrifices for the common good around which presidents traditional mobilized their leadership. This was not our fathers' war.

In that first hour after the collapse of the twin towers, without the speechwriters or the rest of his White House apparatus at hand, George Bush instinctively repeated his father's words from ten years earlier. He told Americans perhaps the only thing he thought he knew for sure: "This will not stand."

Growth: Triumph of the Will

Without a considerable capacity for growth, George W. Bush could never have succeeded politically, let alone reached the White House. His own parents were surprised that it was he rather than one of the other Bush sons who became the next political star of the family. Indeed, those who knew him best were amazed at the transformation he had undergone by the 1990s. His favorite cousin, Elsie Walker, saw the change and could not believe her eyes as she watched the single make-or-break debate between her cut-up cousin and Texas Governor Ann Richards in 1994. As the media star governor goaded, jabbed, and ridiculed him, Elsie's bombastic cousin with the notoriously short fuse was unflappable and unrelentingly on message. Seeing her cousin maintain a steely self-control "like a dog with a bone," Elsie immediately wired her aunt Barbara Bush, "WHAT HAS . . . WHAT DID HE DO?"[21]

What had happened was that George W. Bush had gradually and painfully added a fourth feature that undergirded the other three elements of his political ethos. Broadly speaking, this feature was a growing appreciation for the power that lay in the discipline of his own will and in the application of such willpower to politics. A succession of life experiences had taught him that this was the growth he needed if he was not to be his own worst enemy.

Of course, no one becomes a successful politician without having or developing a strong will, not least of all the will to win power. However, for Bush what was at stake went beyond a politically desirable personality trait. The idea of a disciplined will became a guiding belief in his approach to politics. It shaped his concept of political communication and his interpretation of political events.

It would be tempting, but inaccurate, to portray Bush's growth as some sort of revelation that first served to get his personal life together and then spilled over to shape his political career. In popular accounts, Bush's religious conversations with Billy Graham in the mid-1980s have been given exactly that mythical reading. To be sure, as I will note shortly, this was an important experience in disciplining Bush to live the life he hoped to live. However, it is much truer to say that Bush's was a drawn-out journey, political and personal, with no single Damascus Road experience. Both the private and the public sides of Bush's life haltingly but eventually converged in a workable paradox: a growing recognition of the need to discipline his own willfulness and a deepening conviction of the indispensable value of that will. After 1968 his father had risen politically by serving other public figures loyally, often with that loyalty betrayed. George W. Bush would rise by learning the discipline to serve his family, his father, and above all his own calling with loyalty. At both a personal and a political level, the learning of discipline, self-control, and unblinking perseverance prepared Bush to be a wartime president long before he, or America, knew they were at war.

For a young man endowed by nature with a combustible personality, there were many milestones on the journey to self-discipline as an adult. In one of the earliest, the unfocused quality of much of Bush's school time at Andover and Yale was answered by his clear achievement in the eighteen months of training to earn his pilot's wings and the sheer delight of flying fighter jets. As young Bush experienced it, there was an utterly clarifying focus in that moment when he lit the jet burners.[22] It was a kind of serenity that would settle in as his somewhat sloppy mental, emotional, and physical energies finally became concentrated on a single existential point (though he would never have put it that way).

Finding a physical regimen may seem incidental to the story, but for Bush it was another noteworthy step in the journey of focusing his willful energy. An interesting dissertation remains to be written comparing the physical exercise routines of Bill Clinton and George W. Bush. For

Clinton jogging appears to have been a mostly sociable, hit-and-miss affair through which he made a stab at physical fitness. For Bush jogging (or, more accurately, running) began in his early adult years to become a competitively timed and tightly held regime for disciplining his day. Perhaps more than anything else, Bush's faithfully observed daily run became a physical-psychological space he could always reenter to gain a centeredness within himself.

When Bush's days as a pilot in the National Guard ended, entering Harvard Business School became a way of testing himself and demonstrating his mettle, first by showing he could get in and then by showing that he could stick it out with Harvard's best and brightest, without becoming one of them. All this time Bush's emotional edginess coexisted with a remarkable natural mental ability. Whether it was the mountain of baseball statistics in his youth, the intricate components a jet plane and radar system during pilot training, or the organizational structures and dynamics in his favorite Harvard class on human organization and behavior, Bush excelled at learning vast amounts of information about the internal workings of any particular enterprise that interested him. During his long years of political apprenticeship, this combination of emotional energy and capacious mental particularism turned into a powerful force when disciplined to the service of electoral politics.

An extraordinarily important milestone occurred during George Bush's first attempt at elective office, only two years after he had returned to Texas from Harvard. It is not the intent of this chapter to try to dissect the inner workings of the Bushes' marriage. The point I wish to make here is that George Bush's courting and winning thirty-year-old Laura Welch in 1977 not only brought a more settled and quiet order to his life; it also revealed a man who knew he needed those things in his life. This recognition was an important mark in his personal growth, and it was only enhanced by the birth of twin daughters who then became a new focus of his fatherly attention.

It would be presumptuous to imagine we can know what went on inside George Bush's soul in the mid-1980s, but the external fruits seem clear enough. Out of his conversations and soul-searching with Billy Graham in 1985 there came a new seriousness about religion and about the integrity and possibilities of his own life, apparently more a recommitment than a conversion.[23] The result was not any wholesale transformation of personality, but something more like a redirection of its central and often carelessly spent energies. This appears to be what Bush meant when in a 2000 debate among Republican presidential candidates he could offer no other explanation as to why Jesus was his favorite political philosopher than that "He changed my heart." In a way difficult to explain, Bush's Christian recommitment enabled what was frozen in his cockiness to become newly purposed. A more serious and humble religious view seemed gradually to open the way to a better understanding of himself and his shortcomings. He could acknowledge that he was turning to alcohol rather than to God to deal with his sense of failure in the oil business. His sarcastic impulses to criticize others did not disappear, but he began a more earnest search to discern what was worthy and unworthy, first of all in himself. There was a more genuine self-confidence that could come from admitting insufficiency and depending instead on a something higher and more worthy than oneself. He discovered that, oddly enough, acknowledging his willfulness could free that will for something better.

In the summer of 1986 the forty-year-old George Bush gave up a lifetime of drinking, cold turkey. A short time later, and in the same manner, Bush kept his promise to Laura and willed himself to overcome an addiction to smoking. As we have seen, it was at this time that Bush's political instincts were also becoming more deeply engaged and disciplined (according to some accounts, a major reason for giving up drinking at this time was to avoid the possibility of embarrassing his father as the vice president ran to succeed President Reagan).[24] Working alongside Lee Atwater, the first son learned more about how to control his anger and handle the press, about how political control depends on first controlling one's own impulses. Bush became the disciplinarian in a campaign staff of prima donnas, using his brusque, straightforward manner to leave no doubt that loyalty to his father's best interests in the campaign was non-negotiable. In the younger Bush's own campaigns and governorship, the same sort of determination went on to produce his strategy of tightly focusing on a very few themes, of hammering away on those issues, and of steadfastly refusing to go beyond whatever it is he meant to say. It also eventually produced a Bush White House that was almost monolithic in its discipline of political messages and staff egos, despite many journalists' best efforts to the contrary.

By general report of people who know him, George Bush believes that the events of September 11 revealed to him the mission for which he had become president. The unstated premise may be even more interesting. That September 11 had such an effect suggests that Bush is a person who willed himself to become president without a particularly compelling reason for having done so. Of course as a well-prepared, disciplined candidate, after 1998 Bush was always ready to answer the "Roger Mudd question" (the lack of an answer to which was a mistake that had embarrassed Ted Kennedy in his quest for the White House in 1979) with a pre-programmed explanation of why he wanted to be president. There was the good he could do for America with his policy agenda of tax cuts, educational reform, and aid to faith-based organizations. There was his desire to restore a sense of decency to the White House (subtext: to be the anti-Clinton). More implicit but also important for the candidate was a desire to set right the injustices done to his father as well as to fulfill vague background expectations that had been part of growing up with the Bush family ethos. None of this, however, really amounted to a compelling reason for wanting to be president, nothing that seemed to catch hold of and inspire what George W. Bush likes to call his "fieriness."

On September 11 Bush's long-hidden mission, the purpose for everything that had gone before, seemed to snap into place for the president. In the political ethos of the Bush family, the charge to keep was to behave responsibly. The terrorist attack filled in the blank space as to what responsibility required in the new post–cold war era. It required defending American security against a new kind of threat. This was the principle of political essentialism raised to the *n*th degree. Moreover the events of September 11 also brought the issue of will front and center for interpreting the larger meaning of the event. Now one could see that America had been hit again and again, but had mounted little effective response. The Beirut bombings of the U.S. Embassy and then the Marine barracks in 1983; the 1985 attacks on Americans in Madrid, at the Rhein-Main Air Force Base, and on the cruise ship *Achille Lauro;* the sabotage of TWA Flight 840 in 1986 and Pan Am Flight 103 in 1988; the bombing of the World Trade Center in 1993; the 1995 car bombing of two U.S. military compounds in Saudi Arabia; the simultaneous bombing of U.S. embassies in Kenya and Tanzania; and the bombing of the USS *Cole* in 2000—this roll call of events showed a nation under constant attack. More than that, it demonstrated that America's vacillating and weak responses had been provocative; they had taught terrorists to think they could act with impunity. Indecision had made America vulnerable. Safety required decisiveness. And decisiveness required risking the bold action that Bush as president thought was necessary in Afghanistan, Iraq, or anyplace else. Rogue states supporting terrorists would be treated the same as terrorists. Thus the Bush doctrine of preemption was born. In a sense, the critique of the 1960s found a new focus. For too long the United States had in effect accepted victimhood, ducked responsibility, and lacked the will to respond.

Obstructive actors in the larger world could also easily fit into a narrative about will, or the lack thereof. By proving unwilling to enforce its own resolutions against Iraq, the United Nations had failed to behave responsibly. The essential issue came down to that, even while President Bush held himself back, bided his time, and allowed the diplomatic maneuvering to exhaust itself. But in the end, regardless of others' opinions, Bush would show that he and the nation had the will to act. As he expressed it to the country in the hours before launching war on Iraq, "Under Resolutions 676 and 687—both still in effect—the United States and our allies are authorized to use force in ridding Iraq of weapons of mass destruction. This is not a question of authority, it is a question of will."[25]

After September 11 Bush's political ethos was available to offer the interpretation underpinning a new sense of national purpose. He saw history as having called both the man and the nation to action. Both the man and the nation had to have the will to act rather than wait on threats to fully materialize. The war on terror would not be won on the defensive. "In the world we have entered," the president told the next generation of Army leaders, "the only path to safety is the path of action, and this nation will act."[26] Disciplining his will in personal and political terms had been the preparatory work. Watchwords that had applied to Bush and his own growth were now writ large for the nation: "We will not tire; we will not falter; we will not fail."

Perils: Leading without Educating

The elements discussed in this chapter certainly do not exhaust our subject, and later historians will be able to go much further in evaluating the Bush political ethos. In the preliminary account offered here, I have tried to describe this orientation along four tracks that are—speaking very roughly—(1) ethical, (2) tactical, (3) strategic, and (4) psychological in their emphases.

1. Bush's family legacy taught him that politics was a preeminent arena for testing one's character and doing one's duty. The background presupposition was always that there are firm standards of good and bad character, along with a faith that honor, if not always fame, would ultimately come to those who deserved it. Some have characterized Bush's ethical view as Manichean, but the fact is that the starker language of "evil" was never a prominent feature of the Bush moral catechism. It was a later add-on of his presidency, triggered by September 11 in a rather facile attempt to mimic the more deeply rooted Reagan rhetoric. The ethic of responsibility, not the eschatology of good versus evil, was the building block of so-called moral clarity in the Bush political ethos.
2. The tactical dimension of this ethos found its source in the changing system of partisan politics that overtook America in the latter

twentieth century. As we have seen, Bush served a long and highly educational apprenticeship in this new world of polls, consultants, media relations, and the selling of political personas. He learned the skills and toughness required to manage one's political career, whether in or out of office, as a permanent campaign. Obviously attention to political strategy was an important part of this picture, but since the focus was on how to maneuver in this permanent campaign to get one's way, it seems right to designate this as the tactical aspect of Bush's ethos.

3. Strategy refers to the overarching habits of mind that proved valuable to Bush as he followed in his father's footsteps in a more complex and confusing America. From the mid-1960s onward, Bush encountered a world that often did not function according to the expected rules of the game. Rather than growing a political vision out of the political and cultural confrontations of these times, George W. Bush turned to what he could recognize as familiar and essential. In a culture increasingly heavy with the complexities of self-examination and doubt, Bush refused to get lost in nuances. He honed his natural instinct to cut to the heart of the matter in any task at hand while generally staying on whatever ground was well known to him.

4. Finally, the Bush political ethos has a more psychological dimension, something referred to earlier as the triumph of the will. At both a deeply personal level and a political level, Bush grew to appreciate the immense gains to be realized from allowing his own willfulness to be ruled. The result was a psychological investment in self-discipline that brought Bush into a deeper engagement with the life he hoped to live. Politically speaking, a disciplined will could be expected to resolve itself into a hyperfocused agenda and decisive action. Bush became a man not to hoard political capital but to risk it, build it again, and put it on the line again.

Perhaps it is worthwhile at this point to state the obvious. The inner schema for generating and applying Bush's energy to public affairs—his political ethos—has produced immense political success, especially considering that he has held public office (at this time of writing) for a total of less than nine years. Political opponents and much of the public have consistently underestimated George W. Bush. However, any balanced assessment should assay ways this political ethos may also serve Bush and the country poorly. Rather than offering predictions, these constitute a menu of dangers entailed in his way of doing political business, temptations that leave the forty-third president's leadership vulnerable over the longer run.

It is true to say that Bush has the inner confidence to surround himself with strong, smart people, and apparently the wisdom to listen to them. However, it is not good enough to say that the strengths of presidential advisers will compensate for their boss's vulnerabilities. That itself is a dangerous hope. First, because no one but a president himself can be counted on to protect his power stakes. Second, because the inevitable tendency is for presidential advisers to mirror any president's own style and focus, in short, to reflect rather than challenge his political ethos. It is appropriate, therefore, to conclude by drawing attention to three dangers embedded in the Bush political ethos, moving in ascending order of their imperilment of his legacy.

First, the Bush family's sense of rectitude does not take well to charges that one might not be acting responsibly. If opponents find it opportune to engage in a sustained questioning of Bush's motives, there is a good chance it could arouse a disproportionate sensitivity and anger. Bush has never had much difficulty deflecting attacks on his intellect; it adds to his common touch, and in any event he detests people who think they are smarter than other people. Attacks on character are another thing, as attested by his ballistic responses when charges of being a wimp were directed against his father earlier. If for some reason George W. Bush ever faces serious attacks that he is acting without a moral compass, it could tap emotional forces that would cloud his judgment in responding.

Second, Bush learns quickly and becomes deeply informed about what he is interested in. But this sort of learning capacity turns into a liability when it comes to things that should interest him but do not. Then too much is lost from view. The problem with cutting through nuances by doing what one knows is that it tends to stifle learning about what one does not know. To be sure, it yields a sense of assurance and self-confidence that people value in a leader. But this is a dangerous self-confidence if it exists because one's mind is not burdened with challenging the adequacy of its own conceptions. Then arises the age-old danger for political leaders, the idée fixe locked in the confines of its own idiom, where critical doubt generated from a larger world of facts offers no safeguard. Focusing "when the burners come on" is not the same thing as thinking imaginatively. Always being on message is not the same thing as being on target.

Third, campaigning may be permanent, but it is not synonymous with governing. Bush's political outlook has been steeped in the campaign mentality of modern public life. The mental framework of campaigning invites a preoccupation with single win-lose decision points. It conceptualizes the political world as a purely competitive arena for exploiting one's disagreement with adversaries. It aims to promote one's cause against those adversaries by telling people what they want to hear, not what they need to know. All of this can disserve the needs of governing. There the time horizon needs to be long and steady, not short and discontinuous. Sensible governing involves trying to grasp the larger picture beyond the contests of the moment. While campaigning seeks to defeat enemies to win an unshared prize, governing demands collaboration to bring others along on various paths of action. Campaigning is about selling a product. Governing is about judging how to use the terrible powers of the modern state.

Hints of all these dangers were discernable by the summer of 2003, revealed in George W. Bush's apparent misinterpretation of the lessons of his father. The standard view is that the first President Bush made the mistake of focusing on the Gulf War and neglecting domestic priorities before the 1992 election. In fact the deeper problem was created by Bush's focusing on the parades at home to try to squeeze out domestic credit from the war, meanwhile neglecting the postwar situation in Iraq during 1991 and 1992, a situation that encouraged doomed uprisings against Saddam and stored up huge longer-term problems for the United States (which his son eventually inherited).

When it comes to Gulf War II, George W. Bush's failings do not lie in statements he made during the 2000 campaign that he would avoid ventures in nation building; no politician could have known then what lay in store for Afghanistan or Iraq after September 11. The fault lies in the foreshortened vision with which Bush decided to make war on the Iraqi regime. It is now clear that there was thorough planning for quick military victory, but very meager planning for the long-term rebuilding effort that would be required after our troops reached Baghdad. This sort of blind spot took symbolic form as the difference between "campaigning" and governing in Iraq emerged. On literally the same day in March that George Bush was addressing the Iraqi people from London, expounding on the glorious history and future democratic promise of their nation, American forces were standing by as domestic order in that nation broke down. Oil wells were protected; museums containing the nation's cultural heritage were not.

Likewise, there is the facile view that before the 1992 election Bush senior made the mistake of raising taxes he had promised never to raise. In fact, the mistake lay in succumbing to the campaign temptations of 1988 and making his capacity to govern hostage to the fortunes of an unconditional tax pledge. The heart of his alleged 1992 problem with tax policy lay in having taken short-term campaign profits from the tax issue four years earlier. This is a problem his son also faces. By presenting tax cuts as the one and only way to think about the nation's economic and fiscal problems, President George W. Bush has tended to foreclose future choices for governing. More tax cuts will be no answer when past tax cuts have deprived the federal budget of revenues needed for government activities people actually do want (providing homeland security, health coverage for the uninsured, environmental cleanup, etc.). Still more dangerous in the long term is a blithe disregard of really big and inescapable bills coming due. The underfunding of Social Security and Medicare that looms in the next decade is now projected to be $18–25 trillion, or something roughly amounting to half of all the household wealth of the United States in 2002. Only in the "bizarro world" of comic books does the presidential one-note tax cut strategy have anything to say about that. For Bush and many others, an easy campaign strategy has been to call on Washington to manage its budget the way American families have to; the governing reality is that people are being taught to let government behave exactly as too many households do—mortgaging their future for cheap short-term gratifications.

The point is not to condemn Bush or other politicians for failing to predict the future (even political science professors sometimes fail to do that with perfect accuracy). The point is that it is dangerous to stop with decisive leadership and not take much interest in looking around the corner to teach Americans about the larger and longer-term realities of their situation. For better or worse, a president is always teaching. Not least of all, he is teaching people about himself by teaching them about events. The less hard realism he teaches about events—the more he mistakes selling for educating—the harder it will go for him in the long run.

By all accounts, Bush thinks seriously about the nature of leadership and its exercise in the presidency. In White House meetings he has emphasized his role in explaining issues related to terrorism and educating the public on the long-term challenges they face in this "first war of the twenty-first century." Bush clearly understands the need for persuading the people to his point of view, but it is also possible to sell people on things without broadening their horizons. The paradox is that successful teaching requires ongoing learning on the teacher's part.

Bush's mental style and political ethos are not naturally suited to such broadening of horizons through educational leadership. In the idiom of his internal schema, the purpose of politics is to identify one's mission, keep faith with that charge, and then move on to the next agenda item. It is the sort of decisiveness and disciplined will that can ultimately fail to draw others into an understandable larger narrative of a worthy journey they are on together. The declarative language Bush is drawn to—"We shall prevail," "Our cause is just"—can be seen as no more that a factual statement about power or personal conviction. Listeners are left hanging in a timeless moment.

Insiders like Vice President Dick Cheney have described Bush as "Reaganesque," with a remarkable ability to focus on the heart of a matter.[27] This is a half-truth. For Reagan this ability to avoid getting lost in details stemmed from a clearly defined long-standing system of ideas, his public philosophy and vision of history, for lack of better terms. For Bush it is more a matter of decision-making strategy and disciplined will. Reagan savored the opportunity to remind Americans who they are and what their national story means before telling them what they should do. Bush is by nature inclined to cut straight to the action plan, what needs to be done. Reagan's mental equipment was set up to make him a visionary storyteller; Bush's is set up to make him the straight-talking and politically astute CEO of a permanent campaign.

By Vice President Cheney's account, President Bush immediately understood that September 11 created a new situation for the nation, demonstrating this understanding in his earliest public statement to the effect that rogue states that support terrorists would now be treated as terrorists in a worldwide war. If one accepts this assessment of the situation, it is clear that being even the most brilliant CEO will not be good enough. Protecting the security of the nation—the essence of political essentialism—requires transformative leadership by one who learns and teaches others to think anew and act anew. The logic of the situation implies that preserving the status quo now requires wholesale changes.

For example, since there seems no reliable defense at home against this new kind of enemy, America must be wiling to attack others before it is attacked. Or again, while America desperately needs other countries' cooperation in this war, it must also be willing to go it alone. Multilateralism can be the path to getting the world to act responsibly, and it can also be a device for ducking responsibilities. Unilateralism can demonstrate American arrogance as well as let other participants off the hook, but it can also demonstrate America's taking up its ultimate responsibilities and leading by example. Peace negotiations can be seen as rewarding terrorists, and they can also be seen as a way of refusing to allow terrorists to veto progress.

In short, in the first American war of this century the task of the first president of the century amounts to an immense educational project for the long term, one at least as large as was entailed in teaching the lessons of Munich in the 1930s or those of the containment of communism in the 1940s. Americans are poised to be taught that they are beleaguered and under attack in the world, that their nation's own safety and security is the one thing to think about. But they are also poised to be taught that Americans' safety is bound up with bringing hope to the larger world. America in a mainly defensive posture has never produced very constructive results at home or abroad. Its positive work has flowed out of those times of forward-leaning promise and hope for things that can be. Down this path lies an America going about the larger business of constructing a more just and thus more secure international order, not just nation-building, but world-building.

No one has ever gained the White House promising to take the country into war, and Bush, like all his predecessors, became a wartime president inadvertently.[28] Once at war, men have seen their presidencies wrecked (Madison, Wilson, Truman, Johnson) or apotheosized by the ordeal (Lincoln, F.D.R.). There seems little room for anything in between. Regardless of party, one should hope that the strengths of Bush's political ethos prevail over the dangers of its weaknesses. Our common fate is tied up even more with George W. Bush's teaching than with his leadership. For as Martin Buber observed one hundred years ago in an eerily related context: "Leading without teaching attains success: Only what one attains is at times a downright caricature of what, in the ground of one's soul . . . one wanted to attain. . . . Unhappy, certainly, is the people that has no leader, but three times as unhappy is the people whose leader has no teaching."[29]

Chapter 3

The Bush White House in Comparative Perspective

Karen M. Hult

DURING THE EARLY MONTHS of George W. Bush's presidency, there was widespread speculation about the inner workings of the White House. Even before he was inaugurated, attention focused on whether President Bush or Vice President Richard Cheney actually made the final decisions on staffing the cabinet and organizing the White House. Others speculated about the impact of additional "seasoned veterans" of past Republican administrations, including the elder Bush's. Soon the president's political affairs director, Karl Rove, and Counselor Karen Hughes joined those who received public credit for allegedly shaping most presidential initiatives, including the successful tax-cut package. Of course the September 11 attacks and the president's widely praised performance in its aftermath triggered an almost immediate reconsideration. Some noted that Bush had finally "grown" into his presidency, pointing to a new seriousness and resolve. Others stressed the influence of his religious commitments.

To the extent that it was accurate, such commentary illuminated the dynamics of the Bush White House, although some of it also was influenced by partisan sentiment and the fascination of the media with drama and conflict. Whatever the case, the accounts typically shared an unstated premise. They implied that the organization of the White House was unique to President Bush.

In contrast, this chapter takes a different perspective. The structuring, operation, and activities of contemporary White Houses—and many of the associated consequences—have often reflected the influences of more *systematic* (or predictable, recurring) factors that have affected most recent presidencies.[1] I emphasize two general kinds of systematic influence that have constrained and enabled White House organization and operations: the prevailing *political and policy environments* and longer-term *organizational dynamics* that frequently have transcended administrations. Comparing George W. Bush's White House with the White Houses of his predecessors highlights both continuities with previous administrations and departures from them. Underscored throughout is the resilience of the institutional presidency.

Taking this approach does not mean that the preferences, objectives, and strategies of individual presidents are irrelevant. But it does suggest that presidents pursue their political and policy goals within the constraints and incentives of the institution of the presidency and of given problem contexts.

In the discussion that follows, I begin by elaborating on the conceptual foundations of the analysis. I then focus on three primary tasks of contemporary White Houses: (1) coordination and supervision of the activities and people that comprise the modern presidency, (2) policy formulation and deliberation, or "policy processing," and (3) outreach to external interests and the general public. Based on the information available in the public record, I describe how the Bush White House has handled each of these tasks, identify similarities to and differences from the efforts of previous administrations, and offer tentative explanations for the continuities and discontinuities.

In general, I show that the Bush administration has organized the White House, and supervises and coordinates its activities, in ways that are quite similar to those seen in past modern presidencies. Virtually all of the familiar units and functions of recent administrations appear in the Bush White House. Meanwhile, other features—for example, extensive vice presidential influence and the permeation of policy by political and public relations concerns—reflect the persistence of longer-term trends. Still other characteristics recall the initiatives of previous Republican presidents. Even the catastrophic terrorist attacks of September 2001 influenced the institutional contours of the presidency and the structures and processes of the White House only at the margins.

At the same time, George W. Bush's values and priorities have shaped the focus of new units such as the Office of Faith-Based and Community Initiatives and the Office of Global Communications just as they have affected the emphases of other White House units. His management preferences have helped produce the administration's characteristic discipline and the premium it places on secrecy. On the whole, however, despite a distinctive policy agenda and virtually unprecedented policy challenges, President Bush guides a White House that is defined more by continuity than by discontinuity.

Making Sense of a White House: Conceptual Foundations

Few today would likely dispute Dwight D. Eisenhower's assertion that although "organization cannot make a genius out of an incompetent . . . disorganization can scarcely fail to result in inefficiency and can easily lead to disaster."[2] Numerous factors may shape presidents' organizational choices.

One set of systematic influences is environmental. Events outside the White House clearly can affect what goes on inside. The terrorist attacks of September 11, 2001, are perhaps the most striking and horrific reminder. Perceived crises have led administrations to create new positions (for example, one of Eisenhower's responses to the launch of *Sputnik I* in 1957 was to name a special assistant to the president for science and technology)[3] or to change decision-making processes (as happened with the emergence of the ad hoc "war cabinet" that met in the aftermath of the September 11 terrorist attacks). Other environmental influences may be less abrupt, ranging from the election of new leaders in other countries to global, regional, national, and local economic dynamics; from new communication, information, and weapons technologies to increasingly homogeneous and polarized congressional parties and the rising numbers of interest groups in U.S. politics. Meanwhile, the expectations of external actors may produce pressures for continuity. Some White House staff operations persist mostly because outside actors, such as members of Congress and journalists, come to see tasks such as the maintenance of legislative liaison and press relations as part of "normal" White House activities.

A second cluster of systematic factors taps the organizational dynamics of the institutional presidency. For example, presidential party affiliation has exerted important, if declining, influence on White Houses. "Partisan learning" refers to the tendency of presidents to follow the strategies of predecessors of their own political party while rejecting those of presidents of the other party. Typically partisan learning is transmitted by staffers or transition advisers from previous administrations. George W. Bush, of course, was quite familiar with his father's White House. In addition, Vice President Cheney had worked in earlier White Houses, as had the chief of staff (and one of his deputies), the national security assistant, and the director and deputy director of legislative liaison, among others.[4]

Certain White House arrangements persist across several administrations of both parties. An especially striking illustration is the acceptance by both Republicans and Democrats of what has been labeled a "standard model" of White House governance.[5] In this general approach to White House organization, the activities of numerous specialized units (for instance, those responsible for press and congressional relations) are coordinated and linked to the president through the office of a chief of staff, which occupies the top level of an overall White House hierarchy and links staffers to the president. Among the primary objectives of this arrangement are to help relieve presidents of some of the burdens of managing a White House staff that numbers in the hundreds and to ensure that the information and the decision options that reach presidents have been discussed and reviewed by those with relevant expertise. Despite some variations in specifics, every Republican president beginning with Eisenhower has adopted this approach, as have Democratic presidents since the middle of the Jimmy Carter administration.[6]

Such organizational continuity in part reflects a kind of "nonpartisan learning," as new presidents seek to imitate the successes of their predecessors. Other examples of this dynamic include the existence of press secretaries in all White Houses since Herbert Hoover's and the presence of formal domestic policy staffs dating at least to the administration of Richard M. Nixon. External expectations regarding appropriate White House tasks and structuring no doubt reinforce presidential tendencies to follow precedent. Indeed advice given to new presidents by White House veterans and external observers alike highlights the consensus in favor of the standard model.[7]

Even so, the preferences, objectives, and strategies of individual presidents can scarcely be overlooked. The diverse policy agendas, campaign promises, and political experiences of particular presidents certainly can affect the decisions, organization, and operations of their administrations. Yet one need not be overwhelmed with examining the idiosyncratic characteristics of specific chief executives. Here I view presidents as purposive actors who pursue their objectives given the constraints of both the institutional presidency and the political and policy environments of their particular presidencies. Attention is focused, then, not on the unique features of George W. Bush, but instead on his likely responses as a strategic actor who seeks an identifiable set of political commitments and policy goals.[8]

Running the White House: Variations on a Theme

The first major task that all White Houses must handle is the supervision and coordination of the diverse activities, people, and units that make up the contemporary presidency. A standard model for performing this task has emerged that features numerous specialized units directed and coordinated by a chief of staff. Following an approach first introduced by Eisenhower, later Republican presidents all have relied on a hierarchically organized White House headed by a chief of staff. When Jimmy Carter sought to rescue his presidency, which had been plagued by charges of lack of direction and inept execution, by naming Hamilton Jordan chief of staff in 1979, it signaled the Democrats' acceptance of the need for more centralized and better-coordinated White House operations. The next Democratic administration began with a chief of staff. Bill Clinton initially experimented with a "weak" chief of staff that permitted numerous aides to have direct access to the president but had few mechanisms for coordinating efforts or minimizing conflicts over political or policy turf. As charges of internal disarray mounted, the president abandoned the arrangement; under Chief of Staff Leon Panetta and his successors, responsibility for the supervision and coordination of White House activities explicitly rested in the chief of staff's office.

Clinton's experience and George W. Bush's selection of White House veteran Andrew Card as his chief of staff underscore the institutionalization not only of the chief of staff's office, but also of the "strong" version of that unit. The complexity and volatility of the contemporary presidency "requires discipline and coordination that can only be achieved if there is a central coordinating point, someone other than the president to oversee the operation."[9]

Even so, exactly how individual administrations have implemented the standard model has varied. Unlike Eisenhower, Nixon, and the first President Bush, George W. Bush did not make his chief of staff the only person at the top of the White House hierarchy. Two other senior aides— political strategist Karl Rove and campaign press secretary and public relations adviser Karen Hughes—reported directly to the president and oversaw political affairs and communications activities, respectively. This arrangement in part reflected the new president's unwillingness to have two such valued aides placed in positions subordinate to the chief of staff. Probably also influential was Bush's familiarity with the problems created by his father's first chief of staff, John Sununu, and by Ronald Reagan's second-term chief of staff, Donald Regan, both of whom had sought to dominate the White House and had sometimes prevented useful streams of information and advice from reaching the president.[10] Meanwhile, the younger Bush's senior staffing is consistent with reports of his desire for multiple sources of information.

More than presidential "management style" seemed to be involved, however. A partisan precedent certainly existed for a limited division of power among senior staffers. The Bush arrangement is reminiscent of the "troika" of advisers present in Reagan's first-term White House.[11] In the earlier configuration, Chief of Staff James Baker III managed the White House decision-making process, Edwin Meese was responsible for domestic policy, and Michael Deaver, formally Baker's assistant, had responsibility for presenting the public face of President Reagan.

The emphases of the three top aides in the Bush White House differed from those of their Reagan administration predecessors. Hughes's responsibilities came closest to paralleling Deaver's, although with considerable input from Rove. Card undertook the coordination and management tasks that had been part of Baker's job and shared the more political dimensions with Rove. Rove and Card became involved in policy issues when they intersected with key political concerns.[12] Most notably, none of the three was primarily responsible for the substance of domestic or economic policy.

Although numerous explanations can be offered for this difference in the division of labor, a persuasive account directs attention to changes in U.S. politics. Washington, D.C., has become more politicized, with growing party polarization in Congress and the pressures of a twenty-four-hour news cycle. At the same time, the demands and expectations of organized interests have multiplied, and citizens' ties to political parties and to the federal government continue to erode. Such pressures may well dictate presidential efforts to identify, track, and try to shape public opinion.[13] Although the constituencies to which the Bush White House seeks to be responsive differ from those the Clinton administration stressed, the two administrations pursued quite similar strategies. The disputed 2000 presidential election likely only amplified the emphasis on Bush's having to establish himself with many members of the public as a legitimate and capable president.

In addition, other aspects of the standard model of White House organization appear in the Bush White House much as they have in administrations beginning with Nixon's. Subordinate to the chief of staff, several specialized units (such as the staff secretary's office and the cabinet affairs office) are designed to extend the reach of the president and to maintain orderly processes within the White House. In addition, like most recent chiefs of staff, Card has had two deputies. One deputy (Joshua Bolten, until he became director of the Office of Management in late June

2003) oversees the policy staffs; most remaining White House units report to the chief of staff through the other deputy, Joseph Hagin.[14]

The overall White House organization changed relatively little once the enormous shock of September 11 wore off; throughout the crisis, most routine operations continued. Nonetheless, Card joined the war cabinet, and the focus of policy decision-making became quite different. Deputy Chief of Staff Bolten chaired a "domestic consequences" group that met daily "to deal with fallout from the attacks on the home front."[15] In October 2001, Pennsylvania Governor Thomas Ridge joined the White House Office as assistant to the president for homeland security, charged with overseeing the new Office of Homeland Security in the Executive Office of the President.

The White House confronted another kind of disturbance in July 2002 when Counselor Hughes left the staff. Despite speculation about the "seismic shift"[16] that would take place in the distribution of White House influence, it has been difficult to determine exactly how the internal dynamics have changed. Doubtless becoming more influential were Press Secretary Ari Fleischer, head speechwriter Michael Gerson, and Daniel Bartlett, the White House communications director who had served as Hughes's assistant and took over her operation.[17] Working as a consultant for the Republican National Committee, Hughes continues to work on major speeches; near the end of 2002 she told journalist Elisabeth Bumiller that she "still talks to Mr. Bush two or three times a week, if not more, and she is in daily contact with some of the most important officials in the West Wing."[18] Even so, the troika was reduced to two senior aides, and reports of Karl Rove's increasing influence over both politics and, increasingly, policy have proliferated.[19] Meanwhile, Rove and Card evidently have developed a workable division of labor.

In sum, although the Bush White House is not organized in a way that is identical to the Eisenhower and Nixon arrangements, it falls well within the parameters of the standard model used by recent presidents and advocated by White House veterans and scholars. Moreover, the initial troika recalled a Republican predecessor, and the division of labor among the most senior staffers is responsive to external demands and to presidential preferences for a disciplined operation that is sensitive to politics.

Policy Processing: Innovation and Continuity

With but a handful of significant exceptions, the arrangements of Bush's White House for handling its second primary task—policy processing— also highlight continuity. As in the Clinton administration, the Bush White House includes cabinet councils and associated staffs for formulat-

ing and deliberating over national security, domestic, and economic policies. Some innovations have appeared, such as the establishment of the
Office of Faith-Based and Community Initiatives. Not surprisingly,
the structural change of the greatest magnitude—the creation of an assistant to the president for homeland security, the Office of Homeland
Security in the Executive Office of the President, and the Homeland Security Council—was made in response to an extraordinary and unanticipated shock; yet even these efforts to address homeland security largely
imitated the other main policy-processing mechanisms. Meanwhile, both
the high levels of involvement of the vice presidency and efforts to
achieve policy objectives through non-legislative means recalled earlier
presidencies.

Differing Priorities and Contexts:
Elimination and Creation of Specialized Offices

Like most new presidents, George W. Bush strove to distinguish his White
House from that of its just departed occupant. Such effort had a special
urgency for a chief executive who had received fewer popular votes than
had his opponent. In Bush's case the determination was reinforced by
the fact that he was a Republican replacing a two-term Democratic president and by the controversial way in which Bill Clinton and his staff had
exited.

President Bush's abolition of some White House units and his introduction of others were scarcely unusual. At the outset, he eliminated the
Office of Women's Initiatives and Outreach and the unit supporting the
President's Initiative for One America, which had been established to
promote discussion of race relations. Similarly, John F. Kennedy had abol-
ished all but one of Eisenhower's ten special White House offices,[20] and
the Clinton staff had not retained George H. W. Bush's Points of Light
Foundation.

New presidents sometimes also form new units or create new positions
in either the White House Office or the larger Executive Office of the President to signal high presidential priorities.[21] The Eisenhower White House,
for instance, had included a public works planning unit; J.F.K. had established an office for mental retardation policy; and Clinton had introduced,
among others, an AIDS policy coordinator and an office for environmental
initiatives. On other occasions, the formation of new staff units in the
White House reflects external demands for governmental action and the
absence of readily available ways to respond. Examples include Kennedy's
and Johnson's experiments with consumer affairs advisers and offices as
the consumer movement burgeoned in the 1960s and the Clinton admin-

istration's creation of the Millennium Project to handle possible Y2K problems. Although the Bush administration tried to eliminate the Clinton AIDS office, loud protest led officials to quickly restore it. Finally, crises like September 11 sometimes highlight the need for, and heighten public expectations of, highly visible organizational responses.

The Office of Faith-Based and Community Initiatives. During the 2000 presidential race both candidates expressed support for including religious groups among the providers of federally financed social services. George W. Bush claimed that such integration was a key part of "compassionate conservatism," and he promised that as president he would strive to reach out to so-called faith-based organizations and enlist their help in aiding the needy. It was not a surprise, then, when one of his administration's first actions was to issue an executive order that created the White House Office of Faith-Based and Community Initiatives (OFBCI).[22]

OFBCI suffered numerous difficulties from the start, however. It was "understaffed, under-funded," and lacked a "firm grasp of [its] responsibilities."[23] At least as important, its first director, John J. DiIulio, Jr., "lacked budgetary authority, the ability to staff the Office with his own colleagues, and the power to develop and execute political strategies."[24] Other problems soon arose. One of the unit's initial charges was to secure passage of the Community Solutions Act of 2001, which was designed to make it easier for faith-based groups to qualify for federal funds. DiIulio lost the debate within the White House over the best way to handle the issue; the OFBCI director advocated a "consensus-building" strategy, while others supported what Kathryn Dunn Tenpas dubbed a "'move it or lose it' approach."[25] Moreover, not only was there little coordination of this initiative with the White House congressional relations staff or other relevant offices, but the president's tax-cut and education reform initiatives also received higher priority within the administration. Meanwhile, DiIulio came in for considerable criticism, triggered mostly by his too-candid statements to the press about weaknesses in the White House domestic policy operations.

Nor could environmental influences be ignored. Some church-related organizations expressed strong opposition to the legislation, and numerous others raised a range of constitutional objections. A leaked Salvation Army memo exacerbated the difficulties, claiming that the Bush administration had committed to exempt organizations from state and local gay and lesbian rights statutes. Although legislation supporting the federal funding of faith-based organizations passed the House on July 19, 2001, its prospects in the Senate only worsened with the shift to Democratic control that had taken place in June. Damage from unexpected external events, of course, intensified after the September terrorist attacks. Like much of the rest of the White House, OFBCI shifted its focus.

DiIulio announced his resignation in mid-August 2001, and a replacement, Jim Towey, was not named until February 2002. Not only did Towey come into the White House at a lower level of the staff hierarchy than his predecessor had occupied, but the unit itself was to be overseen by a new White House advisory council headed by John Bridgeland, director of the new USA Freedom Corps Office.[26]

OFBCI redirected its efforts to emphasize implementation and outreach, focusing on making changes in administrative regulations and on developing ties with religious organizations and charities. President Bush sought to strengthen the former strategy by issuing two additional executive orders in December 2002, one that allows religious organizations that refuse to hire individuals of any faith to win federal contracts and one that placed faith-based units in two additional agencies (the Agency for International Development and the State Department).[27]

OFBCI is one of the signature additions of the Bush White House, and the legislation supporting the federal funding of faith-based organizations that it pursued was virtually the only congressional initiative in the first two years that reflected the president's campaign emphasis on compassionate conservatism. Still, it would be difficult to conclude that OFBCI's presence dramatically changed the administration or, at least in the first thirty months, contributed much to its achievements. Even before the terrorist attacks, its emphases could hardly be called among the most significant of the administration.

The Office of Homeland Security. September 11 had myriad effects on the White House, the larger executive branch, and without doubt the president. Still, the initial structural innovation for policy was the creation of the Office of Homeland Security, headed by an assistant to the president and charged with serving as the staff to the new Homeland Security Council.

The administration's first policy responses to the terrorist attacks included numerous meetings of the war cabinet and other ad hoc groups of national security officials. Clearly, however, terrorism directed at Americans is a long-term problem, not a single event. Critically needed, then, was a structural response. In early October the president named then–Pennsylvania Governor Tom Ridge to head a new White House Office of Homeland Security (OHS). In many respects, this approach was "modeled after the current iteration of the National Security Council (NSC) and the Assistant to the President for National Security Affairs."[28]

Like the NSC model, OHS was designed to be a coordinating body, with a director who is a top presidential adviser and a staff located in the Executive Office of the President. Overseeing the operation is the Homeland Security Council, which includes top cabinet members and agency heads as well as Chief of Staff Card. OHS confronted a daunting task: coordinating the activities of the more than forty agencies that were involved in aspects of what the president defined as "homeland security"; state and local government entities also had crucial roles. Yet Ridge had only a small staff and neither statutory nor budgetary authority over these agencies.[29]

By and large, these arrangements proved insufficient. Virtually all assessments of OHS have concluded that, crippled from the start, Ridge and OHS could not succeed, at least in the short run. He "lacked the necessary clout to move the bureaucratic behemoth at anything but a snails' pace."[30] By June 2002, President Bush had abandoned his initial resistance to the idea of elevating the unit responsible for homeland security to the status of a cabinet department. After months in which Bush wrangled with the Senate over his proposal to weaken civil service protections for employees of the new department, the Department of Homeland Security (DHS) was established in the aftermath of the 2002 election.

Although Ridge became secretary of the department, an assistant to the president for homeland security remains in the White House Office, supported by OHS; the Homeland Security Council also survives. How the department secretary and his counterpart in the White House would work together remained to be seen; until March 1, 2003, Ridge retained responsibility for "domestic response efforts otherwise assigned to the Assistant for Homeland Security."[31] At least the potential for overlap exists. For instance, according to a homeland security presidential directive on "management of domestic incidents," the DHS secretary is the "principal Federal official for domestic incident management," with statutory responsibilities for "coordinating Federal operations within the United States." At the same time, the presidential assistant for homeland security is charged with handling "interagency policy coordination on domestic . . . incident management."[32] One can easily imagine the difficulties that might arise in separating coordination of operations from interagency policy coordination.

Institutionalized Arrangements: Cabinet Councils

Despite its newness, the initial organizational arrangement for homeland security closely paralleled the arrangements for processing national security, economic, and domestic policies in the Bush administration and its immediate predecessors: all four areas rely on cabinet councils. In such a council a group of cabinet members (and/or subcabinet officials and agency heads) is the formal governing body, assisted by a staff (formally lodged in the Executive Office of the President) whose top official typically is a White House aide, usually with the title of assistant to the president.[33] The use of cabinet councils to oversee major areas of public policy started with the creation of the National Security Council (and the beginnings of a staff) in 1947. With the creation of the Domestic Council, Nixon first sought to explicitly apply this model to the domestic policy arena. The Economic Policy Board established under Ford followed a version of the same approach in economic policy. Although several domestic and economic policy variants have appeared since then, some type of a cabinet council–presidential staff mechanism has emerged to handle economic and domestic policy issues in virtually all subsequent administrations.[34]

Not only has reliance on cabinet councils become routine in recent presidencies, but their importance also has increased. Complex new issues, such as "intermestic" economic policy and "nation building" abroad, defy traditional categories and established expertise. As a result of both environmental influences and presidential policy objectives, the task of weaving multiple, sometimes novel, policy streams and organizations together has grown more urgent. It is scarcely surprising, then, that the Bush administration has changed relatively little of the overall approach. The arrangements for dealing with national security are quite similar to those in place since the first Bush administration; the Clinton executive orders that created the Domestic Policy Council and the National Economic Council remain in place.[35] As I show later, however, the structural continuities have not always meant that the councils' activities and performance have been identical to those of their predecessors.

National Security Policy. Since the days of Henry Kissinger (under Nixon) and Zbigniew Brzezinski (under Carter), the role of the national security assistant (NSA) has shrunk somewhat. Recent NSAs have moved somewhat closer to Eisenhower's image of the position; they have worked primarily as process managers, seeking to coordinate the policy planning process and to supervise policy implementation. In effect, NSAs have served as chiefs of staff for the foreign and defense policy sides of the presidency, although this has not precluded the greater involvement of White House chiefs of staff in national security.[36] Perhaps the paragon of this latter kind of NSA was Brent Scowcroft, who served under Gerald Ford and George H. W. Bush. The younger Bush sought the same type of NSA, tapping Condoleezza Rice, a political scientist and university administrator who had served on the NSC staff under Scowcroft and the elder Bush. Rice's mandate was not to dominate the advising process, but, with her aides, to coordinate it, presenting a full range of information and options for presidential decision.

At the beginning of the second Bush administration, the NSC staff underwent several changes. Its size dropped by 30 percent, to approximately seventy policy professionals. Moreover, its internal organization was simplified, and tasks like communications and legislative affairs returned to the White House Office.[37] Underscoring the rising importance of international economics, a second NSC deputy was added to "coordinate economic strategy with national security and foreign policy goals," reporting to both the NSA and the national economic adviser.[38]

At the same time, Rice's initial activities were quite similar to those of her immediate predecessors, as she took on a more visible "public and operational role" than many had expected. In the administration's first month, for example, she met with most official foreign visitors to Washington; she also appeared on television news programs and gave interviews to the *New York Times* and the *Washington Post,* sometimes using the occasions to announce changes in U.S. policy. Although observers worried about the possible costs of such activities both to the NSC's process management tasks and to her relationship with Secretary of State Colin Powell, some believed external expectations and organizational inertia helped explain them.[39]

Few evident difficulties have emerged between the secretary of state and the national security assistant.[40] Nevertheless, "despite a disciplined public affairs operation and tighter lips than most of its predecessors," the Bush administration often "had trouble singing from the same foreign policy hymnal," and it struggled to keep the resulting internal conflict out of the public eye; press reports began noting the "two competing foreign policy camps" within the administration.[41] Secretary of State Powell anchored one side; the other, based at the Pentagon, included Secretary of Defense Donald Rumsfeld, Deputy Secretary Paul D. Wolfowitz, and, in most accounts, Vice President Cheney. Both sides claimed the allegiance of the NSA. For the most part, the conflict pitted the more ideologically conservative Defense Department against the more moderate State Department; Defense urged a more "unilateralist" foreign policy, while State argued for the benefits of continued multilateralism. Differences surfaced on a variety of issues, ranging from missile defense to U.S. relations with North Korea and Russia to Middle East peace negotiations to U.N. sanctions policy in Iraq. By September 10, 2001, *Time* picked the most likely loser in many of these struggles, with a cover that asked: "Where Have You Gone, Colin Powell?"

On September 11, of course, everything changed. The Bush White House suddenly became what analyst Paul Light called "an organized anarchy or an organized adhocracy." Light continued, "There's more dotted lines here than on a dress pattern." In the national security area in particular, decision making was hurried, often the product of ad hoc meetings that brought together diverse White House offices and executive agencies "in a collection of interwoven coalitions handling shared tasks."[42] The NSC began to meet daily, supplemented by a war cabinet of top White House officials, including Vice President Cheney, Chief of Staff Card, and NSA Rice, as well as Secretary of State Powell, Defense Secretary Rumsfeld, Secretary of the Treasury Paul O'Neill, and CIA chief George Tenet, along with some of the principals' deputies.[43]

The focus of the administration had shifted irreversibly from domestic and economic concerns to national security and the president's "war on terror." In *Bush at War,* for instance, Bob Woodward provides details on forty-two NSC meetings and sixteen principals' meetings that were held between September 11 and November 13. Woodward's descriptions of the post–September 11 deliberations of the NSC and the sessions of Bush's principal subordinates without his presence are reminiscent of the meetings of President Kennedy's executive committee of the NSC (the "Ex Comm") during the Cuban Missile Crisis.[44] Both arguably are reasonable procedural responses to external threats.

At the beginning, the public conflicts among senior foreign policy advisers faded, even as they continued to give President Bush sometimes contrasting assessments. As the attacks on Afghanistan receded and life gradually returned to a "new normal," however, differences among national security advisers (and their external advocates) again appeared.[45] Numerous other foreign policy issues soon joined the war against terrorism, itself "all-consuming" in geographic scope and appetite for resources. For example, after several Palestinian suicide bombings took place in May 2002, the administration turned its attention to the Middle East. Yet it took several weeks of reportedly fierce internal debate before Bush publicly committed the United States to support the establishment of a Palestinian state within three years. Even after that, Secretary of Defense Rumsfeld was characterized as seeming "deeply equivocal about a Palestinian state."[46]

In addition, arguments in the administration over the wisdom of U.S. policy in Iraq became public as early as June 2002 and continued through the 2003 war and its aftermath. To some, the "factions" in the ongoing debate reflected the ongoing divisions over foreign policy within the Republican Party, carried into the administration by cabinet and subcabinet appointees and reinforced by advocates in Washington think tanks and among the former President Bush's confidants.[47] Such disagreements are amplified in a global media environment characterized by pervasive and virtually instantaneous twenty-four-hour news coverage.

Meanwhile, policy overload may be a problem. The blame for some of the overload might be placed on too heavy a reliance on "multiple-advocacy" decision-making arrangements that emphasize the inclusion of numerous competing views. Complaints about the lack of high-level U.S. attention to the strikes in Venezuela, to plans for an Israeli-Palestinian peace settlement, or to North Korea's nuclear weapons capability frequently pointed to the administration's preoccupation with Iraq.[48]

Economic Policy: A Change in Emphasis. In handling economic policy, Bush again followed precedent, retaining the National Economic Council (NEC) created by Bill Clinton. Established by executive order in 1993, the NEC has as its principal functions "to coordinate policy-making for domestic and international economic issues, to coordinate economic policy advice for the President, to ensure that policy decisions and programs are consistent with the President's economic goals, and to monitor implementation of the President's economic policy agenda."[49]

At the outset, Chief of Staff Card claimed that the Bush NEC was charged with taking a "more international view" than its predecessor had taken. In most ways, however, the current NEC staff bears a close resemblance to that in the Clinton administration. For example, the new deputy NSA, with responsibility for international economics issues, replaced the two NEC/NSC staffers who oversaw a joint international economics staff under Clinton.[50]

The Bush economic team experienced an early initial victory—if one that was expensive in terms of political capital—in helping secure congressional passage of major tax-cut legislation. Immediately after September 11, NEC Director Lawrence Lindsey reported having less "policy time" with the president, something he claimed returned within several months.[51] Still, serious economic problems persisted. Not only did the U.S. economy threaten to plunge back into recession, but other dangers also loomed: international financial contagion (including serious debt problems in Argentina and an economic boycott in oil-rich Venezuela) and continuing effects from major business scandals and stock market losses. Amid the consequent political and economic uncertainties, Bush's economic and financial advisers confronted considerable criticism both in and out of the administration.

In a White House looking toward the 2004 reelection campaign, concern focused anew on highlighting Bush's commitments to addressing ongoing economic weaknesses and to pushing hard for a new round of tax cuts. Among the results were the dismissals in early December 2002 of both Treasury Secretary Paul O'Neill and NEC Director Lindsey; both were faulted for their weak presentations of administration policy. By late February 2003, Council of Economic Advisors Chair R. Glenn Hubbard, the reputed "architect of President Bush's plan to slash taxes on corporate dividends," announced that he, too, was leaving.[52]

The replacements for members of the Bush economic team reportedly were selected for their presumed ability to help "sell" the proposed next round of tax cuts. Whether this—or any other proposed strategy— could do much to revive increasingly complex and volatile national and global economies remained an open question.

Domestic Policy: A Disappearing Act? At least at the start of the Bush administration, continuity also appeared in domestic policy. The White House began by following the pattern of relying on a cabinet council arrangement to coordinate and oversee diverse policy threads. Like its Clinton-era predecessor, the Domestic Policy Council (DPC) staff, headed by Assistant to the President Margaret LaMontagne Spellings, ostensibly supervises policy planning and implementation in major areas of domestic policy while also coordinating with the specialized White House policy units dedicated to drug control, HIV/AIDS policy, and faith-based initiatives. Nevertheless, even though the DPC staff continues to meet twice weekly,[53] neither the council nor its staff has been at the center of White House attention.

At first the DPC staff was charged with translating Bush's policy agenda of "compassionate conservatism" into legislation on such issues as education reform.[54] Yet securing the passage of tax-cut legislation occupied most of the attention of senior presidential aides in the administration's initial months. OFBCI had little contact with the rest of the White House, suggesting a key lapse in coordination by the DPC staff. Other seemingly "domestic policy" issues also were handled outside of the DPC staff. For instance, Jay Lefkowitz, at the time the Office of Management and Budget (OMB) general counsel, oversaw examination of policy on stem cell research.[55] Meanwhile, although the director of the reorganized Office of National AIDS Policy had a formal position on the DPC, the DPC staff did not oversee the AIDS unit's activities, and the responsibilities of the AIDS office soon expanded to include international HIV/AIDS issues.[56] About this early period, former speechwriter David Frum recalled: "Since the tax battle, we had worked harder and harder on less and less—and since the loss of the Senate, the domestic agenda of the administration had filled up with gimmicks and dodges."[57]

The slow start for the DPC staff reflected several factors. First, domestic policy issues are not only diverse and ambiguous, but most were not at the top of President Bush's list of priorities. Second, the one policy area that was salient—faith-based initiatives—was placed in a separate unit. Third, the director of the DPC staff had no Washington experience and relatively little broad policy expertise, having worked for Bush on education issues when he had been governor of Texas. It is perhaps not surprising, then, that others were called on to handle pressing policy concerns such as the debate over federal funding of stem cell research. Meanwhile, domestic policy director Spellings *was* a key participant in the area in which she is most expert: education; she helped formulate and lobbied for the "Leave No Child Behind" legislation, which passed in December 2001.[58]

September 11 pushed domestic policy initiatives far down on the administration's agenda. When the president was able to turn back to the domestic agenda, one of his first acts was to name Jay Lefkowitz, the OMB general counsel, deputy assistant to the president for domestic policy. Lefkowitz, who had served as deputy secretary of the DPC and as director of cabinet affairs in the first Bush White House, replaced John Bridgeland, who became director of the USA Freedom Corps Office. Described as a "hard-nosed litigator . . . attracted to controversial issues," Lefkowitz is "a primary liaison to Christian conservatives." Charged with coordinating domestic policy making, he reportedly meets with the president twice each week.[59]

With renewed presidential attention and a more aggressive and experienced domestic policy adviser, the DPC staff has grown in potential influence. Even so, two other indicators underscore its relatively low status. First, it is located (along with the NEC staff) in the only White House unit that was scheduled for a cut in funding in the proposed fiscal year 2004 White House budget—the Office of Policy Development.[60] Second, alone among the cabinet councils, the DPC does not have a link on the White House Web site.

As in past presidencies, under Bush "'domestic policy' is less a coherent policy area than a collection of odds and ends whose importance will vary with circumstances and with the priorities of each administration."[61] Among the additional casualties of the terrorist attacks may well have been domestic policy initiatives.

Administrative Presidency Redux

Many policy-related activities in the Bush presidency have involved initiatives that focus on the larger federal executive branch or on U.S. district and appeals courts. Recalling especially the "administrative presidency" strategies of the Nixon and Reagan administrations, the current administration has relied on executive orders, administrative rules, and appointments in its pursuit of a variety of presidential policy objectives.[62]

As have most of his predecessors since the 1970s, Bush has employed the first strategy—use of the executive order as a policy tool—throughout his presidency.[63] Like most new presidents who replace a chief executive from the other party, he revoked several Clinton administration executive orders during his first three months in the White House. On the third day in office, for example, Bush issued an executive order that overturned the Clinton policy of providing aid to family-planning organizations outside the United States that offered abortion counseling. Two other early Bush executive orders—both on energy—included language similar to that used in a draft bill and an executive order that the American Gas Association had submitted to the Energy Department.[64] Other orders banned federal financing for research that used new lines of embryonic stem cells, changed the process for releasing presidential papers under the Presidential Records Act, and required faster government environmental assessments of transportation construction projects.[65]

Since then the prevailing policy environment has critically influenced the numbers and types of executive orders that have been issued. Alexis Simendinger of the *National Journal* reported that Bush "signed more [executive orders] in the three-and-one half months after the terrorist attacks than he had in the first eight months of his presidency."[66]

A second strategy of the administrative presidency is the use of administrative rules. Here the Bush administration often has focused on environmental policy, seeking a different balance than its predecessor had among the goals of environmental protection, economic development, and energy production. Among the initiatives have been "easing wetlands rules affecting developers; reducing energy-saving standards for air conditioners; allowing more road-building and power lines in national forests; delaying a ban on snowmobiles in national parks; and easing restrictions on mining on public lands."[67]

The third administrative strategy emphasizes appointments—to positions in both the executive branch and the federal courts. As in the Reagan administration, the Bush White House personnel operation evaluates nominees for subcabinet positions using partisan and ideological standards as well as other criteria. Among those from whom the White House Personnel Office seeks input are Senior Adviser Karl Rove and staffers in the Office of Political Affairs.[68] Other times the White House has decided *not* to fill particular vacancies, arguably signaling the priority it gives to certain tasks. For example, the former director of the Environmental Protection Agency's (EPA's) Office of Regulatory Enforcement (who resigned in the spring of 2001 after having worked at the EPA for twelve years) contended that the administration continued its "stealth attack on environmental protection" by not replacing him for over eighteen months.[69] Like many of its predecessors, the administration has used recess appointments as a means of placing nominees that had triggered Senate opposition; on occasion, this has served as a way of putting those with controversial policy views into key positions.[70]

Furthermore, the stress on appointments of individuals whose policy and political views are congruent with the president's extends to the federal bench. Although presidents have long sought to pay attention to the views of those they have nominated to the U.S. Supreme Court, "prior to the Nixon administration, policy considerations and/or ideological ones didn't often take primacy in lower court selection processes."[71] Systematic presidential involvement in nominations to the lower courts started in earnest under Ronald Reagan, when the selection process became centralized in the White House. Beginning with Reagan, the White House counsel has chaired a selection committee of White House staffers and Department of Justice officials that reviews possible nominees and makes recommendations to the president. By most accounts, evidence of an individual's "ideology" was pivotal to her or his success at being nominated in the Reagan administration and the first Bush administration; Clinton, despite some perceptions to the contrary, focused more on "judicial competence" and on "diversity." Most available evidence indicates that the second Bush administration handles nominations to the lower courts much as its Republican predecessors did, with a judicial selection committee chaired by White House Counsel Alberto Gonzales and with Karl Rove as one of its participants. The highly publicized conflicts over the ideology and policy views of a number of Bush's nominees (such as Charles Pickering, Priscilla Owen, and Miguel Estrada) also are consistent with such a concentration.[72]

Any firm conclusions about the extent, nature, and impact of such administrative strategies cannot be drawn until additional time has passed and there is greater access to relevant information. Nonetheless, George W. Bush appears to be following precedents set by the past two Republican presidents.

Vice Presidential Involvement

Although Vice President Richard Cheney participates in a range of tasks, he is centrally involved in policy discussions. As a former White House aide and Secretary of Defense, Cheney has credentials as a top adviser that are indisputable. Yet his prominence is consistent with a trend in the modern vice presidency that dates back to Walter Mondale's involvement in the Carter administration as a political and policy adviser and continued through Al Gore's work on environmental issues and government reform under Clinton.[73]

Cheney is even more powerful than his predecessors. From the outset, the vice president has been invited to attend any meeting he chooses to, and he was immediately placed in charge of the administration's review of national energy policy. Even more telling, he chairs the President's Budget Review Board, which rules on appeals of OMB decisions regarding proposed funding for executive branch departments; no other vice president has held this position. Two of Cheney's top aides—Lewis Libby and Mary Matalin—were named assistants to the president, a rarity for vice presidential staffers, and the White House and vice presidential staffs work together closely. Meanwhile, as a former member of the U.S. House, Cheney has been called "Bush's emissary to Capitol Hill" and has a vice presidential office in the House as well as the customary one in the Senate.[74]

After September 11 Cheney participated in the war cabinet, and he continued to be active as the administration planned for war against Iraq. After the war started, he was said to be "consumed by planning for the political reconstruction of a post-Hussein Iraq."[75] Also involved in handling issues of domestic security, the vice president both recommended the establishment of OHS and created the initial plan for its design. The structuring of his own office in part reflects Cheney's long-time concerns with bioterrorism; the unit has become almost a "mini-research center" on the subject.[76]

Overall, in the Bush administration the vice presidency is more influential—and, not infrequently, more controversial—than it ever has been. In most ways, however, this continues a trend that can be traced back to the Carter years. Although Cheney's own broad-ranging experience, discretion, and lack of presidential ambition doubtless contribute to his impact, expectations of the vice presidency have grown over time as well. It is too early to declare the Bush vice presidency the product solely of idiosyncratic factors.

Policy Processing: Conclusions

Overall, arrangements for policy processing under George W. Bush exhibit considerable continuity. At the same time, they underscore the adaptability of the White House to external pressures, presidential goals, and organizational precedent. Environmental factors have shaped many of the administration's activities in handling policy. Most obviously, the terrorist attacks drove issues of national and homeland security to the top of the policy agenda, where they continue to occupy the time and attention of decision makers. September 11 also altered the very nature of "domestic" policy and, in damaging an economy that was already slowing, changed the context in which economic and budgetary policies could be sought. Given these constraints, presidential priorities exercised some influence over the kinds of policy initiatives that would be pursued. Although much less important, how policy processing was organized may have contributed to some of the strengths and weaknesses that have emerged in national security and in domestic policy.

Public Relations: The Reagan and Clinton Legacies?

The third major task area for which White Houses have assumed responsibility is outreach. Contemporary presidencies seek to develop and sustain relations with a variety of entities outside the federal government, including voters, organized interests, and the media. Beginning at least with the presidency of Richard Nixon, administrations have devoted increasing resources to boosting public support, both for the president and for presidential initiatives. White House polling (or virtually indistinguishable efforts by the national party committees) is routine and incessant. Press and communications units have expanded, joined by White House offices of political affairs and constituency liaison. To a significant degree, the resulting "public relations presidency" can be viewed as a response to a political environment characterized by fragmenting political parties, multiplying interests, a Washington, D.C., press corps distrustful of government pronouncements, and citizens divided by age, class, race, values, and policy views. Presidential efforts to adjust to developing information and communications technologies and an emerging twenty-four-hour news cycle have only reinforced such emphases.[77]

Under George W. Bush the specific strategies for handling these challenges have differed somewhat from those that past administrations pursued. Still, significant continuities appear. Movement toward a presidency animated by public relations concerns persists and perhaps has even accelerated.

Continuities in White House Responses

As I noted earlier, Counselor Karen Hughes's responsibilities generally paralleled those of her Reagan administration predecessor, Michael Deaver. She oversaw several familiar White House operations, including those of the Press Office, communications, and speechwriting. Moreover, the activities of these units have been much the same as those in earlier administrations, as might be expected given the influences of external expectations, partisan learning, and emulation of previous successes. The White House Media Affairs Office, for instance, which focuses on non–Washington, D.C., media, first surfaced during the Carter years. The regular meetings that Deputy Communications Director Jim Wilkinson holds with press secretaries for Republican leaders in Congress are similar to efforts in past administrations to coordinate messages between both ends of Pennsylvania Avenue.[78]

Many observers spotted a more dramatic change in the creation of the Office of Strategic Initiative (OSI), a unit "designed to think ahead and devise long term political strategies." Even so, Tenpas and Hess compare the unit to the Reagan administration's Office of Planning and Evaluation. In their view, OSI's "unique feature" is that it reports to Karl Rove, the president's leading political adviser, and has been "thoroughly integrated into the White House chain of command."[79]

Yet much as did Hughes, Rove oversees other offices that have appeared in past administrations. These include units such as the Office of Public Liaison (which handles outreach to various organized interests) and the Office of Political Affairs (which is responsible for forging relationships with national and state party officials and candidates, tracking patronage, and preparing for the reelection campaign).[80]

In addition, Rove is the primary White House link to the president's pollsters and to the chief of polling, Matthew Dowd, who is formally lodged at the Republican National Committee. From the outset the Bush White House has sought to appear as though it does not rely on polling, highlighting a key difference between the president and his "poll-obsessed" predecessor as well as "'conveying an impression of leadership, judgment, and substance.'"[81] Still, like most recent administrations, the White House devotes considerable attention and (party) resources to tracking public opinion and to probing ways of more effectively communicating with target audiences.[82]

Finally, once more like most recent chief executives, President Bush has been central in efforts to promote public support for himself and his initiatives. The scope of his domestic travel and speechmaking, for example, are quite similar to President Clinton's. Although some of Bush's initial efforts can be traced to his narrow and (to some) questionable election, both the persistence of his public activities and their resemblance to his predecessor's also point to the impact of more general environmental influences. The volume of travel and speeches is consistent with the not infrequent conclusion that "the permanent campaign is now a permanent feature of the American presidency."[83]

Innovations and Evidence of Discontinuity

The organizational arrangements and activities that focus on public relations and outreach in the Bush White House, then, show a good deal of continuity with those in previous administrations. Clearly, however, there have been notable departures from past practice. Some of these changes might be traced to lessons learned from previous presidencies, to shifting White House staff dynamics, and to the demands of volatile political and policy environments.

From the beginning, senior Bush officials explicitly claimed that they sought to "fix the mistakes of earlier administrations," including those of the new president's father. The establishment of OSI was only part of the response. At least as important was the formation of a committee of senior White House aides—quickly dubbed the "Strategery Group" after a *Saturday Night Live* skit—that was charged with meeting on a biweekly basis to discuss issues ranging from future budget priorities to possible reelection campaign themes. A midlevel deputies' group generated ideas for the senior staff sessions. OSI was designed to "'serve as a secretariat'" for the two groups, "'an operation that sets the agenda, prepares the notebooks and materials and does the research.'"[84]

It is not completely clear how effective these efforts were in generating ideas or improving staff coordination, either in the first several months of the administration or over the longer run. The September 11 attacks reportedly changed OSI's orientation for a time, "from long-term planning . . . to research on how previous presidents operated during times of war or domestic crisis." In the immediate aftermath of the attacks, Rove concentrated on working with the White House's domestic consequences task force and helping manage presidential-congressional relations, even as his political activities continued, albeit less visibly.[85]

Like Rove, Karen Hughes was not a member of the war cabinet. In other ways, though, her job changed less, since more routine White House tasks, such as scheduling the president's appearances and writing his speeches, remained essential. Thus, for instance, the full White House speechwriting and support system, including Hughes, Rove, and speechwriter Michael Gerson, chose a site for the delivery of an early presidential speech to the nation (Congress) and prepared a powerful and well-received televised address.[86]

Over time, as Bush's attention focused on national security issues, reports began to circulate about Rove's increasing involvement in policy issues. Allegedly "expanding his White House portfolio by inserting himself into the debate over how to deal with the Middle East, trade, terrorism, Latin America, and other foreign policy matters," the adviser left his fingerprints on the president's decision to support protection for farmers and steelworkers and to withhold funding for the United Nations Population Fund.[87] Meanwhile, Hughes "created a special White House–based public relations operation aimed at winning international support, particularly in the Islamic world, for the anti-terror campaign."[88]

The impact of Hughes's departure is difficult to determine precisely, in large part because most in the administration refuse to discuss such issues, especially when they concern Karl Rove. Moreover, Hughes remains in close contact with the White House. She campaigned extensively for Republican candidates during the fall of 2002, wrote Bush's speech on the anniversary of the September 11 attacks, traveled with the president to the Azores on the eve of the U.S. war with Iraq, helped draft his March 17 address delivering an ultimatum to Saddam Hussein, and advised him on the communications strategy for the Iraq war.[89] Nonetheless, some observers insist on calling Rove "the most powerful adviser in the White House."[90]

Finally, September 11 at least indirectly led to the establishment of two new outreach units in the White House Office. President Bush announced the first, the USA Freedom Corps Office, in the 2002 State of the Union address as part of his challenge to citizens to pledge to perform four thousand hours of public service over their lives; the unit was charged with coordinating the work of other executive branch programs that work with volunteers. The second, Hughes's initiative to "rebut Taliban disinformation about the Afghan war," the White House Coalition Information Center, was converted into a more permanent Office of Global Communications, which was "designed to coordinate the administration's foreign policy message and supervise America's image abroad."[91]

A "Public Relations Presidency"?

The activities of the George W. Bush administration are consistent with the trend for public relations concerns to increasingly permeate the presidency. Not only does the White House include the now routinely expected staff units for media relations, communications, speechwriting, group liaison, and political affairs; it also counts among its most influential advisers aides responsible for political strategy and message formulation and management. Moreover, several of the new staff offices focus on electoral concerns (OSI), communications (the Office of Global Communications), and public outreach (the USA Freedom Corps Office and the reconstituted OFBCI).

Even more striking may be the questions that have been raised about the extent to which policy deliberation and initiative have been driven by concerns with public relations. Former staffer John DiIulio, for example, has observed that "the domestic politics-to-policy ratio in the White House today is arguably the highest in recent history," adding that "the EOP [Executive Office of the President] offices that matter most (or matter only) are those dedicated to 'strategic' (i.e., political) initiatives—communications, press relations and speechwriting."[92] As the stock market fell in mid-2002, reports surfaced that "President's Bush's economic policy team [was] starting a heightened public relations campaign."[93]

The makeup of key decision-making groups lends additional credence to concerns about the attention paid to public relations rather than to substantive policy. The Budget Review Board, for example, "includes the President's top political and communications advisers."[94] In addition, Karl Rove participates in all domestic policy meetings, and he and Karen Hughes were among those who attended NEC Director Lindsey's thrice-weekly economic briefings of the president.[95]

Certainly substantive domestic and economic policy initiatives have been constrained by other factors, including the president's limited agenda, a closely divided Congress, policy problems with unclear remedies, and the emphases on national and homeland security that followed the terrorist attacks. What remains striking, however, is the degree to which political and public relations concerns weave through most examinations of domestic and economic policy making.

That said, most recent presidents also have incorporated such considerations into their domestic and economic policy decision making. It is the Bush administration's open and explicit attention to public relations in national security affairs that is an innovation. To be sure, there is little evidence that more narrowly "political" concerns have received much attention in policy deliberation. Only after major policy decisions have been made do the various communications and political staffs go to work. Even so, the White House Coalition Information Center, the Office of Global Communications, and the "embedding" of journalists within military units seem designed to extend attention to public relations further into the national security arena. Whatever one's evaluation of such efforts, they are fairly predictable strategic adaptations to a volatile and uncertain global environment in which both domestic and foreign publics are exposed to multiple interpretations of often ambiguous events and actions. That the war on terrorism has heightened public and media interest in Bush's words and actions only strengthens presidential incentives.

Conclusions

Without a doubt, George W. Bush has changed several aspects of the way the White House is structured and in how it operates. New units have appeared, including the Offices of Strategic Initiative, Faith-Based and Community Initiatives, Homeland Security, and Global Communications. The vice presidency is more powerful than it ever has been. And from the start, this administration has stood out for its discipline and the general absence of leaks.

Yet the numerous continuities with previous presidencies in how the overall White House is organized and in its many activities are striking. Presidents pursue their goals mostly within the constraints and opportunities imposed by external actors, events, and forces and by the organizational dynamics of the institutional presidency. The Bush administration has adopted a version of the standard model of White House management, and virtually all of the familiar units and tasks of recent administrations appear in the Bush White House. Other features—for instance, the permeation of policy by political and public relations concerns reflect the persistence of longer-term trends. Still others, such as the pursuit of administrative strategies, remind one of the initiatives of past Republican presidents.

Both the continuities and the changes in the Bush White House point to the impact of environmental and organizational factors. The structuring and activities of this White House mostly resemble those of its predecessors, in part reflecting the influence of external expectations regarding, for instance, press relations or liaison with organized interests. Also clearly important are environmental demands. September 11 is the prime example, producing the need for organizational responses and shaping the dynamics of staff influence. Meanwhile, the political environment of the past two decades has laid the foundation for longer-term trends, such as the emphases of the Clinton and Bush presidencies on public relations. Organizational precedent also is important, as illustrated by the reliance on cabinet councils and partisan learning in the use of administrative strategies.

These sorts of factors have constrained and informed George W. Bush's choices about the structuring and operation of his White House. Nonetheless, his values and priorities have been significant as well. They have shaped the focus of new units such as OFBCI and the USA Freedom Corps Office, just as they have affected the emphases of other offices. The president's management preferences helped foster and sustain the administration's characteristic discipline and the premium it places on secrecy.

Even so, despite President Bush's distinctive agenda and approach to management and the virtually unprecedented environment that he confronts, his White House is defined far more by continuity than by discontinuity. Moreover, many of the changes that have appeared—in, for example, the vice presidency, presidential emphasis on public relations, reliance on administrative strategies, and attention paid to national and domestic security—are consistent with longer-term trends, with the efforts of past Republican presidents, and with expected responses to crisis. Individual presidents can introduce innovations, but the overall impact of such novelty is likely to be marginal or short-lived.

The institutional presidency is remarkable in its resilience. Whether George W. Bush's organizational innovations will endure remains to be seen.

Chapter 4

Bush's Budget Problem

Allen Schick

IT WAS GEORGE W. BUSH'S misfortune to become president just about the time the stock market bubble burst, the economy weakened, and federal revenues plummeted. It will be his successor's misfortune to enter office with an inadequate revenue base and an urgent need to push a tax increase through Congress. But even if the next president reverses course on budget policy, the aftereffects of Bush's government-by-deficit strategy will linger for many years.

Assuming he wins a second term, Bush will be the last president before the front edge of the baby boom generation reaches retirement age. His successor will have to deal with the economic and budgetary implications of an aging U.S. population in ways that Bush has not. The future financing of Social Security and Medicare is not the only problem the current president has slighted; he also has not faced up to the escalating costs of national defense and homeland security. During the first decade of the new century, the security costs added by Bush are likely to exceed the $1.3 trillion his 2001 tax cut subtracted from federal revenues. Less than two years after this tax cut, while the United States was at war in Iraq, Bush pressured Congress to enact another trillion-dollar tax cut that was estimated to reduce federal revenues by $330 billion, but whose full cost may be more than double that amount.[1] When the books are closed on his presidency, a country that at the beginning of the century was moving to liquidate the $3.7 trillion in federal debt held by the public will instead add $1 trillion to $3 trillion to its debt burden. Which end of that range materializes will depend more on the length of Bush's stay in office than on the performance of the economy.

It is easy to tar Bush as fiscally irresponsible, as Democratic leaders and a few rank-and-file Republicans have. The same week that warfare broke out in Iraq, key presidential aides were pressuring ambivalent Republicans in Congress to vote for a budget resolution that ensured passage of his second round of mega–tax cuts in 2003. Bush is the first president in American history to combine a call to arms and a significant tax reduction in the same political package. By some bad-, not worst-case scenarios, Bush's recipe will produce deficits in the vicinity of $500 billion a year, almost double the previous record, set by his father.

How did this president lose his way on fiscal prudence? Why did he not use September 11 to rally support for taxes to finance homeland and national security? Arguably, had he done so Bush might have been in a stronger position to ward off spending demands from Congress, including many from fellow Republicans. It may be that Bush miscalculated, that he did not know that the budget would spin out of control, and that faced with a rush of bad news—a weak economy, spiraling defense costs, and plummeting revenues—he let things drift in the expectation that conditions would improve if he stayed the course. When they did not, he was left with a record budget deficit that could not be trimmed through politically acceptable options. In characterizing George W. Bush's thinking, I mean to spell out the logic of the positions he takes, not to purport to psychoanalyze him.

Yet miscalculation does not fit this calculating president who, in contrast to his father, knows how to use the power of the office. This is a president who has not fought for a lot of things he professes to want—Medicare prescription drug coverage, abortion restrictions, and Social Security reform, to name some of his most prominent aims—but he has twice fought for big tax cuts. This is a president whose eyes are wide open to the short- and long-term fiscal and policy implications of the revenue losses he has imposed on the federal government. Even as he has truncated the budget horizon from ten years to five,[2] he has been aware of the doomsday projections that if current policy continues, a generation from now Social Security and Medicare will claim almost all of the federal revenue, leaving very little for the rest of government. He wants to strip the government of future revenue, not in spite of these dire scenarios but because of them. He sees revenue privation as the only or best weapon to change the course of budgetary history, a history that for him probably began with Reagan's victory in 1980. Bush is an avid student of recent political failures, in particular his father's failed presidency and the failure of both Reagan and his father to halt the expansion of government.[3] George W. Bush wants a smaller government, and he is willing to pay the budgetary price to get it. In contrast to Reagan, he has not launched a rhetorical challenge to big government, preferring instead to let budgetary realities do the job for him. In contrast to his father, George W. Bush is not willing to let adverse budgetary numbers get in the way of his determination to purge the government of revenue. The elder Bush said, "Read my lips, no new taxes" and signed a large tax increase into law. The younger Bush does not want to repeat his father's backpedaling. In contrast to both Reagan and his father, Bush has had a Republican Congress through most of his first term, making it much easier to muscle his tax cuts through the House and Senate.

At times the White House trots out its version of the "It's the economy" defense to argue that the deficit has been the product of an economic force majeure, that the rising tide of red ink has been caused by the plunging stock market and the fragile economy, not by policy changes. This "no-fault" defense does not square with the facts, however. Critical turning points in budgeting—from deficits to surpluses in the 1990s and back to deficits in the present decade—did not just happen; they were driven in substantial part by changes in federal revenue or spending policy. For Bush no less than for his predecessors, policy matters in budgeting. Moreover, policy mistakes—and I consider the current fiscal posture a colossal misstep—take a long time to wash out of the federal budget. It took the federal government twenty-eight years (from 1970 to 1998) to produce a surplus, but only four years to return to a deficit. The asymmetry in budget cycles is due to policy biases, not economic swings. It is far easier for politicians to cut taxes than to raise them, and far easier to boost spending than to curtail it. Economic weakness impels the government to spend more than it takes in; economic strength also impels it to spend more, though not necessarily more than the revenue it produces. At this point, no one knows whether the nation will go through another twenty-eight-year spell of deficits, but it is not too early to predict that the government will not be able to liquidate annual deficits if it stays on the current budget course.

Bush is a president who has learned from the recent past and is looking to change the future, and he is willing to risk the present to accomplish his aims. He has been told that discretionary spending will go up a lot more than his official forecast shows, that his proposal to allocate $400 billion for Medicare prescription drug coverage will not suffice, that in the next decade Social Security surpluses will diminish, and that before 2020 Medicare will be insolvent. He knows that spending on homeland security and national defense will soar tens of billions above budgeted levels and that the new Bush doctrine of preemptive war will be costly. But instead of conceding the need for a more robust revenue base, Bush firmly believes that only a vastly larger, perhaps unmanageable, deficit can curb the relentless expansion of government.

Thus the Bush White House is not clueless on the fiscal course the president has charted; this is not a case of ignorance aforethought. The administration knows what it wants and is setting out to get it. Bush's revenue policy is actually a spending strategy. He wants revenue deprivation to force a truly fundamental change in the course of government. Rather than tinker with Social Security and Medicare so that they can muddle through a few more decades, Bush wants the government to be so depleted of resources that it cannot come to their rescue. Rather than fight and lose on appropriation bills, Bush wants Congress to come to its own realization that the spending culture of Capitol Hill has to be purged.

During the Reagan era, to which the Bush presidency is sometimes compared, serious policy mistakes led to a fourfold increase in the federal debt held by the public, from $700 billion in 1980 to $3 trillion in 1992. At the time, Senator Daniel Patrick Moynihan accused the administration of fabricating the deficit to starve the government of revenue. Moynihan did not have a smoking gun to validate his accusation, but George W. Bush has supplied one. Several weeks after taking office, Bush unveiled his "Blueprint for New Beginnings," which set forth his budget policy. One of the charts in this publication is prominently titled "Budget Surpluses Lead to Bigger Government."[4] The chart noted the surge in discretionary spending that occurred when surpluses emerged in the late 1990s. According to the Bush worldview, since surpluses inevitably spur government to spend more, the sensible thing to do is to get rid of surpluses. Otherwise, government will grow bigger, regardless of whether the Democrats or the Republicans are in command. Many conservatives accept as an article of faith that no matter what rules are applied, a significant portion of the revenue raised to abate a deficit will be spent instead on enlarging government. The critical turning point in their thinking came in 1982, when Ronald Reagan undid some of the tax cuts enacted the previous year by agreeing to a deficit reduction package that he thought would subtract three dollars in federal spending for every dollar added in revenue. When few of the expected spending cuts materialized, Reagan and fellow conservatives felt cheated. This was the "triumph of politics" bemoaned by David Stockman, who understood that Americans and their elected leaders, including many Republicans in Congress, want to spend more, not less.[5] Despite his misgivings, Reagan signed another half dozen, mostly minor, tax increases into law during his long presidency.[6] But the biggest blow to conservatives came in 1990, when the first President Bush agreed to legislation boosting the highest marginal tax rate on individual income as part of a half-trillion-dollar deficit reduction package.[7]

Two decades after Reagan signed his first tax increase and one decade after President Bush signed his only increase, the lessons have been branded into the political mind-set of conservatives and have framed George W. Bush's budget policies. One lesson is that it is better to have a smaller government with a bigger deficit than a bigger government with a smaller deficit. Another lesson is that the political system and the budget process are biased in favor of more taxes and more spending. In the eyes of many conservatives, the expansionary bias of politics arises out of the simple fact that the costs of programs are dispersed among taxpayers, while the benefits are concentrated among those who get the services or payment from government. As a consequence, those who want smaller government in principle nevertheless promote the expansion of government by lobbying for particular programs.

The biases of the budget process also favor government expansion. According to conservative ideology, the appropriations committees buy support in Congress for higher spending by earmarking funds to members, and the congressional budget process propels higher expenditure by incorporating price and (for mandatory programs) workload changes into the official projections that are used to measure the impact of executive and congressional actions on federal revenues and expenditures. The budget rules that were enacted to combat these biases—the Gramm-Rudman-Hollings (GRH) limitation on deficits in the 1980s and the Budget Enforcement Act (BEA) restrictions on tax and spending legislation in the 1990s—did not, in the view of conservatives, have the intended effects.[8] In each year that GRH was in effect (1986–90), the actual deficit exceeded the limit permitted in law. And despite the BEA caps on appropriations and PAYGO (pay-as-you-go) rules for mandatory programs, federal spending continues to rise.[9]

If politics and budgeting expand government and restrictive rules do not counter the trend, the only recourse is to put the federal budget in a predicament that precludes significant expansion. This is the "Starve the beast" strategy that defines George W. Bush's budget posture. Of course to him and other conservatives this means cutting revenues before expenditures, and thereby leaving the government with record deficits until such time as the imbalance compels the contraction of government. Conservatives disagree on whether deficits matter, but many who believe they do think that the alternative—the relentless growth of government—matters even more.

This chapter provides an interim assessment of the Bush strategy. No presidential term ends quite the way it began, certainly not one beset by terrorism at home, a costly war abroad, and an economy struggling to recover from post-bubble trauma. Compared to his recent predecessors, Bush seems the type who values staying the course. It will be difficult to dislodge him from entrenched budget positions, no matter how severe the imbalance between revenues and expenditures. Nevertheless, the longer he is in office, the weaker the claim Bush's original budget doctrine will have on his political calculations.

The next section of this chapter focuses on spending policy because it is the key to understanding Bush's hard line on taxes and his willingness to have oversized deficits. The following section turns to the revenue side of the budget and considers trends in tax collection and the distribution of the tax burden. Distributive questions are critical to the Bush agenda because he inherited a tax structure that virtually ensures that upper-income persons are the principal beneficiaries of tax cuts. The next section examines the deficit that has ensued from Bush's budget policies in the light of current and prospective economic conditions. The final section discusses the politics of the president's budget strategy, in particular his dependence on congressional approval. It concludes with speculation on whether the Bush strategy will survive beyond the Bush presidency.

Cutting Expenditure by Indirection

As a president who wants to reduce the size of government, George W. Bush is reticent about where most of the cuts will fall. In contrast to his father and Ronald Reagan, who listed many of the programs that were to be terminated or curtailed, this president veils his cuts in projections that show appropriations rising about as fast as inflation during his hoped-for two-term administration, and he promises new money for Medicare and some other entitlement programs. One must plumb the budget's accounts to find the many programs that will grow less than inflation or that will lose resources through various reforms. Few of the cutbacks are so dramatic as to provoke the "dead on arrival" verdict that accompanied the budgets of his Republican predecessors. If Bush has his way, during his presidency many programs will be scaled back simply because there will not be enough money to go around, not because he has launched a frontal attack on government.

For example, the 2004 budget proposes to give states the option of switching their Medicaid programs to a block grant. States that switch would get increased funding; those that do not would continue with the existing matching grants, but they would not receive any of the $13 billion increase. However, increased spending would be available only for seven years; afterward federal Medicaid payments would drop significantly below levels prescribed by current law. But inasmuch as the Bush budget shortened the time horizon from ten years to five, only the increases appear in the budget.

Bush knows that although efforts to shrink government may have some short-term success, over the long run the spenders will win out. Evidence for this conclusion can be drawn from Table 4.1, which shows discretionary spending at four-year intervals since 1965, the year before President Johnson's Great Society irrevocably enlarged the federal government. The four-year intervals approximate presidential terms, but inasmuch as the fiscal and budget calendars are not in sync, the figures in the table do not precisely show the spending changes that occurred during each presidential term. The table reports spending in both current

TABLE 4.1 Discretionary Spending Trends, 1965–2008
(dollars in billions)

	Defense			Domestic		
	Total	Constant $	Percent GDP	Total	Constant $	Percent GDP
1965	51	267	7.4	22	119	3.2
1969	83	362	8.7	31	131	3.2
1973	77	257	5.9	49	161	3.7
1977	98	231	4.9	92	220	4.6
1981	158	260	5.2	136	236	4.5
1985	253	331	6.1	145	208	3.5
1989	304	370	5.6	168	212	3.1
1993	292	316	4.5	225	245	3.4
1997	272	266	3.3	257	252	3.1
2001	306	276	3.1	321	287	3.2
2005 Est.	410	347	3.4	412	342	3.5
2008 Est.	460	375	3.3	433	339	3.1

Source: Office of Management and Budget, Budget of the United States Government for Fiscal Year 2004 (Washington, D.C.: Government Printing Office, 2003).
Note: Constant dollars are in FY 1996 dollars.

and constant (1996) dollars and as a share of gross domestic product (GDP). It also distinguishes between defense and domestic discretionary spending, that is, spending controlled by annual appropriations decisions. These appropriations account for only a little more than a third of federal spending, but this is the portion of the budget that requires annual congressional action. The remaining expenditure is mandatory, consisting mostly of entitlements and interest on the public debt. Some of these have permanent appropriations that become available automatically; others require annual appropriations, but the amount spent is controlled by substantive legislation.

Budget conservatives view the trends in this table as confirming runaway government expansion. In fiscal 1965, the last year before the Vietnam War build-up, defense appropriations were more than double those for all domestic programs. By 2000, however, domestic appropriations exceeded defense spending. Much of this shift in relative spending occurred in the 1990s, after the cold war ended but before September 11 triggered a new upsurge in defense spending. Defense poses a dilemma for Bush in working toward his objective of shrinking the size of government; in thinking that the federal government has grown too large, he clearly has domestic programs in mind, but he knows that defense spending opens the door to more domestic spending, first, by building support for tax increases, and second, by increasing overall appropriations, creating a situation in which domestic spending can displace defense appropriations when the threat to national security recedes. This "displacement effect" is one of the leading factors explaining government expansion in democratic countries, and it has been a recurring pattern in American budgetary history.[10] If past trends continue, the surge in defense spending during the Bush administration will facilitate a big expansion in domestic programs sometime in the future. To ward this off, Bush is not paying for additional defense spending with tax increases, as was the case in most past military engagements. Moreover, he has been somewhat tight-fisted in supplementing defense appropriations, resisting demands from military leaders for more resources. In fact, Bush has augmented the defense budget much less than Reagan, to whom he is sometimes compared, did two decades ago. Reagan boosted defense spending from 4.9 percent of GDP in 1980 to a peak of 6.2 percent in 1986; the Bush scenario (which excludes the war in Iraq) projects defense outlays' declining from 3.5 percent of GDP in 2003 to 3.3 percent five years later. Perhaps Bush is a skinflint who dislikes spending any money, or perhaps he has been indoctrinated by Vice President Cheney and Secretary of Defense Rumsfeld in the view that the best way to get military leaders to restructure the armed forces is to squeeze them on money. But it also is likely that Bush is wary of pumping up defense too fast lest Congress siphon off some of the money for domestic priorities.

This pattern is clearly evident with regard to homeland security, Bush's most prominent government initiative. Immediately after September 11, in both regular and supplemental appropriations bills, Bush strongly opposed efforts by congressional Democrats and some Republicans to provide more money for "first responders" and other state and local security-related activities. At first glance, it seems it would have been an easy call for Bush to give state and local governments enough to at least reimburse their out-of-pocket security costs. Bush, however, clearly saw this as a domestic spending issue; he was convinced that giving states and localities money labeled "homeland security" would enable them to spend more on ongoing activities that would have little to do with making the nation more secure.

Bush's parsimony has surprised some who expected his experience as governor of Texas to sensitize him to the fiscal plight of many states whose budgets have been severely imbalanced by the economic downturn and other adversities. His failure to help the states has welled out of an overriding concern: that added expenditure would enlarge both the federal budget and the budgets of state governments. The president views state deficits the same way he views the new federal deficit, as opportunities for the states to curtail spending. If they do not, it is their problem, not the federal government's.

Bush knows that it is hard to curtail spending, as a review of the trends in Table 4.1 indicates. In nominal terms, domestic appropriations rose almost twentyfold, from a little more than $20 billion in 1965 to $400 billion less than forty years later. The rise was relentless in every presidential term, regardless of whether a Democrat or a Republican occupied the Oval Office. The fact that domestic appropriations are about the same share of GDP today as they were before Great Society programs, environmental protection, and many other activities were added to the roster of federal responsibilities does not alter the conservative view that government cannot control its appetite to spend public money. Spending as a proportion of GDP may be the way economists analyze budget trends, but it is not the metric favored by politicians bent on making the case that government has grown too large. The same mind-set pertains to real (inflation-adjusted) expenditure, which grew threefold during the past four decades. Conservatives regard inflation adjustment as one of the key weapons used by spenders to wrest more money from the budget. Although their protests have been to no avail, conservatives believe that CBO's use of an inflated baseline has contributed to the enlargement of government because nominal spending increases below the inflated baseline are labeled as spending cuts.[11] The conservatives may have a valid point here, but they do not apply it consistently. If they had their way, defense spending would be adjusted for inflation, but all the rest would not.

As a student of recent political history, Bush has been most influenced by spending patterns during the three presidencies that immediately preceded his. Reagan succeeded in downsizing real discretionary spending, principally through blitzkrieg victories during his first year in office. But Reagan's successes were not lasting, and by 1996, less than a decade after he retired, real spending was above the level he had inherited at the start of his presidency. How and why did this happen? Bush and fellow conservatives are certain that the large tax increases enacted in 1990 and 1993 fueled the regrowth of government. Rather than paying down the deficit, which is the way economists generally view the tax increases, conservatives argue that they opened the door to bigger government.

To George W. Bush and fellow conservatives, the most telling evidence of fiscal laxity occurred during his father's short presidency. In the elder Bush's single term, the rise in domestic appropriations averaged more that 7 percent a year, almost double the rate during the ensuing Clinton presidency. When George H. W. Bush was defeated, annual appropriations for domestic programs were almost $60 billion more than when he was elected. Worse yet, Bush began his term with Gramm-Rudman-Hollings rules (first enacted in 1985) restraining the deficit and ended his term with Budget Enforcement Act rules (enacted in 1990) restraining appropriations. Evidently, neither worked; GRH failed because it targeted the projected rather than the actual deficit, thereby enabling politicians to assume more favorable conditions than were warranted; BEA failed because it capped domestic appropriations at a high level, allowed politicians to evade the limit by labeling expenditures as emergencies, and (some years) permitted the substitution of domestic appropriations for defense spending.

This is not the full BEA story, however. In terms of constraining federal spending, BEA went through three distinct phases. It was not effective either during the first phase (the period immediately after its enactment) or during the final phase (the last years of Clinton's presidency and the first year of George W. Bush's term). It did not constrain domestic spending at the outset because the House and Senate Appropriations Committees obtained a large, up-front increase in spending in exchange for accepting the caps; it was not effective at the end because the arrival of large surpluses unleashed spending demands in the White House and Congress. But it was effective through most of the Clinton presidency; real discretionary domestic spending was less than 1 percent higher in 1998 than it had been in 1994. The rules worked, but only after the caps had been set at a high level and before the surpluses loosened budgetary discipline. However, it was not Clinton's relative parsimony but Bush senior's failure and the spending spree that welcomed him to the White House that framed George W. Bush's budget outlook.

During the first years of his presidency, Bush has been unable to escape the impact of Clinton's last years. Clinton bequeathed his successor spending momentum that has not been significantly dampened by September 11 and the return of big deficits. To illustrate Bush's problem, let us assume that he had been elected in 1998 rather than two years later. On taking office, discretionary domestic outlays would have been $277 billion; in fact, however, they were $321 billion, almost $50 billion higher, reflecting the disregard of BEA rules triggered by the surplus. The rules remained in place, but political behavior had changed. More important, the spending mood continued unabated with the presidential transition. Bush's first budget for fiscal year 2002 requested $341 billion for discretionary domestic outlays, but by the time the fiscal year had ended, these outlays totaled $359 billion. The same pattern was repeated the next two years, spurred by the funneling of additional resources into homeland security. Fiscal year 2004 discretionary domestic outlays are currently projected to be more than $400 billion, compared to less than $300 billion in fiscal year 2000.

Why does Bush not just say no to more spending? The straightforward answer is that he cannot, possibly because spending pressures are too intense. He succeeded in Texas by agreeing to more expenditure than he professed to want, but that state is reputed to have the weakest executive budget system in the nation. The legislature rules in Texas, and Bush got along by going along, sometimes reluctantly. Like most Americans, Bush wants smaller government but bigger programs, and while he has challenged Congress on budget matters, appropriations usually end up more than he asked for. This is exactly what happened in the tug of war between Bush and Congress over fiscal year 2003 appropriations. Because of conflicts and delays in House and Senate action, eleven of the thirteen regular appropriation bills were folded into an omnibus act that was passed the fifth month of the fiscal year. Despite the fact that Bush and Republican leaders agreed that regular appropriations for 2003 should not exceed $751 billion (in budget authority), the omnibus act resulted in a $766 billion total.

CBO has estimated that this increase added $200 billion in baseline projections of discretionary outlays over the next ten years. It is estimated that other provisions in the omnibus appropriations act affecting agriculture and Medicare will boost mandatory spending by more than $50 billion over the next decade. With higher debt service costs added, this single act increased baseline projections of future deficits by more than $330 billion.[12]

The omnibus experience is important in understanding Bush's budget problem because he announced a top line that he would not cross and then breached it. He did not have the personal or political strength to just say no. He has the same problem with mandatory spending, which, as Table 4.2 discloses, has had much larger increases during the past three decades than those achieved in the discretionary budget. Inasmuch as mandatory spending is driven by eligibility rules and payment formulas written into substantive law, most of these increases are automatic; they occur without new congressional action and regardless of the president's budget preferences. Bush wants to slow the growth of some mandatory programs by inducing the states to convert them into block grants rather than open-ended entitlements. Thus far, Congress has not adopted any of his proposals, but if it were to do so the legislation would likely hold states harmless against a loss of federal aid and might also offer "sweeteners" in the form of additional up-front grants to encourage the conversion.

The federal budget will continue to be dominated by entitlements as far ahead as the eye can see. At times, some entitlements may be adjusted at the margins, but the role of the government in assisting dependent families and households will not diminish significantly. The easy course for Bush, therefore, is to accommodate his budgets to these expenditures. Two problems, however, preclude doing nothing; one is that Medicare and Social Security cannot be endlessly sustained in their current form;

TABLE 4.2 Growth in Major Entitlement Programs (dollars in billions)

	1970	1980	1990	2000	2004	2008
Title payments for individuals	65	279	586	1,054	1,383	1,710
Social Security	30	117	246	406	491	587
Medicare	7	34	107	215	279	340
Medicaid	3	14	41	118	183	233

Source: Office of Management and Budget, Budget of the United States Government for Fiscal Year 2004 (Washington, D.C.: Government Printing Office, 2003).

the other is that, despite deficits, Americans want the government to spend even more on certain entitlements than current law requires. Before September 11 and the return of big deficits, Bush was laying plans to make Social Security over by shifting much of its financing into private accounts. He hoped to use a portion of the $5.6 trillion surplus projected at the start of his administration to finance the cost of transitioning to a partly privatized Social Security system. When the surplus vanished, the president stopped promoting Social Security reform because the government lacked the funds to pay for it. Medicare, however, has remained on the table, both because its financial crisis will come much earlier than Social Security's and because pressure has built to extend coverage to prescription drugs. Bush has tried to straddle the conflicting Medicare pressures by linking reform and expansion, but he has run into criticism from those in his own party who believe that all eligible seniors should receive prescription drug coverage, even if they elect to stay in the traditional fee-for-service system. Moreover, Bush has been impelled to propose $400 billion more for prescription drug coverage, more than his original offer, but only about half the amount sought by congressional Democrats.

If Medicare is a harbinger, the federal government will spend proportionally more on entitlements in the future, not less. A frontal attack on popular entitlements would injure Republican prospects at the polls; accommodating Democratic demands would further enlarge the federal budget. The difficulty of cutting entitlements is illustrated by the Medicare increases enacted in the 2003 omnibus appropriations measure. Some years ago, Congress ordained that Medicare payments to physicians would be cut by 4.4 percent in March 2003. But under pressure from medical groups, the omnibus bill cancelled the cut, adding more than $50 billion to baseline expenditure over the next decade.

Bush's budget problem is a spending problem. But his solution is not on the spending side of the budget. To spend less, Bush is convinced that the government must tax less, which is what he has set out to do through tax cuts enacted in 2001 and likely to be enacted in 2003.

The Power Not to Tax

"Taxation," Richard Rose and Terence Karran wrote, "precedes big government. The development of the capacity to collect large and increasing sums of money in taxes has been a necessary condition of the growth of government."[13] This unsurprising conclusion was drawn for the British government, but it fits the United States and every other industrial democracy as well. The expansionary process has a certain circularity:

government runs an actual or projected deficit, raises taxes to cover the shortfall, spends more because it has more to spend, returns to deficit, and raises taxes again. A generation ago Martha Derthick chronicled how Social Security tax rates, which were set at 1 percent of covered payrolls when the program was established in 1935, soared to more than 6 percent by the 1980s.[14] Congress periodically expanded Social Security benefits, its actuaries then projected a future deficit in the system, Congress raised rates a bit more than was necessary to cover the deficit, the new funds permitted a further expansion in benefits leading to deficit, and the process repeated itself.

Bush wants to break this pattern by cutting taxes rather than raising them. He succeeded in 2001, getting Congress to approve almost $1.3 trillion in tax cuts over a ten-year period. The main features included progressive reductions in marginal tax rates, a rebate to taxpayers, and a phase-out of the estate tax. The estimated cost was held down by budget rules that impelled Congress to make some tax cuts temporary, in the expectation that they would be made permanent in subsequent legislation.[15] Fully effective, the cuts would total almost $2 billion over the next decade and more in the years beyond that. Bush returned to his tax-cutting strategy in 2003, proposing $726 billion in reductions over the next decade, centered on eliminating the tax on dividends and accelerating some of the cuts enacted two years earlier. In addition, he asked for a steep increase in the amount Americans can shelter in tax savings plans. The president's short-term success can be measured by the Democratic response, which proposed to cut the revenue loss to about $350 billion.

In the context of revenue trends over the past several decades and the projected revenue needs for the next several decades, the 2003 tax cut makes no sense. President Bush's fiscal year 2004 budget estimated that, assuming his tax cuts were enacted, federal receipts in that year would be 17.0 percent of GDP, below the average of any decade since World War II. Federal revenues have not been as low as 17.0 percent of GDP since 1965, the last year before the cost of Great Society legislation impacted the budget. The reversion to 1965 revenue levels may be coincidental, but the aim to force the shrinkage of government is not. Looking ahead to future demands on the budget, paring revenue barely a handful of years before the leading edge of the baby boom generation begins to draw promised benefits appears to be a willful disregard of financial realities. It has been estimated that federal spending on Social Security, Medicare, and Medicaid (a rising portion of which goes to assist elderly Americans) will double, from a little more than 7 percent of GDP at the turn of the century to 14 percent by 2030 and 20 percent by 2070.[16] This projection assumes that the current structure of federal pension and health financing programs will remain intact, which is precisely the point that divides those who see tax cuts as imprudent and those who want more of them. One side argues for tax increases because the government will not have enough money to pay the benefits; the other side argues for tax cuts to emphasize that the promised benefits are untenable. In the latter view, the less money the government has, the more evident it will be that fundamental changes in public policy are needed.

In addition to stirring controversy on fiscal grounds, the Bush cuts have stirred controversy over their distributive impacts. Most of the tax reductions enacted in 2001 and 2003 will accrue to upper-income earners. One reason for this is that changes in the distribution of income and in the progressivity of the income tax during the 1990s decreased the tax burden of low-income Americans while significantly raising the tax liabilities of upper-middle-class and affluent households. Drawing on Internal Revenue Service data, the Tax Foundation has calculated that the top 10 percent of taxpayers accounted for two-thirds of individual income tax receipts in 2000, up from half in 1984.[17] The bottom half of taxpayers contributed only 13 percent, down five percentage points from their share in the 1980s. This skewed distribution of the tax burden dictates that across-the-board tax cuts, such as reductions in marginal tax rates, have much greater dollar value for affluent persons than for poor ones. Moreover, most (the earned income tax credit is an exception) are not refundable; the credit is limited to the amount of tax liability. Thus persons who already pay little or nothing in taxes get little or none of these breaks. In fact, millions of Americans did not get the rebates distributed in 2001 because they did not pay income taxes.

Basing his position on the argument that tax cuts should go to those who pay taxes, Bush tilted both the 2001 and the 2003 reductions in favor of upper-income Americans. They would be the main beneficiaries of phasing out the estate and dividend taxes and expanding tax-sheltered savings plans. It has been estimated that a family of four would be able to shift $60,000 a year to these savings plans. This amount exceeds median family income and would be available only to households whose income enabled them to save a substantial portion of their earnings.

Regardless of the merits of Bush's position, it may turn into an economic and political liability, and it certainly impedes efforts to restore budgetary balance. Bush promoted tax cuts in 2003 as necessary to spur economic growth, but tax cuts given to low-income earners have greater stimulative potential than those awarded to upper-income taxpayers. The latter typically increase savings when their taxes are cut; the former increase consumption. Bush does not have to worry about a political backlash if he remains popular, but if the economy continues to languish and the Democrats are able to mount a strong challenge, the concentration of tax cuts on affluent Americans may damage him at the polls. To cover his political flanks, Republicans broke with doctrine in 2003 and made the expanded child tax credits refundable; they go to persons who pay little or nothing in taxes.[18] Inasmuch as the refundable portions of tax credits are scored as outlays, this facet of Bush's drive to cut federal revenue increased federal spending.

The distribution of the tax burden troubles many conservatives, who believe that it encourages Americans who pay little or nothing in taxes to demand more from government. Liberals counter that low-income earners pay a disproportionate share of Social Security taxes and that the maldistribution of the tax burden merely mirrors the maldistribution of income in the United States. This is a debate that has no end, for the history of the income tax indicates that policy swings in one direction, then in another. Bush's tax cuts for the affluent are a reaction to the tax increase imposed on this segment of the population in the 1990s. At some time in the future, taxes on upper-income persons will be boosted in response to the Bush cuts.

Until this occurs, however, the budget may have to bear the brunt of a tax code that collects little from the bottom half of income earners and much less than before from those at the top of the income ladder. If estates, capital gains, dividends, and savings escape taxation or are taxed at reduced rates, the main burden will fall on wage earners who make too much to avoid taxes and too little to evade taxes. This will not be fiscally or politically tenable: the government will not collect enough to pay its bills, and middle-income Americans will pay too much to tolerate their tax bills.

The Economic Deficit

The budget deficit has not been due solely to Bush's tax cuts; it also is the result of a weak economy that has been buffeted by collapsing stock prices, a fall in business investment, and the adverse effects of terrorism and war on consumer confidence. The early signs of weakness appeared during the last half-year of the Clinton presidency, when real growth slowed to barely a 1 percent annual rate. Bush, however, will be judged, both by contemporary observers and in historical perspective, not by the economy he inherited, but by the one he managed. Halfway through Bush's first term, there already is reason to be concerned about the course of economic policy. Part of the concern is short-term: is the president doing the right things to lift the economy out of the doldrums? Surprisingly, however, much of the controversy over Bush's policies pertains to the country's long-term prospects; has the president embarked on a course that will impair the future economic performance of the United States? Tension between short- and long-term considerations is centered on the budget deficit. While it may ease the current economic malaise, if the deficit persists it may lower the economy's potential in the decades ahead.

Bush is not a fan of the economic fine-tuning that was in vogue during the heyday of Keynesian doctrine a generation ago. Like other supply-siders, he believes that active demand management contributes to the progressive enlargement of government. In this view, the size of the deficit does not have much influence on economic development. The deficit does not do much good in the short run, and it does not damage the economy in the long run. What matters is not the size of the deficit, but the structure of federal taxes and expenditure. The budget aggregates have little economic meaning of their own; they are merely the results of the numerous features of the tax code and of public expenditure that encourage or discourage work, saving, investment, and profits. Taxes on the intergenerational transfer of wealth are prominent provisions of tax policy that inhibit economic activity. On the spending side, an over-generous welfare state and the shift of risk from households to government have undermined the vitality of the United States.

The argument that deficits do not matter explains the startling abandonment by Bush and many fellow Republicans of the party's traditional anti-deficit stance. Clearly there is residual unease in Republican ranks about deficits that may approach or exceed $500 billion a year if bad-case scenarios materialize. Yet the president does not defend the deficit on the ground that it will ease economic distress. His 2003 Economic Report makes the case that the deficit has been caused by economic weakness and other factors; it does not claim that recovery will be stimulated by the deficit.[19]

In this construct, the relationship between budget aggregates and the macroeconomy is unilateral. A weak economy causes the budget to spiral into deficit; a deficit does not cause the economy to grow any more than a surplus does. This posture explains why Bush waited until January 2003, more than two years after the economic slowdown began, to announce a stimulus program. Of course the stimulus package consisted almost entirely of tax cuts, and of course the cuts were justified on the ground that they would generate jobs. Democrats and many economists pointed out that the new round of tax cuts would provide little immediate stimulus and that substituting rebates for low-income persons would have a greater short-term impact than would eliminating the dividend tax or provisions enabling affluent persons to protect savings against taxation.

While the immediate economic impact of Bush's tax program is problematic, the long-term implication has troubled many economists, who see it as a ploy to deplete the treasury of sufficient resources in the future. Controversy over its long-term effects parallels the short-term arguments. Critics see chronic deficits as jeopardizing the future economic well-being of the United States; Bush sees them as irrelevant, believing instead that the tax structure matters more than the capacity of revenues to cover expenditures. The Democratic argument, which has been labeled "Rubinomics" after Clinton's influential secretary of the treasury, Robert Rubin, is based on the notion that a robust economy requires a pool of savings to permit investment and productivity gains. Because Americans do not save much, this pool depends on the federal government's saving for them by running a budget surplus. If, however, the government were to incur chronic deficits, its dis-savings would further shrink what is already an inadequate pool of financial resources needed to ensure future economic growth. Here, too, the Republicans' riposte is that deficits do not matter, that future savings depend on incentives built into the tax code. They further argue that the high marginal tax rates enacted in the 1990s, along with the long-standing tax on dividends and other established features of U.S. tax policy, account for the low level of savings. Thus even if certain aspects of Bush's tax cuts will not bring much immediate stimulus, they will promote future economic growth.

In one sense, this is a clash of economic beliefs, neither of which can be truly validated without the passage of years or decades. If the Democrats prove to be right, the economic potential built by having ample savings can cumulate to trillions of dollars of additional GDP over the next half century, enough to finance Social Security and other downstream commitments. If, however, the Republicans are right that aggregate budget savings do not make much of a difference but that eliminating disincentives to save embedded in tax policy does, their plan would pave the way for a more prosperous future. Unfortunately, however, policy cannot wait until the evidence is in, nor can politicians afford to make big mistakes. This is an area where taking the wrong turn may seriously damage America's economic health. Prudence dictates that we not pave the way to the future with trillions of dollars in additional debt.

In another sense, the conflict between Republicans and Democrats is not about the future or over policies to stimulate savings, but over current and future expenditure. One side wants government to have sufficient resources to finance ongoing programs plus some enhancements; the other wants it to have insufficient resources, so that it will be compelled to retrench some commitments. Democrats and Republicans are fighting over today's government, and tomorrow's is at stake.

The Budget Battle in Congress

Not only are the two parties warring over budget policy; Congress has the final word, not the White House. Bush has prevailed by pushing his budget agenda through a Congress in which Republicans have a bare majority in each chamber. They have little margin for defection and little prospect of gaining Democratic support. The Democrats are united in opposition, so Republicans must rally behind their president for him to win. This is an age in which party-line voting is at a near record high, and the budget has become one of the great divides between the two parties. Bush has had easy passage in the House, where the rules favor the majority party and enable it to control floor debate by denying the minority the opportunity to offer amendments. As long as House Republicans are cohesive, they have the votes to pass Bush's budget program. The situation is more difficult in the Senate, where party discipline is weaker and the Democrats can block action by filibustering any tax cut that exceeds the amount provided for in the budget resolution.

Tax policy is one of the few issues that unites Republicans; spending, by contrast, divides them. Some Republicans, however, are troubled by the massive deficits that they see, looking ahead, and they would be willing to defer some of Bush's second round of tax cuts until the budget outlook brightens. Consequently, Bush and party leaders in Congress have to whip wavering members into line by offering standard legislative inducements such as favorable consideration of tax breaks or expenditure earmarks. But the main inducement has been the old-fashioned appeal to rally behind the president in time of national crisis. The Bush White House has artfully turned terrorism and war in Iraq, which have added over $100 billion to the annual deficit, into an argument for enacting tax cuts that would add hundreds of billion more. The budgetary arithmetic may not add up, but the political calculus gave the president a winning hand in Congress.

As impressive as Bush's congressional victory was, it required difficult negotiations between the House and the Senate, tie-breaking votes by the vice president, budgetary ruses that veiled the true cost of tax reductions, and efforts to keep the small numbers of Republican doubters in line. Both the 2001 and the 2003 revenue measures had to go through two legislative processes: (1) a budget resolution that set the outer limits of revenue loss as measured by current budget rules and (2) a reconciliation bill that enacted changes in the tax code. Failure at either of these stages, or in either the House or the Senate, would have doomed the president's agenda. Moreover, for Bush to prevail, the House and Senate would have had to set aside fundamental differences in political makeup and style and agree on a single measure.

During the 1970s, in the aftermath of Vietnam and Watergate, Congress introduced the budget resolution process as a means of staking out an independent position on revenues and expenditures. The president was given no role in the budget resolution; he can neither sign nor veto this measure. It is an internal congressional device, and Congress is not bound to follow the president's lead. As things have turned out, however, the budget resolution serves two very different purposes than those foreseen by its original architects. One is to facilitate passage of the president's budget agenda; the other is to facilitate enactment of a reconciliation bill. Bush, like Reagan and Clinton before him, took control of Congress's own budget apparatus and made it into an instrument of presidential policy. Bush might have won the tax battle even without a budget resolution endorsing tax reduction, but in view of Congress's congenital fragmentation, the battle would have been more difficult.

Nowadays, just about the only purpose served by a budget resolution is to set the stage for a reconciliation bill, which is protected against a Senate filibuster. With reconciliation, the president's tax plan is ensured of passage if he can muster majority support in both the House and the Senate; without reconciliation, the plan can make it through the House, but has no chance of passing the Senate. But in order for there to be a reconciliation bill, Congress must first pass a budget resolution that includes reconciliation instructions and determines the amount of revenue loss that is protected against a filibuster. Thus the key vote on President Bush's budget policy was the vote on the budget resolution, even though enactment was accomplished in separate measures. In 2001, with the Senate divided 50–50 before Republican Senator James Jeffords changed his party affiliation, becoming an independent, the Senate passed Bush's big tax proposal virtually intact because it was in a reconciliation bill. In 2003 the budget resolution reduced the amount set aside for tax reduction, ensuring a tax cut, but not as much as Bush had requested.

The official size of the 2003 tax reduction was further constrained by the defection of several Senate Republicans. While much has been made of the split in the Republican ranks, the more important story has been the high degree of cohesion. True, in a closely divided Senate even a few defections can put the majority party at risk, but it is also true that Bush got most of what he wanted because almost all Senate Republicans stood with him. Arguably, with the full effect of the sunsetted provisions counted in, Bush got more than he bargained for. Tax reduction in 2003 demonstrated that in budgeting less could be more.

Why Bush May Lose Even Though He Won

"This ain't the end of it—we're coming back for more," House Majority Leader Tom DeLay said shortly before the House voted final approval to the 2003 tax cuts.[20] News accounts told of a Republican strategy to make tax reduction an annual occurrence, to both extend sunsetted provisions and cut some other taxes as well. As long as Republicans control both the legislative and the executive branches and are united, they can continue to shrink the government's revenue base. Ultimately, however, tax reduction must be coupled with spending reduction; if it is not, the imbalance in the budget will unbalance Bush's budget objectives.

The coupling of the two sides of the budget was openly displayed in the budget resolution adopted by the House in 2003. Not only did it accommodate the full $726 billion in budget cuts requested by Bush; it spelled out the spending cuts that would restore the budget to balance within the ten-year period covered by the resolution. According to the Center on Budget and Policy Priorities, the resolution would prune an estimated $475 billion from discretionary spending, Medicaid, and certain entitlements.[21] These amounts are calculated against the CBO baseline and would be phased in over ten years. With much smaller tax cuts, the Senate version also had more modest spending cuts.

There are critical differences between the proposed tax and spending cuts, however, which leaves open the strong probability that enacting the former will not ensure approval of the latter. One difference is that tax reductions are enacted up front in a single measure; appropriations cuts must be enacted one year at a time. Entitlements reductions can be enacted up front, but when they are there is a good chance that they will be reversed, as occurred in the case of the reduced payments to physicians that were supposed to become effective in 2003.

An even more important difference between the revenue and spending sides of the budget is that Republican Party unity is much more pronounced in taxes than in spending. While barely a handful of congressional Republicans have deviated from the party line on taxes, many more have done so on spending issues. Of course, almost all Republicans (and many Democrats) espouse the view that the federal government should be smaller and should spend less, but when particular programs are up for a vote, they find it difficult to say "No." In this regard, many congressional Republicans mirror George W. Bush; they would like to spend less, but lack the political will to resist demands for more money. In 2003 the tax reduction law added $30 billion to federal spending in order to attract the votes needed for Senate passage. Thirty billion is not a lot of money in the federal budget, but it does couple tax reduction and spending increases, the exact reverse of Bush's strategy.

Thus the probability is that Bush will meet the same fate that Ronald Reagan did two decades earlier. He will be largely successful on tax matters, but much less so on spending policy. And just as Reagan's success on revenues and his failure on spending opened the door to massive deficits "as far ahead as the eye can see," in David Stockman's famous words, so too will Bush's successes and failures. Just as Reagan was succeeded by presidents who boosted taxes, so too will George W. Bush. It does not even matter whether his successor will be a Republican or a Democrat; taxes will be increased. The only way for Bush to thwart a future president's efforts to push tax increases through Congress would be to do so himself. But then he would be more like his father than he wants to be.

Chapter 5

Bush's Foreign Policy Revolution

Ivo H. Daalder and James M. Lindsay

PRESIDENT GEORGE W. BUSH is leading a revolution in American foreign policy. For a half century after World War II, successive administrations believed that the United States could make the most of its vast power by working closely with allies and through multilateral organizations such as the United Nations (UN) and the North Atlantic Treaty Organization (NATO). This conviction hinged on the belief that cooperation—even at the cost of accepting constraints on the freedom to act—reassured others about Washington's intentions and ultimately extended the reach of American power.

Galvanized by the terrorist attacks of September 11, Bush has abandoned this approach to how America should engage in the world. With terrorists, tyrants, and technologies of mass destruction posing a grave and growing danger, he believes that the best—if not the only—way to ensure America's security is to jettison the constraints imposed by friends, allies, and international institutions. The United States will act as it sees fit to protect itself and its interests. Other countries will either follow or get out of the way.

Bush is, in many ways, a surprising foreign policy revolutionary. During the 2000 presidential campaign many doubted he had the background or the inclination to make a mark on international affairs. He was widely seen as ill informed about and uninterested in the world beyond America's borders. Most observers suspected that he would be guided—if not held captive—by his far more experienced advisers. His insistence during the campaign that Bill Clinton had overextended the United States abroad fueled suspicion that his presidency would drift toward isolationism.

This conventional wisdom proved wildly off the mark. Bush, who came to the presidency with an insider's view of the White House, had a clear understanding of how presidents must lead. Early on in his presidency he established that he was not the pawn of his advisers, but rather their leader. Moreover, he came to office believing that a confident and unilateral exercise of American power was the best way to promote America's national interest. The logic of that belief was evident in the first months of his presidency, when he withdrew the United States from the Kyoto Protocol and the Anti-Ballistic Missile (ABM) Treaty and ended America's participation in a range of other multilateral efforts.

Rather than transforming Bush's beliefs about the world and America's place in it, September 11 confirmed them. He suddenly had both the motive and the opportunity to act on those beliefs and develop them in full. Foreign policy became not just the priority of his administration, but its mission. He dispatched U.S. forces to oust the Taliban from Afghanistan and Saddam Hussein from Iraq. He also made clear that America would confront potential adversaries before they acted against the United States. Terrorists would be brought to justice, tyrannical regimes overthrown, and weapons of mass destruction kept out of the hands of states and groups that would do America harm.

Bush's foreign policy revolution has profound consequences for American security and international affairs. An America that acts as it sees fit may be able to remake the world—for the better. But an America unbound also may be seen by others as arrogant rather than principled. Its friends and allies could balk at following its lead, and some might actively oppose its chosen course. The result could be that America will find itself less able to use its immense power to shape world affairs in ways conducive to its interests.

The Campaign

Presidential campaigns do not reveal everything about how a candidate might govern, but they almost always reveal something. Bush's 2000 presidential campaign was no exception. The impression that most people gleaned was that George W. Bush was uncomfortable discussing foreign policy and dependent on his advisers. Yet anyone listening closely to what Bush and his advisers said could discern something else. The Texas governor had clear views on how to run the White House, how to exercise American power abroad, and how to balance the relative priority of domestic and foreign policy.

The Candidate

It is ironic that foreign policy has come to define the Bush presidency. Throughout the campaign, doubters openly questioned whether Bush was smart enough to be commander in chief. Although he grew up in affluence and was the son of a president and the grandson of a senator, he had traveled little outside the United States. Aside from frequent visits to Mexico during his governorship, his international travel had consisted of a six-week trip to China in 1975, a short visit to the Gambia in 1990 as part of an official U.S. delegation, a trip to the Middle East in 1998, and a few trips to Europe in the 1990s with a group for corporate executives. By his own admission, Bush knew little about foreign affairs when he decided to run for the presidency. "Nobody needs to tell me what to believe," he said on the campaign trail. "But I *do* need somebody to tell me where Kosovo is."[1]

To help him locate Kosovo, Bush assembled a group of eight Republican experts, nicknamed the Vulcans, to tutor him on world affairs. The group was led by Condoleezza Rice, the provost at Stanford University and previously his father's White House adviser on the Soviet Union, and Paul Wolfowitz, the dean of the Johns Hopkins School of Advanced International Studies and undersecretary for defense policy in the first Bush administration. The other Vulcans were Richard Armitage, assistant secretary of defense for international security affairs in the Reagan administration; Robert Blackwill, White House adviser on European and Soviet affairs in the first Bush administration; Stephen J. Hadley, assistant secretary of defense for international security policy in the first Bush administration; Richard Perle, assistant secretary of defense for international security policy during the Reagan administration; Dov Zakheim, deputy undersecretary of defense for planning and resources in the Reagan administration; and Robert Zoellick, undersecretary of state for economic affairs and White House deputy chief of staff during the first Bush administration.

Bush's choice of these eight advisers was significant because it signaled his own foreign policy predispositions. In the mid-1990s the congressional wing of the Republican Party had been captured by what might be called the "sovereigntists." Led by polarizing figures such as Senator Jesse Helms (R-North Carolina), they were deeply suspicious of engagement abroad and saw most international institutions, whether political or economic in nature, as eroding American sovereignty. They favored a mix of isolationism and protectionism. The Vulcans, by contrast, supported international engagement and free trade. Still, they hardly represented the views of all internationalist Republicans. They were instead "intelligent hard-liners."[2] Missing from the foreign policy team were moderate Republicans from the Reagan and the first Bush administrations.

Bush made no attempt to hide his lack of knowledge of the world or his reliance on his advisers. Still, his penchant for confusing Slovakia with Slovenia or referring reporters' questions to Rice did not mean he had no idea how to be president. To the contrary, his views were well developed. They drew in part from his Harvard Business School education and from running a company. They also drew from watching his father's triumphs and failures. In 1988 he had worked to keep his father's campaign staff in line. After the election he had occasionally returned to Washington to play the heavy in intra–White House politics, most notably, in firing John Sununu as chief of staff. Unlike most presidential candidates, then, he had first-hand experience in the White House. And unlike vice presidents who have run for the country's highest office, he had watched a president operate from both a staff and a unique personal perspective.

During the 2000 campaign Bush described how he viewed the position of the president—it was that of the country's chief executive officer (CEO). The job description for that position entailed three things. "The first challenge of leadership," he wrote in his campaign autobiography, "is to outline a clear vision and agenda."[3] A belief in the need for clear objectives is not surprising for a man whose father's reelection campaign had foundered over "the vision thing." He pushed the point further in his first major foreign policy address as a candidate: "Unless a president sets his own priorities, his priorities will be set by others—by adversaries, or the crisis of the moment, live on CNN."[4] Moreover, Bush believed that top priorities had to be bold. Leaders did not merely tinker at the margins. As he said about becoming governor: "I wanted to spend my capital on something profound. I didn't come to Austin just to put my name in a placecard holder at the table of Texas governors."[5] His presidential campaign platform—a $1.6 trillion tax cut, Social Security privatization, and ambitious missile defense—attested to his desire not to spend his political capital on small things.

"The next challenge" of leadership, according to Bush, is "to build a strong team of effective people to implement my agenda."[6] Many of his critics, and more than a few of his supporters, depicted his willingness to rely on others as a sign of weakness. He saw it as a sign of strength. He repeatedly reminded voters, "I've assembled a team of very strong, smart people. And I look forward to hearing their advice."[7] He used his advisers' foreign policy qualifications to deflect questions about his own. "I may not be able to tell you exactly the nuances of the East Timorian situation but I'll ask Condi Rice or I'll ask Paul Wolfowitz or I'll ask Dick Cheney. I'll ask people who've had experience."[8] His job, then, was to be decisive—to pick among the options his advisers presented. "There's going to be disagreements. I hope there is disagreement, because I know that disagreement will be based upon solid thought. And what you need to know is that if there is disagreement, I'll be prepared to make the decision necessary for the good of the country."[9]

Third, Bush would stick to his positions even if polling data moved the other way. His campaign mantra was "We have too much polling and focus groups going on in Washington today. We need decisions made on sound principle."[10] This insistence on standing firm no doubt made for good politics. However, Bush's sentiment, particularly if it is understood as skepticism of conventional wisdom, probably also reflected his true feelings. His personal history demonstrates that experts are often wrong and opinions change. Few took him seriously when he decided to run for governor. Pundits criticized his rote repetition of his four campaign themes and his refusal to go "off message." He proved the skeptics wrong and defeated the popular Ann Richards. Once in office, he succeeded in enacting some of his priorities and failed in enacting others. Still, his governing style was in keeping with his philosophy: "I believe you have to spend political capital or it withers and dies."[11]

Underlying this approach to presidential leadership was tremendous self-confidence. Bush never confronted the obvious question: How would someone who knew little about the world know what the right foreign policy priorities were, decide whom to listen to when his seasoned advisers disagreed on what to do, know when his advisers reached a flawed consensus, or recognize when the conventional wisdom was actually right? Then again, Bush had reason to be self-confident. As Cheney explained it: "Well, but think of what he's done. He's the guy who went out and put his name on the ballot, got into the arena, captured the Republican nomination, devised a strategy to beat an incumbent vice president at a time of considerable prosperity in the country. None of the rest of us did that. And that's the test."[12] Indeed, how many Americans who at the age of forty were running a failing business and drinking too much turned their lives around so completely that within a dozen years they became not just a two-time governor of the nation's second-most populous state, but also a serious contender for the White House?

The Worldview

Bush's lack of foreign policy experience also did not mean that he lacked beliefs. He did not. He sometimes describes himself as a "gut" player rather than an intellectual.[13] But during the campaign he outlined, at times faintly, a coherent foreign policy philosophy. It was visible first in what he said on the campaign trail. But it was also visible in a deeper way in the writings and statements of the people he chose to advise him on foreign policy. These views, while not always identical or consistent, differed significantly from both the policies of the Clinton administration and those of previous Republican administrations.

At the level of broad goals, Bush outlined a foreign policy hardly distinguishable from Bill Clinton's. Like virtually every major presidential candidate since World War II, Bush's foreign policy aspirations were Wilsonian. The United States, he argued, had a "great and guiding goal: to turn this time of American influence into generations of democratic peace." In an implicit rebuke of the sovereigntist wing of the Republican Party, he warned that giving in to the temptation "to build a proud tower of protectionism and isolation" would "invite challenges to our power" and result in "a stagnant America and a savage world."[14] He did criticize what he said was Clinton's excessive use of American military forces overseas, thus prompting suggestions he was peddling a brand of soft isolationism. But when pressed to name a military intervention he opposed, he mentioned only Haiti.[15]

On another level, Bush's foreign policy outlook could be summarized as ABC—Anything But Clinton. His speeches dripped with disdain for the forty-second president. In Bush's judgment Clinton had committed the cardinal sin of leadership—he had failed to set priorities. Bush clearly had Clinton in mind when he declared that presidents would always be tempted to let the nation "move from crisis to crisis like a cork in a current." The result was that Clinton had given the United States "action without vision, activity without priority, and missions without end—an approach that squanders American will and drains American energy."[16] Clinton's mistake, then, was not that he actively involved America in world affairs. It was that he expended America's power on matters of secondary importance.

What Bush promised in contrast was clear priorities based on a hard-nosed assessment of America's national interests: "These are my priorities. An American president should work with our strong democratic allies in Europe and Asia to extend the peace. He should promote a fully democratic Western Hemisphere, bound together by free trade. He should defend America's interests in the Persian Gulf and advance peace in the Middle East, based upon a secure Israel. He must check the contagious spread of weapons of mass destruction, and the means to deliver them. He must lead toward a world that trades in freedom."[17] To read this pledge is to recognize how conventional Bush's foreign policy goals were.

Bush's stands on the two foreign policy issues that would come to define his presidency—terrorism and Iraq—were equally conventional. He vowed in his first campaign speech to "put a high priority on detecting and responding to terrorism on our soil."[18] For the most part, however, he, like Al Gore, seldom mentioned terrorism during the campaign. He did not raise the subject of terrorism in any of the three presidential debates, even though the third debate came just days after the bombing of the USS *Cole*.

Bush's comments on Iraq were scrutinized throughout the campaign. Asked how as president he would respond to the discovery that Iraq had resumed manufacturing weapons of mass destruction, he appeared to say he would "take him out." When the moderator immediately followed up this answer, Bush said he would "take out his weapons of mass destruction." The next day he said his original answer was "take 'em out," which people had misinterpreted because of his Texas drawl. "My intent was the weapons—them, not him."[19] His standard line subsequently became that there would be "consequences" if Iraq developed weapons of mass destruction, though he studiously avoided saying what those consequences might be. He never pledged to use the U.S. military to unseat Saddam Hussein. Instead, like Gore, he supported the Iraq Liberation Act, which provided funds for Iraqi exile groups dedicated to toppling Hussein's government. Bush also agreed with Gore that the policy of containing Iraq with sanctions should continue, insisting that "I want them to be tougher."[20]

What made Bush's beliefs distinctive—and even radical—was the underlying logic about how America should act in the world. This logic, which was more visible in the writings of Bush's advisers than in his speeches—the man from Midland took pride, after all, in being a doer rather than a thinker—has its roots in a strain of realist political thinking best labeled as hegemonist.[21] At its most basic, this perspective argues that American primacy in the world is the key to securing America's interests—and that it is both possible and desirable to extend the unipolar moment of the 1990s into a unipolar era. The intellectual predicate for this worldview was laid in a 1992 Pentagon study prepared for Dick Cheney and Wolfowitz.[22] That study, according to a draft leaked to the *New York Times*, maintained that U.S. national security policy after the cold war should seek to preclude "the emergence of any potential future global competitor."[23]

The hegemonist view rests on five propositions—four of which are familiar to anyone steeped in the realist tradition of world politics. First, the United States lives in a dangerous world, one closer to Thomas Hobbes's state of nature than to Immanuel Kant's state of perpetual peace. "This is," Bush maintained, "still a world of terror and missiles and madmen."[24] Peril to the United States—from China, Russia, Iraq, North Korea, terrorists—was also a staple of Cheney's worldview, laid bare in numerous speeches and conversations.[25]

The second element of the hegemonist worldview is that self-interested nation-states are the key actors in world politics. The 1990s witnessed much talk about how globalization—growing interconnectedness among states—was undercutting national governments, empowering nonstate actors, and reordering the structure of world politics. Bush and his advisers would have none of it. Except when talking about trade, they rarely mentioned globalization when discussing foreign policy. Whenever they mentioned terrorism, they almost always linked the subject back to the threat of rogue regimes and hostile powers. To them, world politics looked no different at the beginning of the twenty-first century than it had to Cardinal Richelieu or Prince von Metternich. States sought to advance their own narrow interests, not to create what Rice called "an illusory international community."[26]

Third, hegemonists see power, and especially military power, as the coin of the realm even in a globalized world. "Power matters," Rice wrote, "both the exercise of power by the United States and the ability of others to exercise it." In this contest, Bush argued, the United States enjoyed "unrivalled military power, economic promise, and cultural influence."[27] But power is about more than just capability. It is also about will. Here Bush and his advisers scorned what they saw as Clinton's hesitance to flex America's military muscles in defense of core national interests. "There are limits to the smiles and scowls of diplomacy," Bush argued. "Armies and missiles are not stopped by stiff notes of condemnation. They are held in check by strength and purpose and the promise of swift punishment."[28]

Bush and his advisers had a decidedly unsentimental view about how to exercise power. Washington should not be afraid of throwing its weight around. The lesson of America's "remarkable record" of building coalitions during the cold war, Wolfowitz wrote, is that leadership consists of "demonstrating that your friends will be protected and taken care of, that your enemies will be punished, and that those who refuse to support you will live to regret having done so."[29] The demonstration of resolve was as crucial for friends as for adversaries. They needed to be convinced that the United States meant what it said. Wolfowitz told the story of how Saudi Arabia rejected the elder President Bush's offer immediately following the Iraqi invasion of Kuwait to send a fighter squadron to help defend the desert kingdom. Only after then–Defense Secretary Cheney traveled to Riyadh and assured King Fahd that the administration would send hundreds of thousands of U.S. troops did the Saudis conclude that Washington was committed to "finish the job."[30] The lesson was clear: If America leads, others will follow.

The fourth basic proposition of the hegemonist worldview is that multilateral institutions and agreements are neither essential nor necessarily conducive to American interests. Bush did not flatly rule out working through international institutions. To the contrary, he occasionally spoke of working to strengthen organizations such as NATO and the UN. However, he articulated a distinctively instrumental view of formal multilateral efforts—they were fine if they served immediate, concrete American interests.[31] As a practical matter, they would usually be found wanting. That would force Washington to look first at forming "coalitions of the willing," an idea that the 1992 draft Pentagon planning document had endorsed. To borrow a metaphor popularized by one prominent Republican foreign policy thinker, the idea was that the United States would be the "sheriff" that organized the townspeople into a posse.[32] If the townspeople did not want to ride out to meet the bad guys, Washington would happily take on the role of Gary Cooper in *High Noon* and face the bad guys alone.

The Bush team was equally worried that many cold war agreements, most notably the 1972 ABM Treaty, had outlived their usefulness. The broader argument, however, was that multilateral agreements had ceased to be a means of achieving American interests and become an end in themselves. Bush and his advisers rejected the notion, popular with many in the Clinton administration and in Europe, that committing good words to paper would create international norms able to shape state behavior. In Bush's view, such agreements constrained only the United States and other law-abiding countries, not rogue states bent on harming American interests. Given this reality, Washington would be better able to maximize its own security by minimizing the constraints on its freedom of action.[33] This policy of the free hand, which had its intellectual roots in the criticisms Senator Henry Cabot Lodge leveled against the Treaty of Versailles, rested on an important assumption: The benefits of flexibility far outweigh the diplomatic costs of declining to participate in international agreements popular with others.

Washington could get away with disappointing its allies because of the fifth tenet of the hegemonist faith: The United States is a unique great power, and others see it so. This is the one proposition alien to the realist worldview, which treats the internal makeup and character of states as irrelevant. But it is a proposition most Americans take as self-evident. "America has never been an empire," Bush argued in 1999. "We may be the only great power in history that had the chance, and refused—preferring greatness to power and justice to glory."[34] The purity of American motives was crucial, because it meant that exercising American power should threaten only those opposed to the spread of freedom and free markets. What Washington wanted was what everyone would want if they were freed from despotic rule.

Most of Bush's advisers accepted this billiard ball view of the world, where the United States was the biggest (and most virtuous) ball on the table and could move every other ball when and where it wished. The one exception was Colin Powell, whom Bush tapped as an adviser more for his biography than for his philosophy. Powell was not a Vulcan, seldom appeared publicly with Bush during the campaign, and did not form a deep bond with the Texan.[35] Powell was a traditional internationalist who understood the importance of power, but worried about flexing America's muscles too freely and alienating other countries. He saw more virtue in multilateral efforts and agreements; he was the only member of the Bush team to have endorsed the Comprehensive Test Ban Treaty. In accepting the nomination to be secretary of state, he implicitly rejected the president-elect's insistence that the White House would set the policy agenda. The former national security adviser and chairman of the Joint Chiefs of Staff warned Bush: "During your administration you'll be faced with many challenges, and crises that we don't know anything about right now will come along." Many of Bush's other foreign policy advisers dismissed Powell's caution as timidity. When Wolfowitz was asked why he had agreed to become deputy secretary of defense, he reportedly gave a one-word answer: "Powell."[36]

While the hegemonists in the Bush campaign were united in their dislike for Powell's worldview, they disagreed among themselves over a key question: To what extent should the United States use its power to promote America's ideals? A minority was made up of democratic imperialists. Led by Wolfowitz, they argued that the United States should actively deploy its overwhelming military, economic, and political might to remake the world in its image—and that doing so would serve the interests of other countries as well as the United States.[37] Most of Bush's advisers, though, were assertive nationalists deeply skeptical that American power could create what others were unable to build for themselves. Led by Cheney and Rumsfeld, they saw the purpose of American power as more limited—to deter and defeat potential threats to the nation's security.[38] Because these threats also affected others, America's willingness to stare them down would enhance not only U.S. security, but international security as well. Or, as the controversial 1992 Pentagon study put it, "The world order is ultimately backed by the U.S."[39]

The Politics

Bush said throughout the campaign that the United States needed clear foreign policy priorities. He did not say, however, that foreign policy was his top priority. Topping his list instead were two domestic initiatives—a $1.6 trillion tax cut and education reform. While Bush provided detailed plans on how he intended to achieve these two objectives, his discussion of foreign policy initiatives—whether military readiness, missile defense, or better relations with Mexico—never went beyond listing aspirations.

Bush's decision to relegate foreign policy to a secondary place in his campaign reflected his own background and political vulnerabilities. Candidates taking remedial courses in world affairs are poorly positioned to tell the country to look overseas. Another factor was that foreign policy was not important to most voters. Polls throughout the 1990s found that fewer than 10 percent of Americans—and often fewer than 5 percent —named any defense or national security issue as the most important problem facing the United States. Even when people were pressed to name a foreign policy problem, the most common response polls turned up was "Don't Know."[40]

What the campaign suggested was that for Bush foreign policy was a not matter of passion. He had to speak about world affairs to demonstrate his political credibility. He attempted to do so in ways that maximized his appeal to voters. On a few issues, most notably better relations with Mexico, he showed genuine enthusiasm and comfort, though here the domestic political benefits given America's rapidly growing Latino population were obvious. But the main message he sent to the American electorate was that his would not be a foreign policy presidency.

The Early Months

World affairs might not have been at the top of George W. Bush's priority list in January 2001, but many Republicans hoped he would act decisively on foreign policy. The White House's actions in the spring and summer of 2001 gave them reason to be both discouraged and pleased. Although Bush did not launch any major new initiatives, he began undoing many of Bill Clinton's. In so doing, Bush showed a keen sensitivity to American domestic politics and almost none at all to politics abroad. He also turned a deaf ear to warnings that Al Qaeda represented a clear and present danger to the United States.

Leaving the Gate Slowly

Many of Bush's supporters expected him to move immediately to overhaul U.S. defense and foreign policy. Hawks expected a massive defense spending increase. Missile defense enthusiasts predicted a rapid U.S. withdrawal from the ABM Treaty and a new Manhattan Project to build a national missile defense. Beijing haters anticipated a push to redirect the U.S. military to counter a rising China, a blunt declaration of the administration's intent to defend Taiwan, and massive arms sales to Taipei. Isolationists on Capitol Hill looked forward to the withdrawal of U.S. troops from Bosnia and Kosovo. Free traders hoped for a revival of talks on a Free Trade Agreement for the Americas and a new round of world trade negotiations. Saddam haters expected aggressive efforts to produce regime change in Iraq.

Bush disappointed these expectations during his first eight months in office. In February he announced that he would not seek to add more funds to the 2001 budget and that he would let the Clinton administration's proposed 2002 defense budget request of $310 billion stand. He did not immediately withdraw from the ABM Treaty or launch a crash project to build a national defense against missile attacks. When Bush finally gave a speech on missile defense in May, he emphasized that he intended to prepare the diplomatic ground for a U.S. withdrawal rather than to present the world with a fait accompli. A month later he met Russian President Vladimir Putin for the first time at a summit in Slovenia, got "a sense of his soul," and declared that Russia "can be a strong partner and friend."[41]

Relations with China were more contentious, but the administration sought to restrain tempters. A Chinese fighter jet collided with a U.S. reconnaissance aircraft on April 1, 2001, destroying the Chinese fighter and forcing the American plane to make an emergency landing on Hainan Island. Rather than escalate the crisis, the administration quietly negotiated with Beijing. That caution continued even after China released the American crew. In late April the administration broke with past practice and announced it had authorized the sale of eight diesel submarines to Taiwan. In what administration officials acknowledged was a clear nod to Beijing's concerns, however, the White House decided against selling Taipei destroyers equipped with the advanced Aegis radar defense system.[42] Two days after the arms sales announcement, Bush told

ABC-TV's *Good Morning America* that the United States would do "whatever it took to help Taiwan defend herself."[43] Within hours the president backtracked, saying he had not changed long-standing U.S. policy toward Beijing. His advisers confirmed that statement publicly and privately. A little more than a month later, Bush extended normal trade relations status for China for another year.

Bush's initial reluctance to undertake major new foreign policy initiatives was evident on other prominent campaign issues. Powell announced in February that the United States would not remove its troops from Bosnia or Kosovo without the agreement of NATO allies, saying: "The simple proposition is: We went in together, we will come out together."[44] Bush made a point of taking his first foreign trip to Mexico, and he declared (just days before September 11) that "the United States has no more important relationship in the world than our relationship with Mexico."[45] Nonetheless, he offered no concrete plans for resolving the outstanding issues in U.S.-Mexican relations. The administration's trade policy remained stuck in the interagency process.[46] Finally, Bush made no moves to unseat Saddam Hussein either through direct U.S. action or by empowering Iraqi exile groups to do so on America's behalf. Instead the administration opted to seek to replace the existing Iraqi sanctions with smarter ones.

Just Say No to Multilateralism

Rather than unveiling new initiatives, during his first eight months in office Bush focused on extracting the United States from existing ones. In March he abandoned his campaign pledge to curtail emissions of carbon dioxide from power plants. Rice subsequently told European Union ambassadors at a private lunch that the Kyoto Protocol on global warming was "dead."[47] Thereafter the administration declared its determined opposition to a string of international agreements: a pact to control trafficking in small arms, a new verification protocol to the Biological Weapons Convention, the Comprehensive Test Ban Treaty, and the treaty establishing the International Criminal Court.

This "Just Say No" foreign policy extended beyond international agreements. Bush reined in a variety of U.S. efforts to broker peace around the world. At the top of the list was the U.S. effort to end Israeli-Palestinian conflict, which administration officials saw as the black hole of U.S. diplomacy. In a break with Clinton, who had enmeshed himself in negotiations between Israelis and Palestinians, Bush put U.S. engagement in the Middle East peace process on hold. He declined to send an envoy to the last-ditch Israeli-Palestinian peace talks at Taba, Egypt, in late January 2001. The White House eliminated the post of special Middle East envoy, and in May the National Security Council still did not have a senior director for Middle East affairs.[48] The reason for this inaction, as Powell repeatedly said, was that "in the end, we cannot want peace more than the parties themselves."[49]

Bush took a similar approach to North Korea. He abandoned the Clinton administration's efforts to strike a deal freezing the North Korean missile program in exchange for food aid, and he signaled that he had no intention of supporting South Korean President Kim Dae Jung's "sunshine policy" toward Pyongyang. Bush's hands-off approach carried over to mediating the conflict in Northern Ireland. Whereas Clinton had repeatedly played the role of peace broker, Bush said, "I am going to wait to be asked by the prime minister" of Great Britain. Tony Blair politely acknowledged the White House's withdrawal by saying, "It's difficult to perceive the exact circumstances in which I might pick up the phone and ask the president to help."[50] Bush also declined Colombian President Andres Pastrana's request for the United States to do more to help end Colombia's long-running civil war.[51]

In short, in his first months in office Bush delivered precisely the presidency he had promised. He had focused on a few key priorities and worked them hard. Those priorities just happened to involve domestic, not foreign, policy. The key legislative initiative was the $1.6 trillion tax cut. The administration's standard response to questions about why it did not seem to have a proactive external policy agenda was that it was conducting a thorough review of American foreign policy.

Politics at Home and Abroad

The steps that Bush did take in foreign policy, however, reflected domestic politics, and especially the demands of core Republican constituencies. On his third day in office Bush reinstated the "Mexico City Policy," the executive order that Ronald Reagan had imposed and Bill Clinton repealed mandating that non-governmental organizations receiving federal funds agree to neither perform nor promote abortion as a method of family planning in other nations. The practical importance of the decision was questionable, but the symbolic importance was not—pro-life groups had demanded the policy's reinstatement. With the stroke of a pen Bush shored up his support from the Republican base, which had previously doubted his conservative credentials.

The decision to proceed deliberately on missile defense was calculated at least in part to deny Democrats a political issue. They believed they had scored significant political points in the 1980s attacking Ronald

Reagan's "Star Wars" missile defense, and they hoped to repeat those successes by accusing the Bush White House of endangering the "cornerstone" of international stability. In contrast, by proceeding deliberately on missile defense and publicly reaching out to Russia, the White House looked to minimize the chances that its policy could be labeled reckless.

Domestic politics figured prominently in other Bush decisions. He based his decision to withdraw the United States from the Kyoto Protocol solely on domestic considerations, arguing that "idea of placing caps on CO_2 does not make economic sense for America."[52] Powell later admitted the decision had been handled badly, arguing that when the international "blowback came I think it was a sobering experience that everything the American president does has international repercussions."[53] The decision to delay action on a major trade initiative reflected a desire not to complicate work on other, higher presidential priorities.[54] Bush also showed he was not above reversing course to accommodate domestic political realities. His decision to stick with Clinton's defense budget proposals infuriated defense hawks on Capitol Hill. They quickly moved to open the spending tap. Rather than being trumped by Congress, the White House changed its tune. By August 2001 Bush had submitted a 2001 defense appropriation supplemental request and raised the 2002 defense budget request to $343.3 billion.

The flip side to Bush's sensitivity to American domestic politics was his insensitivity to foreign reactions. During President Kim's visit to Washington in March, Bush angered the South Koreans when he used a joint public appearance to express his "skepticism" that the North Koreans could be trusted to keep their word.[55] The abrupt announcement of the decision to abandon the Kyoto Protocol set the tone for a world already primed to believe Bush had no interest in the views of other countries. As complaints abroad about American unilateralism grew in the spring of 2001, Bush did not back down. On the eve of his first trip to Europe in June 2001, he reiterated his opposition to the Kyoto Protocol. While admitting that the surface temperature of the earth is warming and that human activity looked to be a contributing factor, he offered only to fund programs to study the problem, not, as his opponents demanded, action to reduce the emission of heat-trapping gases. As White House speechwriter David Frum later wrote, with only some hyperbole, "Bush was extraordinarily responsive to international criticism—but his response was to tuck back his ears and repeat his offense."[56]

Bush's willingness to step on diplomatic toes surprised many observers, who pointed to his campaign pledge to strengthen America's alliances. Nonetheless, his unsentimental diplomacy flowed directly from his core beliefs. If all states pursue their self-interest, if power matters above all else, and if American virtue is unquestioned, then U.S. foreign policy should not be about searching for common policies. Rather, it should be about pushing the world in the direction Washington wants it to go, even if others initially resist. As Powell told European journalists, Bush "makes sure people know what he believes in. And then he tries to persuade others that is the correct position. When it does not work, then we will take the position we believe is correct, and I hope the Europeans are left with a better understanding of the way in which we want to do business."[57] Nor did Bush miss the fact that the allies did not match their harsh words with equivalent deeds. The attitude Bush took to challenges to his domestic initiatives applied here as well: "We aren't going to negotiate with ourselves."[58]

Two other factors encouraged the administration's conclusion that it could ignore foreign capitals. One was the firm belief that Bush was being criticized because countries had grown accustomed to Clinton's eagerness to do what pleased them rather than what was right. Persuading countries that Washington would be doing business in a new way required a dose of "tough love" that would produce vocal complaints, at least for a time. Nonetheless, most officials in the Bush administration believed that if they stuck to their guns, the complaints would fade away as the allies adjusted to the new style of American leadership.

The other factor reinforcing Bush's willingness to ruffle diplomatic feathers was his firm belief that chief executives do not change simply because they get bad reviews. After returning from his first state visit to Europe, he commented: "I think Ronald Reagan would have been proud of how I conducted myself. I went to Europe a humble leader of a great country, and stood my ground. I wasn't going to yield. I listened, but I made my point. And I went to dinner, as Karen [Hughes] would tell you, with 15 leaders of the EU, and patiently sat there as all 15 in one form or another told me how wrong I was [about the Kyoto Protocol]. And at the end I said, 'I appreciate your point of view, but this is the American position because it's right for America.'"[59] Bush's description sounded more fitting for a cold war summit with Soviet leaders than for a meeting with America's closest allies in peacetime. Nevertheless, he was supremely confident in the goals he had set for U.S. policy, and he was willing to exercise patience in his effort to achieve them.

Bush's vision of the president as CEO showed itself in another way—he made clear to everyone that he was in charge. Unlike Reagan, who often could not decide between his oft-feuding friends, or Clinton, who always saw every side to an argument, Bush quickly earned a reputation among his advisers for decisiveness. Contrary to suggestions that he would be a pawn of his more seasoned cabinet secretaries, he dominated them, overturning their decisions or spurning their recommendations. Secretary of Defense Donald Rumsfeld was the first victim. His public commitment in February to seek a supplemental defense appropriations bill was quickly countermanded by the White House. In March, Powell had to retract his statement that the Bush administration would "pick up where the Clinton administration left off" in dealing with North Korea— "I got a little far forward on my skis" he later told reporters.[60] When Powell told Europeans in July that the administration would have a plan for combating climate change by fall, Rice followed by saying that there was no deadline and no plan. Environmental Protection Agency Director Christine Todd Whitman and Treasury Secretary Paul O'Neill saw their recommendation for action to combat global warming rejected. In short, Bush left no question as to who was in charge.

Underestimating the Al Qaeda Threat

In putting his mark on his administration, however, Bush failed to push his advisers to tackle the one issue that would dominate his presidency— terrorism in general and Al Qaeda in particular. He seldom mentioned terrorism publicly during his first months in office. In early May he announced a new Office of National Preparedness for terrorism at the Federal Emergency Management Agency, but gave it no new resources. Except on the handful of occasions on which he justified abandoning the ABM Treaty because of the "terrorist threats that face us," he did not mention the subject of terrorism again publicly before September 11.[61] By all accounts, things were not much different in private. None of this is surprising. Bush and his advisers had always emphasized that America was threatened by states—whether great powers or rogue nations—not stateless actors.

The outgoing Clinton administration—whose own handling of the Al Qaeda threat could be criticized—had tried hard to challenge that assumption. Before Bush took office, Rice met with the man she was replacing as national security adviser, Samuel R. Berger. He told her, "You're going to spend more time during your four years on terrorism generally and Al Qaeda specifically than any other issue."[62] Other Clinton administration officials repeated the same message just as bluntly. About a week before the inauguration, George Tenet, who stayed on as director of central intelligence, met with Bush, Cheney, and Rice. He told them that Al Qaeda was one of the three gravest threats facing the United States and that this "tremendous threat" was "immediate."[63] Brian Sheridan, the outgoing assistant secretary of defense for special operations and low-intensity conflict, says he told Rice that terrorism is "serious stuff, these guys are not going away. I just remember her listening and not asking much." Lieutenant General Don Kerrick, the outgoing deputy national security adviser, sent the National Security Council (NSC) front office a memo on "things you need to pay attention to." About Al Qaeda it said: "We are going to be struck again." During Bush's first week in office, Richard Clarke, the top NSC staffer on terrorism during the Clinton years who was held over by the Bush administration, handed Rice an action plan that said a high-level meeting on Al Qaeda was "urgently needed." A subsequent memo argued: "We would make a major error if we underestimated the challenge al-Qaeda poses."[64]

These efforts did not convince the Bush team to make counterterrorism a top priority. Rice did not schedule the high-level meeting that Clarke had requested. Instead she reorganized the NSC's handling of counterterrorism and effectively demoted Clarke. Kerrick, who stayed through the first four months of the Bush administration, said, "Candidly speaking, I didn't detect" a strong focus on terrorism. "That's not being derogatory. It's just a fact."[65] General Hugh Shelton, whose term as chairman of the Joint Chiefs of Staff ended shortly after September 11, concurred. In his view, the Bush administration moved terrorism "farther to the back burner."[66]

Bush administration officials later argued that they had worked throughout the summer of 2001 to prevent a possible Al Qaeda attack. The intelligence community had picked up "chatter" in late spring indicating greater terrorist activity. These concerns did not, however, prompt more aggressive action. Nor did they revive the Clinton administration's practice of keeping covert military assets on alert near Afghanistan to strike if the intelligence community located Osama bin Laden. Treasury Secretary O'Neill actually suspended U.S. participation in multilateral efforts to track terrorist money flows.[67] Clarke's plan to go after Al Qaeda wound its way slowly through the bureaucracy. Bush's senior advisers met for the first time to discuss the plan—which was dedicated to "rolling back" Al Qaeda—on September 4.

After September 11 administration officials insisted that President Bush had pushed them throughout the spring and summer of 2001 to move faster in confronting Al Qaeda. "I'm tired of swatting flies," he had reportedly said. "I'm tired of playing defense. I want to play offense. I want to take the fight to the terrorists."[68] Bush's own assessment of how he had handled the Al Qaeda threat and Osama bin Laden was far less flattering: "There was a significant difference in my attitude after September 11. I was not on point, but I knew he was a menace, and I knew he was a problem. I knew he was responsible, for the [previous] bombings that killed Americans. I was prepared to look at a plan that would be a thoughtful plan that would bring him to justice, and would have given an order to do that. I have no hesitancy about going after him. But I didn't feel that sense of urgency, and my blood was not nearly as boiling."[69]

Bush had done what he promised during the campaign. He had stuck to his agenda. Counterterrorism just happened not to be prominent on it. He would soon discover the truth of Secretary-designate Powell's warning: Events abroad do not always observe the priorities and schedules of even the most disciplined of presidents.

A Worldview Confirmed

September 11, 2001, shook the president, the nation, indeed the world. The differences that had divided the United States from its friends and allies before the attacks gave way to solidarity and support. *"Nous sommes tous Américains"* declared the left-leaning French daily *Le Monde*. Germany's Chancellor Gerhard Schröder offered "unlimited solidarity."[70] All over the world people stood as one with the United States.

With the global shock and sympathy came an expectation that September 11 would compel President Bush to alter his approach to foreign policy. Many people at home and abroad assumed that the unilateralism of the first eight months of Bush's administration was dead, replaced by a firm embrace of multilateral cooperation. It was an expectation shared even by Bush's father, who three days after the attack predicted: "Just as Pearl Harbor awakened this country from the notion that we could somehow avoid the call to duty and to defend freedom in Europe and Asia in World War II, so, too, should this most recent surprise attack erase the concept in some quarters that America can somehow go it alone in the fight against terrorism or in anything else for that matter."[71] Rather, international cooperation was assumed to be the only effective way to combat what many saw as the dark side of globalization.

President Bush took several steps within hours of the attacks that seemingly corroborated expectations of a new, more multilateral U.S. foreign policy. Washington turned to the United Nations, which on September 12 passed a resolution condemning those responsible for the attacks, holding accountable "those responsible for aiding, supporting or harboring the perpetrators, organizers and sponsors of these acts" and authorizing "all necessary steps" to respond to the attacks.[72] The administration also turned to Europe, where for the first time in its history the Atlantic Alliance invoked its solemn obligation under Article V of the NATO Treaty to come to the defense of a fellow member under attack. Instead of lashing out alone, Bush appeared set to assemble a broad coalition to fight the war on terrorism.

However, the expectation that September 11 would produce a new Bush foreign policy was soon proven wrong. The decisions to go to the United Nations and accept NATO's invocation of Article V were seen to have been tactical responses to the attacks, not a strategic conversion to the multilateralist creed. In fact, rather than seeing the terrorists attacks as repudiating their worldview, Bush and his advisers saw them as confirming it. They had argued throughout the euphoria of the 1990s—a time George Will called a "holiday from history"—that the world remained a dangerous place.[73] As Bush told the nation nine days after the attacks, September 11 had awakened America to danger: "We have seen their kind before. They are the heirs of all the murderous ideologies of the 20th century. By sacrificing human life to serve their radical visions—by abandoning every value except the will to power—they follow in the path of fascism, and Nazism, and totalitarianism."[74]

The reason terrorists had struck the United States was simple— American weakness had invited it. According to many in the administration, the dead at the World Trade Center, at the Pentagon, and in a field in rural Pennsylvania had paid the price for Washington's failure to respond forcefully to a long litany of attacks that had begun with the Beirut embassy bombing in 1983 and run though the bombing of the USS *Cole* in 2000. "Weakness, vacillation, and unwillingness of the United States to stand with our friends—that is provocative," argued Vice President Cheney. "It's encouraged people like Osama bin Laden . . . to launch repeated strikes against the United States, our people overseas and here at home, with the view that he could, in fact, do so with impunity."[75] By implication, the best way to defeat terrorists was to make it clear to all that the United States would respond decisively to any attack.

The Bush administration recognized that defeating Al Qaeda also required better homeland security within the United States and increased intelligence and law enforcement cooperation with other countries. It moved quickly to double homeland security spending and make counterterrorism priority number one at the Central Intelligence Agency (CIA) and the Federal Bureau of Investigation. Still, the focus of the administration's response was on taking the battle to the terrorists.[76] That meant targeting the states that harbored and aided them. "We will make no distinction between the terrorists who committed these acts and those who harbor them," the president declared the night of the attacks, in a statement now remembered as enunciating a new Bush doctrine.[77] Days later, Wolfowitz pledged that the United States would focus on "removing the sanctuaries, removing the support systems, ending states who sponsor terrorism."[78] The link between terrorist organizations and state sponsors became the "principal strategic thought underlying our strategy in the war on terrorism," according to Douglas Feith, the number three official in the Pentagon. "Terrorist organizations cannot be effective in sustaining themselves over long periods of time to do large-scale operations if they don't have support from states."[79]

Bush also made clear that he viewed the war on terrorism as a fight in which there was no room for neutrality. "Every nation, in every region, now has a decision to make. Either you are with us, or you are with the terrorists," he declared.[80] He saw the way other countries put aside their grudges about the Kyoto Protocol and the ABM Treaty to rally to Washington's side as confirming his belief that the rest of the world viewed America as a great power with a unique moral purpose. His task was to provide a clear lead for them to follow: "The best way we hold this coalition together is to be clear on our objectives and to be clear that we are determined to achieve them. You hold a coalition together by strong leadership and that's what we intend to provide."[81]

September 11 did not, however, leave the administration's thinking entirely untouched. One thing it changed was the once firm belief that great power competition constituted the primary threat to U.S. security. That distinction now belonged to terrorists and rogue states armed with weapons of mass destruction. Given that both Russia and China endorsed, with varying degrees of enthusiasm, America's war on terrorism, the White House even suggested that a fundamental strategic realignment among the great powers might be under way. "Today," Bush declared, "the international community has the best chance since the rise of the nation-state in the seventeenth century to build a world where great powers compete in peace instead of continually prepare for war. Today, the world's great powers find ourselves on the same side—united by common dangers of terrorist violence and chaos."[82] With the great powers united by a common cause, the United States would have greater freedom to pursue terrorists and tyrants.

September 11 also made foreign policy not just the administration's top priority, but Bush's personal mission. "I'm here for a reason," Bush had told his chief political aide, Karl Rove, shortly after the attacks, "and this is going to be how we're going to be judged."[83] The president's friends and advisers described the impact of September 11 on his thinking in similar terms. "I think, in his frame, this is what God has asked him to do," said one close friend.[84] According to a senior aide, Bush "really believes he was placed here to do this as part of a divine plan."[85] Once the world is delivered from evil, the good people everywhere will be able to get on with their lives free of fear. America's mission—George W. Bush's mission—is to make this vision come true.

In providing Bush with a motive to act abroad, September 11 also gave him the opportunity to act without fear of being challenged at home. In a replay of a phenomenon that has occurred repeatedly over the course of U.S. history, the attacks immediately shifted the pendulum of power in Washington away from Congress and toward the White House. Three days after the attack, a near unanimous Congress gave the president a blank check to retaliate against the terrorists, authorizing him "to use all necessary and appropriate force against those nations, organizations, or persons he determines planned, authorized, committed, or aided the terrorist attacks that occurred on September 11, 2001, or harbored such organizations or persons."[86] On issues ranging from missile defense to the payment of U.S. back dues to the United Nations to sanctions on Pakistan, Congress checked its previous defiance and deferred to the White House.

The depth of Congress's deference partly reflected the enormity of the attacks and a principled belief that lawmakers should defer to strong presidential leadership in times of national crisis. But it also reflected the Democratic Party's lack of credibility with the American public on foreign policy. For years Americans had told pollsters they had far more confidence in the ability of Republicans than in that of Democrats to handle national security issues. Now Democrats found themselves in a position where their criticisms of Bush's decisions would either not be believed or sound unpatriotic. Most Democratic lawmakers who would have preferred to challenge the White House opted for silence.[87] President Bush and his advisers—all of whom already had expansive views of presidential authority—happily seized on the chance to act without having to clear their decisions with 535 secretaries of state.

The White House also worked hard to keep Congress, and especially congressional Democrats, on the defensive. In a January 2002 speech to the Republican National Committee, Karl Rove, Bush's chief political adviser, urged Republicans to use the war on terrorism as a campaign issue against Democrats. Such political calculations appear to have influenced the decision to propose creating a new Department of Homeland Security. Although Democrats had initially championed the idea and the White House had opposed it, Bush succeeded in turning the issue to his favor. At one point he went as far as to suggest that Senate Democrats were "more interested in special interest in Washington and not interested in the security of the American people."[88] The keen sensitivity to domestic politics that Bush displayed during his first months in office continued as well. His March 2002 decision to impose new tariffs on imported steel was motivated in good part by a desire to shore up his support in the key battleground states of Pennsylvania and West Virginia. In short, September 11 did nothing to neuter Bush's political instincts.

The war on terrorism and its main initial components—the war in Afghanistan and dealing with what Bush would call the "axis of evil"— represented the logical outcome of the Bush worldview following the terrorist attacks of September 11. The world did not change that day, but the threat Bush intended to confront, the relative priority of foreign policy on his agenda, and his political freedom to act on his beliefs, clearly did.

Afghanistan

No one doubted the United States would respond to the September 11 attacks. "Terrorism against our nation will not stand," Bush declared moments after the second jet slammed into the south tower of the World Trade Center.[89] The question was how to respond. Administration officials concluded almost immediately that Osama bin Laden had masterminded the attacks. He and his Al Qaeda network had settled in Afghanistan with the full support of the Taliban, an Islamist regime that had taken power in 1996.

So Afghanistan became the immediate target of any potential military response. On September 17 Bush signed a "top secret" memorandum outlining plans for war against the land-locked Central Asian country.[90] Unfortunately the Pentagon, which has battle plans for almost every conceivable contingency, had no detailed plans for Afghanistan. It had fired cruise missiles at several Al Qaeda camps in response to the 1998 bombings of the African embassies, and U.S. naval vessels had been stationed in the Arabian Sea during the later years of the Clinton presidency, ready to launch cruise missiles in the event bin Laden was located.[91] But aside from these minor contingencies, Condoleezza Rice acknowledged, there was "nothing on the shelf for this kind of war."[92]

The absence of detailed military options became apparent in the NSC meetings convened during the first week after the attacks. Rumsfeld asked probing questions and wondered whether other countries (including Iraq) should to be targeted, but otherwise provided little advice on how the United States should respond. Shelton presented generic military options—attacking with cruise missiles only, adding long-range bombers, and putting boots on the ground alongside air power—that lacked much detail. CIA Director Tenet and his team presented the most developed military option. Armed with a colorful set of PowerPoint briefing slides titled "Going to War" (each slide was illustrated with a picture of bin Laden inside a slashed red circle), Tenet proposed that CIA and Special Operations forces provide direct support (including directing air strikes) to the Northern Alliance, the main Afghan opposition forces seeking to overthrow the Taliban regime.[93]

On September 17 Bush met with his advisers and told them what they had to do. Powell would issue an ultimatum to the Taliban—hand over bin Laden or be disposed. Tenet would have full authority to pursue Al Qaeda members in any way the CIA deemed necessary. CIA agents also were directed to begin providing full support to Afghan opposition forces. Shelton was told to draw up detailed plans for an attack using missiles, bombers, and ground troops. "Let's hit them hard," Bush said. "We want to signal this is a change from the past. We want to cause other countries like Syria and Iran to change their view." For now, Afghanistan would remain the focus. Bush authorized the Pentagon to accelerate planning for possible military action against Iraq, but he said his was a "first-things-first administration," and Afghanistan would come first.[94]

Three days later, Bush told Congress and the world how he intended to respond. "The Taliban must act, and act immediately. They will hand over the terrorists, or they will share in their fate."[95] Despite intense diplomatic pressure, both from the United States and from its neighbors, the Taliban rejected Bush's demands. On October 7, U.S. and British air strikes struck targets in Afghanistan. The campaign had three goals: to capture or kill top Al Qaeda leaders, destroy the terrorist infrastructure within Afghanistan, and remove the Taliban from power.

The Afghan war went through three distinct phases.[96] During the first phase, U.S. bombers and fighters attacked Taliban leadership sites, military installations, and other fixed targets as well as the terrorist infrastructure throughout Afghanistan. CIA operatives, meanwhile, recruited Afghan warlords with offers of money and weapons. Special Operations forces prepared to join the Northern Alliance and other opposition forces in an assault on the Taliban forces around Kabul and other major cities. In the second phase, U.S. troops guided massive air power against Taliban forces on the battlefield, enabling the opposition to break through the government's defensive lines. Within weeks, the Taliban were routed and the opposition took control of all of Afghanistan's major cities. The final phase, which continued into 2003, consisted of U.S. and allied troops', often with the support of local Afghan militias, mopping up Al Qaeda and Taliban resistance. Some of the battles involved intense fighting— including major clashes in the Tora Bora mountains in December 2001 and the Shah-e-Kot valley in March 2002.

The prosecution of the Afghan war flowed from Bush's worldview in three notable respects. First, the war not only highlighted the administration's belief that the best defense is a good offense, but it also underscored how Bush viewed the terrorist threat as largely a problem of state behavior. The ultimatum to the Taliban put responsibility for dealing with Al Qaeda squarely on the shoulders of the Afghan government. Its failure to comply led to its ouster. Yet while the war removed a crucial support structure, it did not end the threat Al Qaeda posed to the United States.

Second, the administration stuck to its instrumental view of multilateral institutions. Despite NATO's invocation of Article V, the White House decided to ignore most initial offers of materiel and combat support from NATO members. A suspicious Pentagon argued that involving the alliance would place too many constraints on America's freedom to act. This stemmed partly from a belief that the Kosovo war had shown NATO to be cumbersome—a classic case of "too many cooks." But it also stemmed from Bush's insistence that other countries not be able to dictate terms for the war on terrorism. "At some point we may be the only ones left," Bush conceded. "That's okay with me. We are America."[97]

Skeptical of the value of calling on America's primary military alliance, the administration decided instead to form a coalition of the willing. "The mission determines the coalition and we don't allow coalitions to determine the mission," Rumsfeld repeatedly insisted.[98] The partners were largely Anglo-Saxon countries—Britain and Australia in particular. They had a demonstrated record of working well with U.S. military forces and, just as important, with the White House. Even so, the planning and execution of the war in its first phases remained essentially an American affair.

Finally, the manner in which the Afghan war was fought demonstrated that, after all the suffering that had already been inflicted on the American people, Bush was extremely reluctant to demand much sacrifice from them. He urged Americans to get on with their daily lives, to hug their kids, to go out and shop—but he did not ask them to join the fight in any real sense. He also did not modify his fiscal policies to help pay the vastly greater expenses of securing the nation against future attack. Moreover, even in war, he went to great lengths to minimize U.S. combat deaths, even to the point of jeopardizing the administration's ability to achieve its strategic objectives. In a fateful decision in December 2001, the administration decided to rely on Afghan and Pakistani forces to pursue Osama bin Laden and many of his Al Qaeda fighters in the Tora Bora mountains rather than risk U.S. casualties. Bin Laden and many others were able to sneak past the poorly trained and motivated Afghan and Pakistani troops.[99]

Overall, the first phase of the war on terrorism produced mixed results. The combination of Special Operations forces, airpower, and local opposition forces was devastating. It also helped that the Taliban was, as

General Wesley Clark noted, "the most incompetent adversary the United States has fought since the Barbary pirates" in the early 1800s.[100] But more than a year after the main fighting ended, the war's broader objectives still had not been achieved. Few of Al Qaeda's leaders were captured or killed during the Afghan campaign, even though Bush had said publicly that he wanted bin Laden "dead or alive" and had told his military leaders, "We have to get UBL and their leadership."[101]

Finally, the administration's success in permanently eliminating Afghanistan as a terrorist base of operations was unclear. Terrorist training camps were destroyed, and terrorists were driven into the mountains or across the border into Pakistan. However, Afghanistan's long-term political stability remained uncertain. Despite promises of a Marshall Plan–like effort, the Bush administration did relatively little to secure the peace in the war-torn country. Indeed, the White House forgot to request funding for Afghanistan's reconstruction in its 2004 budget submission to Congress. Unless Afghanistan's many warlords are disarmed, its economy is restarted, and its government gains control of the countryside, it could again become a security problem for the United States.

The "Axis of Evil"

The Afghan war enjoyed broad international support. After initial resistance, and when for a time it looked as if the fighting might not go well, the Bush administration accepted troop contributions from more than twenty-five countries. Eighteen months after the fall of Kabul, more than half the foreign military forces in Afghanistan were non-American. In August 2003, NATO even took over command of the peace-keeping force. This widespread international support reflected the legitimacy of America's cause in Afghanistan. After September 11, few countries defended Al Qaeda and its Taliban supporters.

Most countries thought that with the end of the Afghanistan war U.S. policy would turn to long-term strategies such as greater law enforcement and intelligence cooperation. President Bush, however, saw the challenge differently. Just how differently became clear in January 2002, when he used his State of the Union address to argue that the threat facing the United States extended beyond terrorists to include rogue states bent on acquiring weapons of mass destruction. He said that states such as Iraq, Iran, and North Korea, "and their terrorist allies constitute an axis of evil, arming to threaten the peace of the world. By seeking weapons of mass destruction, these regimes pose a grave and growing danger. They could provide these arms to terrorists, giving them the means to match their hatred." Using the most dire language heard in any presidential speech since John F. Kennedy's first State of the Union address forty-one years earlier, he declared that the United States could not afford to stand still as this threat grew. "Time is not on our side. I will not wait on events, while dangers gather. I will not stand by, as peril draws closer and closer. The United States of America will not permit the world's most dangerous regimes to threaten us with the world's most destructive weapons."[102]

Identifying the threat to the United States as terrorists, tyrants, and technologies of mass destruction represented a logical evolution of Bush's worldview. As might be expected from someone who believed that states were the primary actors in world politics, the administration argued that tyrants—and not terrorists or technology—were the key to this trinity of evils. Thus Cheney, in making the case for going to war against Iraq, argued that "we have to be prepared now to take the kind of bold action . . . with respect to Iraq in order to ensure that we don't get hit with a devastating attack when the terrorists' organization gets married up with a rogue state that's willing to provide it with the kinds of deadly capabilities that Saddam Hussein has developed and used over the years."[103]

With tyrants as the core of the post–September 11 threat, regime change became the obvious solution. Only when tyrants no longer ruled could the United States have confidence that states such as Iraq, Iran, and North Korea would not seek to acquire weapons of mass destruction or make common cause with the terrorists. To prevent this from happening, the United States had to be ready to use force to topple a regime—perhaps even preemptively. As the Bush *National Security Strategy,* which was released in September 2002, concluded, "Given the goals of rogue states and terrorists, the United States can no longer solely rely on a reactive posture as we have in the past. The inability to deter a potential attacker, the immediacy of today's threats, and the magnitude of potential harm that could be caused by our adversaries' choice of weapons, do not permit that option. We cannot let our enemies strike first."[104]

The "axis of evil" speech and the administration's subsequent emphasis on preemption were profound strategic innovations. The Bush administration effectively abandoned a decades-long consensus that put deterrence and containment at the heart of American—and transatlantic—foreign policy. "After September the 11th, the doctrine of containment just doesn't hold any water, as far as I'm concerned," Bush explained in early 2003.[105]

But did the "axis of evil" speech mean that the United States would henceforth strike first militarily—that it had in effect declared war against each and every rogue state? Some abroad clearly thought so. French Foreign Minister Hubert Védrine complained that U.S. foreign policy had become "simplistic," and EU External Affairs Commissioner Chris Patten criticized the White House for going into "unilateralist overdrive."[106] The administration, however, responded that military force was only one way to deal with rogue threats. Two weeks after the president's "axis of evil" speech, Powell told Congress that, with respect to Iran and North Korea, "there is no plan to start a war with these nations. We want to see a dialogue. We want to contain North Korea's activities with respect to proliferation, and we are going to keep the pressure on them. But there is no plan to begin a war with North Korea; nor is there a plan to begin a conflict with Iran."[107] Despite President Bush's dismissal of containment, the administration left open the possibility that concerted pressure along the lines of the cold war strategy of containment might gradually force regime change, perhaps aided by reform movements within rogue countries.

Iraq, however, was different. President Bush clearly targeted it as the country of greatest concern. But why? North Korea and Iran had more advanced nuclear programs. Pyongyang possessed large stocks of chemical and biological weapons and over the years had sold weapons and technology to the highest bidder. Teheran's support for terrorism was both significant and long-standing. In contrast, Iraq's nuclear program had been dismantled, and its chemical and biological weapons program had been set back by UN inspectors in the 1990s. There was no evidence that Baghdad had proliferated any of its weapons or capabilities to others, and years had passed since it had been directly implicated in sponsoring terrorist attacks.

Yet Iraq became the top priority for four complementary reasons. First, many senior administration officials had come to office intent on toppling Saddam. Most had served in the elder Bush's administration, and they regarded the February 1991 decision not to march on Baghdad as a major mistake. Some (like Wolfowitz) had arrived at this belief early on; others (including Dick Cheney) had done so only later.[108] While many of these officials wanted to take a tougher line on Iraq before September 11, Bush became receptive to their arguments only after the attacks. As Bush explained, "The strategic view of America changed after September the 11th. We must deal with threats before they hurt the American people again. And as I have said repeatedly, Saddam Hussein would like nothing more than to use a terrorist network to attack and to kill and leave no fingerprints behind."[109]

Second, Bush and several of his advisers evidently believed from the start that Saddam Hussein must have had a hand in the September 11 attacks. In public the president denied suggestions of a link between Al Qaeda and Iraq. "I can't make that claim," he replied when asked about it.[110] In private, though, he said otherwise. "I believe Iraq was involved," Bush told his advisers on September 17, 2001.[111] Among Bush's advisers, Wolfowitz pushed the Iraq connection from day one, basing his argument in part on the belief that Baghdad had been behind the 1993 bombing of the World Trade Center.[112] Bush apparently sympathized with Wolfowitz's argument, but decided to focus first on Afghanistan. "I'm not going to strike them [the Iraqis] now. I don't have the evidence at this point."[113] He did, however, direct the Pentagon, in the same September 17 "top secret" memorandum that outlined plans for a war with Afghanistan, to begin planning options for an invasion of Iraq.[114] The anthrax-laced letters delivered to various news organizations in October 2001 and intelligence reports suggesting that Al Qaeda might detonate a "dirty" or radiological bomb in Washington, D.C., reinforced Bush's belief that Iraq was somehow supporting bin Laden's efforts.[115] For years Hussein had sought to acquire weapons of mass destruction, and he had used chemical weapons against both Iran and Iraqi Kurds.

Third, the administration believed Saddam could be ousted with relative ease. Attacking Iran, with three times the population of Iraq and a government that enjoyed broader public support, would be a major military undertaking. North Korea possibly possessed a nuclear weapon or two, and in any event, it effectively held South Korea hostage against an American attack. In contrast, Iraq's army was believed to be much weaker following its defeat in the Gulf War and the twelve years of sanctions that had followed. In the meantime, U.S. military capabilities had grown stronger, as demonstrated in the easy victories against Serbia and Afghanistan. Moreover, Baghdad had few friends—and none that was expected to help it if the United States attacked.

Finally, regime change in Iraq would give the president what he and several of his advisers most wanted: the opportunity for a grand strategic play, the type that establishes presidential reputations. As he said publicly on the eve of war, Bush believed that liberating Iraq could transform the Middle East by ushering in democratic governments throughout the region—making it less fertile ground for terrorists and possibly even creating stronger allies for a peaceful settlement of the Israeli-Palestinian conflict.[116] The White House hoped that, much as Ronald Reagan is remembered as the president who won the cold war, George W. Bush would be remembered as the president who brought democracy and peace to the Middle East. Such an achievement would not only secure another term in office, but would also help secure familial success given that Bush's father had started the confrontation with Iraq and a Middle East peace process that his son would then complete.

For all these reasons, then, Iraq became the first part of the axis of evil to which the United States turned.

The Inevitable War

President Bush appears to have made up his mind to press for Hussein's ouster by late winter 2002. "F___ Saddam. We're taking him out," Bush told Rice as he poked his head in her office as she met with three senators in March to discuss what to do about Iraq.[117] In the months ahead, Bush repeatedly—often bluntly—made the case that only ousting Saddam would eliminate the threat Iraq presented. Many of America's closest allies disagreed, but Bush and his advisers calculated that their views were irrelevant. "The fact of the matter is for all or most of the others who are engaged in this debate, they don't have the capability to do anything about it anyway," Cheney explained.[118] And if confronting Iraq offended key allies and weakened international institutions, that was a price well worth paying. In the long run, Cheney argued, "a good part of the world, especially our allies, will come around to our way of thinking."[119]

An Aspiration, Not a Strategy

Administration officials agreed on the need to remove Saddam from power. They disagreed, however, on how to do it. Cheney and Rumsfeld maintained from the start that military force was the only option—though in the flush of the seemingly easy victory in Afghanistan they believed that the combination of precision airpower, local opposition forces, and a small number of U.S. ground troops would suffice. Powell, in contrast, argued that if Washington convinced the international community to force Saddam to choose between his weapons or his rule, he would give up his weapons. That, in Powell's view, would weaken Saddam's hold on power and enable the Iraqi people to overthrow him.

Administration officials also differed about what Saddam's ouster would accomplish. Assertive nationalists like Cheney and Rumsfeld argued that removing the Baathist regime and disarming Iraq would eliminate a significant threat to regional stability and American security. They worried less about what would happen to Iraqi society once these major security objectives had been accomplished. In contrast, democratic imperialists like Wolfowitz saw the opportunity to democratize Iraq and thereby begin transforming the greater Middle East. Their view was that American security requires more than toppling evil regimes. It also requires supporting the emergence of governments that embrace America's values and principles.[120]

Bush did not initially show his hand for much of this internal debate—and when he did he was as likely to side with one view as the other. The result was considerable confusion. Most administration officials did not realize that the president had in fact decided to seek Saddam's ouster. Richard Haass, the director of policy planning at the State Department and a close confidant of Secretary Powell, met with Rice during the first week of July as part of a regular series of meetings they held to discuss world events and administration policy. Haass asked whether Iraq really should be front and center in the administration's foreign policy. Rice responded that the decision to get rid of Saddam had in fact been made.[121]

This confusion over what the administration was seeking hampered efforts to develop a coherent strategy for taking the country from a statement of policy (the "axis of evil" speech) to Saddam Hussein's ouster. In the weeks following the "axis of evil" speech, the administration did nothing to turn its words into deeds. Cheney traveled to the Middle East in March in an attempt to enlist Arab support for confronting Iraq, but his meetings were dominated instead by the escalating conflict between Israelis and Palestinians. That issue preoccupied the administration throughout the spring. Internal debate on the Israel-Palestinian conflict was settled only in late June, when Bush announced that American involvement in the peace process would be possible only after the Palestinians chose a new leadership "not compromised by terror."[122]

As it slowly became clear within the administration that Saddam's ouster was a top priority, the debate over how to do it intensified. Powell continued to argue that war could be avoided if Baghdad knew that its only alternative was to resume UN weapons inspections and destroy its weapons of mass destruction. As he later recalled, "There was a realistic chance that it could have worked, if [Saddam] realized the seriousness of the president's intent."[123] Powell made his case for coercive diplomacy in a private dinner with Bush and Rice in early August. He argued that by going to the United Nations the United States would be able to gain broad international support for the resumption of tougher inspections and, if necessary, for war.[124]

The administration's assertive nationalists made the opposite case. Not only would weapons inspections fail, Cheney argued in a major speech in late August; they "would provide false comfort that Saddam was somehow 'back in his box.'" Saddam was bent on acquiring nuclear weapons, and once he did, he "could then be expected to seek domination of the entire Middle East, take control of a great portion of the world's energy supplies, directly threaten America's friends throughout the region, and subject the United States or any other nation to nuclear blackmail."[125] The conclusion was unmistakable: Saddam had to be removed before he succeeded in his ambitions. There was little time to waste.

With the administration's internal debate spilling out into public, Bush was forced to choose. This he did in early September, when he essentially decided to take Powell's route to Cheney's goal. He went to the United Nations and challenged the members to stand up to Iraq and enforce the sixteen Security Council resolutions passed over the preceding twelve years. "All the world now faces a test, and the United Nations a difficult and defining moment. Are Security Council resolutions to be honored and enforced, or cast aside without consequence? Will the United Nations serve the purpose of its founding, or will it be irrelevant?"[126] It was a bold speech, and a bold challenge to the world community. Most countries nonetheless applauded it. They concluded that Bush had decided to work through the United Nations rather than outside it.

Despite the speech's boldness, Bush had no strategy for turning his challenge to the world into a workable policy. While he had decided to seek a new Security Council resolution, he had not decided what it would say. When Iraq predictably reacted to his speech by announcing that UN inspectors could return unconditionally, the administration was caught off guard. It took weeks before it finally decided to table a new resolution, and many more weeks before it negotiated a text acceptable to all the members of the Security Council—most of which in the interim had come to doubt Washington's sincerity in seeking the peaceful disarmament of Iraq.

The unanimous passage of UN Security Council Resolution 1441 on November 8, 2002, proved to be the high watermark of U.S. diplomacy. After eight weeks of intense negotiations, the administration persuaded a unanimous council to declare Iraq in material breach of its international obligations, create a tough new inspection regime, and warn that there would be "serious consequences" if Iraq failed to comply. Yet after having invested so much in getting the resolution passed, administration officials once again failed to anticipate the many pitfalls sure to arise with its implementation. To get agreement on the resolution, Washington had had to settle for terms that were subject to differing interpretation.[127] More important, there was no agreement within the Security Council on how much Iraqi cooperation would be enough to avoid war—nor on how much noncooperation would provoke it. The Bush administration itself may have been divided on this score. Whatever the reason, it had no contingency strategies in place for the moment when these different interpretations would come to the fore.

The cost of failing to think ahead became apparent early in 2003. On January 22, Dr. Hans Blix, the chief UN weapons inspector, surprised the Security Council by bluntly criticizing Iraq's halting cooperation with the new weapons inspections. Despite suggestions that it move quickly to exploit the opening Blix had provided by introducing a second resolution laying out the key disarmament tasks, setting a clear deadline, and authorizing the use of force if Baghdad failed to comply, the administration hesitated.[128] While the White House debated what to do, Blix returned to the Security Council for a second time in February with a more optimistic report. The political momentum that Washington had enjoyed only weeks earlier immediately swung to the bloc of member states, led by France and Germany, that opposed war. By early March, when the administration finally moved in to introduce a new resolution declaring that Iraq had failed to grasp its final opportunity to disarm under Resolution 1441, it was too late. Only three countries publicly joined the United States in supporting the new resolution.

So the United States went to war against Iraq on March 19, 2003, without the explicit backing of the UN Security Council. It is possible, perhaps even probable, that nothing the Bush administration could have done would have avoided this outcome. France, Germany, Russia, China, and Syria all adamantly opposed war. But then again, a more vigorous diplomacy and greater tactical acumen might have succeeded in winning Security Council support—or at least the support of a majority of its members. Failing that, the effort would likely have isolated those countries that were unalterably opposed to war. Instead, Bush's approach ended up isolating Washington.

The lack of allies had little effect on the actual conduct of the war. U.S. soldiers, supported by a significant contingent of British troops and a token contribution of Australian and Polish special forces, performed with great speed and skill to oust Saddam Hussein in just three short weeks of fighting. But it was in the aftermath that a broad level of international support would have been welcome. For while U.S. and British forces were able to take control of Iraq with little difficulty, the power vacuum created by the overthrow of the existing order demanded a large security presence throughout the country. In its absence, ministries were looted and many burned to the ground, suspect weapons sites were overrun (and whatever dangerous material might have been there was stolen), and Shi'ite and other groups with very different agendas were able to begin exerting control. To combat an emerging culture of lawlessness, the United States was forced to deploy many more troops—more than two hundred thousand in Iraq and Kuwait alone—than originally intended. And given the lack of international support, there was little prospect of other countries' making troop contributions sufficient to lift part of the burden that had befallen U.S. and British forces.

The Other Evil States

Even as Iraq became Bush's priority in late 2001, Iran and North Korea—the other two members of the "axis of evil"—were emerging in some ways as more immediate threats. In summer 2002 the intelligence community concluded that Pyongyang had secretly embarked on an effort to enrich uranium, violating its 1994 pledge to freeze its nuclear weapons program.[129] Once it admitted to the illicit program in early October, North Korea moved swiftly to put itself on a path to a viable nuclear weapons program. In December it ordered the three International Atomic Energy Agency (IAEA) inspectors to leave the country, shut down cameras monitoring the nuclear complex in Yongbyon, and removed IAEA seals in nuclear facilities. In January, Pyongyang announced its withdrawal from the nuclear Non-Proliferation Treaty (NPT), restarted its small research reactor, and began removing spent nuclear fuel rods for likely reprocessing into weapons-grade plutonium. Once reprocessing starts, North Korea will have the capacity to produce about six bombs' worth of plutonium in as many months.[130]

Iran was not sitting still either. In August 2002 an opposition group revealed the existence of two secret Iranian nuclear facilities—one to produce heavy water and the other to enrich uranium. In early 2003 Iranian authorities admitted these facilities existed and invited the IAEA to inspect them, as it is required to do under its NPT obligations. Inspections confirmed that the two facilities would enable Iran to complete the nuclear fuel cycle, thus giving it an indigenous capacity to produce nuclear weapons. Given that there is no peaceful reason for Iran to possess either facility (Russia has promised to fuel its only civilian reactor indefinitely) as well as Tehran's failure to declare the facilities to the IAEA before beginning construction (as is required under its safeguards agreement with the IAEA), it is clear that Iran has embarked on a program that will enable it to produce nuclear weapons in a very few years.[131]

Neither development surprised the Bush administration. Yet for all the administration's rhetoric about not permitting "the world's most dangerous regimes to threaten us with the world's most destructive weapons," it downplayed the significance of the North Korean and Iranian actions throughout 2002 and into 2003. Iraq remained the top priority. And while the administration might have hoped to use the credibility it had gained from defeating Iraq to intimidate Pyongyang and Tehran, in the meantime it largely ignored the development of threats that in most ways were more dangerous, more immediate, and more challenging.

The reluctance to match deed to word was most evident in the case of North Korea. While administration officials warned about the catastrophic threat a nuclear Iraq might pose years hence, they were either silent about or dismissive of the nuclear threat North Korea posed in 2003.[132] The administration deliberately delayed announcing Pyongyang's admission to U.S. officials of its illicit enrichment program until after Congress voted in October 2002 to authorize war with Iraq. It rejected any suggestion that what was happening constituted a "crisis." It refused to draw clear red lines because, as one senior administration official told the *New York Times,* "the problem with a red line is that North Korea will walk right up to it."[133] It declined to engage with Pyongyang in direct negotiations, arguing that this was a "regional issue" that would best be handled within multilateral forums—ad hoc groups, the IAEA, or the Security Council.[134] And it even suggested that Pyongyang's nuclear threat was less significant than many thought. "You can't eat plutonium," Powell said in dismissing the threat. "Yes, they have had these couple of nuclear weapons for many years, and if they have a few more, they have a few more, and they could have them for many years."[135]

The Bush administration was similarly silent about Iranian nuclear developments. This in part reflected its need for Tehran's cooperation in the war with Iraq. But the silence also reflected a belief that the United States needed a different strategy for dealing with Iran than with Iraq, or possibly even North Korea. Iran, with its large population of young people yearning to be free from the strictures of the religious fundamentalists, offered the possibility of regime change from below. Beginning in the mid-1990s large majorities of Iranians had begun voting in favor of reformist leaders opposed to the ayatollahs who still held tightly on to the reins of power. In July 2002 the Bush administration abandoned hope of reaching a rapprochement with reformist leaders, and instead openly sided with the people against their rulers. "We have made a conscious decision to associate with the aspirations of the Iranian people," said a senior administration official at a briefing on the new policy. "We will not play, if you like, the factional politics of reform versus hard-line."[136] But as with so many other aspects of its foreign policy, the Bush administration did not have a strategy for turning another worthwhile aspiration into reality.

Conclusion

George W. Bush assumed the presidency with many people openly questioning his ability to master foreign policy. By any reasonable standard of judgment, he proved his doubters wrong. Even before September 11, he demonstrated that he understood how to be an effective president. To an extent that surprised even his most ardent supporters, he was decisive, resolute, and in command of his advisers. This is not to say that history will necessarily judge all his choices wise. It is to say that he succeeded, especially after the terrorist attacks on the World Trade Center and the Pentagon, in persuading the country to follow his lead on foreign policy.

September 11 had a profound impact on President Bush. It did not, however, lead him to rethink his view of the world and America's role in it. Rather, he and his advisers saw the attacks as affirming their conviction that the United States can be made secure in a dangerous world only by the confident application of American power, especially its military might. In their view, it might have been possible to debate the threats to U.S. security and America's place in the world before September 11, but not after. As a top White House official explained:

> A few years ago, there were great debates about what would be the threats of the post–Cold War world, would it be the rise of another great power, would it be humanitarian needs or ethnic conflicts. And I think we now know: The threats are terrorism and national states with weapons of mass destruction and the possible union of those two forces. It's pretty clear that the United States is the single most powerful country in international relations for a very long time. . . . [It] is the only state capable of dealing with that kind of chaotic environment and providing some kind of order. I think there is an understanding that it is America's responsibility, just like it was America standing between Nazi Germany and a takeover of all of Europe.[137]

The Bush administration is right to see the trinity of terrorists, tyrants, and technologies of mass destruction as the principal threat to American security. But the strategy it has adopted for dealing with this threat—the focus on tyrants and the emphasis on regime change, by force if necessary—is misplaced. To believe that states are the key to the problem is to ignore the vast changes that globalization has wrought in politics. No doubt Al Qaeda and groups like it can benefit from state support. But their existence and ability to cause harm do not depend on direct state support. If anything, terrorist networks thrive on the weakness and failure of states rather than on their strength—a conclusion Bush has himself acknowledged.[138] Removing tyrants, while perhaps helpful, is no guarantee that terrorists will be significantly weakened.

Similarly, the problem of weapons of mass destruction goes well beyond rogue states. Globalization has dispersed technology around the globe, and with it the knowledge of how to build weapons of mass destruction. Many chemicals and biological pathogens have beneficial as well as harmful uses, so they can be openly acquired. The vast weapons hangover from the cold war—including the many thousands of tons of fissile material, chemical agents, and biological toxins stored throughout Russia, mostly with inadequate security and therefore vulnerable to theft or diversion—compounds the problem. Changing the leadership of rogue countries will provide no solution to these challenges.

Finally, the Bush administration overestimates how much the United States can accomplish on its own. No one can deny that America is powerful and that its power can be useful—even decisive. But having a big hammer does not mean that every problem is a nail—or that a hard hit will not misfire. Take weapons proliferation. If countries around the world were to abandon their export control policies, nuclear and other technologies of mass destruction would become even more widely available. Or consider the problem of terrorism—and what would happen if key allies in the fight against terrorism were to halt exchanging information or end cooperation in law enforcement. Our ability to penetrate terrorist networks and pursue many of their key leaders would be fatally undermined.

The Bush administration argues that international cooperation on terrorism, proliferation, and other crucial matters will be forthcoming even if the United States runs roughshod over the views of others. Countries act in their own self-interest, and it serves everyone's interests to cooperate in the war on terrorism. But what if this calculation is wrong? Arrogance, George Bush warned during the presidential campaign, breeds resentment of the United States.

Such resentment dissipated for a time after September 11. However, once the Iraq debate heated up in the summer of 2002, it reemerged and intensified. Distrust of the Bush administration was a pivotal issue in the German and South Korean elections. President Bush's subsequent failure to persuade a majority on the Security Council, let alone many of America's key allies, to support attacking Iraq resulted in a grave diplomatic defeat. The White House's strained efforts to prove that the war was being fought by a broad and diverse "coalition"—including powerhouses such as Macedonia, Micronesia, and the Marshall Islands—only underscored its international isolation.[139] All of this was reflected in the precipitous drop in foreign opinion of the United States—with America's favorable rating dropping by more than a third in Britain and Poland and by more than half in France, Germany, Italy, Russia, and Turkey in less than one year.[140]

The long-term consequences of the Bush administration's arrogance in exercising American power remain to be determined. Self-interest may drive other nations to follow Washington's lead, even if the United States is not the "humble" nation Bush promised during the 2000 campaign.

But then again, Bush might have been right then and wrong now. Too often, the administration behaves as "the SUV of nations," as Mary McGrory put it. "It hogs the road and guzzles the gas and periodically has to run over something—like another country—to get to its Middle Eastern filling station."[141] At some point, other countries may decide they have had enough and work together to resist American leadership. Some may even actively oppose its chosen course. At that point, America would stand alone—a great power shackled in the pursuit of its most important goals.

Chapter 6

President Bush: Legislative Strategist

John C. Fortier and Norman J. Ornstein

GEORGE BUSH ENTERED the presidency facing formidable challenges. His election was the most controversial in over a century; he won by a razor-thin margin in the Electoral College after thirty-six contentious days beyond Election Day, and then only by a 5-4 decision of the Supreme Court. Seething unhappiness about the controversial election outcome was widespread among Democrats. While Bush's party maintained majority status in the House and Senate, giving Republicans control of the White House and both houses of Congress for the first time since Dwight Eisenhower in 1953–54, it was by the barest of margins; the Senate was divided 50-50, with Vice President Cheney breaking the tie, and Republicans narrowly controlled the House 221-212. In fact, Bush's election had provided negative coattails in both houses, including the largest loss of Senate seats in a president's party in a presidential election in recent history.

To many observers these conditions would suggest a cautious, incremental, bipartisan approach to Congress. On the surface, so did Bush's experience in Texas, where he had worked extensively with Democrats who controlled at least part of the legislature for his entire time as governor. In May 2001, when Senator James Jeffords of Vermont left the Republican Party, control of the Senate switched to the Democrats, and caution and bipartisanship seemed even more likely. After the shock of September 11, as both parties and their leaders rallied around the president, symbolized by the warm embrace in the House chamber between the president and Senate Majority Leader Tom Daschle (D-South Dakota), bipartisanship via a kind of "Grand Coalition" of governance appeared inevitable.

But those predicting consistent bipartisanship or a cautious and incremental approach to policy making were wrong. Bush has been a bold president in the legislative arena. For much of his first two and half years in office, George W. Bush had chosen a tough-minded, sometimes confrontational, and strongly conservative approach to making policy— tossing aside conventional wisdom as to how to approach a narrowly divided Congress. His audacious and partisan tactics often worked—both in achieving legislative success in areas such as tax cuts and in blocking the Democrats in the Senate from achieving many of their goals or from gaining significant leverage over policy negotiations.

Bush has, however, sometimes balanced this approach with more bipartisan measures, in particular education reform at the start of his administration and a prescription drug benefit for Medicare most recently. At these two key junctures, Bush has reached across the aisle and sought Democratic support even at the risk of alienating some in his party. On both of these measures Bush could have fought for a plan more to the liking of his conservative followers, but he chose to give Democrats much of what they wanted and pass legislation by wide margins. This second tactic of bipartisanship is by no means the dominant one for Bush. In fact, there was a long stretch in his presidency when a more partisan strategy with Congress was the only one he pursued. During this period there was a real danger that the bare-majority partisan approach to Congress would not continue to provide legislative successes because it was angering and emboldening congressional Democrats and it was becoming increasingly difficult to keep strict party line discipline in Republican ranks. But just when it seems as if Bush had forgotten how to reach out across the aisle, he appears willing to work closely with Democrats on a prescription drug benefit and endure some criticism from some in his conservative base.

Critics of Bush will call it "politics," and supporters will argue that Bush's "compassionate conservatism" is a mix of traditional conservative positions with more "compassionate" measures. But regardless of how one characterizes Bush's motives, it is clear that Bush has been a tremendously successful legislative president. Bush has not engineered a political realignment of the nation or Congress; Congress still mirrors the 50-50 nation with a nearly even party split, albeit with narrow Republican majorities. However, the president has prevailed time after time in Congress, much of the time with bare majorities, less often with larger bipartisan ones, and has shown political and legislative dexterity that one might not have expected from a man with only six years of elective experience before coming to the presidency.

This chapter was written two and a half years into the George W. Bush presidency. Its aim is to demonstrate how Bush has worked with Congress and what it bodes for the remainder of his presidency. The chapter begins with an examination of how Bush worked with the Texas legislature. Bush's six years as governor provided him with the primary governing experience of his career prior to the presidency, and a look at these years reveals many characteristics that have carried over to his presidency: his focus on a limited achievable agenda, a sense of when and when not to cut legislative deals, and a willingness to use political capital. Bush's governorship, however, was also remarkable for the degree of bipartisanship seen between a Republican governor and Democratic legislators. This bipartisanship has been less apparent for most of the early part of Bush's presidency, with the exception of his early work on an education reform bill and recent attempts to craft a deal on prescription drug coverage for Medicare. The remainder of this chapter traces Bush's work with Congress through several key periods. In the initial six months of his presidency Bush skillfully balanced a partisan initiative (his tax-cut plan) with a very bipartisan education reform bill. He displayed skill in passing both. But in the summer of 2001 Republicans lost control of the Senate, and there were signs that Bush was losing control of the legislative agenda. The attacks of September 11 changed everything, and they were followed by an initial period of extreme bipartisan sentiment, with Congress rallying behind the president. But this bipartisanship masked larger differences between the parties, and Bush began a long period of passing largely partisan initiatives, using the Republican-controlled House of Representatives to back his proposals and cutting deals with just enough senators to garner slim majorities. After the period immediately following September 11, the more partisan strategy became more pronounced. Bush did not have bipartisan initiatives, like education reform, to balance his more partisan agenda items. The chapter examines the legislative history of the issue of trade promotion authority as an example of the way Bush used his narrow Republican majority to his advantage during this period. It then looks at the legislative fight over creation of the Department of Homeland Security and how Bush used the issue to the Republican Party's advantage in the 2002 midterm elections.

The initial version of this chapter was completed just after the U.S. victory in the war in Iraq, with Bush engaged in a fight over another significant tax-cut plan that ultimately passed with narrow partisan margins. Up until that time Bush had shown himself to be a president skillful in handling the legislature, generally successful in getting his agenda through. His initial strategy of reaching out to Democrats on some issues, however, seemed to have faded from view, and his close partisan victories had alienated potential Democratic allies. There were serious doubts as to whether he could hold together his Republican allies in Congress as he had done early in his presidency. In the time it took to revise this chapter, Bush had scored an impressive partisan victory on the tax-cut package, although with a total tax cut just under half of what he had originally proposed. Following the passage of the tax cut, Bush was attempting to employ a more bipartisan approach to a prescription drug benefit for Medicare.

Signs of a Governing Style: How Governor Bush Worked with the Texas Legislature (1994–2000)

Four of our last five presidents had never held political office in Washington before they assumed the presidency. Governor George W. Bush was different in that he was the son of a former president, but in many ways the best information the voters had on how he would govern and how he would work with Congress came from his six years as governor of Texas.

George W. Bush came to the Texas governor's office in 1995, beating incumbent Democrat Ann Richards with a campaign platform of four initiatives: education reform, juvenile justice reform, tort reform, and welfare reform. At the beginning of his first term, Democrats controlled the House and Senate as they had for more than one hundred years. The margins were 17-14 in the Senate and 89-61 in the House.

During the gubernatorial campaign, Bush had focused relentlessly and nearly exclusively on the four issues that were the focus of his platform. His first term as governor was marked by a methodical focus on enacting the four legislative initiatives he had proposed on the campaign trail. His focus on this agenda was so single-minded that when he was asked by a reporter to name a fifth item on his agenda, he replied, "Sure. Pass the first four things."[1] Bush's focus paid off, as he successfully steered each of these proposals through a legislature that meets for a single 140-day session only every two years. It is true that in each of the policy areas Bush delved into significant work had been done by prior administrations and there was a broad consensus around many of the issues. Nonetheless, Bush won over many critics by making policy proposals clear on the campaign trail, picking areas where he had a chance of legislative success, focusing exclusively on his defined political agenda, and allowing the legislature to add its stamp of approval by making changes around the edges.

The flip side of Bush's tremendous focus on key agenda items was that the governor was sometimes blindsided by issues that came into the political arena not at his bidding. Bush was the opposite of Bill Clinton, who lacked a focused, businesslike agenda, but was intellectually engaged in a wide variety of policy matters.[2]

Bush's relations with the Texas legislature were notable because of the good rapport he developed with many Democrats. Bush had the support of large numbers of Democrats on his legislative proposals, and he possessed a personal touch that reached across party lines. His good working relationships extended so far that in the 1996 midterm elections Bush did not campaign against Democrats who had been supportive of his legislative program, even though members of his own party urged him to do so. Bush's relationships with Democrats included rank-and-file members, chairs of committees, and party and institution leaders. His relationship with Pete Laney, the Democratic speaker of the Texas House, was warm enough that Bush asked Laney to introduce him when he gave his presidential acceptance speech in December 2000 after the resolution of the disputed election—a speech he gave inside the state legislative chamber to emphasize his role as a bipartisan "uniter, not a divider."[3]

By far Bush's most significant relationship was with Democratic Lieutenant Governor Bob Bullock. While Bullock was a conservative, the alliance between Bush and Bullock was by no means preordained. Bullock had a reputation for hard-nosed politics, causing Texas Republicans to dub him "Machiavelli in boots." One Republican wag opined that Bullock was "Lyndon Johnson, Sam Rayburn and Lloyd Bentsen all rolled up into one ornery alcoholic."[4] Bullock also had a frosty relationship with Bush's Democratic predecessor, Ann Richards. In Texas the lieutenant governor is an extraordinarily powerful figure—the chief operating officer of the state to the governor's CEO. In other words, the lieutenant governor is the equivalent of a strong city manager in a system with a weak mayor. Many governors, Richards included, had failed to acknowledge that power, preferring to treat the lieutenant governor as a secondary figure or a subordinate. Bush did not.

Bush actively sought out a genuine partnership, wooing Bullock and making it clear to him that he wanted Bullock to be both a partner and a mentor. The relationship blossomed into a close friendship. Part of the reason for the Bush-Bullock alliance was personal, but there were also institutional factors peculiar to the Texas legislature.

In the Texas Senate there is a requirement that two-thirds of the senators consent to a bill in order for it to pass. For many years the two-thirds rule was not an obstacle to one-party Democratic politics, as Democrats controlled the vast majority of seats. But in 1992 Republicans increased the number of Senate seats they held from eight to thirteen out of a total of thirty-one, overcoming the one-third hurdle and making themselves players in the Senate. Bullock, serving with a Democratic governor, was forced to acknowledge the Republicans, and relations, while not friendly, became professional and more productive. Thus when Bush came to office, Bullock had already worked across the aisle. That practice increased substantially under Bush. Bullock and the Democrats could easily have blocked any Bush proposals; they had majorities in both chambers at the outset of Bush's governorship. But if either wanted to gain legislative achievements, the parties had to work together. Bush's first session with the legislature was generally hailed as a success. Bush had a defined focus on the four issues on which he had run for office, he worked with Democrats, and he passed legislation in all four areas.

Although the first legislative session of Bush's governorship was marked by success and a focused and limited agenda, Bush took a more aggressive approach in the second session in 1997. He tried to capitalize on his accomplishments with a bold play for a plan to revamp the way schools were funded in Texas. While the Bush of the first legislative session had pushed initiatives that had a history and a good chance at success, the school funding issue was more controversial, and there was no consensus on a plan to solve it. Texas, like many states, relies on local property taxes for funding of schools. The result is that poorer communities cannot fund their schools as well as richer ones can. While this had been an issue in Texas, it was not a crisis that needed to be fixed immediately, as in other states where courts had required changes in funding structures by a specific date.

Bush introduced his school funding plan without thorough consultation with the legislature and against the advice of some of his Republican allies in the legislature. When Republican State Senator David Sibley told Bush that he should not introduce the plan and that he could not win, Bush replied with a message that has become a familiar theme of his presidency: "I've got this political capital. If you're not going to do something with it, there's no sense in having it."[5] The urge to use political capital and the need to have an active domestic agenda is a lesson that was, according to his associates, impressed upon him by his father's experience after the Gulf War. As reported in the *Wall Street Journal,* associates say Bush "draws that lesson from his sense that his father, former President Bush, wasted the popularity he had banked during the Persian Gulf War, failing to push a domestic agenda as a recession hit and then losing his re-election effort."[6]

Bush's plan went beyond the simple issue of school funding; it encompassed a broad set of changes in the tax base of the state. He proposed using an existing budget surplus to cut property taxes and direct a higher percentage of state funding to local school districts. At the same time, the plan would also raise the state sales tax and institute new business taxes, including taxes on professionals such as lawyers and doctors. While there were some tax increases in the plan, the use of the surplus for tax cuts meant a net tax cut, as well as a shift in funding for education from local governments to the state.

Democratic House Speaker Pete Laney created a special committee to deal with the issue. The committee moved the bill in a more liberal direction with greater state funding and larger tax increases. Despite misgivings and the objections of conservative Republicans, Bush ended up supporting the effort of Democrats to pass such a bill in order to get it to conference with the Senate. Tough opposition from business and professional groups led to the bill's demise, although Bush did get the legislature to pass a scaled-back plan to use the surplus to cut property taxes.

Some Democrats were emboldened by the failure of the Bush initiative, believing that the governor showed vulnerability, that he was not invincible as he had been during the first session of the legislature. But it is not clear that Bush's gamble hurt his overall standing with the legislature or the people. Some gave Bush credit for trying to solve a difficult problem, and he did cut his losses by accomplishing the simple property tax cut. Nonetheless, it was a setback, and one in which his acquiescence to the majority Democrats' actions had cost him significant support from his base.

The third legislative session of Bush's gubernatorial administration was overshadowed by his run for the presidency. His legislative agenda was not as ambitious as in the first two years, but it is notable that Democrats in the legislature did not mount an aggressive campaign to push bills that would embarrass Bush.

A short summary of the key points of Governor Bush's legislative strategy in Texas provides a touchstone with which to compare the early part of his presidential administration. First, Bush as governor had a focused and disciplined start. He ran on a discrete number of issues, and he was successful in passing his legislative program through the legislature. Second, Bush's initial legislative program consisted of initiatives that had been started on by the legislature before he came to office and where a rough consensus had developed. Third, Bush was concerned with the big picture on his agenda, and he allowed the legislature to work out details and change his plans in small ways. In the end, Bush was able to claim credit for legislation that looked much like what he had proposed, but the legislature was also able to put its stamp on the programs.

Fourth, Bush's narrow and disciplined approach succeeded because he did not take on too much, spread his attention too thin, or clog up the legislative committees with too many bills. However, Bush was not as informed or flexible as he might have been when issues outside his agenda were forced onto the public stage. Fifth, Bush succeeded not only in the legislature, but also in the election booth, gaining seats for Republicans in the legislature in 1994, 1996, and 1998. But notably, Bush did not campaign directly against Democratic incumbents who had been supportive of his agenda. Despite their partisan differences, many of the same Democrats repaid him with support, or at least enthusiastic assessments of his governorship, during his presidential campaign. Sixth, Bush demonstrated an understanding of, and sensitivity to, the concept of political capital. Winning in the legislature gains an executive political capital, capital that must be spent or it dissipates. That understanding was honed by his gubernatorial experience, but dated at least back to his father's presidency and failed election bid, which Bush interpreted as coming in significant part because his father had failed to use his political capital after the first Gulf War.

Seventh, when he had the chance, Bush opted for boldness, making a play for global reform of the Texas system of funding schools with property taxes, but his endeavor faltered when he failed to bring in the legislature during the formulation of the plan and when he subsequently lost the support of his business and conservative Republican political base. Eighth, Bush worked successfully with Democrats in Texas, in particular Bob Bullock. But the parallels of Texas Democrats with Democrats in Washington are limited. Texas Democrats are much more conservative than their national counterparts, and in Washington there is no obvious Bob Bullock–like figure, someone who wields power and builds coalitions while sharing ideological compatibility with the president.

The Two-Pronged Strategy: Bush and Congress (2001)

In the 2000 campaign Bush described himself as a "compassionate conservative." Many of his positions resonated with the conservative base of the Republican Party, but he also emphasized issues such as education reform that appealed to Democrats and independents. In the first nine months of his presidency Bush employed a two-pronged legislative strategy that mirrored the two aspects of his compassionate conservatism. He employed a mostly partisan strategy, relying very heavily on Republican votes, to pass his tax cut. At the same time he forged a bipartisan coalition in Congress to pass his education reform package.

The Two Sides of Compassionate Conservatism

On the presidential campaign trail Bush defined himself as a compassionate conservative. He was conservative in recognizable ways on both economic and social issues, advocating less government and traditional values. However, he emphasized that conservatism was not harsh or uncaring, but that it was compassionate in a different way than the traditional welfare state model. In particular, compassionate conservatism emphasized character and individual responsibility. Government might be called upon to alleviate suffering, but part of the solution was to hold institutions responsible for improvement and to help foster better character and self-reliance in the individuals that government would help. Education reform became his signature issue to underscore the Bush direction of compassionate conservative government.

Education reform was by its nature better suited to action at the state level, as the federal government provides only a small portion of public school funds. It was an important issue for many of the Republican governors, who portrayed themselves as more pragmatic than congressional Republicans in Washington who were in opposition to the Clinton administration. Bush, like many governors, took this issue to heart. While education reform was a more effective issue at the state level, where most of the funds were provided, it was also true that reforms in testing and accountability had not been implemented by all of the states, and federal money for education was not related to these reforms. Bush's intensive focus on education during the campaign paid off politically, as his polling numbers on handling education equaled or surpassed those of the Democratic nominee, Al Gore, quite unheard of for a Republican presidential candidate.[7]

President Bush's Start: Highlighting Two Priorities

As in his run for governor, Bush promoted a clear and limited agenda on the presidential campaign trail. He emphasized a few issues, among them a tax cut, education reform, a patients' bill of rights, Social Security and Medicare reform, an end to the Anti-Ballistic Missile Treaty, faith-based initiatives, and military modernization. But of this short list two received the most emphasis on the campaign trail. Bush was first and foremost for cutting taxes and for improving education.

In a number of important respects, Bush's start as president resembled his initial days as governor. He deviated little from the clear limited agenda that had been laid out on the campaign trail. The two issues that were his prime legislative focus were his tax cut and his education reform proposal. President Bush's two-priority strategy avoided a problem that had plagued a number of his predecessors. The legislative agendas of Bill Clinton and Jimmy Carter, for example, were more ambitious and less focused. Carter, in particular, suffered from too many proposals competing with one another for public attention, congressional support, and space on the agenda, with most up for consideration before the same committees. Bush's administration could work both initiatives because the players were different in each policy area and because their momentum would not be diluted by other issues.

In addition, the two issues represented political balance, as the new president faced an evenly divided political system. The tax cut was a partisan issue that excited the president's base. The education reform package, on the other hand, was bipartisan, cutting across ideological lines, with a good chance of passage with 80 percent support in both houses. It reinforced Bush's image as a compassionate conservative and appealed to moderate voters.[8]

The Tax Cut: Appealing to the Republican Base

Bush had proposed a large tax cut during the 2000 campaign, a position popular with his conservative base. After the election there was widespread speculation that he would cut back on the size and dimensions of the tax cut to respond to the close partisan margins in Congress. But in January 2001, before taking office, Bush signaled that he would not scale down his tax cut and that he might propose accelerating parts of the tax cut to stimulate the economy.[9] Bush's campaign proposal was projected to cost $1.6 trillion over ten years.[10] The major features of the plan were a reduction and consolidation of income tax rates, a doubling of the child tax credit, alleviation of the marriage penalty, and repeal of the estate tax. Bush made it clear that he would make his tax cut his top priority and push for early action in the Congress.

Institutional differences between the two chambers made it clear that President Bush would have an easier time passing his tax cut plan through the House than through the Senate. The rules of the House allow the leadership to set strict rules on debate and to limit amendments by the minority. But even given the powers of the House leadership, the Republican majority was slim (only six seats), and it would be a tremendous task to hold almost all of the Republicans together. The Senate, however, was even less favorable to action on the president's plan, because it had less favorable rules and a large percentage of Republicans who might not wholeheartedly support the president's plan. Given these dynamics, the president pursued a strategy to use the House of Representatives to pass his plan more or less as proposed, with a very narrow margin of victory and almost exclusively Republican votes.

Once the House had acted, the president would bargain with key Senate moderates to secure a majority. This meant cutting House Democrats out of the process. It also meant dealing with individual Democratic senators, but not with the Democratic Senate leadership. This strategy was designed to get a bare majority with very few Democratic votes. This bare majority strategy was first employed on the tax cut, but was duplicated many times in the following two years. In the case of the tax cut, however, Bush was also pursuing an education reform bill, using a much more bipartisan strategy. The two-pronged approach of the bare majority tax cut and the bipartisan education reform bill was effective and disarming to his political opponents, helping Bush keep his conservative base and reach out to Democrats in the legislature.

Republican leaders in the House were eager to take up Bush's tax cut. Despite their bare six-vote margin, the House Republican leaders aimed to achieve perfect or near-perfect unity among their members. The Democratic congressional leadership opposed the Bush tax cut's size, breadth, and duration. But, unwilling to appear opposed to all tax cuts, they offered an alternative. The Senate's Democratic leader, Tom Daschle, indicated in January that Democrats would support a $300 billion tax cut.[11] By late February they had coalesced around a $700 billion (or $900 billion) plan.[12] It was clear that the Senate, with a 50-50 division, less party discipline, and rules more generous to the minority than the House, would be the battleground for the plan. After these initial moves, Bush and House Republicans began a procedure that has been duplicated many times in the course of his administration—passing the president's plan with a narrow majority of Republican votes in the House and making some compromises with the Senate to get just enough moderate Democratic and Republican votes to ensure final passage.

The action on the tax cut began in the House. While Republican House leaders were instrumental when the tax bill made it to the House floor, the key player in Congress making sure that the plan got to the floor quickly and nearly intact was Bill Thomas (R-California), the chairman of the House Ways and Means Committee. To expedite action and maximize support, Thomas split Bush's proposal into parts. The Ways and Means Committee first addressed a bill that included the largest part of the Bush tax cuts (about $950 billion over ten years), the income tax rate cuts. On March 1 the committee voted to approve the rate cuts by a 23-15 vote, with all Republicans voting in favor and all Democrats against.[13] As the House committee was voting in favor of the rate tax cuts, Bush went public, going directly to voters in states that he had won where there were wavering Democratic senators.[14] Bush traveled to more states in the early part of his presidency than any other president.[15]

On March 8 the tax-cut plan came to the floor of the House, and it was passed 230-198. Every Republican voted for the bill, and all but ten Democrats opposed it. (By contrast, the Reagan tax cut of 1981, which had been much larger adjusting for inflation, had garnered significantly more Democratic votes.) Bush attracted very few of the conservative Democrats, who call themselves the "Blue Dogs," some of whom, like Charlie Stenholm of Texas, had voted for Reagan's tax cuts. The major part of the tax-cut plan was thus passed with scant Democratic support and with virtually no Democratic input.

The House Ways and Means Committee then quickly took up another part of the Bush tax cut, the marriage penalty and child tax credit provisions. Bill Thomas's proposal altered the president's tax plan by adding a provision to strengthen the earned income tax credit, which benefits lower-income workers, and to add more relief from the marriage penalty. The bill passed out of committee on March 16, once again on a strict partisan vote (23-16).[16] The package was estimated to cost $400 billion over ten years. On March 29 the House voted 282-144 in favor of the bill. This time, attracted by the Thomas provisions, sixty-four Democrats voted for the package and no Republicans voted against it.[17] But the key vote was one to reject a substitute amendment proposed by Democrat Charles Rangel, which would have made the package smaller and more heavily targeted toward lower-income earners. Some 231 members, including twelve Democrats, voted against the Rangel amendment; 196, all Democrats, voted for it.[18]

That same day, March 29, the Committee on Ways and Means voted for a third part of the Bush tax proposal, the elimination of the estate tax ($192 billion over ten years), by a vote of 24-14, with only one Democrat supporting the proposal.[19] On April 4 the House passed the bill 274-154, with fifty-eight Democrats voting for the measure and three Republicans voting against it.[20] The bill eliminated the estate tax (or, as Republicans preferred to call it, the death tax), but phased in its demise more slowly than the president's plan, thereby lowering its cost.

The overall effect of the House's maneuverings was that Bush's tax cut was passed more or less as he had asked for it. To be sure, the House had put its own stamp on it, but via marginal changes. The House package was for approximately the same dollar amount as the Bush proposal, and it encompassed the major areas the president had proposed. While a few parts of the plan garnered some Democratic support, it was the unanimous Republican backing, combined with the restrictive House procedures, that made for the early and thorough presidential victory.

Meanwhile, in the Senate there was little formal action and much behind-the-scenes bargaining. Republican Phil Gramm (Texas) joined with Democrat Zell Miller (Georgia) to introduce the president's plan. However, it was clear that the president's bill could not pass the 50-50 Senate without modification, as only a few moderate Democrats (maybe only Miller) might support the president's plan, while some moderate Republicans might oppose it. In this atmosphere Majority Leader Trent Lott (R-Mississippi) and Minority Leader Tom Daschle exerted pressure on their rank and file to respectively support or oppose the president's plan.

In this contentious atmosphere the chairman and the ranking member of the Finance Committee, Iowa Republican Charles Grassley and Montana Democrat Max Baucus, began working together on a compromise. Both were discouraged from doing so by members of their own parties. Baucus, in particular, was heavily criticized by Democrats for not holding the party line on the tax cut.[21] Baucus, a moderate Democrat from a conservative state that frequently voted Republican for president and for statewide offices, was up for reelection in 2002 and was uneasy about opposing the president generally or his tax cut specifically.

While Democratic leaders had hoped to slow down the bill's progress in order to dull the president's early momentum, Grassley and Baucus quickly came to a compromise, one much closer to the president's plan than to anything Senate Democratic leaders had contemplated. The plan called for $1.3 billion in tax cuts over ten years, and it was slower and less generous in lowering the rates for the highest income brackets and slower in phasing out the estate tax.[22] On May 15 the bill passed out of the Finance Committee with the votes of all ten Republicans and four of ten Democrats.[23] On May 17 Majority Leader Trent Lott brought the bill for debate to the Senate floor, where a number of amendments to the Grassley-Baucus compromise were defeated.

Republican leaders expected that the debate would conclude the week of May 21 and the Senate would pass a bill that would go to conference rapidly to iron out differences with the House.[24] But the week turned out to be more momentous than anyone had expected. On May 21 there were rumors that Senator James Jeffords, a Republican from Vermont, would leave his party and become an independent, but vote with the Democrats, thereby shifting control of the Senate to the Democrats. The next day Jeffords met with Vice President Cheney and then later with President Bush and made it clear that he would leave the party. Bush asked him to delay the date of the switch until after the tax cut had passed.[25] The Senate voted on the Grassley-Baucus tax package on May 23. All of the Republicans (including Jeffords) and twelve Democrats voted for the package, sending the bill to a House-Senate conference. On May 25 the conference met to work out the details of a compromise; given the realities of a Democratic majority in the Senate, the size of the package and the major features of the tax cut closely resembled the Senate's version. Final passage was on May 26. In the House no Republicans voted against the package and twenty-eight Democrats voted for it. In the Senate twelve Democrats voted for the tax cut and two Republicans voted against it.

In a substantive sense, the president had a huge victory. The tax cut that was enacted into law was more than 80 percent of the size he had proposed and much larger than Democrats had wanted. Most of the details resembled those of the president's original plan. The political victory for Bush was enormous as well—he had achieved his top legislative goal more rapidly than Ronald Reagan (elected by a landslide in 1980 with huge coattails in both houses) had been able to achieve his in 1981. Still, as Bush celebrated signing the tax cut into law, the Jeffords switch continued to reverberate.

Education Reform: Reaching Out to Moderates

On a parallel track to the tax-cut proposal was President Bush's proposal for education reform. From the beginning it was clear that education reform would take quite a different path to passage than the tax cut. The basic purpose of Bush's education reform proposal was to provide more money to states and more flexibility in spending it, but to require them to be accountable for improved performance, especially by instituting state testing plans and improving student test scores. The most controversial provision in the Bush plan was for giving parents a form of school vouchers, which would allow them to use public money that it would take to educate their children in public schools and apply it to private school tuition. In the particular plan proposed by Bush, if an individual school underperformed for a number of years the federal funds provided to that school could be given to the parents of children in that school so that they could pay for their children to attend other schools. Other points of potential disagreement between Republicans and Democrats were funding levels and a Republican interest in using block grants to the states to give the states flexibility to use money for many education purposes versus the Democratic approach, which favored targeting money for specific purposes.

The education plan was initially welcomed with warm bipartisan comments from the Democratic side. Early on, the president worked closely with liberal Democratic Senator Edward Kennedy (Massachusetts) and Representative George Miller (California), the ranking Democrat on the House Education and the Workforce Committee. Bush designated a close Texas friend, a moderate named Sandy Kress, to be his education reform coordinator. Kress formed solid and warm relationships with these key Democrats. On March 8 Senator Jeffords, who before his party switch had chaired the Senate Health, Education, Labor, and Pensions Committee, moved the bill out of committee quickly by leaving out the provisions regarding vouchers and block grants to the states, saving the debate on those issues for the Senate floor. Without these provisions the measure passed 20-0 in the committee.[26] The House began working on education reform shortly thereafter and unveiled a plan that was closer to the president's.

On March 22 Representative John Boehner (R-Ohio), chairman of the House Education and the Workforce Committee, introduced the bill, including among other measures the president's school voucher program. Democrats planned to introduce their own bill. But both Boehner and ranking committee member Representative George Miller made it clear that differences could be worked out.[27] For the next month both the Senate and the House tried to fashion bipartisan compromise bills. In each case the bill moved significantly in the Democratic direction; vouchers were stripped out, the block grant flexibility was significantly reduced, and the funding levels were increased. The majority of the public grumbling over the bill came from conservative Republicans. After vouchers were more or less taken out of the bill, several conservative groups including the Family Research Council, the Eagle Forum, and the Traditional Values Coalition said they would not support it.[28] Nonetheless, the House Education and the Workforce Committee passed this compromise bill out of committee on May 7 by a vote of 41-7. Among the seven dissenters were six conservative Republicans and one Democrat.[29]

At this point it appeared that the bill would sail to victory quickly. On May 23 the House passed its bill, rejecting amendments that would have changed it from the version passed out of committee. The vote was 384-45, with thirty-four Republicans, ten Democrats, and independent Virgil Goode voting against the bill. Those who voted against the bill were among the most conservative and the most liberal in each party. It seemed likely that the Senate would pass its version the same week, but on May 24 Jeffords left the Republican Party, switching the Senate to Democratic hands. The education reform bill would languish until after September 11, finally passing in December with some more concessions in the Democratic direction. The final vote then was 381-41 in the House and 87-10 in the Senate.

The Results of the Two-Pronged Strategy

After all of the twists and turns of the legislation, Bush's two-pronged strategy was successful. Bush succeeded in getting his tax-cut and education reform packages passed into law, and he was able simultaneously to appeal to his conservative base and to moderate voters. But for the Jeffords switch, Bush might have received greater credit for these successes. If all had gone according to plan, Bush could have had the double boost coming from passage of a large tax cut very similar to his original proposal and over intense Democratic opposition, followed by a Rose Garden ceremony for the signing of an education reform bill, with the president flanked by conservative House Whip Tom DeLay and liberal Senate icon Ted Kennedy!

Bush had been more or less on target to achieve these twin goals, but the historic Jeffords defection had changed the political and policy dynamics. A midstream change of party control of the Senate had not been completely unexpected, although most observers had morbidly anticipated that the change would result from the death of one of the older senators, not from a single middle-aged senator's renouncing his lifelong affiliation with the Republican Party. Both the manner of Jeffords's switch and its timing on the eve of passage of the tax cut had been particularly unhelpful to the Bush agenda. Instead of chronicling Bush's first major legislative victory on the tax cut, media accounts underscored the tension between the conservative and moderate wings of the party.

The longer-term consequences of the Jeffords switch also impacted the Bush agenda. The membership of the Senate did not change, but majority status means control over the timing and the substance of the policy agenda, and Democrats quickly took advantage of that power, scheduling votes on issues such as patients' rights that the White House wanted to delay. Once Democrats gained control over a branch of government in Washington, however, they also inherited a new responsibility for governing—giving Bush some opportunity to cajole them into bipartisan agreements or face the prospect of being blamed successfully for gridlock.

Other Issues in Congress in Bush's
First Nine Months in Office

While the twin issues of the tax cut and education reform dominated the agenda, there were other legislative initiatives that were taken up in Congress. Bush showed skill in staying out of fights he could not win, cutting his losses when initiatives were not succeeding, and offering alternatives to popular Democratic proposals. These smaller congressional issues were energy, faith-based initiatives, campaign finance reform, and a patients' bill of rights.

In March 2001, when California's energy crisis worsened to the point of rolling blackouts, energy policy vaulted upward on the priority list. Bush's plan included contentious issues such as drilling in the Arctic National Wildlife Refuge (ANWR) and a provision to block an increase in CAFE (fuel efficiency) standards. A number of the Bush measures were seen as anti-environment, which spawned a backlash, and the energy crisis in California cooled as quickly as it had heated up. For a time it appeared that the president might suffer a politically damaging defeat of his energy package. But, fitting a pattern, Bush turned to the House to save his plan. House leaders, Tom DeLay in particular, put together a coalition of most Republicans, along with Democrats from oil and gas states, and also gained the support of the Teamsters Union and other building trade unions. Bush staved off amendments to block drilling in ANWR and increase CAFE standards, and he achieved an impressive win in the House, 240-189 on final passage. There was little chance that the Senate, now in Democratic hands, would compromise on the issue. There would be no passage of the Bush plan, but Bush was able to get a tough House victory to avoid political defeat.

Bush also brought faith-based initiatives onto the national stage. The central idea was that religious organizations would be able to provide government services. For example, a drug rehabilitation clinic might be run by a religious charity that stressed faith as well as providing services. Individuals might choose this option among other government-run options or those run by private secular groups. Bush's general concept of involving religious charities in providing government services had bipartisan support, but questions of implementation and constitutionality hampered the passage of legislation. It was reported that the administration was considering making faith-based initiatives the next big legislative item after tax cuts and education, but because of the difficulty of maintaining a coalition and the resignation of the director of the newly created Office of Faith-Based and Community Initiatives, John DiIulio, the White House began to look at smaller, discrete initiatives that could be implemented administratively rather than as a large legislative package.

Finally, there were two issues—campaign finance reform and patients' rights—that Bush would have preferred not to be on the legislative agenda in his first six months in office. His campaign rival, John McCain, had pushed both, and both had more support from Democrats than from Republicans. Bush did not control the legislative agenda on these items, but he skillfully managed to avoid ending up on the losing side of the issues. On campaign finance, Bush announced early on that he would sign a bill, but would not actively participate in the congressional deliberations. This had two consequences. First, Republicans opposing campaign finance reform would have to kill the bill in the House or the Senate, or they would have to pass a bill they could live with. Second, the no-veto promise meant that Bush was largely absent from the debate. Negative publicity focused on the opponents of campaign finance reform in Congress, not on him. His rival McCain did steal the spotlight, but Bush avoided directly opposing him.

On patients' rights, Bush had hoped to delay action until after the first six months, and ultimately to pass a more business-friendly version of the measure. His hand was forced when the Senate switched to Democratic control. Again McCain was his nemesis, as he allied himself with Democrats. In this case Bush did issue a veto ultimatum. He would oppose a bill without sufficient limits on employer liability. For a time in the summer, it looked as if Bush would be forced to take the unpopular step of vetoing a patients' bill of rights passed by both houses. But at the last moment he persuaded the key House Republican patients' advocate, Representative Charlie Norwood (Georgia), to agree to a compromise that narrowly passed the House and forced a stalemate in a conference committee. Thus Bush was able to stake out the position that he supported a version of patients rights without having to sign a bill that would have alienated many of his conservative supporters.

The time from inauguration to the August recess of Congress is a key time for a presidency. It is the transition or "honeymoon" period when a president can highlight an initial agenda and might expect greater unity in his own party in Congress and some deference from the opposition. Except for the relatively rare times of crisis, however, as in Franklin Roosevelt's initial presidential period, or after sweeping landslides, like Lyndon Johnson's in 1964 and Ronald Reagan's in 1980, it is not a foregone conclusion that a new president will accomplish some of his agenda in this early period. But even those presidents who are successful in implementing key parts of their agendas in the initial period may face a difficult time sustaining that momentum after Labor Day. After a successful first act, it is hard for a president to focus the attention of Congress and the public on a second set of agenda items.

When Congress returned from the summer recess in September 2001, one could look back and see that Bush had been extraordinarily skillful in shepherding through a tax cut, and it was clear that his education reform package would be agreed to that fall. But the prospects for a future agenda were cloudy. The Jeffords switch had taken some of the shine off of Bush's tax cut and delayed a victory on education reform. Further, the Senate was now in Democratic hands. From that early September perspective, it looked as if the fall would most likely be spent arguing about how much the Bush tax cut diminished the Social Security trust fund, along with issues such as campaign finance reform and the patients' bill of rights that were not high on the presidential priority list. Bush might have negotiated these hurdles, but it was not clear that he could have had an active legislative agenda of his own. In short, on Labor Day 2001 the honeymoon was over.

September 11 and the Days After: Hyperbipartisanship in Congress (September 11 to the end of 2001)

Then came September 11. President Bush said that September 11 would define the rest of his presidency, and it has. Strong leadership and inspiring presidential rhetoric dominated the initial days. And the four months after September 11 were extremely rare in presidential-congressional relations, a period of hyperbipartisanship, a period of nearly unanimous consent in votes on the final passage of many important pieces of legislation. There were also hugs, tears, and regular breakfast meetings with the congressional leaders of both parties. However, beneath this veneer of near unanimity lay the same patterns of legislating that had preceded and would follow it. Partisanship was evident in the actions Congress took before final passage votes, and the president still relied heavily on the partisan leadership of the House of Representatives to keep Republicans loyal to his plan.

The immediate aftermath of September 11 was a series of stirring speeches by the president: at the National Cathedral prayer service, at Ground Zero, and, most notably, before a joint session of Congress. Anyone who watched the speech before Congress knew that everything had changed. There was rousing bipartisan applause for the president, a prolonged tearful public embrace between Tom Daschle and the president, and resolve by members from both sides of the aisle to work together. The public display of friendship between Bush and Daschle was a signal of a new, more significant relationship between Bush and the congressional leadership.

In the first nine months of his presidency Bush had reached out to Democrats by making personal appeals to individual Democratic members, seeking out allies such as Ted Kennedy and George Miller on education, and seeking the broader support of moderate and conservative Democrats such as Senators John Breaux (Louisiana) and Zell Miller

(Georgia). Bush, however, had not made much of an effort with the Democratic leadership, especially when one considers how close he was to Speaker Laney and Lieutenant Governor Bob Bullock in Texas. Before September 11 he had held no individual meetings with Daschle or Gephardt and had had little more that a distant relationship with either of them. Perhaps even more striking and more indicative of a great partisan divide in Washington had been the lack of a relationship between Democratic and Republican leaders, especially in the House. Speaker Dennis Hastert (Illinois) and Minority Leader Richard Gephart (Missouri) had not spoken to each other in months. September 11 forced Democratic and Republican members together, sometimes literally, as in the case of Hastert and Gephart, who were taken to the same undisclosed location for a number of hours after the attacks. Bush further brokered a relationship by instituting weekly meetings with Hastert, Gephart, Lott, and Daschle. The time after September 11 was obviously a time for both sides of the aisle to come together.

In the four months following September 11, Congress was active in passing legislation to respond to the Al Qaeda threat. The new bipartisanship or hyperbipartisanship was evident in that most of these measures passed by nearly unanimous votes. The psychology of that time was that almost no member of Congress wanted to vote against the final passage of bills to authorize force in Afghanistan, give law enforcement additional tools to combat terrorism, rebuild New York, or beef up airport security. While there might be disagreements over the details, all members of Congress wanted to be identified with the large concepts put forth.

This hyperbipartisanship, however, masked deep-seated underlying differences between the parties. It covered over the fact that the president still wanted to rely on the congressional strategy that had worked on the tax cut, one where the House would be the president's chamber of support, dealing him a tough, bedrock conservative hand for him to use as leverage with the Senate. It did not take fully into account the changed dynamic of a Democratic Senate that could use its own agenda control to influence events.

Take, for example, the airline security bill, which passed the House 410-9 and passed the Senate by voice vote. This bill created a new agency for transportation security that was to institute security measures in airports and other transportation facilities to prevent terrorist attacks. Despite the near unanimity of the final passage of the bill, there was one significant contentious issue that stood between the parties on this bill. Republicans and Democrats divided on the issue of whether baggage screeners should become federal employees or remain private contractors.

Democrats favored the former approach; the Bush administration and many Republicans favored the latter. The familiar political dynamic was in evidence again, as the Republican-controlled House was likely to support the president's proposal and the negotiation would take place in the Senate.

However, the House did not act first as it had in a number of other cases. The Senate tried to preempt the process and cut a deal with Bush behind the scenes. Various proposals were floated. For example, the president proposed that a maximum of 25 percent of screeners be federal employees. A group of Senate Republicans negotiating with the president proposed that a minimum of 60 percent of screeners be federal employees. Ultimately, the two sides could not bridge the gap, and the prospect of a deal fell apart.

On October 11, 2001, the Senate passed a version of the bill including the Democratic proposal to federalize all screening employees. The vote was 100-0.[30] On November 1, the House passed a bill including the president's proposal to allow some screeners to be private contractors with federal supervision by a vote of 286-139.[31] There was a key vote to substitute the Democrats' version of the bill with the provisions for federalizing the screeners. Republicans defeated this substitute 218-214 on a nearly party-line vote, with only eight Republicans voting for the substitute and six Democrats voting against it.[32] Again the House had taken Bush's position.

But ultimately the political pressure was too strong to pass a bill bolstering aviation security. With the Democrats in the Senate using their agenda control to define the terms of the issue, Republicans looked as if they were holding up the bill because of their insistence on keeping screeners in the employ of private contractors. In the end, the conference report federalized screeners, making a few modest concessions to the Bush position. Democrats had won the day. On the larger issue of airline security, there had been great agreement between the parties. However, on one subsidiary issue, federalizing airport screeners, Bush had again relied on the House to pass his plan by a narrow margin. The difference here was that the president had ultimately lost the fight and had to accept the Senate Democrats' policy on that issue.

A second piece of legislation in the post–September 11 period showed that there might be some doubts as to whether the House as a whole would reflexively back the president. But in the end it illustrated that the House leadership, in particular Dennis Hastert, was still able to overcome individual members' doubts and keep Republican members in line with the president's agenda.

The Patriot Act: Increasing Law Enforcement
Powers in the Wake of September 11

After September 11, Congress began considering legislation that would give the Justice Department greater powers to combat terrorism—the Patriot Act, as it was later named. This bill was more controversial than the authorization of force in Afghanistan or transportation security, as it dealt with heated questions such as the proper line between privacy and government investigation to prevent terrorist attacks. Controversial or not, the vote for final passage was an overwhelming 357-66 in the House and 98-1 in the Senate. Again the final passage vote did not reflect the divisions in Congress.

Shortly after September 11, Attorney General John Ashcroft proposed a sweeping measure designed to give law enforcement greater tools for discovering and disrupting terrorist operations—wiretaps, secret wiretaps, easy detention of noncitizens, internet tracking, and other measures. After a contentious exchange between Ashcroft and the Congress in which Ashcroft accused his former colleagues of dragging their feet on a matter of national security, both chambers sought to pass legislation in this area. In this case, however, it was the Senate that was closer to the White House's position on what would become the Patriot Act. The Senate Judiciary Committee's chairman, Patrick Leahy (D-Vermont), and ranking member, Orrin Hatch (R-Utah), negotiated a deal with the White House. Once the deal was struck, Leahy and Hatch agreed to let the bill come to the Senate floor, bypassing committee hearings and votes. By contrast, the House Judiciary Committee, under Chairman Jim Sensenbrenner, reworked Ashcroft's proposal significantly. The vote was an astonishing 36-0. Perhaps in the context of September 11, unanimity should not seem that striking, but this committee is one of the most polarized in the House, with almost all of its members among the most liberal or the most conservative in the chamber. The product of the committee showed the more populist character of the House, with liberals and conservatives suspicious of the expansion of government intrusion into personal privacy. It removed an administration proposal relating to the conduct of secret searches, and, most important, it provided that the additional powers given to law enforcement would last for only two years. The Bush administration, which had negotiated a deal with key senators, found itself in an unfamiliar position, supporting the Senate bill and opposing the House Judiciary Committee's bill.[33]

At a point where it looked as if the House would be at loggerheads with the president and the Senate, Speaker Hastert stepped in and fashioned an alternative bill much closer to the president's, which went to the House floor instead of the Judiciary Committee's bill. It was reported that Hastert did so, notwithstanding the preferences of Representatives Richard Armey (Texas) and Tom DeLay (Texas), the number two and three Republicans in the leadership. The Hastert provision adopted a number of the administration's search and wiretap provisions that had been removed or watered down by the Judiciary Committee, and, more important, it extended the sunset provision of the laws for several more years. Ultimately a House-Senate conference resolved the differences and produced a bill that the administration could support.

As a more general matter, September 11 may have replaced compassionate conservatism as the defining theme of Bush's presidency. The George W. Bush of the campaign trail had reached out to moderate swing voters with soft issues such as education. The post–September 11 Bush emphasized law and order and security concerns that have been the staple of Republicans in the past, but that Bush had not emphasized on the campaign trail. Security issues are not simply the province of one party, so these issues allowed Bush to reach across party lines, but not in the same way as had his compassionate conservative message.

The Return of Partisan Differences (2002)

The period of bipartisanship directly following September 11 was short lived. By January of 2002 politics began to return to normal—acrimonious and partisan. There were, of course, security issues remaining, and the aura of September 11 hung over the Capitol, but it became typical for the parties to oppose each other more openly and for votes for final passage on significant bills to reflect partisan differences. In this period, extending to the 2002 midterm elections, Bush and congressional Republican leaders again showed their skill in maintaining party unity, especially in the House. Attracting sizable Democratic support at the same time was another matter. During this time there were important policy successes for the president, notably achieving trade promotion authority. But as the congressional elections neared the White House and its congressional lieutenants increasingly played the role of blocker, acting to stymie Senate Democratic initiatives rather than working toward compromises that would lead to bills' being enacted into law. The campaign theme the Republicans used to punctuate its message in the fall of 2002, hitting the obstructionist Democratic Senate and its obstructionist leader, became a theme during congressional deliberations as well.

Trade promotion authority (TPA) is the new name for an issue with a long history in Congress. In the past it has been known as fast-track authority. In essence, Congress promises that if the president negotiates free trade agreements they will be brought to Congress and be given an up or down vote on an expedited schedule without amendments. At various times Congress has extended this authority to the president, sometimes with conditions regarding workers, training, displacement, the environment, and so on. President Clinton actively sought this fast-track authority during his administration; despite (or perhaps because of) his success in passage of the North American Free Trade Agreement (NAFTA) and the General Agreement on Tariffs and Trade (GATT), he was unable to stitch together the bipartisan coalition necessary to prevail.

In general the Senate, filled with members who represent statewide constituencies rather than particular economic interests, has been the body more inclined toward free trade. In addition, as representation is by state, the farm states have a higher proportional representation in the Senate than in the House, and farmers export their products and tend to favor free trade. For these reasons, the Senate has typically supported trade promotion authority, and the House has been the harder sell.

During the 2000 campaign and in his presidency, George W. Bush made TPA a significant priority. But it was clear that on this issue he could not follow his familiar pattern of persuading the House, with perfect GOP unity, to pass a Bush initiative, then using its leverage to bargain with the Senate. In this case, although the House acted first, it represented the real challenge for the White House. To be sure, the White House did start out with some advantages. Most Republicans in Congress are inclined to support free trade. But there are regional and economic factions of each party that make the issue more complicated. If most Republicans with a traditional business orientation or farm state allegiance support free trade, many Southerners, particularly in textile areas in the Carolinas, support protectionism and tariffs. There are also a small number of Republicans who represent districts in the Midwest or Northeast with a heavy union presence who are not partial to free trade. At the same time, while Democrats with ties to unions are more skeptical of free trade, so-called New Democrats, those representing suburbs, high-tech industries, and professionals, lean toward free trade.

The diversity of constituencies meant that Bush's allies in the House had to stitch together a very unusual bipartisan coalition. Success in the House was by no means a sure thing. TPA had failed to pass under Clinton. A number of Democrats who would be potential supporters of the bill were eager to see such trade promotion authority cushioned by conditions that other nations must meet higher worker labor and safety standards. Some of these provisions had been included in NAFTA. And President Clinton had negotiated a bilateral agreement with Jordan that included these measures. This agreement was still pending before the Senate, and Democrats in both houses pointed to it as a model for their support. On the other side, Republicans did not want there to be a precedent for including these protections in all trade agreements. Ultimately, Bush asked Congress to ratify the Jordan trade agreement as a matter of national security in the aftermath of September 11, but he made promises to Republicans that inclusion of worker protections would not serve as a precedent for future agreements, including TPA. This position solidified Republican support, but drove away some Democrats.

The first major action on TPA in the House was taken in the fall of 2001 in the House Ways and Means Committee, when Chairman Bill Thomas attempted to pass a bill out of committee. Thomas found two Democratic allies on his committee, John Tanner and William Jefferson. He made several deals to get their support, in the process bypassing senior committee Democrat Charles Rangel (New York) and the Democrats' top trade expert, Robert Matsui (California). They represented a larger group of Democrats on the committee who had supported free trade in the past and who might have supported TPA if it had included worker protections provisions such as those in the Jordan trade bill. The key figure on the committee was Matsui. Matsui represented a Sacramento-based district that included city as well as suburbs and had experienced the influx of Silicon Valley high-tech businesses and suburban growth. He had been a key supporter of NAFTA and of fast-track authority in efforts in 1997 and 1998 to pass it. Matsui and most of his fellow Democrats felt that there had been no attempt to bargain with them to satisfy their concerns and that Thomas had cut a mostly partisan deal. Republicans claimed that Matsui and other Democrats were not willing to make any proposal short of a full package of worker protections that Republicans would not support. Whatever the merits of these arguments, the end result was that the Bush White House and House Republicans proceeded to the floor with a bill that was sure to lose support among many Democrats generally disposed toward free trade.[34]

After delaying the vote for several weeks, the House Republican leadership brought TPA to the floor without a guarantee that it had the votes for final passage. The vote was one of the most dramatic of the Bush presidency, with TPA prevailing 215-214. The normal fifteen-minute period allowed for the electronic vote on the House floor was extended by Republican leaders by nearly thirty minutes to win the final vote they needed, bringing howls of protest from Democrats.

To get to the final tally, Republicans had to persuade several of their members who were traditionally against free trade initiatives to support it. In the 1990s Republicans had usually been able to get approximately

165 Republican votes for fast-track authority; a robust 194 supported TPA. These additional Republicans were brought on with promises on specific matters "such as agriculture, textiles, and steel in future trade pacts." The most striking changes of heart came from Republicans Jim DeMint (South Carolina) and Robin Hayes (North Carolina), who represented textile districts in the Carolinas. There were predictions at the time that this vote would hurt their reelection efforts (both won reelection). On the Democratic side, only twenty-one Democrats supported the bill, half the number that had supported fast track in the 1990s. Strikingly, the Democrats who supported the bill were more "blue dog," or conservative, Democrats from culturally conservative parts of the country, rather than New Democrats from the professional and upscale East and West Coast suburbs.[35]

Bush's victory in the House was stunning. The president would have been deeply embarrassed by a loss; he was shielded from that embarrassment by a single vote. Once again, Bush did much better than expected in keeping his own Republican troops loyal, but far worse in attracting Democrats than he might have.

Even though the Senate is traditionally more in favor of free trade than the House, the political dynamic of a Democrat-controlled Senate complicated the prospects for final passage. First, Majority Leader Tom Daschle delayed consideration of the matter until the spring of 2002. Senate Democrats united around a strategy of linking TPA to the reauthorization and expansion of legislation that would provide displaced workers benefits for training, relocation, and medical insurance coverage. It also included provisions that would make it easier to amend trade agreements than the House had provided for. The Senate passed such a bill. In an intense conference, Max Baucus and Bill Thomas worked out a deal. Republicans agreed to most of the additional funds for displaced workers, but were able to strip out several provisions that would have allowed agreements to be amended more easily. Ultimately, on August 1, 2002, the Senate passed TPA 64-34 and the House passed it 215-212.

Creating a Homeland Security Department and Its Effect on the Midterm Elections (October–December 2002)

A report issued in 2000 by a commission on threats to the United States, co-chaired by former Senators Gary Hart (D-Colorado) and Warren Rudman (R-New Hampshire), called for the creation of a homeland security department encompassing such agencies as the Immigration and Naturalization Service, the Border Patrol, and the Customs Service. That recommendation was turned into a bill introduced by Senator Joseph

Lieberman (D-Connecticut). However, the report and this recommendation were largely ignored by the public, the president, and Congress until after September 11, when the salience of the issue of homeland security was made manifest to all.

After September 11, Lieberman renewed the call for enactment of his bill, using his position as chairman of the Senate Governmental Affairs Committee as a platform. The Bush administration resisted the move to create a department, settling for a homeland security adviser, former Pennsylvania Governor Tom Ridge. Many members of Congress in both parties repeatedly challenged the efficacy of an office in the White House with an adviser lacking cabinet rank or line authority. But while publicly resisting calls for creation of a department, Bush asked several senior aides to begin a secret effort to come up with a plan for a major reorganization that would create a Department of Homeland Security and transfer existing functions from other departments to it.

Bush unveiled the plan on June 6, 2002. Despite his long, vigorous opposition to the idea, the Bush plan instantly became the agenda of the nation and of Congress, and the idea became his. The creation of a homeland security department would by its nature be complex and controversial, but Bush boldly chose a plan to create an extensive department with more functions than most congressional plans had envisioned. Among opponents and proponents of creating a homeland security department, there were significant arguments about jurisdiction and logistics, along with security and privacy concerns.

With only a few months before the midterm elections, the time to consider a massive government reorganization was very limited. The House decided to bypass the jurisdiction of committees that might have a vested interest in the status quo, and instead created a Select Committee on Homeland Security chaired by Majority Leader Dick Armey. His committee ultimately ignored many changes recommended by various committees and came up with a bill similar to the White House's original proposal.[36] The House passed its version 295-132 on July 26.[37]

In the Senate the Governmental Affairs Committee had jurisdiction over the bill. Chairman Joseph Lieberman fashioned a bill that gave Bush much of what he sought structurally, but his bill included strong worker and union protections, in contrast with the House bill, which granted the president extraordinary flexibility in personnel matters. Besides this difference, there were other signs that the issue might take a different path in the Senate than in the House. In particular, Senator Robert Byrd (West Virginia), president pro tempore of the Senate, senior Democrat, and chairman of the Appropriations Committee, made it clear that he had grave misgivings about the entire enterprise and favored moving slowly to make such a sweeping change. The stated goal of the president and many in the House was to have a bill ready for signature by September 11, 2002—the one-year anniversary of the terrorist attacks. In part because of extended debate on the Senate floor led by Byrd, the bill moved slowly in the Senate.

On September 3, as the bill neared the Senate floor, the White House issued a threat that it would veto the Senate version of the bill because it did not provide the president enough personnel flexibility to ensure national security protection.[38] The original Lieberman proposal gave greater protections to workers in the homeland security department than to those in other departments. The president's proposal, by contrast, gave the president much greater flexibility in transferring, rewarding, or removing personnel than he had in other departments, even for other national security–related functions.

On the Senate floor the battle was over which version of the Homeland Security Department Bill could get the fifty-one votes needed for passage. During the Senate debate a small group of moderate Republicans and Democrats proposed a middle ground. The White House agreed to modest modifications in its flexibility proposal to satisfy most of the moderate Republicans.[39] Moderate Democrats John Breaux and Ben Nelson (Nebraska), however, were not satisfied with the president's modification. The partisan battle lines were drawn.

Since Democrat Zell Miller supported the president and chastised his own party for not giving the president what he wanted (Miller said the party would be slitting its throat if it did not vote for the bill), the main question was over the vote of Republican Lincoln Chafee (Rhode Island).[40] Chafee ultimately sided with the Democrats, giving them the one-vote majority needed for passage and required to get the bill to a conference committee with the House version.[41]

To prevent that occurrence—and the Senate Democrats' declaration of victory on this important issue—Republicans invoked a filibuster, managing to block cloture and prevent a vote on the Democratic plan. Democrats retaliated in kind and prevented a vote on the Republican version.[42] Ultimately, no agreement could be reached between the sides, and both parties went into the November midterm elections without a deal. While the Homeland Security Department Bill languished in Congress, Bush made a decision to put his prestige on the line and actively campaign for Republican candidates. Bush's job approval ratings had soared to over 90 percent after September 11, but had gradually fallen over the next year—but to a level that was still historically high for presidents at this stage of office. The decision to campaign vigorously was a bold and risky one. Bush's continued high approval was clearly due to his standing as commander in chief in the war against terrorism, a nonpartisan role. If he emerged as a partisan leader, it could easily tarnish his public image and his approval ratings.

At the same time, Bush faced the history of midterm elections, which are usually inhospitable to presidents and their parties. Only twice since the Civil War had a president's party gained seats in the House of Representatives in midterm elections, and the last president to gain seats in the House in his first-term midterm elections had been Franklin Roosevelt in 1934.

Other presidents had campaigned for congressional candidates in midterm elections, but Bush's effort was unprecedented. He made a record ninety campaign appearances, including campaign stops for twenty-three congressional candidates, sixteen Senate hopefuls, and candidates in a number of hotly contested gubernatorial races. Along the way he attended nearly seventy-five fund-raisers and raised a record of more than $144 million. His campaign trips had him on the road nearly nonstop in the weeks leading up to the November 5 election, including a whirlwind tour of fifteen states in the last five days before the election.

Enough time had passed since September 11 that domestic concerns, many of which favored Democrats, were back on the agenda. But the president still used September 11 as a rallying point. Congress's agenda before the election had been taken up by homeland security, but more visibly by the vote to authorize the use of force in Iraq. There was some division on the Iraq vote, but many Democrats who had tough reelection prospects had voted in favor of the war, and the vote itself was not a major factor in the election.

Bush focused instead on the creation of a homeland security department, criticizing Democrats for blocking the measure. It became a standard theme as he traveled the nation to campaign for Republican Senate candidates, bolstered in the message by a barrage of television ads run by individual candidates and the Republican Senatorial Campaign Committee, under chairman Bill Frist (Tennessee), that aggressively attacked individual Democratic incumbents for failing to support homeland security. Some of these ads, in places like Georgia, juxtaposed the picture of the Democratic target (in this case Max Cleland) with pictures of Osama bin Laden and Saddam Hussein.

The attack themes and ads enraged Democrats, but worked in many states, including Georgia. Going against every historical trend, Republicans picked up seats in the House, retook the majority in the Senate, and did well in gubernatorial and state legislative races. While the overall change in the number of seats in the Republican direction was not large, Bush and the Republicans had exceeded expectations and gained seats in a midterm election where almost all presidents and their parties had lost them. Bush had personalized the election, asking voters to put in a team of Republicans who would help him succeed. Most observers believed his efforts—his coattails—made the difference.

After the election Congress returned for a lame-duck session, and the president moved quickly to take advantage of his new political leverage. He insisted that a homeland security bill be passed immediately by the lame-duck Congress, and it was, with nearly all the flexibility for dealing with workers that Bush had sought. Bush also got the Senate to confirm a number of judges whom he had nominated earlier in his term.

Bush and the 108th Congress (2003)

Following up on his aggressive moves in the lame-duck session of the 107th Congress, Bush also prepared for an ambitious agenda in the new Congress convening in January 2003. The boldest proposal he made was for a tax-cut/economic stimulus plan that would cost $726 billion over ten years. The centerpiece was the abolition of the double taxation of corporate dividends, a move favored by many economists but not a populist message or one that would be stimulative in the short term. Republicans in Congress had not vetted the Bush tax plan. Its announcement by the White House was the first they knew of it; many, including Ways and Means Chairman Bill Thomas, reacted negatively at first. Also in the tax plan was a set of proposals favored by nearly all congressional Republicans, including an acceleration of tax cuts that had already been passed in 2001: the cut in personal income tax rates and the child tax credit.

Reports suggested that many of the president's advisers, surveying the close margins in both houses of Congress, had recommended a much smaller tax-cut plan, in the range of $350 billion—a suggestion rejected by the president for the bold alternative. Once Bush had put out the $726 billion tax cut, he was unwilling to entertain suggestions that he lower the number. His answer was, "We don't negotiate against ourselves."

Given the expanding deficit, the looming war with Iraq, the expected opposition of Democrats, and the stated position of many moderate Republicans that they would not support a large tax cut, this was a very risky approach. It reflected the approach to governing that Bush had assumed regularly in the White House: use your political capital (in this case, enlarged with his election win); go for big and bold goals; stake out outsized and dramatic positions; hold to them as long as you can; rely on your House Republican base to pass bills reflecting your goals early in the process, by narrow partisan margins; and use that leverage to persuade the Senate to go along. But by failing to notify or consult congressional leaders before the plan was announced, Bush evoked the approach he had taken as governor with his ill-fated education tax plan.

Early in the 108th Congress there were signs suggesting that Bush's familiar approach might need significant revision. The predictions of many pundits and politicians that the new Republican monopoly on the reins of power in Washington would quickly open the floodgates on Bush judicial nominees, moving them through the Republican Senate and onto the courts, quickly was disabused. Using a variety of Senate procedures and customs and a new disciplined cohesiveness, Democrats held up several nominees and effectively blocked the president's top judicial priority, Appeals Court nominee Miguel Estrada, with a filibuster on the Senate floor that new Majority Leader Bill Frist was unable, repeatedly, to overcome.

House Republicans managed to prevail on a budget resolution that included the president's tax cut, but barely, and only after Herculean efforts by new Majority Whip Roy Blunt (Missouri) and Majority Leader Tom DeLay. In the meantime, moderate Senate Republicans Olympia Snowe (Maine) and George Voinovich (Ohio) signed a pledge to oppose any tax cut greater than $350 billion, joined with Democrats in blocking a larger tax cut in their budget resolution vote, then held firm against intense White House pressure to increase the number to at least $550 billion. The long-sought presidential goal of mandating oil drilling in the Arctic National Wildlife Refuge was blocked in the Senate because of opposition by Republican senators such as Norm Coleman (Minnesota), infuriating both the White House and long-time drilling champion Senator Ted Stevens (Alaska), the new president pro tempore of the Senate, senior Republican, and chairman of the Appropriations Committee.

The president was faced with a reality that had also hit his predecessor, Bill Clinton: holding all the reins of power in Washington is not an unadulterated plus. Clinton's first two years in the presidency, with Democrats controlling both houses of Congress, had been difficult and contentious ones. Clinton could count on zero Republican support for his top priority, a budget and tax plan, and needed agonizing and sometimes humiliating months of negotiations to get one-vote majorities from among his own partisans. Despite comfortable majorities in both houses, Clinton saw his prized health care reform plan summarily rejected by Congress. His political fortunes turned ironically for the better when the Republicans subsequently swept into power in the 1994 midterm elections. With Speaker Newt Gingrich as a foil and congressional Republicans to blame for any gridlock, the president had an easier time making compromises and achieving legislative success.

The parallels for President Bush are clear. Freed from the responsibility of governing and the need to get fifty-one votes to be in the ballgame, Senate Democrats can fully use the levers of the minority in the Senate, with little fear of being blamed by voters for policy constipation—after all, the president and his party have the power, so they should be able to make things work. Moreover, Senate Democrats had changed by the last months of the 107th Congress and by the 2002 campaign, becoming more recalcitrant and suspicious of a president they believed cynically attacked them and exploited the homeland security and national security issues for naked partisan advantage.

The White House has also experienced a change in the attitude of congressional Republicans, what some have called the price of hubris. The White House attitude, often treating congressional Republicans as field lieutenants and generals carrying out orders coming from Central Command at 1600 Pennsylvania Avenue, met with considerable resistance early in the 108th Congress. Many Republicans, facing their own level of accountability and their own constituent needs and demands, began to push back, at least rhetorically.

Postscript

In May and June of 2003, Bush's tax cut passed Congress. In the end, the president had to settle for less than 50 percent of the amount of his original proposal, and there was significant tinkering with the details, including a reduction of the tax on dividends rather than its elimination. In a fashion similar to that seen in dealing with many of his earlier initiatives, Bush used a narrow majority strategy, attracting nearly all Republican votes and few Democratic ones. Although in the end Bush had to settle for half a loaf in terms of the size of his tax cut, the president showed his political agility by embracing the plan, declaring victory, and successfully maintaining that perception of victory.

Following the narrow win on the tax cut, the president abandoned the narrow majority strategy, at least in part, for his next majority initiative. Bush felt the need to secure a policy victory on Medicare prescription drugs, a vexing political issue that had been used against Republicans in the 2000 and 2002 campaigns, and one that the president and his congressional allies deeply wanted to neutralize in the 2004 campaign.

After a long period of strongly partisan legislating, Bush's return to a more bipartisan approach on prescription drugs surprised many observers. Bush once again worked closely with Senator Ted Kennedy of Massachusetts to build bipartisan support for a bill in the Senate. As with the education bill, it was clear that Bush was less interested in passing every detail of his plan than in having a deal that could be supported by a significant fraction of Senate Democrats. But unlike in the case of the education reform bill, on which the president had worked closely with House Democrats like George Miller, the White House eschewed compromise or serious communication with House Democrats on prescription drugs. Instead it built a majority with the Republican base in the House.

As we write this chapter, the House prescription drug bill has passed 216-215, with the final margin provided by a Republican visibly upset at having to switch her vote to "Yes" at the last minute. After House passage, forty-two conservative House Republicans signed a letter pledging to vote against any compromise with the Senate that tilted toward the Senate's more moderate and bipartisan bill (which passed 76-21).

While no comparable Senate letters were crafted, it was equally clear that a compromise tilting more to the House bill would have great difficulty mustering a majority in the Senate or that it could fall victim to a filibuster. The final stages of the Medicare prescription drug issue promises to be a new, interesting, and rather different chapter in Bush's legislative history, testing the president's ability to maintain discipline among his Republican troops in Congress while also satisfying enough Democrats in the Senate to secure passage of a bill.

Conclusion

The political twists and turns facing President George W. Bush and Congress since November 2000 have been astonishing in number and nature. From a controversial, disputed, and close election delayed in its outcome for thirty-six days, to a tied Senate and nearly tied House, to a sudden shift in Senate control four months into Bush's presidency, to the stunning developments of September 11, to the historic results in the midterm elections of 2002, to the extended lead-up to war in Iraq and the remarkable conclusion of that war, the tides of power and opportunity in Washington have changed regularly and not according to any predictable cycle.

Early on, as president-elect and then president, Bush showed agility in strategy in dealing with Congress, using dramatically different approaches to achieve his initial two top priorities: tax cuts and education reform. But he also showed a marked preference for an approach that was quite ideologically conservative and quite partisan, trying to use perfect party unity in the closely divided House to pass strongly conservative measures and then use that passage as bargaining leverage with the Senate. His preference in the Senate was to lure over one or a handful of Democrats, regularly starting with Zell Miller, to join the Senate Republicans and form the fifty-vote majorities necessary for passage, then use his public campaigning and the House position to force Senate Democratic leaders to shun filibusters and bend to his will.

Although the president had some success with that formula, it showed clear signs of wear before the end of the 107th Congress. His successes in the House tended not to lead to bills enacted into law, but more to protection against attacks claiming that he opposed popular measures like patients' rights. He was more successful at the end of that Congress at blocking Senate Democrats from passing their preferred bills than at persuading them to pass his.

Any expectations that regaining control of the Senate in the 2002 elections would result in major breakthroughs for the president in his legislative goals were dispelled quickly. His successes at the end of the 107th Congress and his formidable campaign presence led to a sharp increase in Democrats' animosity toward him. In private conversations in 2003, Senate Democrats regularly invoke the name of Senator Max Cleland (D-Georgia), a decorated veteran and amputee, whose patriotism Democrats believe was unfairly challenged in the 2002 elections by a Republican Party using the homeland security issue to its advantage. The anger of Democrats over the tactics of the 2002 election and their minority status has led them to display greater unity than they had been able to achieve while in the majority. Senate Republicans have found their ability to garner fifty votes for the president's plans often elusive and their ability to garner sixty votes to overcome Democrats' filibusters even more unattainable.

While the president found early in 2003 that he could still fall back on the House Republicans for majority support, there were signs, though the size of the majority doubled from six to twelve in the 2002 elections, of some resistance to his agenda among the small but significant number of moderates. And the fury of House conservative Republicans at Senate moderates like Olympia Snowe (for her opposition to the Bush tax-cut plan) suggested that any White House compromise with Senate moderates might lead to a revolt among the conservatives. But Bush ultimately prevailed with a definitive win on his tax-cut package. He followed up this victory with a push for a prescription drug benefit that may very well succeed.

Two and a half years removed from the 2000 election, the Congress and the country are still closely divided along partisan lines. Even with Republican control of both chambers of Congress, the close margins and Senate rules will make it difficult for Bush to achieve major legislative victories with the support of his party alone. He has shown the ability to secure nearly unanimous Republican support for his initiatives. Bush has also been presented with several extraordinary events that have allowed him to expend political capital, and he has consistently been able to press the advantage. His initial legislative program benefited from the unity of a Republican Party out of the White House for eight years. September 11 raised the president's job approval ratings to stratospheric heights, and the president used that popularity to pass numerous emergency bills. The surprising Republican win in the midterm elections provided another boost that yielded the Homeland Security Department. And the successful prosecution of the war in Iraq gave the president momentum to follow through on a second large tax-cut stimulus plan.

Bush has confounded many of his critics with his ability to keep his party loyal and pass partisan initiatives while occasionally reaching across the aisle for a bipartisan achievement. But, given the close margins in Congress, the various strategies that Bush has employed are part of an intricate balancing act. It is not at all clear that Bush will be able to keep Republicans loyal or win over necessary Democratic votes in the future. With the continuing war on terrorism and an election on the horizon in 2004, it became possible that Bush would focus his efforts on foreign affairs and domestic security, where the executive branch has its greatest scope and is relatively unimpeded by the legislative branch. It also was possible that Bush's popularity would fall and his own party would become divided.

Bush is a man of his agenda, as has been evidenced by his efforts to pass a prescription drug benefit. But other tasks he set for his administration, such as passage of a patients' bill of rights, Social Security reform, and dealing with increasing deficits, were not easy to accomplish in the closely divided Congress. Bush has been keenly aware that his father lost the presidency because he was unable to follow up his victory in Iraq with a domestic agenda that won the confidence of ordinary people. The parallel for George W. Bush is obvious. In the run-up to the 2004 election and his possible second term, he would require all of his political talents and an effective strategy for dealing with Congress, almost certainly under different circumstances than he faced earlier in his presidency.

Chapter 7

Capitalizing on Position in a Perfect Tie

Charles O. Jones

POSITION, THE STATUS of being president, has been crucial for George W. Bush in his initial years of service in the White House. Lacking commanding political standing, Bush promoted the bearing and benefits of office. He has fashioned a strategy to cope with the competitive partisanship of split-party and small-margin politics. The effectiveness of this approach was enhanced by a period of crisis-induced bipartisanship.

The politics of the last two decades of the twentieth century dramatically challenged U.S. presidents. Consider Richard E. Neustadt's formulation that professional reputation and public prestige provide sources of influence.[1] By these tests, recent presidents have had to be adaptable and resourceful, even nimble, in exercising power. Their reputations and prestige have waxed and waned as measured quantitatively in polls or qualitatively by the perceptions of other power holders. Associated with these sources of influence are the objective realities of split-party and small-margin politics. From 1981 through 2003, only President Bill Clinton worked with a Congress in which his party had majorities in both houses, a condition that lasted just two years (1993–95). The personal victories of presidents in this time varied substantially. President Reagan had two landslide wins and Republicans won the Senate between 1981 and 1987. President George H. W. Bush won handily, but was the second president of the twentieth century to assume office with his party in the minority in both houses of Congress (Nixon had been the first in 1969).

President Clinton failed to get a majority of the popular vote in either of his elections, and his party lost control of both houses of Congress in the first midterm election of his tenure. And President George W. Bush won a tie with help from the U.S. Supreme Court and his party had a net loss of seats in both houses while retaining majority status in the House and organizational control in the Senate, with the tie-breaking vote of Vice President Dick Cheney.

During this period presidents also experienced substantial differences in the types of events affecting their power and their impacts. Reagan benefited from an improved economy domestically and the decline of Soviet influence internationally while enduring embarrassment, even ridicule, over the Iran-Contra debacle. The economy worked both ways for the first Bush—as his friend at the start, his albatross in the end. The Gulf War produced record-high job approval ratings for its brief life, but was of limited value as a source of power domestically. Good economic times likely saved Clinton's presidency after his party's loss of both houses of Congress and many state houses in the 1994 elections. Personal problems of his own and several in his administration prevented him from enjoying greater political advantages.

How presidents have won, and with whom, as well as what has happened along the way, has affected their reputations and prestige as sources of power in working with Congress and other power holders. Less variable has been position, or what Neustadt has referred to as the president's "vantage points in government."[2] My argument is that *position* as a source of influence has been vital for President George W. Bush.

As used here, *position* refers to the status of being president. Various synonyms aid us in grasping the application of the term in this context, notably *rank, title, station,* and *status. Location* and *site* are also helpful, as both are commonly associated with power. *Position* incorporates the vantage points one has in government (à la Neustadt) and, for want of a better label, the qualities normally related to the presidency. The vantage points are essentially objective, including as they do those powers allocated to the office by the Constitution, Congress, and custom, powers that authorize the president to act in certain ways. The consequence is that he is depended on by others in government to initiate important actions; to say "Yes," "No," or "Try again" in regard to lawmaking in its many stages; to command the military; to make critical appointments; to manage the bureaucracy; and so on. He has these powers because he occupies the Oval Office. Government can operate for a time without his exercising some of these powers (or doing so poorly), but the set-up is such that system actors expect him to perform, and they conduct themselves accordingly. Their expectations ascribe legitimacy to his position and therefore are of the very essence of power for the office holder.

The second element—the qualities of the presidency contributing to the position of the president as a source of power—is more intangible and subjective. And yet a familiar adage applies: "You know it when you see it." It is more behavioral. It is also based on the expectations of others, but the focus here is on the president himself and the extent to which he behaves presidentially. That is the subjective part, for it is based on his conception of fulfilling the role and doing the job of president. I argue that this quality is incorporated into the concept of position. I will make the point that George W. Bush has attempted to promote this quality as an asset in the exercise of presidential power. That effort is particularly interesting because Bush was judged by many not to be of presidential quality during the campaign and after.

The relatively low estimates of Bush's capacity to perform competently as president may have influenced his strategic choice of emphasizing position. For if expectations are perpetually kept low, exceeding them is potentially quite easy. Presidential performance beyond prospects is typically treated by observers as exceptional. After all, Bush exceeded expectations. Once past, such a lesser view of a president's capability is reset as he deals with the next challenge. And so the cycle is repeated, with little scoring for cumulative exceptions. Harry Truman had to wait decades for historians to tote up his score.

Often judgments about a president-elect's competence are based on a president-centric—"the president is the presidency"—perspective. In Bush's case, whatever the preconceptions of the man himself, there was ample evidence to suggest that he could create a capable team-structured presidency—evidence from the Bush governorship in Texas, the management of the presidential campaign, the experience of his likely appointees to major positions, his familiarity with the White House and its place in the government, and the acknowledged abilities of his closest aides.[3] In fact, few presidents have entered the White House having had more opportunities to acquaint themselves with the presidency, the White House, and Washington or to avail themselves of more mentoring from those with experience in national government (including, of course, a father who had served as president and vice president and a mother who had served as first lady).

What Did He Learn? Bush's Conception of Position

George W. Bush's power ranking, based on measures of political and legislative standing, was second to last of the postwar presidents; Bush was dead last behind Richard M. Nixon in political standing alone upon first entering office.[4] He could rely neither on reputation nor on prestige as sources of power. But he had position, and, whether by instinct, experience, heritage, mentoring, or a combination thereof, Bush had as well-defined a concept of the job as any recent president.

In his account of the workings of the Bush White House, David Frum, a former George W. Bush speechwriter, described a meeting with Andrew Card, the president's chief of staff. Card told a story about his experience in the Reagan White House where staff were identified with either James Baker or Ed Meese. Frum continued as follows:

> This, Card pleaded, must never happen here. "You are not Karl's people or Karen's people," referring to the two most powerful of all the presidential aides, Karl Rove and Karen Hughes. "You are all the president's people."
> There must be no bickering. . . .
> Aides must resist the temptation to self-aggrandizement.[5]

Frum described the Bush White House as basically "un-Clinton," that is, designed to be the opposite of the Clinton White House. "The Bush team lived clean . . . upright and hygienic." The cabinet was "able, solid, and reliable," but no "really high-powered brains."[6] Others, too, have concluded that the Bush team was primarily motivated to make Bush appear to be the "un-Clinton." Perhaps so. Surely the Clinton White House was an unlikely model for Bush and his staff. But predecessor aside, a strong case can be made for the type of cabinet and staff that was created by Bush and Cheney. Lacking the prestige and political standing of a substantial presidential and congressional win in 2000 or impressive professional credentials to enhance his reputation, Bush wisely stressed establishing competence in administration. He wanted the White House to work efficiently and well, thus promoting the viewpoint that the Bush team was capable of doing the job. The team was successful in this quest, measured by the early reactions of the media and the Washington community. And that success was in sharp contrast to the early weeks of the Clinton administration in 1993.

Frum's portrait of Bush is of a highly disciplined, demanding, and confident manager, yet one lacking a clear vision and a "big organizing idea" prior to September 11, 2001. Bush's virtues upon entering office, according to Frum, were "decency, honesty, rectitude, courage, and tenacity."[7] But he had the "bad timing" of a recession, and he was unsuccessful during his campaign in fashioning a "compassionate conservative" coalition more inclusive of minorities and women. Frum judged that the problems were too great for Bush to have a successful presidency, measured primarily by the metric of the conservative agenda. September

11 established a different metric. The "uncertain peacetime president" was transformed into a "superb wartime leader" who was moderate, persistent, and bold.[8] As I will discuss later, the issue would become that of whether leadership in an amorphous national security crisis (fighting terrorism) could be effectively applied as well to domestic matters (including those that arose from September 11).

How does Bush view the job of president? And how do his impressions comport with the stress he has placed on position as his principal advantage? Two *Washington Post* reporters, Dan Balz and Bob Woodward, conducted interviews with Bush that aid in clarifying the president's concept of his job. The purpose of the interviews (one conducted by the two together, another by Woodward alone) was better to understand Bush's post–September 11 decision making. The following quotes are taken from Woodward's book *Bush at War*.[9] Woodward offered them not as I have used them here—to display Bush's conception of the job of president. That was not Woodward's purpose. Rather, the quotes are scattered throughout the book (I have cited the pages).

> One way you're not impulsive is to make sure you listen to an experienced group of national security advisers. If I have any genius or smarts, it's the ability to recognize talent, ask them to serve and work with them as a team. (74)

> I think my job is to stay ahead of the moment. A president, I guess, can get so bogged down in the moment that you're unable to be the strategic thinker that you're supposed to be, or at least provide strategic thought. And I am the kind of person that wants to make sure that all risk is assessed. (136)

> One of my jobs is to be provocative, seriously, to provoke people into—to force decisions, and to make sure it's clear in everybody's mind where we're headed. (144)

> [On sensing when to act:] One of the interesting things about being the president is you don't see much mail, curiously enough. The only thing I can tell you is that I rely on my instincts. I just knew that at some point in time, the American people were going to say, Where is he? What are you doing? Where's your leadership? Where is the United States? You're all powerful, do something. (168)

> [Referring to lines of responsibility:] I like clarity. You can design a system so that nobody is held accountable. If there is failure nobody shows up to—who do you look to to fix it. (244)

> All power should not go through an individual to the Oval Office. I believe that a president must give people access . . . that part of the job satisfaction of being a White House staffer is the capacity to talk to the president one-on-one. (255)

> I know it is hard for you to believe, but I have not doubted what we were doing. I have not doubted. . . . There is no doubt in my mind we're doing the right thing. Not one doubt. (256)

> First of all, a president has got to be the calcium in the backbone. If I weaken, the whole team weakens. If I'm doubtful, I can assure you there will be a lot of doubt. If my confidence level in our ability declines, it will send ripples throughout the whole organization. I mean, it's essential that we be confident and determined and united. (259)

> If there's going to be a sense of despair, I want to know who it is, and why. I trust the team, and it is a team. And I trust them because I trust their judgment. And if people are having second thoughts about their judgment, I needed to know what they were, and they needed to lay them on the table. (259)

These statements were made in reference to the decisions regarding the war plans in Afghanistan, and yet they are consistent with more general observations regarding Bush's concept of the presidency and his role. Further, his views are consistent with the idea of capitalizing on position; indeed, they provide a working definition of that notion. Central to the Bush approach is a team concept. Bush views himself very much as an active and interactive leader of the team upon which he is heavily reliant. It is his job to choose the right people and be accessible; to provide forward ("ahead of the moment") thinking; to provoke and, above all, to expose doubts and express confidence prior to making decisions. This is as coherent a perspective of the position of the president in the presidency as has been articulated in recent decades. Effectively realized, position in this sense should then enhance professional reputation and prestige. In Bush's case, it has, although, as noted earlier, there has been frequent resetting of expectations originally set low.

Preparing to Govern

It is widely accepted that one test of a new administration is the extent to which the team is prepared to govern on the first day, whether they are "hitting the ground running," as the phrase has it. The transition period is the time for making preparations. Two tasks in particular are vital: making appointments and designating an agenda. How, and indeed whether, these tasks are performed provide first impressions of the competency of a president and his team. And these first impressions may influence subsequent judgments about an administration. A transition poorly managed by standard criteria, like that of Clinton in 1992, can form a template that is difficult for an administration to alter, and having to do so diverts precious staff time during the first critical months.

The Bush transition team had to operate under what were thought to be the most difficult conditions of modern times. The time available was cut in half, the delay the result of an uncertain election outcome, and the resolution by the U.S. Supreme Court was bound to raise questions of legitimacy—questions that would dog the administration for weeks, even months in some cases. The Bush team responded by seeking to capitalize on position even before the Florida recount was settled.

In the period prior to the declaration of a winner in Florida, politics was dominated by legal battles. Status in this struggle was primarily based on background in the law. Winning would be achieved by gaining a favorable decision in the courts, local, state, and federal (sometimes by a single judge, more commonly by a majority). This arena was not accommodating to the two nonlawyer, near presidents, George W. Bush and Al Gore. Yet they behaved very differently. Bush began to take on the position of president-elect, leaving the direction of the lawyerly work in Florida to James Baker. Gore, on the other hand, got personally involved in the legal skirmishes in Florida.

These contrasting roles can be attributed to the differing conditions for each contestant. Bush had several advantages that permitted him to concentrate on a transition. He was in the lead in Florida, however small the margin; Gore had to concentrate on overturning that result. Bush benefited from the Florida Secretary of State's certifying his win on November 26; Gore then had to challenge that certification. Polls began to show public acceptance of Bush as the winner; Gore then had to devalue these results by conducting awkward news conferences.

One important consequence of the Bush advantages was that he and Dick Cheney could proceed with transition planning. In fact, the Bush team invited photographers to a meeting just three days after the election to hear that Cheney would be in charge of transition planning and that Andrew Card would be appointed as chief of staff. Bush stated: "The country needs to know—that this administration will be ready to assume office and be prepared to lead. I think it's up to us to prepare the groundwork for an administration that will be ready to function on Day One."[10] The meeting was criticized by the Gore camp and lampooned in the media. But it illustrated an important difference in the strategies of the two contenders at that juncture (front page photos in the *New York Times* on November 11, 2000, showed a well-dressed Bush meeting with aides and Gore in jeans playing touch football).

Once the Supreme Court made its decision in *Bush* v. *Gore,* the Bush team was prepared to announce major appointments in a relatively short period of time. All cabinet secretarial appointments were announced in just seventeen days (though one appointee, Linda Chavez, withdrew and was quickly replaced). Those appointed were uniformly acknowledged to be well qualified, nearly all with substantial executive experience. And though little was made of diversity as a criterion in the selections made, the result was a rich variation in backgrounds. White, Anglo-Saxon men were in the minority. Most of those nominated had experience in working with or in legislatures—seven had experience in federal service (two as cabinet secretaries), five in state service (three as governors), and five in legislative service. Cheney and Donald Rumsfeld had previously served as White House chiefs of staff. Those who had doubts about Bush's experience and qualifications for his job typically conceded that he had created a competent presidency in the truncated transition period. Such was the short-term positive effect of stressing position in nominating the cabinet and filling key White House jobs.

Position and the Congress

How has President Bush used position in his interactions with Congress? Answering that question requires a review of the partisan strategies that characterize presidential-congressional relations. With modifications, these are the strategies identified in my book *The Presidency in a Separated System*.[11] Competitive partisanship and cross-partisanship have been notably dominant in recent decades, fostered by split-party and small-margin politics.

Competitive Partisanship

As used here, *competitive partisanship* refers to those cases in which leaders of both political parties are motivated to participate actively in all phases of lawmaking. These impulses may be a result of split party control, substantial or surprising electoral gains, narrow margins, expectations of future success, or a combination of these factors. The point is that leaders of both parties have solid electoral reasons to justify their competitive mood and to encourage their members to unify in support of party alternatives. And the evidence of public support lends legitimacy to their claims to be actively, even aggressively, involved.

The 2000 presidential and congressional elections resulted in ideal conditions for competitive partisanship. Both parties could legitimately claim victories, and did. It was "the perfect tie"[12] all around—the presidential election result having to be settled in court, the Senate split evenly, and the House Republican margin just 51 to 49 percent. Some analysts interpreted these results as favoring bipartisanship, presenting an opportunity for President Bush to work with the Democrats to produce a unified agenda and proposals. It is difficult to conceive how this might have happened, given the political realities of the time. The president and his team had just completed an intense campaign based on policy positions developed over a period of months and representing preferences among Bush's staff and supporters. Presumably a mechanism for developing new proposals would have to be created (perhaps a bipartisan commission) if a revised agenda were to be developed. Yet there was no precedent for such an action.

Timing would have been an issue given that certain critical budget imperatives had to be dealt with immediately. And, however narrow the margins on Capitol Hill, offering the Democratic minority leaders coequal status in shaping a common agenda would not have been welcomed by the Republican majority leaders. Finally, the matter of determining the agenda itself would have been awkward. Who would have spoken for the Democrats? The defeated presidential candidate? One or other of the minority leaders, or both? Ranking committee members?

Perhaps the president and his team could have acted alone to prepare an alternative program sensitive to Democratic Party interests. That way of proceeding would at least have obviated the need to create a new process or forum. But it is unlikely that Democrats would have accepted any such effort as representing their preferences, which might shift anyway with adjustments made in the White House. The practice of compromising in advance of bargaining has been referred to as negotiating with oneself. The president often warned against doing so: "There's the problem in this town. The temptation is to get the president to negotiate with himself. And the minute I negotiate with myself, I lose."[13]

Much more likely was a scenario in which President Bush would fashion proposals from his campaign promises, expecting counterproposals from House and Senate Democrats—that is, the model of competitive partisanship. Both parties were unusually well prepared for proceeding in that way. Many of the issues of the 2000 election had been developed and debated, with legislation perhaps even passed in one house, during the preceding 106th Congress (1999–2000). Preparatory work had been done on health care (including prescription drugs and patients' rights), energy, Social Security reform, tax cuts, and trade agreements.

Congresses typically are scored based on legislation enacted, and the 106th was found lacking by this measure. But lawmaking requires substantial preparatory work, and the product of that effort does not evaporate with the end of a session or a Congress. The unfinished work of the House and Senate debating chambers frequently becomes the source of the campaign agendas for presidential and congressional elections, as it did in 2000. Accordingly, one could expect competitive point-counter-point lawmaking in the 107th Congress, with substantial attention to the carryover issues from the 106th Congress and the issues that had formed the platforms of both Bush and Gore. To further emphasize this point, I might add that this same agenda would likely have been featured in a Gore administration, too, though with different proposals.

Bipartisanship

As used here, *bipartisanship* refers to those cases in which leaders of both parties cooperatively participate in the several stages of the lawmaking process. Typically this strategy has characterized international or domestic crises. It is also standard that the president initiates the cooperation of House and Senate leaders, often designating and defining the crisis and proposing actions.

Domestic policy issues rarely generate bipartisanship as the term is used here. Typically in the domestic sphere the two parties have incentives to forge proposals suited to differing constituency, programmatic, and ideological interests. As a matter of practice, however, reference is often made to bipartisanship if there is cross-party endorsement of a proposal or if leaders of one party are successful in attracting some support, however limited, from the other party. I interpret these cases as examples of cross-partisanship, discussed later.

The events of September 11, 2001, invited bipartisanship in near textbook form. The intensely competitive partisanship of Congress when it returned from the August recess was instantly transformed into cooperation in support of a series of military actions and security proposals. The prospect was, however, that once the urgency of the crisis passed, competitive partisanship would resume unless specific proposals could be associated with the war on terrorism.

Cross-Partisanship

This strategy refers to occasions when the president or a congressional leader cooperates with a segment of the other party to produce a regular or super-majority. The issues inviting cross-partisanship cut across party lines, as with trade, environmental, and civil rights issues. Calculations are typically made in advance, with support from the other party balanced against possible losses in one's own party.

Two forms of cross-partisanship are pursued in lawmaking. First is that in which a segment of support is known in advance to exist on an issue due to constituency or other interests. Examples would be the availability of certain southern Democrats to Republican presidents on social and economic issues and that of northeastern Republicans to Democratic presidents on environmental issues (or a larger segment on trade matters). This first brand of cross-partisanship very likely involves cooperation at the early stages of lawmaking, given the certainty of position taking, as evidenced by past behavior on the issue. One can understand why cross-partisanship of this type is mistaken for bipartisanship.

The second type typically emerges in the playing out of competitive partisanship. As compromises are made, party leaders learn who on the other side supports an agreement. When successful in enacting law, competitive partisanship produces a cross-party coalition of sufficient strength to carry the day, as when President Bush won the votes of twelve Senate Democrats for his tax package in 2001.

Competitive partisanship and cross-partisanship are interactive strategies. What begins as classic party competition on an issue may, and frequently does, result in a cross-partisan agreement. Conversely, what begins as cross-partisanship may break down as lawmaking proceeds. The work done on the patients' bill of rights in 2001 provides an interesting example. House and Senate Democrats initially attracted enough Republicans (though not the leaders) to support their version of the bill. Later House Republican leaders were successful in winning back party members, and competitive partisanship characterized the efforts to get a bill passed.

It is important to note that competitive partisanship often fails to produce a cross-party coalition sufficient to enact law. So-called gridlock may occur. Even in such cases, however, the full story of an issue may not have been told. A subsequent Congress may enact legislation that had failed for lack of a majority (regular or super) in a previous Congress. As Sarah A. Binder shows, gridlock often can be attributed to bicameralism —differences between the chambers.[14] Accordingly, partisan strategists need to acknowledge and accommodate these differences. Few Congresses better illustrate this point than the 107th.

Partisan Patterns and Presidential-Congressional Relations, 2001–2003

As I indicated in the preceding review, the Bush administration has experienced a fascinating array of strategies associated with political standing and events. Competitive partisanship characterized the early months of the administration, though with a shift in party advantage. Relying on position, President Bush designated the agenda and its sequence following his inauguration. Enactment of the tax-cut package was the principal win for the president during this time. President Bush lost his agenda edge in the Senate when Senator James Jeffords (R-Vermont) left the party and assumed independent status, voting with the Democrats for organizational purposes. The new majority leader, Senator Thomas Daschle (D-South Dakota) gained the advantage of agenda designation and sequence for that chamber. Coordination between the House and Senate leaders was lost with this shift, forcing the White House to be reactive to Daschle's initiatives and variable in plotting strategies for the two chambers—and thus a fine illustration of Binder's observations.

Senate passage of a patients' bill of rights was the principal legislative action to which the White House had to respond during this time. Preferred bills sent over from the House were shelved in the Senate. Frum refers to this time as the "summer of our discontent," citing "stalemate, stumbles, and defeats."[15]

September 11, 2001, dramatically altered the politics of agenda management. It created a new agenda that submerged all items being considered on the day previous. Competitive partisanship gave way to bipartisanship. Democratic Party leaders were quick to join their Republican counterparts in support of the president. Predictably, bipartisanship motivated by crisis enhanced the president's status. Cooperation was featured, typically in support of the president's design. He assumed a role for which there is no congressional equivalency—commander in chief. Here, then, was the definitive case of the distinctiveness of position or official standing within the separation of institutions. As long as the president could legitimately and effectively justify his actions as taken to fulfill this role, he had a leadership advantage in working with Congress. But cooperation on Capitol Hill did not mean acquiescence. Members of Congress of both parties contributed materially to the substantial amount of legislation directly related to the war on terrorism that was enacted in the weeks following September 11.

The president also sought to associate certain items from his pre-September 11 domestic agenda with the war on terrorism (notably proposals related to energy, homeland security, economic stimulus, and trade promotion authority). The Senate Democratic leaders were not willing to extend bipartisan cooperation to this extent. However pervasive was the impact of September 11, it did not alter the narrow margins in either the House or the Senate. The principal change in the president's political standing was in his job approval rating, which soared to record heights and remained at a high level (see the chapters by Jacobson and Brody for details). Though well aware that the poll numbers favored the president, congressional Democratic leaders interpreted this support as applying to the president as commander in chief, not as domestic czar. After all, many of the domestic items that the president sought to bring under the umbrella of the war on terrorism had been vetted earlier, with divergent partisan preferences fully declared.

Accordingly, once Congress resumed consideration of the pre–September 11 agenda, competitive partisanship was restored. Two patterns then were observed: bipartisanship on matters directly related to the war on terrorism; competitive partisanship on other issues, with mostly unsuccessful efforts by the administration to associate some of the latter with the former, as noted earlier. One further point. Having enacted most of the legislation directly linked to the war on terrorism, there were fewer objects of cooperation. Bipartisanship was limited to rhetorical support for the war on terrorism, and that, too, began to erode in 2002. Competitive partisanship resumed as the dominant pattern with the near completion of Afghanistan operations. The issue of Iraq never so clearly invited bipartisanship for one simple reason: it lacked a specific event. The policy promise was that of prevention, not revenge.

There appeared to be little domestic policy bonus for the president for having led a successful venture. Further, his policy initiative regarding the threat of Iraq's weapons of mass destruction drew increasing criticism from members of Congress, mostly Democrats. Pressure was exerted on him to get congressional approval for military action and a resolution from the Security Council of the United Nations. He did both. However, the consequence of his yielding to the Democrats was that their preference that domestic issues, especially the economy, dominate the fall congressional campaign was thwarted by the debate on Iraq. The president got the resolutions on Iraq that he wanted, from Congress before the midterm election and from the Security Council after. Bipartisanship was not achieved on Capitol Hill, but a substantial cross-party coalition supported the president's position.

The 2002 elections joined other events of the Bush years in producing unprecedented results. Republicans had net gains in both houses, a first-ever result for a Republican president in his first term. Republicans recaptured majority control of the Senate. And the president campaigned vigorously for key candidates, afterward encouraging analysts to write about a "mandate." Oddly, he was said not to have had a mandate in 2000 when he had been on the ballot, but to have achieved one in 2002 when he was off the ballot. In fact, neither election produced a mandate for President Bush, though 2002 strengthened his political and legislative standing.

The consequence of the election was to produce for the Republicans the first one-party government in fifty years (discounting the few months of the Senate tie in 2001). The 108th Congress promises to display one of the most fascinating patterns of partisan strategy in a period of captivating variations. Comparisons with the last all-Republican government, in 1953–55, will surely be made.

Discretionary Use of Position

Split-party and small-margin politics encourages presidents to employ their discretionary powers, thereby bypassing the intensity of partisan conflicts with Congress. Save for his power to act as commander in chief (and often related to that role), the president has the most discretion in issuing executive orders (EOs). Kenneth R. Mayer has directed attention to the growing importance of these directives as illustrative of the "gradual expansion of presidential power." He stresses that this growth has occurred in large part because of the imperatives of institutional developments in a complex government: "With the advantage of superior information and the capacity to act unilaterally or 'go first,' modern presidents have succeeded in creating institutional capabilities for influence—over budgets, over agency rulemaking, over foreign affairs and intelligence —that have far surpassed those of their predecessors." While recognizing the potential for misuse of EOs, Mayer doubts that their use "resurrects the imperial presidency." As he writes, "The key is that the use of executive orders is conditioned on presidents' overall political situation: presidents balance the benefits of issuing an order against the costs of doing so."[16]

Table 7.1 shows the EOs issued during the first two years of the Clinton and Bush presidencies. A review of the substance of the orders issued by Bush does not suggest either misuse or excessive reliance on this option, though several orders were expectedly controversial. Orders during the first months of his tenure were of the housekeeping variety, several creating administrative or advisory units (for example, the Office of Faith-Based and Community Initiatives) suited to the president's program priorities. Others rescinded orders previously issued by Clinton, much as Clinton had done in regard to orders issued during the previous Bush administration.

As with so much else in 2001 and 2002, September 11 could also be expected to affect the discretionary powers of the president. The war on terrorism was the subject of several EOs. With the possible exception of EO 13228, establishing the Office of Homeland Security, none matched in importance either legislation being enacted or decisions made by the president as commander in chief. Much the same was characteristic of the orders issued in 2002, during which just nineteen orders were produced, nearly half of which were issued to provide an order of succession in the cabinet departments.

TABLE 7.1 Executive Orders Issued by Presidents Clinton and Bush, Years 1 and 2

President	Year 1	Year 2	Total
Clinton	56	53	109
Bush	53	19	72
Pre–September 11	(24)*		
Post–September 11	(29)*		

Source: http://www.archives.gov/federal_register/executive_orders/executive_orders .html.
* In an e-mail communication Kenneth R. Mayer called nine orders "significant" in 2001, three prior to September 11, six following September 11 (five of which were related to the war on terrorism). Mayer relied on criteria used in identifying significant orders in his book. See Mayer, *With the Stroke of a Pen*, 103–8.

Accepting Mayer's conclusion regarding the growth in the number and function of EOs in modern government, it appears that President Bush has not added greatly, if at all, to this authority. His use of such orders to rescind or amend previous orders or to seek implementation of that on which Congress has failed to act have been as controversial for Bush as for previous presidents. But Bush's EOs have been neither so numerous nor so extraordinary as to warrant special notice, possibly because September 11 enhanced his status and redirected his and the nation's focus. In an e-mail communication Mayer offered a caveat: "This is a case . . . in which executive orders by themselves don't capture everything that is going on. The military tribunal order [issued in the president's role as commander in chief] has implications that run all over the place, as do the claims about designating the two American citizens as enemy combatants [Yasser Hamdi, captured in Afghanistan, and José Padilla, dirty bomb suspect] on the basis of an executive finding." Clearly a crisis of the magnitude of September 11 expands the president's powers to act more or less across the board.

Productivity or Gridlock? The 107th Congress

The 107th Congress was generally acknowledged to be among the most competitive and contentious in recent decades. Gridlock was widely predicted as the likely outcome of a near fifty-fifty split in Congress, the shift in party control in the Senate, and the narrowness of the president's win in the Electoral College, plus the manner in which he won and his failure to produce a bipartisan agenda. The results belie these predictions.

David R. Mayhew provided a count of major legislation between 1946 and 1990 in his book *Divided We Govern.*[17] Relying on his "sweep one" methodology,[18] Mayhew has continued to update his count of major legislation enacted (now extended to the final years of the George H. W. Bush presidency, the Clinton years, and the first two years of the George W. Bush presidency). Mayhew counts fifteen laws and two resolutions as "major" for 2001–2002 (the 107th Congress). He discussed the matter of resolutions as legislation in his most recent update (http://pantheon .yale.edu/~mayhew/DWG2001-02.html). He concludes that he should have included major congressional resolutions and notes to the effect that omitting the post–September 11 and Iraqi resolutions "may not pass the don't-be-ludicrous test given the political reality of 2001–02."

Table 7.2 shows the annual production of major legislation, including those resolutions Mayhew advises that, upon reflection, he might well have included (those regarding Formosa in 1955, the Middle East in 1957, the Tonkin Gulf in 1964, and the Persian Gulf in 1991, as well as the two issued during the 107th Congress). Table 7.3 provides a ranking (most to least) of the production of major legislation in the first two years of newly elected presidents (thus excluding Johnson, who was an incumbent when elected in 1964, and Ford, who was never elected).

Of particular note for our present purposes is the ranking of President Bush—second among the newly elected presidents. Just as interesting, and clearly relevant, is the fact that President Nixon had the highest ranking by Mayhew's measure, a finding Mayhew found counterintuitive. After all, Nixon was the first president in modern times to enter office with his party in the minority in both houses of Congress. Under these and other circumstances, high productivity did not fit the "script." Gridlock should have prevented passage of major legislation.

With modifications, this analysis applies as well to the Bush presidency. Though candidate Bush did offer a program, his winning at all was in doubt, and no analyst spoke or wrote of a mandate. Defying what Mayhew refers to as the "deadlock-between-the-institutions script," Bush staged an active hundred days of promoting his legislative program, with mixed success.[19] In both cases, the broader lesson from Mayhew's data is as straightforward as it is profound: *The production of major legislation in a separated system does not follow a standard script.*

Table 7.4 lists the legislation in the 107th Congress that fit Mayhew's "sweep one" criteria. Note how production followed the events of 2001 and 2002. As expected following September 11, the president and Congress worked on and enacted legislation directly associated with the war on terrorism. The first set of actions in 2001 dealt with the immediate threat. Those related to issues such as airport security, bioterrorism

TABLE 7.2 Major Legislation Enacted, 1947–2003, by President
and Year in Office

President	Year in Office								Total	Mean*
	1	2	3	4	5	6	7	8		
Truman (1945–53)	na	na	6	4	5	7	3	3	28	4.7
Eisenhower (1953–61)	1	8	3	4	3	9	3	2	33	4.1
Kennedy (1961–63)	9	6	6	—	—	—	—	—	21	7.0
Johnson (1963–69)	—	—	—	8	15	7	6	10	46	9.2
Nixon (1969–74)	6	16	5	11	11	5	—	—	54	9.5
Ford (1974–77)	—	—	—	—	—	6	6	8	20	8.6
Carter (1977–81)	7	5	3	7	—	—	—	—	22	5.5
Reagan (1981–89)	2	7	3	4	2	7	5	7	37	4.6
G. H. W. Bush (1989–93)	2	7	3	5	—	—	—	—	17	4.3
Clinton (1993–2001)	7	4	4	11	4	4	3	5	42	5.3
G. W. Bush (2001–2002)	7	10	na	na	—	—	—	—	17	8.5

Sources: Compiled from data in Mayhew, *Divided We Govern,* 52–73, and at http://
pantheon.yale.edu/~dmayhew/.
* Nixon's total has been divided by 5.67 years, Ford's by 2.33 years.

TABLE 7.3 Ranking of Presidents by Mean Number of Major Laws
and Resolutions Enacted, by First Two Years of an Elected President
(Highest to Lowest)

President	Total	Mean	Unified/Divided*
Nixon (1969–71)	22	11	Divided I
G. W. Bush (2001–2002)	17	8.5	Divided II
Kennedy (1961–63)	15	7.5	Unified
Carter (1977–79)	12	6.0	Unified
Clinton (1993–95)	11	5.5	Unified
Eisenhower (1953–55)	9	4.5	Unified
Reagan (1981–83)	9	4.5	Divided II
G. H. W. Bush (1989–91)	9	4.5	Divided I

Sources: Compiled from data in Mayhew, *Divided We Govern,* 52–73, and at http://
pantheon.yale.edu/~dmayhew/.
* Divided I = president and Congress of different parties; Divided II = president and
one house of different parties (Senate for Bush, House for Reagan).

TABLE 7.4 Major Legislation Enacted, 107th Congress:
Mayhew's "Sweep One"

Enactments	Especially Noteworthy
2001 (7)	
Tax cut	×
Education reform	×
Resolution on use of force*	
Patriot Act*	×
Emergency spending ($40 B)*	
Airline bailout*	
Airport security*	
2002 (10)	
Campaign finance reform	×
Bioterrorism defense*	
Agriculture subsidies	
Corporate Accountability Act	×
Trade authority	×
Election reform	
Resolution on Iraq*	×
Homeland Security Department*	×
Terrorism insurance*	
September 11 Independent Commission*	

Source: http://pantheon.yale.edu/~dmayhew/DWG2001-02.html.
* Items addressing terrorism or Iraq (10).

defense, the Homeland Security Department, and terrorism insurance were directed more at future threats. Note also that several pre–September 11 items began to work their way back into the agenda in late 2001 (education) and 2002 (campaign finance reform, agriculture subsidies, corporate accountability, trade authority, and election reform).

Some of these matters, however, were not high priority for President Bush. As noted, he had lost his premier position as domestic agenda designator for the Senate when the Democrats assumed nominal control of that body. He made an effort to reestablish that status, where possible, by associating his domestic proposals as war on terrorism priorities—for example, the energy proposals, an economic stimulus package, and trade authority. The president's job approval ratings remained at record high levels during this period. But Democrats gambled that his public support was limited to the president's role as commander in chief and was not transferable to matters not clearly and directly linked to that role. Accordingly, a common pattern developed whereby the Republican House would pass a bill favored by the president and drawn from his domestic program and the legislation would then stall out in the Senate for lack of sixty votes or because Majority Leader Daschle had other priorities in scheduling floor action.

Then there is the issue of legislative production had there been no September 11 and no declaration of a war on terrorism. As noted in Table 7.4, ten of the seventeen major legislative actions addressed either terrorism or Iraq. So the following question arises: What would Bush's ranking have been without September 11? Frum's answer to that question in *The Right Man* was this: Unimpressive. He judged that the Bush administration was mostly adrift over the summer of 2001, and he observed few, if any, bright spots.

If one were to subtract the ten items in Table 7.3 related to the war on terrorism and Iraq, Bush would have ranked dead last in that table, even below his father. We will never know what might have happened. It is impossible to replay the months between September 11 and the adjournment of the 107th Congress. And yet it seems unlikely that no other legislation among the priorities of either Bush or Daschle would have passed during those many months. A significant amount of work had been done in one house or both on a patients' bill of rights, faith-based initiatives, energy, bankruptcy reform, tort reform, pension protection, corporate corruption, and immigration. Competitive partisanship could be expected to have functioned through the remainder of the first session and during the second session. Gridlock was possible, as it always is in either one-party or split-party circumstances. But it is not inevitable, as Mayhew has shown. And a review of Table 7.3 shows that major legislation was enacted during the second session—five bills not directly related to the war on terrorism. There is no reason to believe that the months immediately following September 11 would have produced a void (as it did not, education reform having passed during that time even with the concentration on the war on terrorism).

Still, it is very likely that the number of major enactments would not have been as high without September 11. That observation invites another, however. One weighty purpose of any political system is to acknowledge, engage, and act on major issues. Many are predictable, arising from existing programs and ordinary social and political life. I would so classify most of the Bush agenda prior to September 11. Indeed, it was so predictable that Gore's agenda would likely have been very much the same, though with very different proposals in an altered sequence.

The challenge of September 11 was to define, engage, and act on the unprecedented and unpredicted events of that day. It is notable that during those first weeks competitive partisanship gave way to bipartisanship with no alteration in the legislative standings of the two parties. Perhaps the one major change in the president's political standing, a dramatic increase in his job approval rating, explains the shift. A more likely account, however, was that all power holders recognized the overarching and extrapartisan crisis at hand. The public support for the president was a numerical indicator of that widespread understanding of the common threat; the increase in the job approval rating for the Republicans (+15) and the Democrats (+11) in Congress after September 11 complemented the rise in the president's rating (CNN/*Time* Poll, November 7–8, 2001; see also the chapter by Jacobson, Figure 9.2). It is also worth mentioning that this bipartisanship featured significant two-party participation in the development and passage of the anti-terrorism legislation.

The 107th Congress was unable to complete its work prior to the election, and therefore it had to return for a lame-duck session. The weeks prior to the midterm election witnessed two versions of preemption. The president set forth a justification for preemptive military action against rogue states that possessed weapons of mass destruction. His remarks targeted Iraq. Democrats and opinion leaders in the media pressured him to seek the support of Congress and the United Nations Security Council. He acceded to these requests and thereby activated a second form of preemption—that of a national security debate forestalling attention to domestic issues. Democrats preferred to campaign on "kitchen-table issues," as they sought to hold the Senate and recapture the House of Representatives. However, the congressional debate on the Iraq resolution borrowed precious legislative and campaign time from issues on which Democrats were favored, while inviting several in both houses to support the president on a vital foreign policy matter. This debate was then followed by a high-profile debate in the UN Security Council that carried through the campaign and beyond. These advantages then permitted the president to campaign actively as the commander in chief, asking for support in that role and avoiding the more partisan posture that would have been necessitated by a purely domestic issues campaign.[20]

The successful military action in Iraq was followed by questions regarding the reliability of the intelligence upon which preemptive action was based. U.S. troops failed to find a stockpile of weapons of mass destruction in the weeks after the war, as predicted. And it was later revealed that the president's claim in the 2003 State of the Union address that Saddam Hussein had bought uranium from Niger was based on forged documents. These matters demonstrate the problems of preemptive (Iraq) over reactive (September 11) military actions. Preemption depends heavily on trust that leaders have the correct information regarding a pending threat or reward. Evidence of bad or bogus intelligence undermines confidence and can therefore negatively affect that which is basic to position as a source of power. Similar effects may be observed domestically if a president seeks to preempt the other party's issues only to lose the trust of his own party. In other words, he had better be right that poaching on the other side of the aisle will reap the benefits promised or forestall the greater harm warned against.

Concluding Analysis

President Bush has capitalized on the one advantage that was made available to him by his contentious win in 2000—that of position. Many Democrats and analysts in Washington questioned his legitimacy. His capabilities for doing the job were doubted. His party had a narrow majority in the House and a tie in the Senate. Inapt for our system anyway, the term *mandate* was absent from post-election commentary. Expectations were low, if an exhausted press and op-ed corps were prepared to predict at all. And yet it was George W. Bush who put his hand on the Bible on January 20, not Albert C. Gore. Accordingly, the position of president belonged to him.

As I have noted, Bush and his team activated "position" as a strength even at the start of the post-election struggle. Their posture throughout was that of preparing to assume office and serve. It was as though they had knowledge of this prescription of a Kennedy aide for taking office:

> I think it's important that the president get off to a running start. That means that he should have people in place before the end of the year, and in all the key positions. It means he should have his priorities for legislation and for executive action, and for foreign policy action clearly in mind. He should go to the country and the Congress early in the first month of his presidency with these initiatives. He should not permit a vacuum which Congress and the pressure groups and others will fill while he's trying to figure out which way to go.[21]

The record and practices of President Bush and his team before and after September 11 reveal a strategy for capitalizing on position, one adjusted to competitive partisanship, cross-partisanship, and bipartisan conditions. The strategy appeared to feature these operating rules:

1. Seek to control the agenda so as to make the other party work on the problems you identify and in the order you specify. Control priorities and sequence.

2. Acknowledge that every problem is susceptible to more than one solution. Be ready with yours. Get there first if possible, but be prepared to respond if the initiative is lost.

3. Know your advantages, and press them to the maximum. (Note: Political capital that cannot be used was not there in the first place.)

4. Do not start where you think you may finish, or you may finish where your adversary started. (Bush's advice: Do not negotiate with yourself.)

5. Win where you can and when you can. (For Bush that meant winning in the House, given Republican Party discipline there and the likely boost from having bills pass in one house for passage in the other.)

6. Be ever alert to the potential for cross-party support. (Cross-partisanship is an important strategy, too, in split-party governments. Oddly, it may be more difficult to achieve where the margins are narrow due to the premium placed on discipline under those circumstances—a matter that requires careful study.)

7. Compromise when you must on what you can. (Judging the point of compromise requires detailed knowledge of the process, awareness of the advantages, and sensitivity to the costs of trade-offs. Competitive partisan politics is not for the faint-hearted.)

8. Corollary: Do not miss an opportunity to close on a good deal. (Split-party politics is not for ideologues.)

9. Remember that agreements are victories, not defeats. (It is difficult to claim credit if you say you lost. Shared credit claiming is the legitimate outcome of competitive partisanship.)

10. Remember this, too: The Constitution provides for just one commander in chief.

Colloquially, it can be said that President Bush played the hand he was dealt, finessing where possible. It was apparent by the end of the summer of 2001 that position alone was insufficient to allow him to win the day very often. That is hardly surprising, but presidential triumph in the politics of a separated system such as ours is not the only test of success. Competitive partisanship, sharpened substantially when Democrats took over the Senate in late May 2001, was functioning to produce policy alternatives for many issues on the domestic agenda.

The shocks the system suffered on September 11 and subsequently with the anthrax incident required significant adjustments in split-party politics. Bipartisanship was brought to bear on the issues and during the time necessary to enact needed legislation. Efforts by the president to make it work where it could not (as in the case of energy and a stimulus package) were less a defeat for him than a display of the effectiveness of the 2001 version of separated-system politics. The same might be written about the president's preemption of the Democrats' campaign agenda in 2002. That is, his effectiveness was less a win for him than a sign of national and international debate over a new, aggressive, and risky policy of preemptive military action.

How may we expect President Bush to rely on position in the years ahead? The 2002 elections did produce change in his legislative standing. And yet the margins remain razor thin—he has a 51 percent party advantage in each chamber. It seems apparent that the president and his advisers have mastered what is perhaps the greatest benefit of position —designating the agenda. Having lost the initiative in the Senate with Jeffords's switch and regained it with September 11, they sought to maintain this advantage. Leadership by the president in the immediate aftermath of September 11 was judged to be so effective that his job approval ratings were sustained at a high level for the longest period of time enjoyed by any president so measured. The issue for the White House (and for Democrats) was whether this mark of public support applied generally to Bush's leadership or was limited to his management of the war on terrorism, perhaps even to the one event—September 11. Evidence in late 2001 suggested that support was generalized, as the president received a positive evaluation on his handling of a less than robust economy. In 2002 Bush's approval score declined, but the development of the Iraqi issue and the subsequent war prevented the economy from dominating the agenda of worries in the same way as in the first Bush administration following the Gulf War.

Sustaining presidential priorities is a principal reason for the president's maintaining agenda designation preeminence, but complementary to that purpose is the preemption of the main interests of the opposition (see earlier). The tactics of the Bush strategists appear to include getting bills passed in the House ("Win where you can"), getting there first with proposals on Democratic issues (education, welfare, prescription drugs, health care), capitalizing on the president's role as commander in chief, designing proposals sufficiently inventive as to invite debate (for example, dividend tax elimination), and continually campaigning for favored policies. Properly implemented, this strategy maximizes position as a means for maintaining the president's competitive edge. It does not ensure supremacy. The challenge for the president in fifty-fifty politics is to seek and sustain advantages for bargaining so as to be taken seriously by the opposition because of demonstrated effectiveness. The measure of success is continuity in maintaining and benefiting from position. Accordingly, achievement is less having won in the classic sense than having designated the agenda, determined the sequence of agenda items, prepared credible proposals that serve as the basis for legislative action, and inoculated yourself on issues of vulnerability.

Pressing forward, staying "ahead of the moment," being aggressive beyond perceived support—these behaviors can be seen as arrogance or even ignorance. Senator Dianne Feinstein (D-California) expressed her frustration with the Bush style this way: "There is a kind of noblesse oblige, a sense that he knows best and we should all just fall into line. I do not believe he takes the Unites States Senate seriously at all." A Democratic aide was quoted as stating: "He treats us like he treats France."[22] It is difficult to assess the policy effects of these reactions. A president has the advantage as the designator of the agenda and initiator of proposals. It is one of the prime benefits of the position, there for the taking should a president and his team have the skills to acquire it. The minority party in Congress has traditionally lacked the status of a unified opposition, especially with a presidential election year pending (four presidential candidates in the Senate and two in the House at this writing). Thus it is not surprising that coverage of congressional Democrats in the early months of the 108th Congress stressed the problems they have had in projecting a unified message on either international or domestic issues.[23]

I have stressed position throughout this chapter. I now pose a question for which it is too early to supply the answer: Can position that is sustained as a source of power primarily by national security issues be transferred to domestic concerns? Evidence from the Bush 41 presidency suggests that the answer is no. The Bush 43 presidency may modify that response, but no one can say for certain at this point, particularly given the risks of preemption internationally and domestically. If position so fortified contributes to reelection and increased party margins in Congress, the president's political and legislative standing will have improved. And should the national security issues persist *and* contribute to presidential status, it may well be that domestic concerns will come to be seated in a national security context. Prestige and reputation are tests that can be employed in tracking whether position has been effective, or at least politically beneficial. At the same time, it is relevant for the president and his staff to recall that position enhanced by greater prestige and acknowledged reputation will contribute to his competitive advantages in separated-system politics. It most assuredly does not, and should not, be interpreted by this or any other president as having revoked the separation of powers. For, as I state elsewhere, those who "believe that the president is the presidency, the presidency is the government, and ours is a presidential system . . . will be proven to be wrong."[24]

Chapter 8

The Bush Presidency
and the American Electorate

Gary C. Jacobson

GEORGE W. BUSH entered the White House with the electorate evenly divided between the parties and sharply polarized along party lines, not least on the legitimacy of his victory. After the terrorist attacks of September 11, 2001, Americans of all political persuasions rallied around the president, and questions about the legitimacy of his presidency no longer even appeared in public opinion polls. Bush subsequently enjoyed the longest stretch of approval ratings above 60 percent of any president in forty years.[1] On the strength of Bush's popularity and leadership in the war on terrorism, his party avoided the usual midterm decline in 2002; Republicans picked up seats in both houses and took undisputed control of Congress.

Clearly the national trauma inflicted by the attacks and Bush's response to the crisis radically altered the president's standing with the American people, to the manifest benefit of his fellow Republicans in 2002. The question remains, however, whether September 11 and the public's strong endorsement of the president's response to the crisis have had any lasting effect on partisan attitudes, the partisan balance, or the degree of polarization of the electorate. The same question, of course, applies to public responses to the war in Iraq. In this chapter I examine the rich trove of public opinion data from the hundreds of national surveys taken during the Bush administration in considering both the immediate and the longer-term electoral effects of the president's first two years in office and, more speculatively, the military victory in Iraq.

George W. Bush and the Electorate before September 11

The 2000 election crowned three decades of growing partisan polarization among both American politicians and the voters who elect them. By every measure, politics in Washington had become increasingly polarized along partisan and ideological lines in the decades between the Nixon and Clinton administrations.[2] The fierce partisan struggle provoked by the Republicans' attempt to impeach and remove Clinton during his second term epitomized the trend.[3] Indeed partisan rancor in Washington had grown so conspicuous that it became a central target of Bush's 2000 campaign. Promising to be "a uniter, not a divider," Bush emphasized his status as a Washington outsider with "no stake in the bitter arguments of the last few years" who could "change the tone of Washington to one of civility and respect."[4]

Bush's implicit premise, that partisan polarization is an inside-the-beltway phenomenon with little popular resonance, was belied by the conditions of his election. Extending the long-term trend toward greater partisan and ideological coherence in the electorate,[5] the 2000 presidential election produced the highest levels of party-line voting in the forty-eight-year history of the National Election Studies. Ticket splitting fell to its lowest level since 1960; the number of districts delivering pluralities to House and presidential candidates of different parties was the smallest since 1952.[6] The elections also highlighted the emergence of distinct regional and cultural divisions between the parties' respective electoral coalitions at both the presidential and the congressional levels.[7] In short, George W. Bush entered the White House on the heels of the most partisan election in half a century.

Any hope Bush might have entertained of bridging the partisan divide was dashed by the denouement in Florida, which not only put politicians and activists on both sides at each other's throats, but also decisively split ordinary citizens along party lines. Surveys found self-identified Republicans and Democrats in nearly complete disagreement on who had actually won the most votes in Florida, how the candidates were handling the situation, whether the Supreme Court decided properly and impartially, and who was the legitimate victor.[8] The sense among Democrats that Bush had not won legitimately diminished only slightly during the first few months of the Bush administration, and the gap between the parties on the issue thus remained huge.[9]

Bush's singular route to the White House cost him the winner's customary honeymoon period.[10] His initial reception by the public showed the widest partisan differences in approval experienced by any newly elected president in polling history. In the twenty-eight Gallup and CBS News/*New York Times* Polls taken prior to September 11, Bush's approval ratings averaged 88 percent among self-identified Republicans, but only 31 percent among Democrats.[11] This fifty-seven-point difference marked Bush as an even more polarizing figure than the former record holder, Bill Clinton (with an average partisan difference in approval of 52 percentage points for the comparable period of his administration). Among Democrats, at least, Bush's competence and legitimacy remained in doubt until September 11. Responding to a survey taken in June, for example, 68 percent of Democrats thought Bush could not be trusted to keep his word, 59 percent thought he did not have strong leadership qualities, 78 percent doubted his ability to deal wisely with an international crisis, 70 percent thought he did not have the skills needed to negotiate with world leaders, and 54 percent doubted his judgment under pressure. In contrast, from 73 to 88 percent of Republican respondents expressed positive views of the president on these questions.[12]

The partisan split on Bush extended to most of his policies. Majorities of Democrats opposed and majorities of Republicans favored his proposals on taxes, energy development, Social Security, military spending, and budgeting more generally. Democrats supported only plans to spend more on education and to provide government funds to faith-based organizations to deliver social services.[13]

In Congress, too, there was little sign during the first eight months of Bush's administration that partisan conflict had subsided (except on education, where the administration effectively adopted the Democrats' position).[14] The administration's strategy of moderating its conservative proposals only far enough to peel off the moderate Democrats needed to win 60 votes in the Senate paid off in a victory on the $1.35 billion tax-cut bill, but was not designed to diminish partisan conflict.[15] Exceedingly narrow House and Senate majorities put a premium on party discipline. The dramatic political impact of Senator James Jeffords's defection underlined the primacy of party. (In May 2001, Jeffords switched from Republican to independent and, siding with Democrats on organizational votes, broke the 50-50 tie left by the 2000 election, giving Democrats control of the Senate.)[16] In short, national politics under the Bush administration showed every prospect of extending rather than moderating the contentious partisanship of the recent past.

September 11

This prospect, like almost every other assumption about the continuity of national political life, was thrown into question by the terrorist attacks of September 11, 2001. The bipartisan unity displayed by Congress in its response to Bush's call for action against terrorism was echoed in the public, as Americans of all political stripes rallied around the president. Bush's approval ratings shot up from the 50s to the highest levels ever recorded for a president, topping 90 percent in some September and October polls (Figure 8.1). The largest change by far occurred among Democratic identifiers, whose ratings of Bush jumped by more than 50 percentage points, from an average of 30 percent in the period before

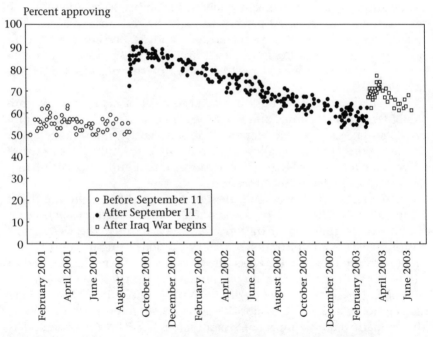

FIGURE 8.1. "Yes" answers to poll question "Do you approve or disapprove of the way George W. Bush is handling his job as president?" 2001–2003.

Sources: Gallup, CBS News/*New York Times,* ABC News/*Washington Post, Los Angeles Times,* NBC News/*Wall Street Journal, Newsweek,* CNN/*Time,* Pew Research Center for the People and the Press, and Marist Polls, available at http://www.pollingreport.com/bushjob.htm and /bushjob2.htm (accessed July 7, 2003).

September 11 to an average of 81 percent in the month following the attacks. Support also rose among Republicans (to 98 percent in polls taken through October), but it had already been so high (89 percent) before September 11 that the Republican contribution to the overall rise was only modest.[17] The rally was not sustained indefinitely, of course, but it faded slowly, with Bush's approval declining by an average of about 1.8 percentage points per month over the next sixteen months.

The rally was by no means confined to the president, however. Approval of Congress reached 84 percent in one October poll, topping its previous all-time high by 27 percentage points. Ratings of congressional leaders also rose steeply (Figure 8.2), as did positive views of the direction of the country, trust in government, satisfaction with the United States, and even assessments of the economy. The surge in support expressed for the country, its government, and its leaders reflected the radical change

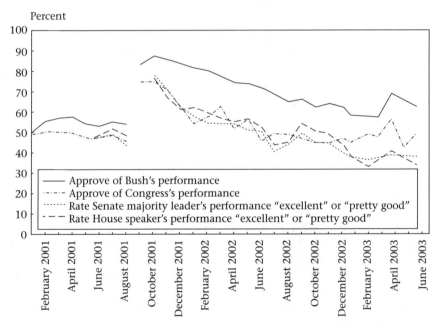

FIGURE 8.2. Ratings of Congress, its leaders, and George W. Bush, 2001–2003 (monthly averages).

Sources: Gallup, CBS News/*New York Times, Los Angeles Times*, NBC News/*Wall Street Journal*, Public Opinion Strategies, Harris, Ipsos-Reid/*Cook Political Report*, Fox News/Opinion Dynamics, *Washington Post*, and CNN/*USA Today*/Gallup Polls, available at http://www.pollingreport.com (accessed July 7, 2003).

in the context in which people responded to such survey questions. The president was now to be evaluated as the defender of the nation against shadowy foreign enemies rather than as a partisan figure of dubious legitimacy. Congress appeared as the institutional embodiment of American democracy rather than as the playground of self-serving politicians addicted to petty partisan squabbling.

For a time, politicians and government institutions enjoyed the kind of broad public support normally reserved for such national symbols as the flag and the Constitution. Not for very long, however; by the summer of 2002 the effects of the rally had all but disappeared—except for approval of the president. As Figure 8.2 shows, prior to September 11 Bush's approval rating had been only slightly higher than that of Congress, which had been close to the other standard measures of public satisfaction. After September 11 the other indexes gradually returned to where they had been before September 11, while the president's approval rating, which had risen further to begin with, declined more slowly. In March 2003, just before the war in Iraq provoked another spike in approval (of Congress as well as the president), Bush's rating was still about 5 percentage points higher than it had been before the terrorist attacks.

The 2002 Elections

There is no question that the political fallout from September 11 and its aftermath dramatically improved the Republicans' electoral prospects for 2002. Despite its steady decline from its lofty peak, Bush's approval rating remained an impressive 63 percent on election day.[18] While not as high as Bill Clinton's rating in November 1998 (66 percent), it tied Ronald Reagan's 1986 rating for the second highest in any post–World War II midterm election. Bush's high level of public approval, like that of Clinton and Reagan before him,[19] clearly helped his party's congressional candidates. Indeed, it helped in just the way that standard aggregate models of midterm congressional elections would predict.[20]

The crisis benefited Republicans in ways that went well beyond its contribution to the president's popular standing on Election Day. Bush's meteoric rise in public esteem shielded his administration from the consequences of financial scandals, epitomized by the collapse of Enron, involving Bush's political cronies and campaign contributors.[21] It is not hard to imagine how Democrats would have exploited the president's vulnerability on the issue had his status as commander in chief in the war on terrorism not put partisan criticism beyond the pale at the very time the scandals surfaced. Bush's popularity also scared off high-quality

Democrat challengers. His sky-high approval ratings during the period when potential candidates had to make decisions about running evidently convinced politically experienced and ambitious Democrats that 2002 was not their year. As a result, Democrats fielded the weakest cohort of House challengers (in terms of prior success in winning elective public office) that they had in any postwar election except the 1990 midterm.[22]

September 11 also shifted the political focus from domestic issues to national defense and foreign policy, moving the debates from Democratic turf to Republican turf. In preelection polls most respondents thought the Democrats would do a better job dealing with health care, education, Social Security, prescription drug benefits, taxes, abortion, unemployment, the environment, and corporate corruption. Most thought Republicans would do the better job of dealing with terrorism, the possibility of war with Iraq, the situation in the Middle East, and foreign affairs generally.[23] Republicans enjoyed the advantage because voters put terrorism and the prospect of war at the top of their list of concerns. Without September 11 the election would have hinged on domestic issues, and the talk of invading Iraq would have seemed like "wagging the dog," a transparent ploy to deflect attention from the economy.[24] Instead the Democrats' inept handling of legislation establishing a Department of Homeland Security (delaying passage until after the election) gave Republicans an issue that played to their strength and that they exploited effectively in several close Senate races.

The war on terrorism also helped deflect blame from the administration and its congressional allies for the return of budget deficits. The extraordinary expense of dealing with the physical and economic damage inflicted by the September 11 attacks and of tightening homeland security against future threats was unavoidable. Wars, after all, are always fought on borrowed money.

Most of all, however, September 11 and its aftermath insulated the administration and Republican congressional candidates from the full force of economic discontent. Although the president sought to blame the terrorist attacks for aborting the recovery from the mild recession of 2001, he could not escape generally negative public reviews of his economic performance. Despite his less than stellar grades on the economy, however, his leadership in the war on terrorism kept his overall ratings high. Normally a president's overall approval rating does not differ by much from his rating in specific policy domains, and economic perceptions help determine levels of presidential approval.[25] As Figure 8.3 indicates, this was the case with Bush before, but not after, September 11. Prior to the attacks his overall rating was, on average, only 6 percentage points higher than his rating on the economy; afterward it ran an average of 17 points higher. The initial rally in approval of Bush's handling of the economy after September 11 had totally dissipated by the election, but his overall rating was buoyed up by enthusiasm for his leadership in the war on terrorism. Had the terrorist attacks not occurred, Bush's overall approval rating would almost certainly have remained much closer to his rating on the economy, and, if standard midterm referendum models are to be believed, this alone might have cost Republicans control of the House.[26]

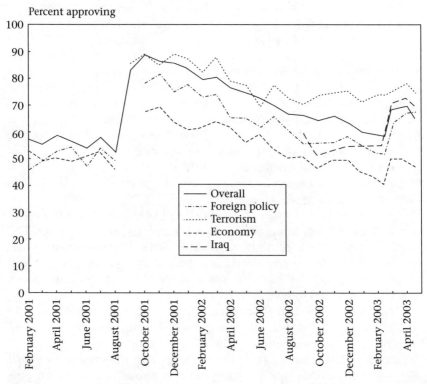

FIGURE 8.3. Approval of George W. Bush's performance by policy domain, 2001–2003 (monthly averages).

Sources: Gallup Polls, available at http://www.gallup.com; CBS News/*New York Times* Polls, available at http://www.cbsnews.com/sections/opinion/polls/main500160.shtml; ABC News/*Washington Post* Polls, available at http://www.washingtonpost.com/wp-srv/politics/polls/polls.htm; and *Los Angeles Times* Polls, Polls, available at http://www.latimes.com/news/custom/timespoll (all accessed July 7, 2003).

Bush's popularity, although crucial, was not the only reason Republicans enjoyed modest but consequential gains in the 2002 congressional elections. The public held a sour view of the economy,[27] but the economy was not, by the usual objective measures, in especially bad shape. The numbers on economic growth, real per capita income change, inflation, and even unemployment were closer to those for midterms under Republican administrations when the party suffered small rather than large losses.[28] In addition, Republicans did not have a surplus of vulnerable House seats to defend, for Bush, loser of the popular vote in 2000, had had no coattails. More important, redistricting after the 2000 census had favored Republicans. The states gaining seats were more Republican than the states losing seats,[29] and Republicans used control of the redistricting process in several large states set to lose or gain seats to improve on the already superior efficiency with which their supporters were distributed across districts.

A convenient way to assess the redistricting-induced changes in district party balances is to compare the distribution of the major-party presidential vote from 2000 in the old and the new districts. The Bush-Gore vote division provides an excellent approximation of district partisanship. Short-term forces had been evenly balanced in 2000, and party line voting had been the highest in decades; hence both the national and the district-level votes reflected the underlying partisan balance with unusual accuracy.[30] Thus districts won by Gore lean Democratic, while districts won by Bush lean Republican. By this measure, the net effect of redistricting was indeed to give Republicans more favorable terrain, as it increased the number of House districts where Bush won more votes than Gore by nine, from 228 to 237.

Table 8.1 offers further detail on these changes. The first section shows that the reduction in Gore-majority districts was concentrated in the states that lost seats. The number of Bush-majority districts actually grew in these states despite their total loss of twelve House seats. This lopsided outcome reflects successful Republican gerrymanders in Michigan, Ohio, and Pennsylvania. The general consequences of partisan control of redistricting are shown in the second section.[31] Plainly, both parties used control of redistricting to improve their candidates' prospects, but Republicans more so than Democrats, and Republicans also came out ahead in states where neither party had full control of the process.

The pattern of House election results in 2002 reflects these redistricting patterns with remarkable fidelity (Table 8.2). Democrats suffered a net decline in states that lost seats (and where redistricting was controlled by Republicans) that was only partially offset by additional victories in states that gained seats. Republicans actually managed to add a seat among the

TABLE 8.1 Effects of Redistricting on the Partisan Leanings
of House Districts, 2000–2002

	Gore-Majority Districts			Bush-Majority Districts		
	2000	2002	Change	2000	2002	Change
All seats	207	198	−9	228	237	9
I. Seat reallocations						
State lost seats	80	65	−15	63	66	3
No change	65	66	1	85	84	−1
State gained seats	62	67	5	80	87	7
II. Partisan control of redistricting						
Republicans	41	30	−11	59	68	9
Democrats	64	69	5	69	66	−3
Shared or neither party	100	97	−3	95	98	3
At-large states	2	2	0	5	5	0

Source: Author's compilation.

states losing representation and won eight additional seats in the states
gaining districts. The similarity between Tables 8.1 and 8.2 is not coincidental. Eight of the ten seats switching party control in 2002, including
all four seats lost by incumbents, went to the party with the district presidential majority.[32] In eight of these districts the incumbent party had
been weakened by redistricting (by an average loss of 5.6 percentage
points in that party's presidential vote share); in the remaining two the
incumbent party was already on the minority side of the presidential
vote (less than 46 percent in both). Thirteen of the eighteen newly drawn
districts for which an incumbent party could not be identified also went
to the party enjoying a presidential majority.

By this analysis, and contrary to the consensus of postelection commentary crediting the Bush administration with a stunning, unprecedented victory, the Republican House gains in the 2002 midterm were
neither surprising nor historically anomalous, but entirely consistent
with models treating midterm elections as referenda on the administration and the economy, conditioned by the president's party's level of
exposure (seats at risk). The effects of September 11 and its aftermath registered, to be sure, but mainly by influencing the value of a key variable,
presidential approval, and shifting attention to defense issues. Despite

TABLE 8.2 Redistricting and Election Results, 2000–2002

	Won by Democrats			Won by Republicans		
	2000	2002	Change	2000	2002	Change
All seats	211	205	–6	223	229	6
I. Seat reallocations						
State lost seats	72	59	–13	71	72	1
No change	70	73	3	79	76	–3
State gained seats	69	73	4	73	81	8
II. Partisan control of redistricting						
Republicans	40	31	–9	60	67	7
Democrats	74	79	5	59	56	–3
Shared or neither party	96	94	–2	99	101	2
At-large states	1	1	0	5	5	0

Source: Author's compilation.
Note: Independent Bernard Sanders was also reelected; for this table, districts held by Virgil Goode (Virginia 5th district), elected in 2000 as an independent but switching to Republican in 2001, and Randy Forbes (Virginia 4th district), Republican elected in 2001 to replace deceased Democrat Norm Sisiky, are treated as Republican districts.

the dramatic change in the electoral context wrought by the terrorist attacks, the aggregate election results provide no evidence of any fundamental shift in American electoral politics.

Other data from the 2002 House elections show far more continuity with than departure from the stark, closely balanced partisan divisions exposed by the 2000 election. Republican redistricting was so effective because of the extraordinarily high degree of partisan consistency in 2002 voting patterns, extending a fundamentally important trend in American electoral politics. Normally the incidence of split results—district majorities supporting different parties in House and presidential contests—rises between a presidential election and the following midterm elections.[33] The opposite occurred in 2002, with the number of split districts dropping from eighty-six in 2000 to sixty-four, the fewest for any election in the entire half century covered by the data.

The district-level data imply a high degree of individual party-line voting, and the survey evidence available is entirely consistent with this interpretation. Moreover, the regional, ideological, and policy divisions expressed so clearly in 2000 emerged once again in 2002. In national polls taken immediately prior to the election, party loyalty among respondents likely to vote and declaring a choice ranged from 91 to 95 percent.[34] The sharp partisan division on the House vote reflected large partisan differences of opinion on the administration and its performance. The gap between Republican and Democratic approval ratings of Bush's performance, which had narrowed from as many as 67 percentage points before September 11 to as few as 14 points immediately afterward, had by November 2002 grown back to an average of 54 points (Figure 8.4), comparable to that for Clinton in 1998 (55 points) if not 1994 (60 points). It was even wider among likely voters, with one poll showing 95 percent of Republicans, but only 30 percent of Democrats, approving of Bush's performance.[35]

Partisans in the electorate were also far apart in their views on the state of the nation. For example, 63 percent of self-identified Republicans

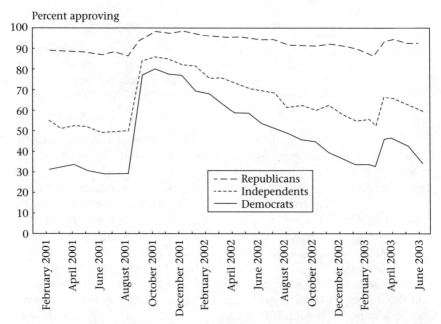

FIGURE 8.4. Approval of George W. Bush's performance, 2001–2003 (monthly averages).

Sources: "Bush Approval by Demographics13.xls," available from the Gallup Organization (contact maura_strausberg@gallup.com); and CBS News/*New York Times* Polls, available at http://www.cbsnews.com/sections/opinion/polls/main500160.shtml (accessed July 7, 2003).

thought the country was moving in the right direction; 67 percent of Democrats thought it was on the wrong track (Table 8.3). Sixty-one percent of Republicans thought the economy was good or very good; 67 percent of Democrats thought it was fairly bad or very bad. Republicans were also more confident that the United States and its allies were winning the war on terrorism. Perceptions of national conditions, like presidential approval ratings, were thus distributed in a way that reinforced rather than challenged partisan inclinations.

The same tendency appears in assessments of the parties' strengths, although here each party demonstrated some appeal to the other party's voters on its issue turf. Republicans favored their party overwhelmingly on defense and terrorism; Democrats generally preferred their own party on terrorism, but conceded defense to the Republicans. Democrats favored their own party overwhelmingly on Social Security and making prescription drugs more affordable for the elderly; Republicans favored their own party on the former, but gave Democrats an advantage on the latter. Very large majorities of partisans on both sides believed their own party was more likely to make the country prosperous.

Neither party got much help from issues ceded by the opposition's voters, because partisans on both sides believed that the issues that mattered most were the ones their own party handled best. Asked in early October to specify "the single most important problem for the government . . . to address in the coming year," Democratic respondents put the economy and jobs at the top of their list; 51 percent chose a domestic economic issue, while only 28 percent mentioned terrorism, national security, or Iraq. Republican respondents inverted this pattern, with 49 percent listing terrorism, national security, or Iraq and only 30 percent listing a domestic economic issue.[36] The economy became more salient to Republican voters closer to the election, but this did not help Democratic candidates win Republican votes, because Republican voters thought their own party would be more likely to deliver prosperity.

Turnout

For partisans on both sides, then, the election's frame—what the election was thought to be *about*—was far more conducive to party loyalty than to defection. As a result, the proportion of party loyalists among all voters (including independents) surveyed in the 2002 National Election Study was the highest since 1964 in House races (79 percent) and the highest since 1958 in Senate contests (83 percent).[37] Aside from reapportionment, what kept the election from duplicating the 2000 stalemate was turnout. Republicans did a better job of mobilizing their core supporters.

TABLE 8.3 Opinions on National Conditions and Party Performance, October 2002

Questions and responses	Republicans	Democrats
1. Do you feel things in this country are generally going in the right direction, or do you feel things have gotten off on the wrong track?		
Right direction	63	27
Wrong track	29	67
2. How would you rate the condition of the national economy these days? Is it very good, fairly good, fairly bad, or very bad?		
Very good or fairly good	61	33
Fairly bad or very bad	38	67
3. Who do you think is winning the war against terrorism—the U.S. and its allies, neither side, or the terrorists?		
U.S. and its allies	50	24
Neither side	39	51
The terrorists	9	19
4. Regardless of how you usually vote, do you think the Republican Party or the Democratic Party is more likely to		
a. make sure the U.S. military defenses are strong?		
Republican Party	83	46
Democratic Party	5	36
b. make the right decisions when it comes to dealing with terrorism?		
Republican Party	72	29
Democratic Party	2	46
c. make the right decisions about Social Security?		
Republican Party	64	5
Democratic Party	14	83
d. make prescription drugs for the elderly more affordable?		
Republican Party	31	5
Democratic Party	40	86
e. make sure the country is prosperous?		
Republican Party	75	9
Democratic Party	7	74

Source: CBS News/New York Times Poll, October 27–31, 2002, available at http://www.cbsnews.com/htdocs/c2k/election_back.pdf (accessed November 20, 2002).

Superior mobilization was central to the victories in Minnesota, Missouri, and Georgia that gave Republicans control of the Senate, as well as in several states where Republican Senate seats had been at risk.[38] Bush's near-universal approval among Republicans, his energetic fund-raising, and his frenzied last-minute campaigning in competitive states, combined with effective Republican grassroots drives to get out the vote, put Republicans over the top.[39]

The president's standing with Republicans was the key to the success of the Republicans' mobilization effort. His 91 percent approval rating among his own partisans in the final Gallup Poll before the election was the highest of any president in any postwar midterm election, while his 37 percent approval rating among opposition partisans had been matched or exceeded in half of the previous dozen midterms.[40] Republicans endorsed Bush with enthusiasm; given the option, more than 80 percent said they approved of Bush's performance "strongly," compared to only 10 percent of Democrats.[41] Bush was thus remarkably effective in solidifying his party's base for the 2002 election, but he was considerably less successful in broadening it. Senate outcomes, like those of House contests, generally reflected the constituency's underlying partisan balance; of the thirteen Senate races rated as "tossup" or "leaning" in *CQ Weekly*'s October preelection review, ten went to the party that had won the state's presidential vote in 2000.[42] The only state won by Gore (barely, with 51 percent of the vote) was Minnesota, where Republicans took a Senate seat from the Democrats, and even that victory came only after the front-running Democratic incumbent, Paul Wellstone, died in a plane crash ten days before the election.

Electoral results and polling data from 2002 recapitulated the regional and demographic divisions evident in 2000.[43] Democrats won 62 percent of House seats in the Northeast, Mid-Atlantic, and West Coast regions (compared with 61 percent in 2000); Republicans won 63 percent of House seats in the South, Plains, and Mountain West regions (compared with 64 percent in 2000). The only notable difference was in the Midwest, where the Republicans' share of seats went from 52 percent to 59 percent, mostly because of redistricting.[44] Preelection polls showed that Republicans continued to be preferred by whites, men, married people, rural dwellers, the devout, and the prosperous. Democrats were preferred by women, minorities, urban dwellers, the secular, and the less prosperous. The marriage gap was even larger than the nine-point gender gap, with one poll showing 68 percent of unmarried women favoring Democrats, compared with 42 percent of married women.[45] The distinct regional and cultural divide between the parties' respective electoral coalitions displayed in the 2000 election was again fully evident in 2002.

There is, in short, no evidence that the electorate was any less polarized in 2002 than it had been in 2000.

Longer-Term Implications

The initial political effects of the terrorist attacks of September 11 and the president's leadership in response to the national trauma they inflicted were huge, and these effects decayed slowly enough to have a major impact on the 2002 elections. But the elections themselves offer little evidence that the partisan stalemate revealed so strikingly by the 2000 elections had been broken. Still, the question remains whether the radical reorientation of national politics after September 11 will continue to shape the electorate's view of the president and the parties in ways that might have durable electoral effects.

One potentially consequential effect would be a change in the balance of Republicans and Democrats in the electorate. Even if partisan divisions have reemerged unaltered, the political landscape would be quite different if post–September 11 events were to shift the distribution of partisans in the electorate in favor of the president's party. Models from the research literature on "macropartisanship" raise this possibility, for they show that changes in the aggregate distribution of partisans in the electorate reflect the same forces that shape presidential approval, and thus predict that the proportion of citizens identifying with the president's party will rise during a period of sustained high approval levels.[46] However, the same models show that macropartisanship is also sensitive to the economic conditions that affect consumer sentiment, which has been less than bullish during the Bush administration. Indexes of consumer sentiment and consumer confidence fell after Bush took over from Clinton, and they remained at comparatively low levels through June 2003 (Figure 8.5).[47] The public's net ratings of the economy (the proportion seeing it as "excellent" or "good" minus the proportion seeing it as "fair" or "poor") has also been decisively on the negative side (Figure 8.6), although so far not as negative as during the first Bush administration. Up-ticks after September 11 and during the spring of 2002 were short-lived.

If high presidential approval ratings reflect forces promoting Republican identification, economic conditions have had a contrary thrust. What has been the net result? Gallup detected a pro-Republican surge from the fourth quarter of 2001 through the second quarter of 2002 that dissipated before the election.[48] Data from the CBS News/New York Times Polls display a similar pattern (Figure 8.7). Time series data from the major surveys uniformly show that the Democrats' long-term advantage in party identifiers dipped noticeably after 1984;[49] since then macro-

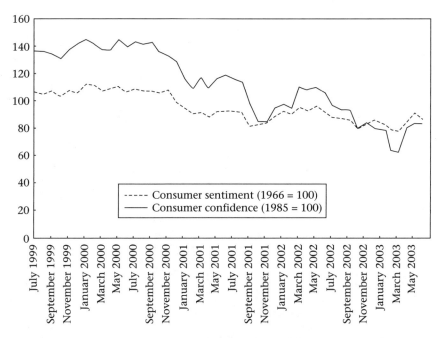

FIGURE 8.5. Consumer sentiment and consumer confidence, 1999–2003.
Sources: University of Michigan Survey of Consumer Sentiment, available at http://www.sca.isr.umich.edu/data-archive/mine.php; and Conference Board Consumer Confidence Index, available at http://www.pollingreport.com/consumer.htm (accessed July 7, 2003).

partisanship has fluctuated, but followed no sustained trend. There was a visible shift to the Republicans after September 11, but the distribution of partisans soon returned to its long-run equilibrium. The mean for the fourth quarter of 2002, 55 percent Democratic, is identical to the average for the entire post-1984 period.[50]

Just as the war on terrorism kept Bush's approval rating high despite the sagging economy, it may well be that economic discontent limited the attractiveness of the Republican Party despite the continuing high level of public regard for its leader. Whatever the reason, experience with the Bush administration has had only modest effects on how the public regards the parties. For example, perceptions of which party is better able to handle domestic policy challenges have, if anything, shifted in favor of the Democrats during the Bush years (Table 8.4).[51] Responses to questions about which party is more likely to ensure prosperity, protect Social

Percent "Excellent" or "Good" minus
percent "Fair" or "Poor"

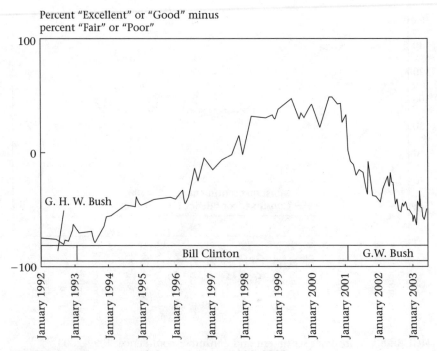

FIGURE 8.6. Net rating of the economy, 1992–2003.

Sources: Gallup Polls, available at http://www.pollingreport.com/consumer.htm
(accessed July 7, 2003) and http://www.gallup.com/poll/releases/pr020213.asp
(accessed February 17, 2003).

Security, and produce a fair tax system show fluctuations, but no systematic change between 1999 and 2002. Republicans gained on education
during Bush's first year in office, but the old pro-Democratic distribution
on this issue was back by the middle of 2002. Preferences for the Democratic Party actually increased noticeably on health care and the environment. Only on national defense do we observe a significant increase in
the proportion of respondents preferring Republicans, adding about 10
percentage points to the party's already substantial advantage.

When partisans are viewed separately, the degree of continuity across
these surveys is also impressive (Table 8.5). So, too, are the partisan differences on most of these issues. Partisans on both sides continue to favor
their own party overwhelmingly on prosperity, Social Security, education, and taxes. Large majorities of Democrats prefer their own party on
health care and the environment, with Republicans divided but moving,

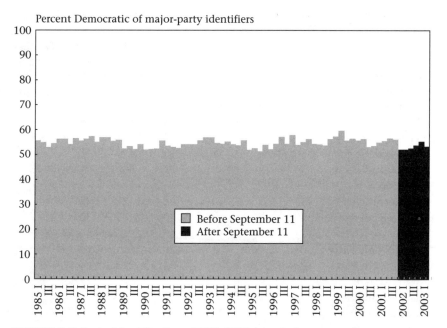

FIGURE 8.7. Party identification, 1985–2003 (quarterly averages).

Sources: Compiled by author from CBS News/*New York Times* Polls archived at http://www.icpsr.umich.edu/access/index.html and available at http://www .cbsnews.com/sections/opinion/polls/main500160.shtml (accessed July 7, 2003).

in both cases, toward favoring Democrats over this period. This pattern is inverted on defense, with even Democrats favoring the Republican Party after September 11. However, the Republicans have lost their initial advantage among Democrats on dealing with terrorism.

These data offer little reason to believe that the partisan terrain has shifted significantly during the Bush administration. September 11 made defense concerns much more salient, playing to a major Republican strength, and the president and his party will continue to benefit whenever defense issues remain at the forefront. But Democrats remain in the stronger position on domestic issues and in policy areas that become more pressing when the economy is in the doldrums. Trends in the distribution of public opinion on policy issues have also been relatively flat. The Bush administration's positions on energy development, taxes, abortion, and prescription drug benefits did not become more popular after September 11, and support for substituting individual investment accounts for part of Social Security declined along with the stock market. Partisan

TABLE 8.4 Party Superiority on Issues, 1999–2002, All Respondents

	1999*	July 2000	March 2001	January 2002	July 2002	October 2002a	October 2002b
Prosperity							
Democratic Party	43	41	41	38	39	41	37
Republican Party	39	41	39	41	39	38	41
Social Security							
Democratic Party	50	43	46	48	49	51	46
Republican Party	32	35	38	31	30	27	33
Education							
Democratic Party	53	46	40	· 42	48	49	
Republican Party	30	32	42	39	33	30	
Health care							
Democratic Party	54	51	51	58	62		
Republican Party	26	28	28	22	22		
Fair tax system							
Democratic Party	46	42	49	47			
Republican Party	37	33	36	34			
Environment							
Democratic Party		52	57	60	63		
Republican Party		24		23	19	19	
Defense							
Democratic Party	27	23		18	20	23	18
Republican Party	57	56	67	64	64	66	
Terrorism							
Democratic Party				15	22	28	20
Republican Party				57	49	47	52

Source: CBS News/*New York Times* Polls.
*The question on education was asked in January 1999; the question on health care was asked in January and July 1999; the question on Social Security was asked in January and November 1999; the questions on prosperity and defense were asked in November 1999. When a question was asked twice, the entry is the average of the percentage from the two polls.

differences on these issues remain as strong as ever.[52] Finally, the belief that the administration's domestic policies are biased toward the wealthy is as widespread as it was before September 11 (Table 8.6). A large majority of Democrats express this view, and it has also become increasingly common even among Republicans.

TABLE 8.5 Party Better Able to Handle Issues, 1999–2002,
Partisan Responders

Issues, responders, and responses	1999*	July 2000	March 2001	January 2002	July 2002	October 2002a	October 2002b
Prosperity							
Democrats							
Democratic Party	75	73	75	70	69	76	74
Republican Party	13	12	9	13	15	14	9
Republicans							
Democratic Party	13	7	10	8	8	10	7
Republican Party	73	79	78	78	75	75	75
Social Security							
Democrats							
Democratic Party	81	77	78	79	80	80	83
Republican Party	8	9	8	6	7	8	5
Republicans							
Democratic Party	16	10	12	19	19	18	14
Republican Party	68	70	79	65	64	59	64
Education							
Democrats							
Democratic Party	75	69	70	63	74	76	
Republican Party	14	13	15	20	14	12	
Republicans							
Democratic Party	24	26	15	21	23	20	
Republican Party	59	58	76	65	59	62	
Health care							
Democrats							
Democratic Party	83	83		79	83	89	
Republican Party	6	6		8	6	5	
Republicans							
Democratic Party	15	24		26	37	35	
Republican Party	59	58		54	46	45	
Fair tax system							
Democrats							
Democratic Party	77	71		79		81	
Republican Party	11	10		11		8	
Republicans							
Democratic Party	15	15		22		14	
Republican Party	71	67		67		71	

(continued)

TABLE 8.5 *Continued*

Issues, responders, and responses	1999*	July 2000	March 2001	January 2002	July 2002	October 2002a	October 2002b
Environment							
Democrats							
Democratic Party		64		71	79	73	
Republican Party		13		14	7	13	
Republicans							
Democratic Party		40		47	44	52	
Republican Party		44		37	37	33	
Defense							
Democrats							
Democratic Party	48	38		28	33	37	36
Republican Party	38	39		54	48	51	46
Republicans							
Democratic Party	6	11		6	6	9	5
Republican Party	84	78		88	87	86	83
Terrorism							
Democrats							
Democratic Party				23	36	46	46
Republican Party				43	29	27	29
Republicans							
Democratic Party				7	6	4	2
Republican Party				79	76	81	72

Source: CBS News/*New York Times* Polls.

*The question on education was asked in January 1999; the question on health care was asked in January and July 1999; the question on Social Security was asked in January and November 1999; the questions on prosperity and defense were asked in November 1999. When question was asked twice, the entry is the average of the two polls.

Assessments of George W. Bush

Unlike his party, President Bush has derived some sustained benefits from his leadership in the war on terrorism. The percentage of Americans who see him as a strong leader has remained high and a full 20 percentage points above its pre–September 11 level; belief in his honesty and ability to understand complex issues also remains higher than before the attacks (Table 8.7). He is viewed as relatively more concerned with the interests of ordinary Americans (42 percent) than is his administration as a whole

TABLE 8.6 Answers to Poll Question "In general, do you think the policies of the Bush administration favor the rich, favor the middle class, favor the poor, or do they treat all groups the same?" 2001–2003

Respondents and answers	June 2001	January 2002	July 2002	October 2002	January 2003a	January 2003b
All respondents						
Rich	57	50	53	55	59	58
Middle class	8	14	18	14	11	10
Poor	2	2	1	2	2	1
All the same	27	28	24	25	23	26
Democrats						
Rich	82	75	77	73	82	82
Middle class	6	7	11	6	8	8
Poor	1	1	0	2	0	0
All the same	8	12	10	15	6	7
Republicans						
Rich	24	22	25	23	36	38
Middle class	12	20	29	24	16	13
Poor	3	2	3	3	3	1
All the same	55	48	38	42	41	47

Source: CBS News/*New York Times* Polls.

(30 percent), although majorities believe both he and his party care more about the interests of large corporations than about those of ordinary citizens (51 percent and 60 percent, respectively).[53] On the other hand, the proportion thinking that Bush understands their problems, which increased significantly after September 11, fell back to near its initial level and was not augmented by the Iraq War triumph, once again suggesting that the domestic side of his presidency has not so far been a rousing popular success.

Even on foreign affairs the president's public image had begun to tarnish a bit prior to the invasion of Iraq. Although approval of his performance remained higher on foreign policy than on the economy, it declined at about the same rate over time (Figure 8.3). The erosion has been particularly notable among Democrats, falling from nearly 70 percent at its peak to 32 percent in March 2003, before getting a boost by initiation of the Iraq War (Figure 8.8). In contrast, Republican approval rates continue to exceed 80 percent. Indeed, partisan differences on this question had by

TABLE 8.7 "Yes" Answers to Poll Question "Please tell me whether the following statement applies to Bush or not."

	(percent)					
Answers	April 2001	July 2001	January 2002	July 2002	December 2002	April 2003
He's a strong leader	53	55		75	75	74
He is honest and trustworthy	62	63		71	70	
He understands complex issues		53			63	
He understands problems of people like you	47	45	61	57	51	51

Source: Washington Post/ABC News Polls, available at http://www.washingtonpost.com/wp-srv/politics/polls/vault/stories/data040203.htm and /data121802.htm.

early April 2003 grown as large as partisan differences on Bush's economic performance (50 points).

Perhaps more surprising, the proportion of the public confident of Bush's ability to deal wisely with an international crisis, which had jumped by 34 percentage points after September 11, eventually reaching 76 percent, was by November 2002 back down to 53 percent, only 5 points above its average for the six precrisis polls (Figure 8.9). In April 2003, after the victory in Iraq, confidence in Bush rose again, but only halfway back to its earlier peak. The modest partisan convergence that had followed the terrorist attacks of September 11 was completely reversed by the time the war with Iraq began; even after that, Democrats' confidence in Bush's handling of an international crisis remained 50 points lower than that of Republicans. Faith in Bush on this score is evidently subject to the same partisan bias and to the same erosion as presidential approval.

Public support for making war on the Al Qaeda terrorists, whose threat was anything but hypothetical, did not automatically extend to support for a preemptive war against Iraq. Backing for military action in Afghanistan aimed at bin Laden's network and its Taliban protectors was overwhelming and bipartisan, as was approval of Bush's leadership in this campaign.[54] Most Americans, convinced that Saddam Hussein was hiding weapons of mass destruction, also approved of using military force to drive him from power in Iraq. But prior to the war large majorities pre-

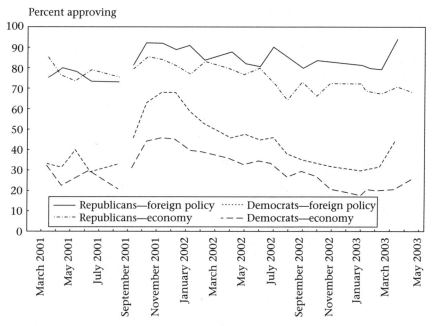

FIGURE 8.8. Partisans' approval of George W. Bush's performance by domain, 2001–2003 (monthly averages).

Sources: Gallup Polls, available at http://www.gallup.com; and CBS News/*New York Times* Polls, available at http://www.cbsnews.com/sections/opinion/polls/main500160.shtml (accessed July 7, 2003).

ferred a diplomatic solution if at all possible, and support for military action was much lower if it was to be taken without strong international support. Most wanted to allow the United Nations (UN) weapons inspectors all the time they needed to complete their investigations before initiating war.[55] No small portion of the public seemed to be looking to America's European allies and the UN weapons inspectors to provide independent confirmation of the Bush administration's arguments for the necessity of war in Iraq before giving it their complete backing.

There was also a noticeable partisan divide on going to war with Iraq. A majority of the public supported such a war, although support was in slow decline until the administration began its unsuccessful campaign to persuade the UN Security Council to authorize military action against Saddam's regime (Figure 8.10). Democrats were considerably less supportive than Republicans, and the partisan gap widened over time as Republicans became more supportive while Democrats became less so

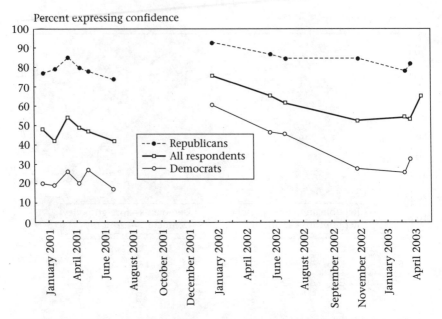

Percent expressing confidence

FIGURE 8.9. "Yes" answers to poll question "Do you have confidence in George W. Bush's ability to deal wisely with an international crisis, or are you uneasy about his approach?" 2001–2003.

Source: CBS News/*New York Times* Polls, available at http://www.cbsnews.com/ sections/opinion/polls/main500160.shtml (accessed July 7, 2003).

until the war began (Figure 8.11). Democrats were also much more partial to diplomacy,[56] putting them at odds with the Bush administration as they perceived it.

Popular support for military action in Iraq rose by an average of about 9 percentage points after the war began and by another 2 points a couple of weeks later, when success in the field seemed ensured (Figure 8.10). Still, Republicans remained much more united in their enthusiasm for the war than Democrats. For example, Gallup Polls taken March 20–24 found 93 percent of self-identified Republicans supporting the war, compared with 53 percent of Democrats (and 66 percent of independents).[57] The March 26–27 poll also reported a 40-point partisan gap, with 83 percent of Republicans, but only 43 percent of Democrats, saying that removing Saddam was worth the cost.[58] Later polls found somewhat smaller partisan divisions. The ABC News/*Washington Post* Poll taken April 3 reported that 95 percent of Republicans supported the war, compared to about 65 percent of Democrats (up from about 60 percent in the

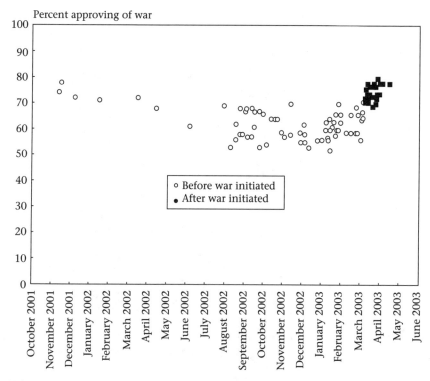

FIGURE 8.10. Support for war in Iraq, 2001–2003.

Sources: Gallup, CBS News/*New York Times,* ABC News/*Washington Post, Los Angeles Times,* NBC News/*Wall Street Journal, Newsweek,* CNN/*Time,* and Pew Research Center for the People and the Press Polls, available at http://www .pollingreport.com/iraq.htm#Program, /iraq2.htm, /iraq3.htm, /iraq4.htm, /iraq5.htm, and /iraq6.htm (accessed July 7, 2003).

same poll two weeks earlier); the CBS News/*New York Times* Poll taken in late April found 93 percent of Republicans and 67 percent of Democrats endorsing the war.[59] Even after statues of Saddam had fallen in Baghdad, partisan differences over the Iraq War remained much wider than partisan differences over fighting terrorism in Afghanistan, and the rally in presidential support among Democrats (and independents) provoked by the fighting in Iraq was much smaller than the one inspired by September 11 and its aftermath (Figure 8.4). The temporary 14-point average rise in Bush's approval among Democrats still left a partisan divide of 50 points, which

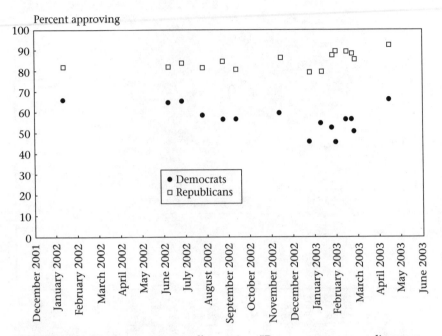

FIGURE 8.11. "Yes" answers to poll question "Do you approve or disapprove of the United States taking military action against Iraq to try and remove Saddam Hussein from power?" 2001–2003.

Source: CBS News/*New York Times* Polls, available at http://www.cbsnews.com/sections/opinion/polls/main500160.shtml (accessed July 7, 2003).

by June had grown back to 58 points. By comparison, the senior Bush's level of approval among Republicans after victory in the 1991 Gulf War had matched his son's 95 percent, but was much higher among Democrats, averaging 74 percent in February and March 1991, compared with 47 percent for George W. Bush in the seven Gallup Polls taken between March 22 and April 23, 2003. The military action in Iraq was a popular as well as a strategic success, but it did inspire the kind of national unity that had emerged for a time in the wake of the terrorist attacks of September 11.

Prospects for 2004

At this writing, George W. Bush remains a clear favorite for reelection. His approval ratings for June 2003 averaged 64 percent, and if they are anywhere near this level in the fall of 2004, history suggests that he will be very tough to beat.[60] Bush runs well ahead of every potential Democratic rival in early horse-race polls. His reelection is by no means a foregone conclusion, however. His father's experience is sufficient proof; the elder Bush's approval ratings, which exceeded 80 percent in January 1991, had fallen to 35 percent by the time Bill Clinton defeated him in 1992. Like the trend in Bush's approval ratings, the trend in responses to a generic question about the current President Bush's reelection showed considerable erosion of support after the post–September 11 rally (Figure 8.12). The proportion of registered voters saying that, if the election were held on the day of the poll, they would definitely vote for Bush fell from 56 percent in December 2001 to 38 percent in early March 2003, while the proportion saying they would definitely vote for someone else grew from 16 percent to 37 percent. The Iraq War rally restored Bush's lead, but only to its level of a few months earlier, well below its post–September 11 peak, and by June 2003 it had already narrowed once more.

There is, of course, no more reason to extrapolate any of the trends examined here into the future than there is to believe that the June 2003 ratings of the president's performance, generally or on specific policy areas, will remain where they are through Election Day 2004. Uncertainties about terrorism, establishing order in Iraq, North Korea, the stock market, and the domestic economy more generally—not to mention the possibility of other, unanticipated, shocks—are far too great, and plausible scenarios could render George W. Bush anything from invincible to unelectable. At this writing, however, Bush's standing with the public appears solid, if not unassailable. Generally favorable evaluations of Bush's personal qualities give him an edge, but the close partisan balance and strong partisan differences could easily make for a competitive presidential race in 2004 if the economy stays weak and if—and this is by no means a sure thing—an effective Democratic challenger emerges.

Bush continues to enjoy nearly unanimous support from his Republican base, while his approval rating among Democrats (and independents), although a bit higher at this writing than before the Iraq War (Figure 8.4), are clearly subject to erosion now that the fighting has subsided. The economy remains a problem for the administration; Bush's approval rating on the economy rose modestly as part of the wartime rally, but by June 2003 had fallen below 50 percent, remaining 20 points below his overall approval rating (Figure 8.3). As attention shifts from war to the domestic economy (and assuming it stays there), the glow of victory is likely to fade, except, perhaps, among Republicans, leaving the public as divided along partisan lines about the president's performance as before September 11.

The Bush administration's domestic agenda for the 108th Congress promises to intensify rather than diminish partisan divisions. The heart of

Percent

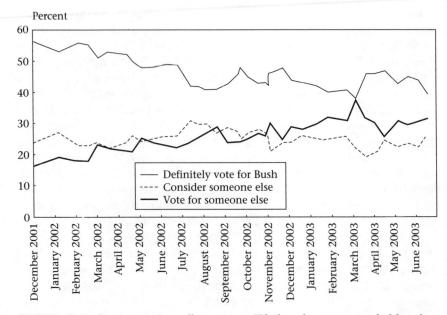

FIGURE 8.12. Responses to poll question "If the election were held today, would you definitely vote to reelect George W. Bush as president, consider voting for someone else, or definitely vote for someone else as president?" 2001–2003.

Source: Ipsos-Reid/*Cook Political Report* Poll (registered voters), available at http://www.pollingreport.com/wh04gen.htm (accessed July 7, 2003).

Bush's economic stimulus package is a set of tax cuts (most important, an end to taxes on dividends) dear to supply-side conservatives, but rightly viewed by ordinary Democrats as mainly benefiting wealthy investors. Domestic social programs bear the brunt of the fiscal damage the tax cuts will inflict. Controversial plans for revising Social Security and Medicare are on the agenda, too. The push to open environmentally sensitive public lands to mineral exploration and other commercial activities continues apace, further offending a Democratic-leaning constituency.[61] Attempts to impose additional restrictions on abortion rights are also in prospect. And Bush pointedly renominated judicial candidates rejected by Senate Democrats in the previous Congress as too conservative.

With conservative Republicans in their strongest position in Congress since the 1920s and eager for action, Bush is poised to test the limits as to how far he can push an aggressively conservative agenda, relying on party discipline and, after the Iraq War, his rise in public esteem to make narrow

Republican majorities prevail. Democrats in Congress, gearing up for the 2004 election, are just as eager to highlight party differences on domestic issues, if not defense issues. Despite the unifying national trauma of September 11 and the positive public response to military victory in Iraq, the George W. Bush administration seems likely to leave the country as polarized as it was at the time of his ascension to the White House.

As long as Bush retains near-unanimous support among Republican identifiers, a partisan standoff should be enough to keep him in the White House. It should also be enough to keep Republicans in control of Congress, given the structural advantage conferred by the more efficient distribution of Republican voters. Not only did Bush, running 540,000 votes behind nationally in 2000, outpoll Gore in 237 of the 435 current House districts; he also outpolled him in thirty of the fifty states, including twenty-two of the thirty-four states with Senate seats at stake in 2004.[62] For Democrats to have any chance to win control of either house of Congress or the White House in the next election, they will need more than a continuation of the current partisan stalemate; they will need the lift of a strong pro-Democratic national tide.

Conclusion

George W. Bush's leadership in response to the terrorist attacks of September 11, 2001, raised his standing with the American people dramatically. The rally in approval was sufficiently durable that, with the help of the shift in national priorities from domestic to defense issues and a pro-Republican reapportionment, the president's party was able to pick up seats in both houses of Congress in the 2002 elections. But aside from altering attitudes toward the president himself, September 11 and its aftermath (including successful wars in Afghanistan and Iraq) have yet to show any lasting effect on partisan attitudes, the partisan balance, or the degree of polarization in the electorate. Despite Bush's national leadership in a time of crisis and widely popular military triumphs, his first thirty months in office have left the electorate, like the Congress, as divided and polarized as when he entered the White House.

Chapter 9

President Bush and the Public

Richard A. Brody

IN JUST HALF A TERM, President George W. Bush has scored record gains in public support and seen his extraordinary level of approval ground down in reaction to diplomatic difficulties, corporate corruption, and the country's woeful loss of economic vigor. His high standing with the American people over the first two years of his presidency is both familiar and novel. We can see in it patterns that are similar to those of many of his predecessors, including his father. The novel elements are by and large matters of degree—shifts in support that have been more extreme and perhaps more enduring than those we have encountered before. This chapter traces and tries to explain these patterns of public support.

Three phases relating to public support emerged during the first 111 weeks of the Bush presidency (see Figure 9.1):[1] The first phase was the period early in the term—from Inauguration Day to September 11—which may have included a brief "honeymoon"; a rally following the terrorist attacks on September 11, 2001; and a postrally period that is ongoing and, until the war in Iraq, found President Bush back at his pre–September 11 level of support.

These phases are considered in turn so that we can determine whether and to what extent the public is responding to President Bush as it did to his predecessors.

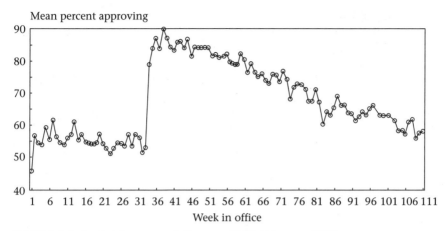

Mean percent approving

FIGURE 9.1. Bush job approval, January 2001–February 2003.

Sources: All figures in this chapter have been compiled from reports of ten media and commercial polling organizations that use the traditional Gallup Poll item, namely "Do you approve or disapprove of the way President Bush is handling his job as president?" to measure public support for President Bush. The charted coefficients are averages for those of the ten polls taken during a given week. These data are available at http://www.pollingreport.com.

The Early Term

Assessments of a president's "job performance" during the early months of his first term are formed without the benefit of a great deal of hard information. News on a fledgling administration is dominated by stories about organizing the White House and the executive branch, the cast of characters who comprise the administration, the executive branch's internal struggles over controlling resources, and the setting of priorities among the issues that define the president's policy agenda. To this ordinary news the media added, in the early days of the Bush presidency, stories of the president's unusual route to the White House, as well as pieces questioning whether he had actually been elected and whether the aftermath of the Florida debacle would affect his ability to govern.

For President Bush and those who held the office of president before him, this early period gave the public little information about the success or failure of the president's program. Later on, in developing its opinion of the president, the public can and will make use of news reports describing and evaluating the effectiveness of his agenda and the results of presidential policy initiatives. But such news is scarce in the initial weeks after a new president has taken office.

From the perspective of citizens trying to judge whether a president is doing well or badly, news typical of the early term is full of ambiguity. In consequence, early in a presidency the public's assessment is constructed on a foundation of ideological and partisan predispositions and elaborated on the basis of cues given the public by respected political leaders and trusted figures in the media.

Roughly speaking, this means that those who voted for the newly elected president are likely to give him the benefit of any doubt arising early in his term and to "approve" of his "handling of his job as president." As the early weeks of the term pass by, continuing "approval" by the president's initial supporters will be affected by the support of his fellow partisans in Congress and, to a lesser degree, by the evaluative comments of respected media figures.

The initial evaluations of those who voted against the winning presidential candidate are not the mirror image of those of the president's electoral supporters. At the outset some of those who voted against the new president—consider them "hard-core" opponents—register "disapproval" of his job performance. Other presidential opponents in the electorate, about equal in number to hard-core opponents, withhold evaluation of the president's performance and report that they "don't know" or "have no opinion" when asked to assess his performance. Of this latter group, about a third (7 to 12 percent of a typical sample) will never offer an opinion of the president's job performance. However, the bulk of those who initially fail to express an opinion will come to express approval or disapproval depending upon evidence of the success or failure of presidential policy and/or the opinions expressed by party and media elites. How does this account square with the early period of the Bush presidency?

Tracing Opinion on Bush's Job Performance
before September 11

The fraction of the American public "approving" of Bush's handling of the presidency in his first twenty-three weeks in office shows that the opinion of the current president followed a pattern similar to the patterns observed in previous administrations: immediately after his inauguration President Bush's "approval" percentage (48 percent) approximated his share of the two-party popular vote. Just over half of the public (52 percent) did not approve of his "job handling," but only a third of this group (17 percent) expressed disapproval (see Figure 9.2). Thirty-five percent of the public failed to express an opinion in the first week of the Bush presidency. The immediate post-inaugural polling showed that the new president's level of approval was statistically indistinguishable from that of President Clinton in 1993 (48 percent versus 51 percent, respectively). President Bush's being "elected by the Supreme Court" may have traumatized the elite of the Democratic Party, but it does not appear to have affected his standing with the public at large.

The pattern of public opinion in President Bush's second week in office was also similar to that of previous presidents:[2] in Figure 9.1 we observe a jump in the fraction of the public approving of the president's performance; the president enjoyed an 18 percent increase in the proportion of the public giving him positive marks.

Between the first and second weeks of the president's tenure the fraction of the public offering a negative assessment of Bush's performance increased by more than 40 percent, from 17 to 25 percent. With levels of both approval and disapproval increasing, it is obvious that by the president's second week in office, opinion on the Bush presidency had begun to crystallize. The increase in the ranks of those with an opinion came at the expense of the group withholding judgment. By the second week the group of those without an opinion shrank by nearly 50 percent, from 35 percent the first week to 18 percent the second week of the Bush presidency. The level of public uncertainty about the Bush presidency—indicated by the fraction of the public without an opinion—increased

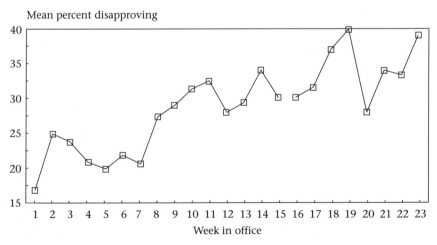

FIGURE 9.2. Bush job "disapproval," January 21–June 30, 2001.

slightly during February, declined fairly steadily during March, and leveled off at 12 percent in April, May, and June. By the end of March (the
beginning of Bush's third month in office), nine Americans in ten had an
opinion about President Bush.

Because "approval," "disapproval," and "no opinion" all varied week
to week in the early part of the term, it is difficult to get a clear picture of
what was happening to public assessments of President Bush. If we set
aside those without an opinion and focus on those approving of the president as a fraction of Americans with an opinion of the president's job
performance—think of it as "relative" approval[3]—a clearer picture of
opinion dynamics emerges (see Figure 9.3).

For the first seven weeks of Bush's presidency, between 70 and 75 percent of those expressing an opinion on President Bush were positive in
their assessment of his performance. Despite the questions raised about
his election, the president had a "honeymoon," and this is when it took
place. Over the next ten weeks, from early March to mid-May, the level of
"relative" approval dropped more than 8 percentage points. However,
support for President Bush did not come to rest at the level it had reached
in March to mid-May; the polls for the remainder of May and for the last
three weeks of June showed a further erosion of 5 to 7 points in his level
of relative approval.

President Bush finished his first six months in office 17 percentage
points of relative support below where he had started; one in four of his

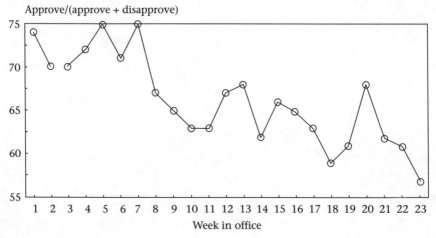

FIGURE 9.3. Bush's relative approval," January 21–June 30, 2001.

initial supporters changed their assessment of his job performance. What provoked this shift in opinion?

Sources of the Decline in Support

The timing of the decline in support for President Bush suggests the sources of the decline: the first precipitate drop in the president's approval rating came between the seventh and eighth weeks of his presidency —between the weeks of March 4 and March 11. The most notable political news event of that period was the delivery to Congress of the president's budget.

The budget represented hard news: it was the president's campaign promises and policy agenda made manifest in billions of dollars. It also signaled that the administration was not cowed by the circumstances of Bush's election. The country may have had its doubts, but the White House's budget was built on the assumption that the president had received a mandate from the voters.

Few members of the public read the budget, but it did not have to be read by individuals in order to influence their opinion of President Bush: the budget received heavy coverage in the press and in the electronic news media. It also was the topic of a large volume of commentary by political leaders; this commentary also was widely reported in the media. Many organized interests brought to their members' attention the connection between members' policy preferences and relevant sections of the budget. By whatever means and via whichever medium, public opinion at the time the budget was introduced became both more crystallized—after this period fewer Americans withheld their assessment of President Bush's performance—and, on balance, more negative.

The decline in President Bush's support in the wake of the introduction of his budget continued for four weeks. The first week of April the drop in support was arrested, temporarily, by a small rally. The increase in support is associated with the forcing down, by China, of an electronic surveillance plane from the United States that had been flying a mission along the southern coast of China and with the subsequent release of the plane's personnel. For the second half of April and into May the president's relative approval ratings fluctuated in a fairly narrow band— between 60 and 65 percent. Then in June President Bush's support began a slow but steady decline.

Over these ten weeks news appeared that, from the president's perspective, was both good and bad. By far the most positive story was Congress's acceptance, with minor modifications, of his tax-cut proposal; the president was able to sign the tax cut into law just as what I have referred to as the early stage of his term was coming to an end. On the negative side, the Middle East, Northern Ireland, and Macedonia were on a slow boil and threatening to create real problems for American foreign policy. The negative reception by our allies in the North Atlantic Treaty Organization (NATO) and by Russia of President Bush's "missile shield" proposal and the testing program designed to back it up gave rise to concerns about a new "unilateralism" in foreign affairs; those concerns have not gone away.

The worst political news of the period, from President Bush's perspective, was the change in partisan control of the Senate occasioned by Senator James Jeffords's switch in party loyalty. When we add to these stories the small but steady increases in unemployment and inflation, it is a bit surprising that the decline in the president's support was not deeper and more rapid.

Summary

President Bush had a "honeymoon" with the American public, but it was, compared to those of his predecessors, short-lived. Seven weeks into his presidency, at the time he submitted his budget to Congress, the standard by which his performance was judged began to shift. His electoral supporters had given the new president the benefit of the doubt throughout the early stage of his term, and those who had voted for his opponent were as likely to withhold their opinion as to judge him negatively. With the introduction of President Bush's budget, the standard shifted. Supporters apparently liked what they saw and correspondingly "approved" of what he was doing. Opponents used the same sources of evidence to consider whether they now knew enough to form and report an assessment.

There is nothing unusual in judging a president using readily available information; typically that is the way it is done. The judgment is based on evidence as to whether the results of the president's political and policy actions satisfactorily meet citizens' expectations. These expectations result in part from their partisan and ideological predispositions and from their taking in the views of trusted opinion leaders, including the president. From the end of the honeymoon period on, as in the previous twelve to fifteen weeks, President Bush began to be evaluated on how well he met the public's expectations. Getting his program passed would help, as would being seen as reducing tensions in the world's trouble spots, and so would a vigorous economy. Congressional gridlock would hurt, and so would being seen as catering to special interests rather than the common good. The American people give presidents a fair amount of latitude, but going into the first week of September 2001 the public appeared to be dividing along partisan lines in its assessment of the success of the Bush presidency. Republicans overwhelmingly liked what they saw, and accordingly expressed approval of President Bush's job performance. Democrats and independents were divided in their assessment of President Bush; by the end of the summer of 2001, majorities of these two groups gave the president negative marks.

Public opinion polls taken during July and August 2001 indicated that the decline in support observed in the late spring was not illusory. The erosion in President Bush's job approval continued between June 30 and September 10, 2001. His average level of support in the first twenty-three weeks of his tenure had been just over 55 percent[4]; his approval ratings for the next ten weeks averaged just under 54 percent. Comparing the mean of the twenty-three averages for the weeks following January 20 with the mean of the ten weeks between June 30 and September 10, we find a difference of 1.62 percentage points. The erosion in the president's support in the summer of 2001 was slight, but, by the usual statistical criteria, real. And then came September 11.

Most measures of public approval of President Bush's job performance during his first twenty-three weeks in office fell between 50 and 60 percent. Only one of the twenty-three observations fell to below 50 percent, and two scored above 60 percent. Toward the end of this period the early signs of a decline in his support, fueled by questions raised about the president's foreign and defense policies and by the movement of the economy toward recession, could be observed. In most respects, public support for President Bush between the time of his inauguration and the end of June 2001 was very much what we would have expected from studies of the public's responses to his predecessors.

The Rally after September 11

The destructive attacks on the World Trade Center and the Pentagon dramatically altered the public's assessment of how well President Bush was "handling the job of president." The eleven polls gauging the public's evaluation of President Bush's job performance that were taken between September 11 and September 21, 2001, showed a mean level of approval in excess of 81 percent. On average, in the first ten days following the September 11 attacks, nearly three Americans in ten (28.3 percent) changed their opinion of the president's job performance. Seven polls were taken during the next two weeks (September 22–October 5); the average level of approval for President Bush in these polls was 87 percent. Support was significantly higher in the second fortnight of the crisis than in the first ten days after the attack ($\Delta = 5.7\%$; $t_\Delta = 2.94$; $p_t < .01$).

This was a rally if there ever was one! This sudden shift in support raises two questions that we will have to answer if we want to understand the pattern of support for President Bush in the months following September 11. What produces rallies in public opinion? And how long do they last?

The "rally" phenomenon was first brought to our attention by Nelson Polsby. Polsby pointed out that "invariably, the popular response to a president during an international crisis is favorable regardless of the wisdom of the policies [the president] pursues."[5] John Mueller provides us with a taxonomy of rally events and an explanation of the source of a rally—that the threat to the United States inherent in an international crisis provokes a patriotic response that is manifested in the public's reluctance to criticize and its predilection to praise the president.[6] Kernell refines Mueller's taxonomy and implicitly raises questions about the patriotism explanation by pointing out that some international crises have been accompanied by a decline in public support.[7] Brody and Shapiro build their explanation of the rally phenomenon on the assumption that the confusion accompanying an international crisis predisposes the public to take its evaluative cue from trusted opinion leaders.[8] If opinion leaders are outspokenly supportive of the president or if they acquiesce to the president's policy response to a crisis without comment, members of the public who theretofore had disapproved of his job performance will tend to switch their evaluations from negative to positive. A precrisis negative assessment of the president is more likely to be found among identifiers with the opposition party and among partisan independents. Accordingly, we would expect these two partisan groups to be prominent among those producing the rally. Absent the active support or passive acquiescence of the opposition elite, no rally should take place.

This explanation of the rally phenomenon has been useful in distinguishing international crises that produce rallies from those that do not.[9] However, analyses of the rally in public support following Iraq's invasion of Kuwait in August 1990 suggest that both "patriotism" and opinion leadership may be responsible for the reshaping of public assessments of President George H. W. Bush's job performance in August and September of 1990.[10] The pattern of elite commentary in the August phase of the Gulf crisis suggests that Democratic leaders in Congress may have been reluctant to appear to be making common cause with Saddam Hussein and other foreign critics of our response to the invasion. This "reluctance" manifested itself in Democratic leaders' both tacitly and actively supporting the first President Bush's response to the invasion. When opposition commentary changed to criticism of the president's reliance on military means to end the invasion, the rally came to an end.[11]

The duration of rallies also appears to depend upon the actions of opinion leaders and the clarity of the situation "on the ground": rallies cycle with the support and/or silence of these elites. When negative commentary emerges, public support begins to decline. In essence, we can say it appears that international crises produce rallies unless or until the opposition elite criticizes presidential policy. Analysis of the rally following the attacks on the twin towers of the World Trade Center and the Pentagon find that both patriotism and opinion leadership affected public support for President Bush. Manifestations of community feeling and patriotism were seen everywhere; flags were displayed where they never had been before, blood donors endured long waits to make their donations, and contributions to the Red Cross vastly increased. Opinion leadership was virtually unanimous in its rhetorical support of the president's actions. Congress went beyond rhetoric and voted without dissent to put money into New York City, the Pentagon, and anti-terrorism activities.

Rallies also cycle with information about whether the actions taken to deal with a crisis are being effective. Surprise and uncertainty about what is going on contributes to a rally, because it tends to centralize information and interpretation in the White House. When information about response to the crisis moves away from the control of the White House, the public can begin to reach its own conclusions about the effectiveness of policy.

The first small signs of a breakdown in the elite consensus following September 11 began to emerge early in October. This was noticeable in very polite debate over the civil liberties implications of Attorney General John Ashcroft's plans for intercepting terrorists before they entered the United States, choking off resources being transferred to potential terrorists, and monitoring intercourse between such individuals. Incidentally, questions about the wisdom of his proposals were raised by members of both political parties.

Be that as it may, the military response in Afghanistan came to dominate the news. Dissent over the threat to civil liberties and questions about the efficacy of anti-terrorist activities in the United States were supplanted in the news by questions about the effectiveness of the military campaign to eliminate the fountainhead of terrorist activity in Afghanistan and, through that means, to eliminate terrorism. News of the defeat of the Taliban, the establishment of an Afghani regime opposed to Al Qaeda, and other military successes in Afghanistan sustained President Bush's extraordinary level of support through December 2001.

The week of October 11, 2001, may be thought of as marking the end of the "rally phase" of the September 11 crisis and the beginning of the "war/policy" phase. That was the week in which air strikes were initiated against the Taliban and Al Qaeda. These actions signaled the end of the period in which citizen support was a response to individual "patriotism" and the actions of opposition elite opinion leadership. In the war phase of a crisis the public's assessment of presidential performance responds to "good" and "bad" policy results news—defined respectively by a match or a mismatch between policy expectations and policy performance.[12] In the early weeks of the battle in Afghanistan, expectations were met and the news was good: the Taliban were routed, and the forces of Al Qaeda were in retreat. All of the good news about the results of our policy in Afghanistan makes it appear that this phase was part and parcel of the post-September 11 rally, making it a rally of extraordinary endurance.

In the 1990–91 Persian Gulf crisis the rally phase and the war phase were separated by more than three months. By contrast, the transition in the crisis following the September 11 attacks took place over a weekend. This difference in timing may not be important,[13] but the differences in the stock of public support when the transition took place is worth considering. In the 1990–91 crisis the rally in support for President George H. W. Bush had been totally dissipated well before the war began. The war/policy phase of the present crisis began with President George W. Bush at the peak of his popularity.

Other differences between the two crises are sources of analytic uncertainty. In the Gulf War the satisfaction of policy expectations was possible to demonstrate: air superiority could credibly be claimed, the occupation of Kuwait could be seen to have ended, an invasion of Saudi Arabia could be precluded, Iraq's army could be pinned down and defeated, and so on. The successful attainment of goals in the wake of the September 11 attacks was inherently ambiguous. Pursuing terrorism by attacking the Taliban made the attainment of policy goals more concrete and visible; ending terrorism, as such, is harder to demonstrate: bringing Osama bin Laden to justice may be demonstrable, but is difficult to achieve; creating a "stable" alliance with Muslim states against terrorism depends on getting the public, the media, and opinion leaders to accept a particular, if not a peculiar, definition of stability, and so on. Does a popular president get the benefit of this ambiguity, or is opinion leadership the key to how the lack of demonstrable success gets interpreted?

Public Support after the Rally

Two facts are important to bear in mind as we move from the "rally" to the war/policy phase of public opinion.[14] The abrupt and massive shift in public support did not take place in all groups in the electorate. Rather, it was largely a product of opinion change on the part of Democrats and partisan independents. Republican partisans, in overwhelming numbers, had registered their approval of President Bush long before the attacks in New York and on the Pentagon took place.[15] The post–September 11 rally was fueled by an instantaneous and massive opinion shift from negative to positive by Democrats and independents. Apart from their agreement on the need for security and domestic tranquility, Republican and Democrat party adherents have different preferences as to the direction of policy. After September 11 the change in the focus of news away from security issues would have led us to expect that Democrats and some independents would leave the bipartisan coalition that supported the president.

In fact, the rally gains in support for the president were not preserved. Among other things, this raises questions about journalistic speculation about whether September 11 permanently altered the relationship between President Bush and the electorate. The president may now be seen as tougher, more decisive, and more resolute, but he has not gotten a pass from the American people. Americans generally like, or even admire, their presidents, but they still judge their performance on the success or failure of their policies. During the year after the attacks in New York and Washington, partisan independents' support for President Bush declined at a rate of 1 percentage point per month. Over the same period the president lost support among Democrats at double that rate. However, the president retained the increased support of his fellow Republicans. The decline in support for President Bush after the rally resulted from Democrats' and independents' changing their assessments of the president's job performance. What brought this change in Democrats' and independents' opinion?

The short answer to this question is that changed opinion was probably linked to changes in the focus of the daily news. In the first twelve weeks after the September 11 attacks the *Facts on File* weekly news summaries were dominated by news of the attacks, the actions in Afghanistan, and the possibility of anthrax bioterrorism. In early December 2001, September 11–related stories begin to share space in the weekly summaries with stories related to domestic politics and foreign policy news that were not part of the September 11 news frame—for example, stories about the expansion of NATO and hostilities between Israel and the Palestinians began to get coverage. At the end of January 2002, the collapse of Enron created a new news frame related to corporate corruption and scandal. The multiple links of the Bush administration to the corporate community, especially in the energy business, meant that negative business news could erode support among those predisposed to be critical of the president, which is to say Democrats and some independents. Brody and Jackman report that in the spring and summer of 2002, the period in which news of corporate corruption became an important continuing story, support for President Bush was eroding at an accelerating pace.[16] The accelerating decline in support appears to have been a response to news stories such as those on the kidnapping and murder of Daniel Pearl, the bombing of a church next to the U.S. embassy in Pakistan, the killing of an American soldier in Afghanistan, intelligence failures and a lack of coordination between the Central Intelligence Agency and the Federal Bureau of Investigation preceding September 11, and the misdirection of "friendly fire" in Afghanistan. It was also a response to repeated stories on the declining economy, corporate corruption, and difficulties for U.S. diplomacy in Israel.

The erosion of support for the president continued, but its acceleration stopped with the shift of the administration's foreign policy focus from Afghanistan and Al Qaeda to Iraq. We can date the end of the acceleration fairly precisely (see Figure 9.4).[17] About a year after September 11 and six months before the end of the period covered by this chapter, the accelerating decline in approval for President Bush ended. News commentaries pointed to a rally in support for the president that accompanied the shift of attention to Iraq. These accounts were correct, but only in the limited sense that the new foreign policy news frame boosted President Bush's approval back to a path that was no longer trending downward at an increasing rate, but was trending downward nonetheless.

Over the twenty-eight weeks that completed the second year of the Bush presidency, support for the president declined a further 12 percentage points. A review of the dominant news stories in this period suggests that those predisposed to be critical of the president, especially Democrats, could find a lot of evidence on which to base their now negative opinion of his handling of his job. News of corporate corruption was among the top three stories for nine of those twenty-eight weeks. The politics of Iraq diplomacy gave a mixed picture: domestic political leaders gave the president qualified support for his intention to use military force; many Democrats called for President Bush to abjure unilateral action and act through the United Nations (UN); our European allies, apart from Britain and Spain, were critical of the president's Iraq policy even after it shifted to an emphasis on arms inspections and UN Resolution 1441; France maintained its opposition to the UN Security Council; and even the UN's arms inspectors gave ambiguous testimony, on the one hand lending support to the Bush administration's contentions, and on the other raising questions about the validity of the assumptions used by the administration to justify using armed force to disarm Iraq. A mixed picture of the "war on terrorism" also emerged: on the negative

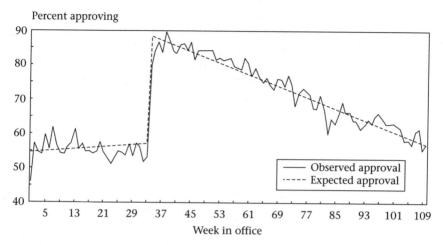

FIGURE 9.4. Bush approval, January 2001–February 2003.

side, evidence of intelligence lapses prior to the September 11 attacks was brought out in congressional hearings; on the positive side, Pakistani forces captured important Al Qaeda leaders. But eighteen months beyond September 11, Osama bin Laden remained at large. A war without end ground on in Israel. The economy showed no sign of improving, and the president's "economic stimulus package" generated a large amount of partisan criticism.

Over the weeks filling out the first two years of the Bush presidency, the most prominently featured domestic and foreign news stories could have served to encourage those predisposed to support the president or, by the same logic, provided ample evidence for those predisposed to score his performance negatively. The trend in approval suggests that the latter group was larger than the former. However, considering the lability of the judgments of these Americans of President Bush, they were apparently not implacably disposed to evaluate him negatively. As the post- September 11 period wore on, large numbers of these citizens found sufficient evidence to give him poor marks. But their opinions proved changeable.

Approval for the President after March 19, 2003

Taking the story of President Bush's public support beyond the first two years, into the Iraq War period, is irresistible. We can extend our examination of Bush's approval with data from March through May 2003 (see Figure 9.5).

It was widely speculated that war with Iraq would again rally Americans behind the president and increase the ranks of those who approved of his performance. This speculation proved correct. But it is not clear that the public responses to events in the past upon which this speculation was grounded were appropriate guides to the likely response to an Iraq war. We have not previously had wars that resulted from American preemption.[18] Nor have we had a war with a long build-up, a war that was justified, debated, and protested. A war with Iraq would have at least two other aspects that could affect its consequences for public opinion: Saddam Hussein was feared and loathed, so Americans would be delighted to see him gone and might well approve of President Bush for acting to achieve that outcome; and the attack also might be seen as directly relevant to the war on terrorism begun in response to September 11.

The second Gulf War began on March 19, 2003, and ended six weeks later. The onset of war and the euphoria produced by the U.S.-led coalition's initial military successes was accompanied by an 8 percentage

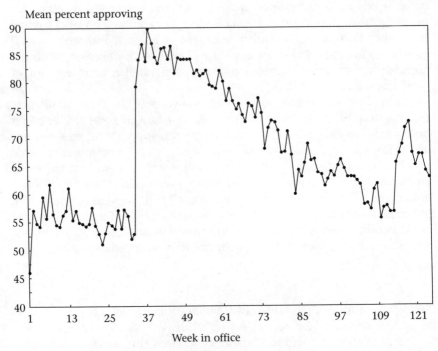

FIGURE 9.5. Bush job approval, January 2001–May 2003.

point gain in approval of the president's handling of his job. The rapid success achieved by the coalition forces and the rapid disintegration of Saddam Hussein's regime added a further 10 percentage points to the president's level of support.

The most recent polling covers the period in which the Iraq War story was transformed from one of unalloyed success to a more mixed picture. The "initial success" story was typified by rumors of the "decapitation" of the Iraqi military effort that arose from the "busting" of Saddam's bunker in the very first strike of the war. This was followed by a week in which the American public was introduced to the latest in weapons technology by reporters who were embedded in military units and appeared on camera dressed in full battle gear. Everything seemed to be going smoothly that week. Troops were arriving and moving out toward battles to come. Even though widely denied, the news in this week gave rise to the hope that it would all be over very soon with minimal casualties.

The story changed during the second week of the war: suddenly a well-oiled machine got some sand in its gears. Saddam may have lived through the bunker busting. The advance toward Baghdad was moving too fast for resupply convoys to keep up. Iraqi attacks on unprotected convoys led to coalition dead, wounded, and prisoners of war. The uprising of groups suffering from Saddam's regime failed to materialize. As March turned into April, stories of dissent in the Pentagon, a failure to meet battle timetables, and questioning of the appropriateness of Secretary of Defense Donald Rumsfeld's overall defense strategy began to accompany news of military success. Democratic voices were largely silent, indeed timid, perhaps because of the furious reaction to Senate Minority Leader Tom Daschle's criticism of President Bush's timing of the start of the war. The Democrats used the occasion of the president's request for a special appropriation to supplement the budget to cover the costs of the war as an opportunity to argue for curbing the president's tax-cut proposals; the war was becoming a serious drag on the economy.

With the official end of the war to "free" Iraq the story shifted from the success of armed force to the frustrations attendant to maintaining order in the country. This shift was nicely captured in television footage of the literal toppling of Saddam's images throughout Iraq, which turned into scenes of rioting and looting. Even more potentially damaging was failure to uncover any of Iraq's weapons of mass destruction (whose presumed existence had been the reason Bush claimed that war was necessary) or hard evidence of links between Iraq and Al Qaeda (another of Bush's arguments for war). At this writing the administration is trying to reduce the centrality of weapons of mass destruction and the Al Qaeda link as justifications for the war and justify it as a means of ridding Iraq of a very bad dictator. By that standard, our policy toward North Korea is inexplicable.

By the time of this writing, the end of May 2003—124 weeks into Bush's first term—mixed news appears to have capped the rise in support for the president. But it may not be followed by a dramatic decline in his support, for several reasons: Iraq continues to be important news, the administration dominates (but does not own) coverage of the war, the Democrats have no institutional base in Congress from which to call attention to problems with the administration's rationale for invading Iraq, the press is positive about Bush's foreign policy initiatives in the Middle East, and the president's domestic agenda has received congressional support.

Looking Ahead

The aim of this chapter, apart from documenting where the president now stands with the American people and how his standing got to this point, is to offer a way to think about how the public will respond to the second half of the Bush presidency. Like his predecessors, George W. Bush will be judged both on outcomes that are within his control and on results over which he has little control. Like most presidents, he will be held to account for outcomes—for example, the presence or absence of peace, safety, and prosperity—about which there is near total consensus.

Unlike many previous presidents, President Bush is quite explicit about what he expects from his policy initiatives. For example, the president claims that his proposed tax cuts will create jobs and in time reduce the deficits it initially creates; "privatization" will save the Social Security system and guarantee its availability for generations to come; cuts in the education budget will "leave no child behind"; a proposed reformed prescription drug program will guarantee the availability of affordable medication to needy seniors; the Department of Homeland Security will reduce our vulnerability to terrorist attacks; the end of Saddam Hussein's dictatorship will help develop democracy throughout the Middle East; and so forth. This explicitness will make it easier for opinion leaders and the public to judge whether or not Bush is making progress. As in the past, policy progress will bring more support, and failure will lead to an erosion of support for the president.

Chapter 10

A View from Within

John J. DiIulio, Jr.

DURING MY ACADEMIC LEAVE in 2001 I had an opportunity that most political scientists who study American government and domestic public policy can only dream about. I served as assistant to the President of the United States and first director of a new Executive Office of the President (EOP) entity, the White House Office of Faith-Based and Community Initiatives (OFBCI). Several authors in this volume cite a book celebrating Bush's leadership penned by a conservative journalist who served the administration as a junior speechwriter.[1] To date, however, no former administration official who attended senior staff meetings and had regular access to both senior staff and the president has written at length—in fact, none has yet written at all—on the Bush presidency. Even if and when those former Bush aides who were truly top insiders (for example, Karen Hughes) offer their public reflections, caution will still be in order, as it always must be. George E. Reedy, a former junior assistant to President Lyndon Johnson, observed that while "the White House staff has an inner political life of its own," most senior staff feel "one purpose in life and one purpose only—to perform personal services for the man in charge" and to do all in their power to see that he is "happy and pleased."[2]

Even a short-term outsider-insider like me sometimes felt that tug. To be clear, while I was on the senior staff, I purposely did not function as a first-rank adviser. For health reasons and because I had only just moved to a new university and launched two new programs there, I had publicly agreed to serve only six months, but ended up serving about eight. I entered with a profile as a centrist Democrat public intellectual in a conservative Republican administration. Still, I did attend scores of senior staff meetings, talk routinely to other senior and junior EOP staff as well as cabinet officials, brief the president, organize several presidential trips and events, meet with House and Senate leaders both on Capitol Hill and beyond the Beltway, and help to shape many domestic policy speeches and decisions that were well beyond my purview as "faith czar."

From day one, the intense controversy and constant press interest surrounding the president's faith initiative thrust me into a highly visible role. Despite my frank public disagreements with a small group of religious conservatives important to the administration's political base, I was asked to stay on, and even entreated in July 2001 to take a leave of absence or move the office to my native Philadelphia if that would permit me to remain for another year or so. But I declined, and we announced my resignation on August 20, 2001. I treasure the president's two-page hand-written letter to me on the occasion of my final decision to leave as scheduled and his other forms of personal outreach. Through February 2002 I pitched in when asked to help keep various OFBCI-related things in play and to provide counsel on assorted other domestic policy initiatives. Since then I have publicly criticized various aspects of the administration's homeland security and social policy efforts and issued, but then apologized for and retracted, criticisms of its West Wing domestic policy apparatus.[3] Just the same, I have maintained close personal ties to and remained in communications with several senior and junior White House and cabinet officials. All policy differences and concerns aside, I remain very much a true believer in the president's moral character and generous heart.

As co-author of an American government textbook, I keep up with the presidential studies literature and did a little writing on the subject early in my academic career.[4] Unlike so many other contributors to this volume, however, I am by no means a presidency scholar. Nonetheless, on many occasions during my White House tenure—early on when my senior colleagues were organizing the EOP and discussing cabinet appointments; later on when they and "the Hill people" (my term for top House Republican staff) were discussing political strategy; at moments when the president would call, button-hole me in the hall, drop by my building, relay questions, or say "get on my dance card" (i.e., arrange to see him); during weeks when important speeches on "faith-based" or other domestic issues were being vetted and finalized; on days when the daily media barrage or the occasional crisis was being managed; and at other times—I found myself focusing on how what I was witnessing fortified or falsified this or that academic concept or theory about presidents and the presidency. Indeed, I even found myself doing certain mental bean-counting exercises, silently coding or content-analyzing senior staff comments, presidential speeches, personnel decisions, communications strategies, or legislative tactics as evidence for or against given ideas or schools of thought.

In what follows I discuss my White House experiences as they relate to what certain of the volume's other authors have written, loosely organizing my reflections around three concepts in presidential studies: presidential character, the modern presidency, and the permanent campaign.

Presidential Character: The Small-*d* Texas Democrat

Little as I expected my time near the Oval Office to bug me with big ideas about the contemporary presidency, I was even more surprised to leave Washington convinced that presidential character is absolutely critical to everything from White House organization and staff relations to military policy decision making. I had never agreed with scholars who insisted that, given the massive growth in the EOP and other institutional factors, the White House is home to a "plural presidency" in which the president is best viewed as "but one of the individuals in the executive."[5] But I was always also deeply skeptical about efforts at "predicting performance in the White House" derived from biographical or psychological insights into how a given president "orients himself toward life," including "how much energy" he invests in the job and "how he feels about what he does."[6]

By the time I left the White House, however, I was converted by experience to the view that presidential character, most especially the sitting president's "worldview"—"his primary, politically relevant beliefs, particularly his conceptions of social causality, human nature, and the central moral conflicts of the time"—probably explains as much or more about everything from domestic agenda setting and legislative-executive relations to foreign policy than does any other single variable.[7]

So what is the essence of Bush's presidential character? Plainly, he is what some scholars, following James David Barber, would term an "active-positive" president: he loves the job and is very energetic and focused.[8] Likewise, Karen M. Hult is right when she says in this volume that Bush's "management preferences have helped produce the administration's characteristic discipline and the premium it places on secrecy."

But to conceive Bush as an active-positive president with a penchant for CEO-style operations is to miss what is, in my view, a far more fundamental aspect of his presidential character. Fred I. Greenstein notes Bush's disdain for "intellectual snobs." What Bush really dislikes are academic or other elites who, as I heard him phrase it on occasion, "are" or "come off" as "smart without any heart," who are "down on average Americans" who "just believe in this great country" and its "great goodness." Thus, compared to other presidencies since that of Franklin D. Roosevelt, the Bush administration is largely bereft of policy intellectuals.[9]

Ivo H. Daalder and James M. Lindsay explore how September 11 confirmed rather than transformed "Bush's beliefs about the world and America's place in it." But the president's main moral rationale for what they term the "Bush revolution" in foreign policy is democratic. Both in public speeches and in private conversations, Bush has deemed it "presumptuous and insulting to suggest that a whole region of the world—or the one-fifth that is Muslim—is somehow untouched by the most basic aspirations of life." He once said, "Human cultures can be vastly different. Yet the human heart desires the same good things, everywhere on earth. . . . In our desire to care for our children and give them a better life, we are the same."[10]

It is, I think, impossible to understand Bush's presidential character without fully appreciating his profoundly small-*d* democratic beliefs and sensibilities. Let me offer a homely example relating to my own experiences with the Texan and the administration's faith-based program proposals.

I first met George W. Bush in February 1999. After declining several invitations to visit with the likely Republican presidential aspirant at the governor's mansion in Texas, several friends, including former Indianapolis mayor Stephen Goldsmith, prevailed upon me to attend a small-group meeting with Bush. The general topic was social policy. Bush greeted me very warmly, singling me out for a hug and repeatedly calling on me to give the final word on the issues that generated disagreements. "I can see you're governor's pet," joked one colleague in a whisper.

Bush became noticeably quite animated when, in reply to his request for "one big new idea on compassion," I suggested a national initiative to match low-income children of prisoners with loving, caring, year-round, life-long adult mentors mobilized from inner-city churches. He seemed genuinely stunned, and stung, to learn that on any given day America was home to over two million children with (as he would later often phrase it) "a mom or dad in jail." He cringed as I rapidly recited the grim statistics on how much more likely these children were than otherwise comparable impoverished urban youth to suffer abuse and neglect, fail in school, abuse drugs, get arrested, and wind up behind bars themselves. At a later one-on-one meeting he smiled broadly when I summarized evidence showing that the vast majority of urban community-serving congregations and grassroots religious groups perform such social services as I had suggested without proselytizing and often work via interfaith, religious-secular, and public-private partnerships. "That's exactly how this ought to go," he exclaimed.

In almost every subsequent communication I had with Bush before he became president, and at least a half-dozen times thereafter while I worked with him in the White House, we discussed mentoring for the children of prisoners. For example, it came up July 22, 1999, when he tracked me down and called me on vacation to thank me for helping to draft his maiden campaign speech, "The Duty of Hope." It was the primary topic of a nearly two-hour meeting and lunch we had together in Philadelphia in June 2000. He lamented the "proliferation of prisons" (a phrase I helped turn) in his inauguration address, and subsequently spoke about "young, innocent kids" with "moms or dads in jail," including "decent dads who made a mistake but want to help their children grow up right and live better." "These children deserve a fair start," he would say, "somebody to love them" and help their families. His homespun sincerity was obvious and inspiring.

On July 4, 2001, Bush gladly came to a Philadelphia barbecue and block party and spent several hours with the children, youth, families, and church volunteers associated with the local Big Brothers Big Sisters of America mentoring program for the children of prisoners that I had helped to develop and launch. On December 12, 2002, he returned to Philadelphia and met once again with those served and mentors in the program. In his 2003 State of the Union address he proposed a $150 million initiative to mobilize a hundred thousand mentors for prisoners' children. In May 2003 the federal Family and Youth Services Bureau announced the availability of funds and issued a request for applications for its "Mentoring Children of Prisoners Program." After nearly three years, this was the one major new program produced by the so-called Bush faith initiative.

In the months that followed the February 1999 meeting in Austin, Goldsmith, in his role as the campaign's senior domestic policy adviser, faxed me every paper on domestic issues, including but not limited to "faith initiatives," generated by ever-expanding cadres of campaign consultants and would-be advisers. My job, essentially, was to read the papers critically, both as a data-demanding social scientist and as a centrist Democrat with a skeptical but hopeful perspective on "compassionate conservatism." As time went on, I became more skeptical than hopeful. Among the things I wrote in the months before being asked to join the administration were an essay in which I expressed doubt whether "compassionate conservatism" would be translated into effective social policy and another criticizing the court majority in the case of *Bush* v. *Gore*.[11]

Bush was aware of my positions and often kidded me about being the in-house Democrat. My president-bestowed nickname, for the record, was "Big John," and—as he joked when he surprised me with a visit to my office on my birthday—the "big isn't for tall!" There was, indeed, a quasi-corporate culture to the White House staff, but the "CEO" was, more often than not, warm, relaxed, quick to joke and laugh, and quite respectful of all, including the most junior staff people. Meetings generally ran on time, but only generally. Staff got chewed out if they failed to turn off cell phones or made other irritating mistakes, but no heads ever rolled, at least not publicly. The president's nightly briefing book was prepared with care, but we got scolded every morning for failing to get things in on time.

By the same token, the administration's press communications were tightly controlled, but the weekly message meetings were large and improvisational, and they became so unscripted that they were an issue at the July 9, 2001, six-month senior staff retreat. The staff, like the president, was buttoned-down, but he often functioned more like an academic department chairman than a CEO, inviting brief but free-ranging discussions and hearing diverse views. He was subtle about letting staff know what he knew or suspected, and not infrequently seemed purposely to create circumstances that would test their honesty as well as their diplomacy.

For instance, on the day Bush announced the new drug czar, John Walters, we had an Oval Office pre-briefing before heading to the Rose Garden for the event. The president asked a junior staff person whether he was correct in understanding that as much as two-thirds of all illicit drugs is consumed by less than a quarter of all illicit drug users. The aide was caught off guard and mumbled an affirmative. The president then turned to me and asked, "Big John, that so?" He knew I had helped his father's administration with research on drug policy and that I had once been a fairly active student of criminal justice. He also knew—or so I suspect to this day—that the statistic he had cited was possibly way off. I replied that, while some such statistics are cited in the relevant research literatures, the data on which they are based are dated, so we really cannot say. He gave a little laugh, and out we went. As I told one reporter, being on the Bush senior staff was just like being in an academic department, with only three exceptions: the issues were mostly real, the people were usually nice, and the meetings normally started on time.

During the aforementioned July 4, 2001, block-party gathering with the children and families of prisoners in Philadelphia, the president engaged the crowd with unusual passion and warmth, even by his normal standards. They responded in kind. The event ran over timewise. The day's main press event, a speech at Independence Hall, awaited Bush. Despite the cloud cover, it was extremely hot and humid. The back of the president's open-collar blue shirt was soaked with sweat. A staff colleague advised me that we really needed to move him out in order to get him "hosed down back at the hotel" and rejoined by First Lady Laura Bush before the speech. The president picked up the pace, but in front of the church through which we were to exit for the motorcade back to the hotel there stood two male cooks and a huge pile of barbecued ribs. Conceding that the ribs looked good, the president was ready to accept my (public-interested, of course) suggestion that we eat as many as possible before departing; but the staff was getting a bit frantic, so we were hurried along.

Suddenly, however, the president paused. "C'mon," he said, "those guys have been doing hard work all day there. Can't eat, but we can say thanks." We walked over to take a picture with the two cooks. Bush lifted the table aside himself, squeezed us in behind it, and took several pictures with the men, pulling me by my super-sweat-soaked shirt into one shot. For senior staff, being in White House photos with the president, including, in my case, several in the Oval Office, is common. But that photo with Bush and the barbecue guys is the one that speaks loudest and speaks most about his core small-*d* democratic presidential character.

Why, then, I am often asked, has the administration made few major social policy efforts on behalf of the needy and neglected? I do not know, but there are at least two possibilities. One explanation relates back to presidential character. Veteran journalist Joe Klein contends that while Bush "used words like love and heart more than any other presidential candidate" he had ever seen, when "suffering became an abstraction—a budget item—Bush lost the sensitivity he had when he confronted poor people directly."[12] Another possibility is that, like most other recent White House teams, Bush and his team have few meaningful political incentives to develop detailed policy plans or worry about administrative matters related to anything other than their one or two top priorities.

The Modern President: Agenda-Setter-in-Chief

As an in-house policy wonk I might have been expected to covet policy and administrative details more than most; and, after all, one thing that sold me on doing the job I did at all was the chance to help produce a substantive report on the extent to which selected federal agencies were following extant laws governing participation by religious organizations in the grant-making process as well as cognate legislatively mandated protocols for program performance and evaluation.[13] Still, I was struck by how, for example, Medicare reform issues would rapidly give way to a narrower focus on prescription drug plans or arguments favoring a patients' bill of rights. I was not surprised, therefore, when in April 2003 the administration produced an eleven-page Medicare reform blueprint and sent it to Capitol Hill.[14]

After its health care policy debacle the Clinton administration had begun framing issues in the broadest possible terms such that multi-faceted policies on which, in fact, it had detailed plans were nonetheless presented for public consumption as representing one simple proposal (for example, an enormously detailed crime bill sold as "a hundred thousand cops"), and an almost daily series of symbolic initiatives were developed and communicated with gusto (for example, uniforms for public school children). As Klein has argued, some of the Clinton administration's greatest domestic policy victories, most especially increased spending on programs that benefit the working poor, were "invisible, in fact, hidden in the massive, incomprehensible budget 'reconciliation' packages negotiated each fall."[15] A former Bush aide quoted by Charles O. Jones in this volume states that the Bush administration was basically "un-Clinton." In many respects, I suppose, it most certainly was and is, but as I have come to believe, no modern presidency can do other than favor agenda setting and flexible public communications over specific legislative and administrative initiatives on most issues.

Why? Start with the political incentives faced by modern presidents. Gary C. Jacobson suggests that more than two years into the Bush presidency the electorate was "as divided and polarized" as it was in 2000. I have every confidence in Jacobson's sophisticated analysis, but I would surmise that the public was not only as divided and polarized, but also as inattentive to policy details, as ever. Most citizens, even among the segment of the public that is attentive, know very little, and care even less, about legislative process. Most news organizations, even the elite ones, do not delve very deeply into the competing perspectives and empirical evidence surrounding any given policy pronouncement, and only a few reporters know a thing about the most basic aspects of intergovernmental relations and public administration. Yet nearly everybody knows and reports whether the president has "said something" about a given topic and whether the administration is "for" a "patients' bill of rights" or whatever. Likewise, hardly anybody knows whether, or how, or why the administration has, in turn, engaged "in detailed negotiations—with the departments, the Hill, and major interest groups—that will produce the administration's proposals and that will clarify the administration's bargaining positions as the proposals move through the legislative process" into public law and administrative action.[16]

The concept that best captures how the presidency has evolved since the days before Franklin D. Roosevelt (F.D.R.) into the institution Bush leads today is that of the modern presidency. Different presidency scholars have emphasized different features, but most would agree that, by "contrast with the traditional (pre-F.D.R.) presidency, the modern president is expected" to "propose legislation and make budget recommendations to Congress, and secure congressional endorsement of his proposals"; be "active in defending and advancing America's interests abroad"; be "a visible national leader, projecting personality and ideas through the media"; and command "the political and national resources to meet these expectations."[17]

Arguably, the modern presidency's signature institutional manifestation was the Executive Reorganization Act of 1939 and the concomitant Executive Order 8248, which created the EOP. The Bureau of the Budget (forerunner of the Office of Management and Budget) and many other agencies were placed within the EOP, not only to serve the traditional presidency's core administrative functions (which, by the 1930s, included new executive branch activities and growing numbers of activities performed by the cabinet and other federal agencies), but also the modern presidency's legislative leadership priorities (which, by the early 1970s, had become so significant that the Nixon White House tried, but failed, to use EOP entities, in conjunction with new political appointees in the cabinet and other agencies, to gain near-complete political control over domestic bureaucracies).[18]

Simply stated, what my EOP tenure dramatized for me was that, in this day of multiple twenty-four-hour-news channels and the Internet, it is truer than ever before that the modern presidency, as Greenstein succinctly states, is about "setting the nation's policy agenda." Modern presidents have fewer and fewer incentives to step beyond symbolic politics and agenda setting to detailed legislative proposals and administrative strategies. Today "a president cannot wait for the perfect proposal any more than a surfer can wait for the perfect wave."[19] Given the complex realities of intergovernmental relations and the rise of so-called government by proxy, a president cannot, in all but the rarest of cases, have much real impact on how or how well most domestic policies and social programs are administered.[20]

Obviously, while presidents must have ideas and policies for everything, it would be impossible, even in periods of unified party government and relatively minor partisan polarization in Congress, for presidents and their administrations to translate every policy idea into legislative language, every favored bill into law, and all law into effective administrative action. According to John Kingdon, "The president may be able to dominate and even determine the policy agenda, but is unable to dominate the alternatives that are seriously considered, and is unable to determine the final outcome."[21] Precisely because of the polarized, partisan character of legislative politics as analyzed by Jones and Jacobson and by John C. Fortier and Norman J. Ornstein in this volume, why would any administration invest scarce White House resources on any save its few very top policy priorities?

Take, for example, the Bush faith initiative. During the 2000 presidential campaign Bush called for expanding and implementing the so-called charitable choice laws that had been enacted under President Clinton. The bipartisan laws were intended to ensure that community-serving religious organizations could apply to administer federal social service delivery programs on exactly the same basis as all other nonprofit organizations. Charitable choice first appeared as a provision (Section 104) of the Personal Responsibility and Work Opportunity Reconciliation Act of 1996, better known as the federal welfare reform law. A charitable choice provision was added to the Community Services Block Grant program when it was reauthorized in 1998. In 2000 another charitable choice provision was added to the Substance Abuse Prevention and Treatment Block Grant and Projects for Assistance in Transition from Homelessness program.

In nearly two dozen public statements and over a dozen public events during the administration's first eight months, Bush strongly promoted faith initiatives. He called for expanding and implementing charitable choice laws and often explicitly embraced the four key principles of charitable choice.[22] First, faith-based providers that compete for public funds should be subjected to the same accountability standards as all other nonprofit organizations, no more, no less. Second, government may not require a religious provider to remove religious art, icons, scripture, or other symbols in order to compete for public funds. Third, religious organizations operate under the civil rights laws, including Titles VI and VII of the 1964 Civil Rights Act and other laws and court decisions affording faith-based organizations with fewer than fifteen employees a broad but not unlimited right, and those with more than fifteen employees a narrow but not trivial right, to take religion into account in making hiring decisions (the so-called ministerial exemption). Fourth, diverse partnerships between government and religious institutions are permissible, but no government funding can be diverted to any inherently religious activities such as worship, sectarian instruction, or proselytizing.[23]

I had been given ample reason to expect that a charitable choice bill would be crafted by the administration, but only after the aforementioned report on extant federal grant-making processes was completed and only after key Senate Democrats had been persuaded that the administration would not instead endorse measures that would promote proselytizing with public funds, unfettered hiring discrimination, or other constitutionally suspect, administratively unworkable, or politically infeasible ideas. As several published accounts have reported, after House Republicans drafted a bill prominently featuring such measures, any chance of expanding or implementing charitable choice, save by the ultimately unsustainable use of executive orders, was lost.[24]

The bill passed the House on July 19, 2001, on a virtual party line vote (with fifteen Democrats plus all Republicans present voting in favor) and was pronounced dead on arrival by Senate Democrats. On July 26, 2001, we brought Democratic Senator Joseph Lieberman, long a supporter of charitable choice, into the Oval Office. The president and Lieberman, joined by Republican Senator Rick Santorum, another respected leader on the issue, agreed to support a bill that would track closely with the 1996 charitable choice law. My staff and I worked with the two senators' staffs on this effort throughout the summer. But rather than draft a fresh bipartisan bill unburdened by the more controversial features of the House bill, some senior staff wanted to back off charitable choice legislation altogether in favor of a "communities of character" initiative.

Of course September 11 put almost everything other than the war on terror and homeland security on the back burner for months. From January 2002 through June 2003 Bush made fewer than a dozen statements, and attended only a half-dozen events, promoting faith initiatives. In 2003 Congress passed an administration-backed bill to encourage charitable giving. It was a decent little bill, but a far cry from the president's initial call for making tens of billions of dollars in tax credits available to the over 80 million taxpayers who do not itemize deductions on their tax returns. The bill contained no charitable choice provisions at all.

Just to be clear, in my view the OFBCI continued to do important and valuable work under my super-able successor, James Towey, most especially with regard to supplying faith-based and community organizations with timely information about how best to access public support for their civic good works. Likewise, the volunteerism and other "compassion agenda" alternatives to faith initiatives that the administration went on to develop after September 11 are worthwhile. In particular, the USA Freedom Corps, under the strong direction of Bush's former chief domestic policy counsel, John M. Bridgeland, showed early signs of success in mobilizing volunteers to assist schools and was also responsible for launching the aforementioned program for mentoring the children of prisoners. The point is simply that faith initiatives got on the president's policy agenda and remained there without concerted effort to draft proposals that could pass and, once passed, effect administrative and funding changes in keeping with the president's public positions on the issue.

A concomitant point is that among the substitute agenda items several were supported by the administration, but without accompanying legislative or administrative exertions. For instance, on day one of the faith initiative, kicking off the self-same event at which the president signed the executive orders establishing the OFBCI, Bush announced that he was nominating Stephen Goldsmith to join the board of the Corporation for National and Community Service (CNCS). The idea was that CNCS would work in tandem with the OFBCI and would prove vital in supplying technical assistance to the faith-based and other community groups seeking support under charitable choice laws. Goldsmith became CNCS chairman, but CNCS was further defunded by House Republicans, even as the agency was heralded yet again as a major pillar of the administration's new volunteer mobilization initiatives.

Viewed from the outside, not the inside, following September 11 the administration faced mounting congressional and public pressures to address homeland security challenges. At first President Bush rebuffed calls by Lieberman and others to create a new "Department of Homeland Defense." Instead, by executive order he created within the EOP a new Office of Homeland Security. By spring 2002 the office had released a homeland security blueprint, and, predictably, Congress began badgering the White House for more details. In particular, congressional leaders insisted that Director Tom Ridge testify before Congress about how homeland security budgetary priorities were to be set by the White House in relation to the Department of Justice and other key agencies. The administration refused, citing Ridge's status as a senior presidential adviser not confirmed by the Senate.[25]

But, as became more obvious with each press conference, even to administer its own general homeland security strategy Ridge's office would need to coordinate personnel and budgets across scores of agencies. The homeland security devil, like the faith initiatives devil, was in the details. After spending nearly nine months defending the position that no new department was necessary, the White House reversed itself on June 6, 2002. It proposed the creation of an umbrella-level cabinet bureaucracy with nearly 170,000 employees (third behind Defense and Veterans Affairs) and a total of about $40 billion in budgets (fourth behind Defense, Health and Human Services, and Education). The proposal passed late in 2002, but nobody, not even Director Ridge himself, pretended that what one report termed "Bush's Swift, Sweeping Plan" could be implemented anytime soon or that the new department had been conceived with all due regard for limiting, rather than multiplying, administrative problems, both present and future.[26]

In sum, my experiences inside the Bush presidency, in conjunction with reflections on other modern presidencies from F.D.R.'s to Clinton's, caused me to recognize how the political and institutional incentives to spend presidential time, staff, and other scarce administration resources on stepping beyond broad agenda setting to detailed legislation and (last and least) effective administration seem to have grown progressively weaker over the past several decades. Or, to state the same point in the affirmative and in the somewhat more technical language of Bryan Jones and colleagues, early "in the policy process, when proposals struggle to gain agenda access, cognitive costs are high but transaction costs are low. The scheduling of a policy topic for a hearing is indicative that policymakers are taking the topic seriously—the topic has accessed the policy or governmental agenda."[27] Whether what appears to be an important institutional trend is real—whether, alas, the next incumbents of the modern presidency will behave ever more as agenda-setters-in-chief—remains to be seen.

The Permanent Campaign: Courting Valence Voters

Hugh Heclo suggests in this volume that Bush's "political ethos" needs to be understood in the context of media-induced pressures and contemporary campaign tactics that have institutionalized negative advertising and strident smash-mouth politics. Heclo's argument is well made and well taken. But while the permanent campaign invites smash-mouth politics, it also involves large doses of mealy-mouthed politics and a strong propensity to adopt slogans and address issues in abstract ways that offend nobody save, perhaps, detail-oriented public policy wonks and results-oriented public administration experts.

Until the dawn of mass electronic communications media, politicians could often get away with saying one thing in public in one place while adopting a distinctly different position, or at least a distinctly different tone, in another. Today, however, the challenge is how to say things in a way that can be interpreted favorably by people with distinct views on a given issue. Sometimes that is impossible. For example, in mid-2003 the administration tried unsuccessfully to deflect criticism of its failure to support a child tax credit proposal.[28] But, to a degree that surprised me, politicians at both ends of Pennsylvania Avenue, and in both parties, have become masters of the art, and often do say things in ways that excite ideological or partisan supporters without alienating others.

I should not have been so surprised. My late Princeton University colleague Donald E. Stokes, a founding father of national election studies, had long since taught me that contemporary American politics involves a mix of what he termed position issues and valence issues. In fact, we co-authored an article on the subject in 1992, and I returned to it in an essay written in his honor in 1996.[29]

Simply defined, a position issue is a policy question that divides the electorate on which rival parties or candidates reach out for the support of the people by taking different positions—an issue such as slavery, high tariffs, abortion, and so on. But many, perhaps most, issues that powerfully interest people do not present even two alternative positions that divide the parties and candidates on the one hand and the electorate on the other. There are issues on which voters distinguish parties and candidates not by their real or perceived differences in position on policy questions, but by the degree to which they are linked in the voters' minds with conditions, goals, or symbols that are almost universally approved or disapproved by the electorate. These are called valence issues.

The economy is a prime example of a valence issue—everybody favors prosperity; nobody is for depression—and so are such issues as political corruption, irresolute leadership, unpatriotic beliefs, weak national defense, wasted tax dollars, and failure itself. In valence politics and campaigns, parties and candidates mount their appeals by choosing from a large set of potential valence issues those on which their identification with positive ideas and symbols and their opponents' identification with negative ones will be most to their advantage.

In the modern presidency the permanent campaign is run almost entirely as a valence campaign, and over the past several decades the EOP has evolved accordingly. Like the Clinton administration before it, the Bush administration has adapted to the relative efficacy and importance of valence issues over position issues, and the dramatic results of the midterm 2002 congressional elections, including the president's campaign messages about defeating terrorism, were all of a piece with this reality. As one magazine phrased it, "Bush was the driving force behind the Republican breeze that blew across the country in 2002."[30]

As political scientists Marc J. Hetherington and Michael Nelson have concluded, "Bush's personal popularity affected the voting for Republican congressional candidates."[31] Many speeches that Bush made on behalf of Republican office seekers in 2002 were centrally concerned with the war against terrorism. News stories stated that "some GOP candidates worked with the White House to challenge the patriotism of Democrats who contested details of Bush's homeland security department plan."[32] As that example shows, valence appeals and smash-mouth politics can sometimes go together and prove quite effective in courting voters.

Jacobson concludes that Bush's post–September 11 popularity has "yet to show any lasting effect on partisan attitudes, the partisan base, or the degree of polarization in the electorate." I am sure that my fellow academic is right, but tell it to the Democratic leaders who, three years into the Bush presidency, saw little hope at countering the political appeal of the small-*d* democrat from Texas, and all but said so in public.[33]

Notes

Chapter 1: The Leadership Style of George W. Bush

1. Fred I. Greenstein, *The Presidential Difference: Leadership Style from FDR to Clinton* (New York: Free Press, 2000.)
2. The most balanced biography of Bush is Bill Minutaglio, *First Son: George W. Bush and the Bush Family Dynasty* (New York: Times Books, 1999). See also Elizabeth Mitchell, *Revenge of the Bush Dynasty* (New York: Hyperion, 2000). During the 2000 presidential campaign there were a number of useful investigative reports on Bush's life. One of the best was the *Washington Post* series "The Life and Times of George W. Bush," which appeared in six parts in July 2000.
3. George W. Bush, *A Charge to Keep: My Journey to the White House* (New York: HarperCollins, 1999), 182.
4. A manner that is engagingly captured in the 2002 HBO documentary *Journeys With George.*
5. Bush, *A Charge to Keep,* 180.
6. Minutaglio, *First Son,* 295–303.
7. Alan C. Miller and Judy Pasternak, "Records Show Bush's Focus on Big Picture," *Los Angeles Times,* August 2, 2000.
8. For an official elaboration see Marvin Olasky, *Compassionate Conservatism: What It Is, What It Does, and How It Can Transform America* (New York: Free Press, 2000).
9. Commission on Presidential Debates, Second Bush-Gore Presidential Debate, October 11, 2000, http://www.debates.org/pages/debhis2000.html, 2.

10. George W. Bush, "Bush's Remarks on the End of the Race," *New York Times*, December 14, 2000.
11. For a succinct summary of this event see *Facts on File World News Digest Yearbook, 2001* (New York: Facts on File News Services, 2002), 304.
12. David S. Broder, "The Reticent President," *Washington Post*, April 22, 2001.
13. Dana Milbank, "With Fanfare, Bush Signs Education Bill: President, Lawmakers Hit 3 States in 12 Hours to Tout Biggest Schools Change Since '65," *Washington Post*, January 9, 2002.
14. Leo Weiland, "Bush's New Image," *Frankfurter Allegemeine* (English language edition), October 20, 2001.
15. A list of the post–September 11 NSC meetings can be found in the index of Bob Woodward's *Bush at War* (New York: Simon and Schuster, 2002), 367. In the early period of the Iraq War, Bush was receiving three hours a day of briefings. Elisabeth Bumiller, "President, No Matter Where, Keeps Battlefield Close," *New York Times*, March 30, 2003. See also Judy Keene and Laurence McQullan, "Bush Dives into Details of Iraq Conflict," *USA Today*, March 21, 2003.
16. Daniel Goleman, *Emotional Intelligence* (New York: Bantam, 1995). Goleman cites as his source Peter Salovey and John D. Mayer, "Emotional Intelligence," *Imagination, Cognition, and Personality* 9 (1990), 185–211.
17. Woodward, *Bush at War*, 158.
18. "Interview of President Bush by Tom Brokaw, NBC," April 14, 2003, http:// www.talkingproud.us/EditorChoice04603.html.
19. Stephen Thomma, "Growing on the Job," *Miami Herald*, December 9, 2001.
20. "President Bush, Prime Minister Blair Hold Press Availability," March 27, 2003, http://www.whitehouse.gov/news/releases/2003/03/20030327-3.html.
21. Woodward, *Bush at War*, 177, 332–34.
22. Dwight D. Eisenhower, Columbia University Oral History Interview, July 20, 1967, uncorrected transcript. The last sentence of the quotation was unaccountably omitted in the corrected final transcript. The classic discussion of the importance of rigorous debate in presidential adviser systems is Alexander L. George, "The Case for Multiple Advocacy in Making Foreign Policy," *American Political Science Review* 66 (1972), 751–85.

Chapter 2: The Political Ethos of George W. Bush

1. Quoted in Woodward, *Bush at War*, 145–46.
2. Speech presented at the National Religious Broadcasters' Convention, Nashville, Tennessee, February 10, 2003.
3. Quoted in James C. Humes, *Confessions of a White House Ghostwriter* (Washington, D.C.: Regnery Publishing, 1997), 168.
4. Minutaglio, *First Son*, 145.
5. Ibid., 98.

6. In his father's 1988 campaign biography George W. Bush was quoted as telling a close friend, "Those were the sternest words to me, even though he said them in a very calm way. . . . When you love a person and he loves you, those are the harshest words someone can utter. . . . He has never been the type of person to put our failures in the context of his life and all that he has achieved. It's our failures in the context of our *own* lives." Quoted in George Bush with Doug Wead, *Man of Integrity* (Eugene, Ore.: Harvest House, 1988), 118.

7. In the early 1930s George Bush's grandfather, George Herbert Walker of Brown Brothers Harriman, had been one of the group of twelve leading businessmen who had met privately with New York Governor Franklin D. Roosevelt to press him to run for the presidency.

8. Quoted in Minutaglio, *First Son*, 120.

9. George Bush's athletic gifts at Andover and Yale were only a small piece of the family's commitment to sports. Prescott Bush's father, Samuel, the industrialist and adviser to President Herbert Hoover, was credited with initiating and coaching the Ohio State University football program. On the maternal side, the sporting Walker clan eventually sponsored the Walker Cup in golf and assisted with the creation of Madison Square Garden, the Belmont Race Track, and the New York Mets.

10. Two books that describe and usefully bracket this period of development are Anthony King, ed., *The New American Political System* (Washington, D.C.: AEI, 1978), and Norman Ornstein and Thomas Mann, eds., *The Permanent Campaign and Its Future* (Washington, D.C.: AEI and Brookings, 2000).

11. Elizabeth Mitchell, *W: Revenge of the Bush Dynasty* (New York: Hyperion, 2000), 87.

12. The paper and the campaign are described in Mitchell, *W*, 91–95.

13. Quoted in Minutaglio, *First Son*, 178.

14. Lou Dsubose, Jan Reid, and Carl M. Cannon, *Boy Genius: Karl Rove, the Brains Behind the Remarkable Political Triumph of George W. Bush* (New York: Public Affairs Reports, 2003), 17.

15. Elizabeth Mitchell, *W*, 54 ff.

16. As in military intelligence on the national level, here the term *essential* corresponds to those elements of information a commander requires to act responsibly.

17. *National Review,* December 1, 1964, 1053–55.

18. Minutaglio, *First Son*, 197–98.

19. Stephen Skowronek, "The Orthodox Innovator in Wartime," paper prepared for the CIDE conference American Politics in a New Millennium, Mexico City, April 26–28, 2002.

20. "Remarks by the President on His Agenda," press release issued by the Office of the Press Secretary, August, 3, 2001, available at http://www.whitehouse.gov/news/releases/2001/08.

21. Minutaglio, *First Son,* 9 and 286.
22. Bush's feelings were expressed in publicity materials produced by the National Guard. Cf. Mitchell, *W,* 130, and Minutaglio, *First Son,* 120.
23. J. H. Hatfield, *Fortunate Son* (New York: Soft Skull Press, 2001), 71.
24. Minutaglio, *First Son,* 210.
25. George W. Bush, televised speech to the nation, March 17, 2003.
26. George W. Bush, commencement address delivered at the United States Military Academy, West Point, New York, June 1, 2002.
27. Dick Cheney, television interview on *Meet the Press,* March 16, 2003.
28. Southern voters for James Polk offered the strongest exception to this rule in 1844. William Dusinberre, *Slavemaster President: The Double Career of James Polk* (New York: Oxford University Press, 2003).
29. Buber was contrasting the leadership of Theodor Herzl and Ahad Ha'am as they debated the founding of a Jewish state in the Middle East. Quoted in Maurice Friedman, *Martin Buber's Life and Work: The Early Years 1878–1923* (New York: E. P. Dutton, 1981), 73.

Chapter 3: The Bush White House in Comparative Perspective

I am grateful for the comments and suggestions of Fred I. Greenstein, Henry Tom, Colin Campbell, Kathryn Dunn Tenpas, and Charles E. Walcott.

1. The emphasis here is on the White House Office (WHO) and the policy staffs lodged in the larger Executive Office of the President. Several of the latter (e.g., the staffs of the National Security Council, National Economic Council, and Office of Homeland Security) are directed by presidential assistants housed in the WHO who help to link the presidency to associated cabinet councils.

   My focus on *systematic* factors is based on the distinction between the systematic and the nonsystematic components of political phenomena. "Systematic" elements are predictable and recurring. Looking for the impact of systematic factors, for example, would lead one to expect that the same variables will influence the activities of presidents or the structuring of White Houses. In contrast, a view of individual presidents as unique would emphasize the influence of nonsystematic factors. See, for example, Gary King, Robert O. Heohane, and Sidney Verba, *Designing Social Inquiry: Scientific Inference in Qualitative Research* (Princeton, N.J.: Princeton University Press, 1994), esp. 55–63, 79–82.
2. Dwight D. Eisenhower, *The White House Years: Mandate for Change, 1953–65* (New York: Doubleday, 1963), 114, quoted in John Burke, *The Institutional Presidency: Organizing and Managing the White House from FDR to Clinton,* 2nd ed. (Baltimore: Johns Hopkins University Press, 2000), 64.
3. Charles E. Walcott and Karen M. Hult, *Governing the White House: From Hoover through LBJ* (Lawrence, Kan.: University Press of Kansas, 1995), 194.

4. Vice President Cheney served as President Gerald Ford's chief of staff; in the Nixon White House, he was a deputy to presidential counselor Donald Rumsfeld. For more on partisan learning generally, see Walcott and Hult, *Governing the White House;* Karen M. Hult and Charles E. Walcott, *Empowering the White House: Governance under Nixon, Ford, and Carter* (Lawrence, Kan.: University Press of Kansas, in press).

5. For further discussion of a "standard model" of White House organization see Hult and Walcott, *Empowering the White House,* Chap. 2; Charles E. Walcott and Karen M. Hult, "The Bush White House and Cabinet System," in *Considering the Bush Presidency,* ed. Mark J. Rozell and Gary L. Gregg (New York: Oxford University Press, 2003).

6. Sherman Adams did not have the formal title chief of staff, but he had the same authority and responsibilities as later chiefs. The first White House aide with the title of chief of staff was H. R. Haldeman, who served under Richard Nixon; see, for example, H. R. Haldeman with Joseph DiMona, *The Ends of Power* (New York: Times Books, 1978), 50; Melvin Small, *The Presidency of Richard Nixon* (Lawrence, Kan.: University Press of Kansas, 1999), 43–50.

7. As the 2000 election approached, for instance, many in the Washington establishment sought to avoid a repetition of the early days of the Clinton administration. Think tanks—from the Brookings Institution through the American Enterprise Institute to the Heritage Foundation—sponsored seminars and produced books and articles on presidential transitions and White House organization. An example of the kind of advice that was offered can be found in Martha Joynt Kumar and Terry Sullivan, eds., *The White House World: Transitions, Organization, and Office Operations* (College Station, Tex.: Texas A&M University Press, 2003).

8. Such an approach is consistent with that of many "rational choice institutionalists." See, for example, Terry M. Moe, "The Politicized Presidency," in *The New Direction in American Politics,* ed. John E. Chubb and Paul E. Peterson (Washington, D.C.: Brookings Institution, 1985); Thomas J. Weko, *The Politicizing Presidency: The White House Personnel Office, 1948–1994* (Lawrence, Kan.: University Press of Kansas, 1995); Andrew Rudalevige, *Managing the President's Program: Presidential Leadership and Legislative Policy Formulation* (Princeton, N.J.: Princeton University Press, 2002). Probing for systematic influences on White Houses is a strategy for isolating presidential idiosyncrasy (or "nonsystematic variance"); see James Farr's argument for starting with assumptions about "rational" individuals in "Resituating Explanation," in *Idioms of Inquiry: Critique and Renewal in Political Science,* ed. Terence Ball (Albany: SUNY Press, 1987), 52 ff.

9. Charles E. Walcott, Shirley Anne Warshaw, and Stephen J. Wayne, "The Chief of Staff," *Presidential Studies Quarterly* 31 (September 2001): 467. See also Samuel Kernell and Samuel L. Popkin, eds., *Chief of Staff: Twenty-Five Years of Managing the Presidency* (Berkeley: University of California Press, 1986).

10. See, for example, Woodward, *Bush at War,* 255.

11. Not everyone agrees that the Reagan troika (or the initial Bush arrangements) was a variation of the standard model. Colin Campbell, for instance, considers the first-term Reagan White House to have been organized in a "modified spokes-in-a-wheel pattern"; see his *Managing the Presidency: Carter, Reagan, and the Search for Executive Harmony* (Pittsburgh: University of Pittsburgh Press, 1986), 93 ff. Yet the three senior staffers occupied the top of an overall White House hierarchy, and they were collectively responsible for coordinating and overseeing the many specialized units and presidential aides. Moreover, much like Chief of Staff Andrew Card in the Bush White House, Chief of Staff James Baker III was at the center of the information and people that flowed in and out of the Oval Office.

12. Reporter Dana Milbank, for example, examined the ways that Card and Rove tried from the start "to make strategy everybody's concern in the White House." Among the mechanisms for accomplishing this were the "Strategery Group," biweekly deputies' meetings held to "generate ideas," and the Office of Strategic Initiatives. See Dana Milbank, "Serious 'Strategery': As Rove Launches Elaborate Political Effort, Some See a Nascent Clintonian 'War Room,'" *Washington Post,* April 22, 2001, A1.

13. See, for instance, Corey Cook, "The Permanence of the 'Permanent Campaign': George W. Bush's Public Presidency," *Presidential Studies Quarterly* 32 (December 2002): 753–64; Hugh Heclo, "Campaigning and Governing: A Conspectus," in *The Permanent Campaign and Its Future,* ed. Norman Ornstein and Thomas Mann (Washington, D.C.: American Enterprise Institute and the Brookings Institution, 2000); Karen M. Hult, "Strengthening Presidential Decision-Making Capacity," *Presidential Studies Quarterly* 30 (March 2000): 27–46.

14. John F. Harris and Dan Balz, "A Question of Capital," *Washington Post,* April 29, 2001, A6. On the similarities with past chief of staff operations see, for example, Walcott, Warshaw, and Wayne, "The Chief of Staff."

15. Mike Allen and Alan Sipress, "Attacks Refocus White House on How to Fight Terrorism," *Washington Post,* September 26, 2001, A3.

16. Carl M. Cannon and Alexis Simendinger, "The Evolution of Karl Rove," *National Journal,* April 27, 2002, 1214.

17. Mike Allen, "Hughes to Sign on with GOP: Contract with Departing Aide Allows Continued Advice to Bush," *Washington Post,* July 5, 2002, A19. Fleischer's departure in the summer of 2003 introduced additional uncertainty; he was replaced by his deputy, Scott McClellan.

18. Elisabeth Bumiller, "White House Letter: Still Advising, from Afar and Near," *New York Times,* October 21, 2002, A12.

19. For example, Richard L. Berke and David E. Sanger, "Some in Administration Grumble as Aide's Role Seems to Expand," *New York Times,* May 13, 2002, A1; Dana Milbank, "Karl Rove, Adding to His To-Do List," *Washington Post,* June

25, 2002, A17; Adam Nagourney, "Shift of Power to the White House Reshapes Political Landscape," *New York Times,* December 22, 2002, A1; Mike Allen, "Bush Fills Key Slots with Young Loyalists," *Washington Post,* May 29, 2003, A1.

20. Bradley H. Patterson, Jr., *The Ring of Power: The White House Staff and Its Expanding Role in Government* (New York: Basic Books, 1988), 272.

21. Cf. Bradley H. Patterson, Jr., *The White House Staff: Inside the West Wing and Beyond* (Washington, D.C.: Brookings Institution, 2000), 263 ff.

22. Executive Order (EO) 13199. A companion order (EO 13198) established units in five executive-branch agencies and charged them with easing participation by such organizations in delivering federal social services.

23. Kathryn Dunn Tenpas, "Can an Office Change a Country? The White House Office of Faith-Based and Community Initiatives, a Year in Review," report prepared for the Pew Forum on Religion and Public Life, updated October 5, 2002, http://pewforum.org/events/022002/Tenpas.pdf.

24. Ibid., 7.

25. Ibid., 12.

26. Towey is a deputy assistant to the president; DiIulio had been an assistant to the president. Jonathan Peterson, "Faith-Based Initiative Gains Unusual Leader," *Los Angeles Times,* February 2, 2002, A12.

27. For an overview of these administrative efforts see, for example, Linda Feldman, "Faith-Based Initiatives Quietly Lunge Forward," *Christian Science Monitor,* February 6, 2003, 2. The executive orders are EO 13279 and EO 13280. On the involvement of the Office of Faith-Based and Community Initiatives (OFBCI) in outreach see Tenpas, "Can an Office Change a Country?"

28. David B. Cohen and Alethia H. Cook, "Institutional Redesign: Terrorism, Punctuated Equilibrium, and the Evolution of Homeland Security in the United States," paper presented at the 2002 Annual Meeting of the American Political Science Association, Boston, August 29–September 1, 2002, 12.

29. See William W. Newman, "Reorganizing for National Security and Homeland Security," *Public Administration Review* 62 (September 2002): 129–31. The Office of Homeland Security (OHS) was created by EO 13228, signed on October 8, 2001. The Homeland Security Council was comprised of the secretaries of the treasury, defense, health and human services, and transportation; the attorney general; the directors of the Office of Management and Budget, the CIA, the FBI, and the Federal Emergency Management Administration; and the chiefs of staff to Bush and Cheney. Cf. David B. Cohen, Chris J. Dolan, and Jerel A. Rosati, "A Place at the Table: The Emerging Policy Roles of the White House Chief of Staff," *Congress and the Presidency* 29 (Autumn 2002), 131–32; Allen and Sipress, "Attacks Refocus White House."

30. Cohen and Cook, "Institutional Redesign," 15.

31. Section 3, EO 13284, signed January 23, 2003.

32. Homeland Security Presidential Directive/HSPD-5, February 28, 2003,

http://www.whitehouse.gov/news/releases/2003/02/print/20030228-9.html (accessed March 6, 2003). Sections (4) and (11) focus on the secretary of the Department of Homeland Security (DHS) and the presidential assistant for homeland security, respectively.

33. See, for example, Hult and Walcott, *Empowering the White House,* Chap. 2.

34. Under Carter the cabinet feature was removed from the domestic policy arrangements, and the administration relied on a Domestic Policy Staff instead of the Domestic Council it inherited from the Nixon and Ford years. See Hult and Walcott, *Empowering the White House,* Chap. 7.

35. See, for instance, *U.S. Government Manual,* 2002–3, 100–101. The Domestic Policy Council was established by EO 12859, signed on August 16, 1993; the National Economic Council was created by EO 12835, signed on January 25, 1993.

36. Fred I. Greenstein and Richard H. Immerman, "Effective National Security Advising: Recovering the Eisenhower Legacy," *Political Science Quarterly* 115, no. 1 (2000): 335–45; Cohen, Dolan, and Rosati, "A Place at the Table."

37. Ivo H. Daalder and I. M. Destler, How Operational and Visible an NSC? Brookings Institution, February 23, 2001, http://www.brook.edu/views/op-ed/Daalder/20010223.htm (accessed April 15, 2002). Even so, Daalder and Destler note that the staff remained "larger than any NSC staff prior to 1996." Nor is it unusual for an administration to try to cut the NSC staff; both Ford and Carter, for instance, sought to downsize it (Hult and Walcott, *Empowering the White House,* Chap. 7). In the Bush administration, Vice President Cheney "assembled a staff of 14 foreign policy specialists, creating what officials say amounts to a mini-National Security Council [staff]" (Glenn Kessler and Peter Slevin, "Cheney Is Fulcrum of Foreign Policy: In Interagency Fights, His Views Often Prevail," *Washington Post,* October 13, 2002, A1).

38. Tom Raum, "Bush Creating New White House Post," *Salon,* January 16, 2001, http://www.salon.com/politics/wire/2001/01/16/security_post/print.html (accessed January 17, 2001).

39. Daalder and Destler, "How Operational and Visible an NSC?"

40. It is not unusual for the secretary of state and the NSA to have a good relationship. Just as Rice and Powell have had good relations with each other, "reasonably cordial and constructive relations between the [NSA] and the secretary of state have been the rule rather than the exception for both the [H. W.] Bush and the Clinton administrations" (Alexander L. George and Eric K. Stern, "Harnessing Conflict in Foreign Policy Making: From Devil's to Multiple Advocacy," *Presidential Studies Quarterly* 32 [September 2002]: 498).

41. Jack R. Binns, "Weighing Bush's Foreign Policy," *The Forum* 1, no. 1, article 3 (2002) http://www.bepress.com/forum/vol1/is (accessed November 20, 2002); Jane Perlez, "Bush Team's Counsel Is Divided on Foreign Policy," *New York*

Times, March 27, 2001, A1. Conflicts among national security officials became public in part due to key players' ties to conservative writers and think tanks outside the administration and to the former President Bush and his national security assistant, Brent Scowcroft. The ideological divide permeated the higher levels of both departments as well as the vice president's staff, expanding the numbers of potential "anonymous" sources.

42. Dana Milbank and Bradley Graham, "With Crisis, More Fluid Style at White House," *Washington Post,* October 10, 2001, A4.

43. Cohen, Dolan, and Rosati, "A Place at the Table," 131–32; Allen and Sipress, "Attacks Refocus White House"; Woodward, *Bush at War.*

44. On the Kennedy administration's handling of the Cuban Missile Crisis see, for example, Graham Allison and Philip Zelikow, *Essence of Decision: Explaining the Cuban Missile Crisis,* 2nd ed. (New York: Addison Wesley Longman, 1990); Ernest R. May, Timothy Naftali, and Philip D. Zelikow, eds., *The Presidential Recordings: John F. Kennedy, the Great Crises* (New York: Norton, 2001).

45. See, for example, Dana Milbank, "Who's Pulling the Foreign Policy Strings?" *Washington Post,* May 14, 2002, A19. Milbank's answer was Brent Scowcroft, representing the "foreign policy establishment," and Richard Perle, "the intellectual guru of the hard-line neoconservative movement in foreign policy."

46. Morton Abramowitz, "Foreign Policy Infight . . . ," *Washington Post,* August 19, 2002, A13. On disagreements over Middle East policy see Todd S. Purdum, "Bush Mideast Policy Delayed by Staff Debate," *New York Times,* June 22, 2002, A6; Martin Indyk, "A White House in Search of a Policy," *New York Times,* August 11, 2002, section 4, 13.

47. On publicized disagreements over Iraq see, for example, Christopher Marquis, "Bush Officials Differ on Ways to Force Out Iraqi Leader," *New York Times,* June 19, 2002, A7; Ivo H. Daalder and James M. Lindsay, "It's Hawk v. Hawk in the Bush Administration," *Washington Post,* October 27, 2002, B3; Doyle McManus, "The World Casts a Critical Eye at Bush's Style of Diplomacy," *Los Angeles Times,* March 3, 2003, A1; John B. Judis, "Why Iraq?" *The American Prospect,* March 2003, 12. On the factions within the administration see, for example, Steven R. Weisman, "Division in Past Bush White House Echoes in Current Struggles," *New York Times,* November 24, 2002, A18; McManus, "The World Casts a Critical Eye." Morton Abramowitz, who served as an assistant secretary of state under Ronald Reagan, observed that by the summer of 2002 the Bush administration's "foreign policy wars" once more were mostly over ideology. Moreover, "the differences between the top team seem to stretch over major issues—from Iraq to Afghanistan to China, from the Arab-Israeli issue to North Korea, from alliance management to public diplomacy" (Abramowitz, "Foreign Policy Infight . . .").

48. For example, Karen DeYoung, "Recent Statements Muddle U.S. Stance on Venezuela: Confusing Remarks a Symptom of Iraq Focus, Some Say," *Washington Post,* December 21, 2002, A20; E. J. Dionne, Jr., "Heed the Hawks," *Washington Post,* March 4, 2003, A23.

49. A description of the National Economic Council is available at http://www.whitehouse.gov/nec/. See also Kenneth I. Juster and Simon Lazarus, *Making Economic Policy: An Assessment of the National Economic Council* (Washington, D.C.: Brookings Institution, 1997); Alexis Simendinger, "The Broker's Burden," *National Journal,* April 26, 2003, 1306–8.

50. Dana Milbank, "A Loyalist Calls White House to Order: Chief of Staff Card Streamlines Bush's Agenda, Staff, Schedule, and Message," *Washington Post,* February 20, 2001, A1; I. M. Destler, *The National Economic Council: A Work in Progress* (Washington, D.C.: Institute for International Economics, November 1996), 11.

51. John Maggs and Alexis Simendinger, "White House: 'The President Has Confidence in Me,'" *National Journal,* July 27, 2002, 2252–54. Bush and Lindsey reportedly met two to three times a week.

52. See, for example, the range of comments reported in Howard Kurtz, "A Very Public Outing: White House Trashing of Economic Team Was Unexpected," washingtonpost.com, December 9, 2002, 8:23 A.M.; Jonathan Weisman, "Bush Tax-Cut Adviser Resigns: President Nominates Harvard Economist to Replace Hubbard," *Washington Post,* February 27, 2003, A9.

53. Eric Umansky, "Who Is Director of the Domestic Policy Council?" *Slate,* January 18, 2003, http://web.lexis.nexis.com/universe/document?_m=a39b28 dble669abb60e2c33941a9cb7c (accessed March 15, 2003).

54. Dana Milbank, "A Hard-Nosed Litigator Becomes Bush's Policy Point Man," *Washington Post,* April 30, 2002, A17.

55. U.S. Newswire, "Press Briefing by Karen Hughes, Counselor to the President, and Jay Lefkowitz, General Counsel, OMB," August 10, 2001, search for "Domestic Policy Council" at http://web.lexis-nexis.com/universe (accessed March 15, 2003).

56. Scott Lindlaw, "President Reorganizing White House AIDS Office," Associated Press Worldstream, April 9, 2001; "Office to be Expanded," *AIDS Policy and Law,* April 27, 2001, search for "Domestic Policy Council" at http://web.lexis-nexis.com/universe (accessed March 15, 2003).

57. David Frum, *The Right Man: The Surprise Presidency of George W. Bush* (New York: Random House, 2003), 111.

58. David S. Broder, "Long Road to Reform: Negotiators Forge Education Legislation," *Washington Post,* December 17, 2001, A1. Cf. Timothy Noah, "Meet Bush's Domestic Policy Chief: Where's She Been Hiding?" *Slate,* December 4, 2002, http://slate.msn.com/default.aspx?id=2074869 (accessed December 5, 2002).

59. Milbank, "A Hard-Nosed Litigator"; Dana Milbank, "A Time to Be 'Citizens, Not Spectators': Administration Hopes September 11 Will Be Catalyst for Innovative Service Initiative," *Washington Post,* March 17, 2002, A6.
60. Dana Milbank, "White House Seeks 9.3 Percent Funding Increase: Bush Had Asked for a 4.1% Federal Limit," *Washington Post,* February 7, 2003, A25.
61. Hult and Walcott, *Empowering the White House,* Chap. 7.
62. On the idea of and justifications for the administrative presidency see, for instance, Richard P. Nathan, *The Administrative Presidency* (New York: John Wiley and Sons, 1983), and *The Plot that Failed: Nixon and the Administrative Presidency* (New York: John Wiley and Sons, 1975).
63. Kenneth R. Mayer, *With the Stroke of a Pen: Executive Orders and Presidential Power* (Princeton, N.J.: Princeton University Press, 2001), 85–86.
64. Don Van Natta, Jr., "Executive Order Followed Energy Industry Recommendation, Documents Show," *New York Times,* April 4, 2002, A18. EO 13211 "established a task force 'to streamline regulation of exploration and production on federal lands'"; EO 13212 "involved government regulations that affect energy supply and distribution." Both were signed on May 18, 2001. More generally, six Clinton administration executive orders were revoked between the start of the Bush presidency and April 4, 2001; see "Executive Orders Disposition Tables, George W. Bush—2001," http://www.archives.gov/federal_register/executive_orders/2001_wbush.html (accessed March 7, 2003).
65. Alexis Simendinger, "How Bush Flexes His Executive Muscles," *National Journal,* January 26, 2002, 233.
66. Alexis Simendinger, "White House: Power of One," *National Journal,* January 26, 2002, 230–35.
67. Simendinger, "How Bush Flexes His Executive Muscles."
68. James A. Barnes, "Bush's Insiders," *National Journal,* June 23, 2001, 1870. That 72 percent of the early Bush appointees had experience working in the federal government might suggest that individuals' performance in earlier administrations also was a criterion.
69. Eric Schaeffer, "Clearing the Air: Why I Quit Bush's EPA," *Washington Monthly* 34 (July–August 2002): 21.
70. For example, in March 2002 the president named a "vocal critic of preferences for minorities" as head of the Office of Civil Rights in the Education Department (Neil A. Lewis, "Bush Names Affirmative Action Critic to Civil Rights Post," *New York Times,* March 30, 2002, A12).
71. Elliott E. Slotnick, "A Historical Perspective on Federal Judicial Selection," *Judicature* 86 (July–August 2002): 14.
72. For example, Charles Lane, "Nominee for Court Faces Two Battles: Senate Panel to Focus on Ideology, Immigrant Past," *Washington Post,* September 24, 2002, A1; Lisa Holmes and Elisha Savchak, "Judicial Appointment Politics in the 107th Congress," *Judicature* 86 (March–April 2003): 232–40. On the activ-

ities of previous White Houses see, for example, Slotnick, "A Historical Perspective"; Sheldon Goldman and Elliott Slotnick, "Clinton's First Term Judiciary: Many Bridges to Cross," *Judicature* 80 (May–June, 1997): 254–73; Sheldon Goldman, Elliott Slotnick, Gerard Gryski, and Gary Zuk, "Clinton's Judges: Summing Up the Legacy," *Judicature* 84 (March–April, 2001): 248–54; MaryAnne Borrelli, Karen Hult, and Nancy Kassop, "The White House Counsel's Office," *Presidential Studies Quarterly* 31 (December 2001): 561–84.

73. See, for example, Kathryn Dunn Tenpas and Stephen Hess, "The Bush White House: First Appraisals," background paper, Brookings Institution, January 30, 2002, http://www.brook.edu/dybdocroot/Views/Papers/Tenpas/20020130.htm (accessed March 5, 2003); James A. Barnes, "The Imperial Vice Presidency," *National Journal,* March 17, 2001, 814–15. On the earlier evolution of the power of the vice presidency see Paul C. Light, *Vice Presidential Power: Advice and Influence in the White House* (Baltimore: Johns Hopkins University Press, 1984).

74. Barnes, "The Imperial Vice Presidency." See too Carl M. Cannon, "The Point Man," *National Journal,* October 11, 2002, 2956–64.

75. Elisabeth Bumiller and Eric Schmitt, "Cheney, Little Seen by Public, Plays a Visible Role for Bush," *New York Times,* January 31, 2003, A1.

76. On Cheney's activities see Bumiller and Schmitt, "Cheney, Little Seen by Public" and Tenpas and Hess, "The Bush White House."

77. See, for example, Kathryn Dunn Tenpas, "The American Presidency: Surviving and Thriving amidst the Permanent Campaign," in *The Permanent Campaign and Its Future,* ed. Norman Ornstein and Thomas Mann (Washington, D.C.: American Enterprise Institute and Brookings Institution, 2000); Martha Joynt Kumar, "The Office of Communications," *Presidential Studies Quarterly* 31 (December 2001): 609–34; Martha Joynt Kumar, "The Office of the Press Secretary," *Presidential Studies Quarterly* 31 (June 2001): 296–322; Hult and Walcott, *Empowering the White House,* Chaps. 1, 3–4, et passim.

78. On the activities of Hughes and her subordinates see, for instance, Jodi Enda, "Bush Aides Push His Message: Mantra Spread across the Nation from One GOP Mouth to Another," *Detroit Free Press,* March 6, 2001, http://www.freep.com/news/politics/bush6_20010306.htm (accessed March 12, 2001); Mike Allen, "Hughes Keeps White House in Line: Veteran Bush Aide Makes Sure Official Message Is the Only One," *Washington Post,* March 19, 2001, A1; Mike Allen, "Hughes to Sign on with GOP: Contract with Departing Aide Allows Continued Advice to Bush," *Washington Post,* July 5, 2002, A19; Howard Kurtz, "Bush Using End Run around Capital Media," *Washington Post,* February 16, 2001, A4.

79. Kathryn Dunn Tenpas and Stephen Hess, "The Bush White House: First Appraisals," *Presidential Studies Quarterly* 32 (September 2002): 579. Other units that were established with objectives similar to those of the Office of Strategic

Initiative (OSI) include Howard Pyle's office in the Eisenhower administration (Walcott and Hult, *Governing the White House*) and Herb Klein's in the Nixon White House (Hult and Walcott, *Empowering the White House*); neither of those attempts, of course, succeeded, but they provide evidence of partisan learning.

80. Cannon and Simendinger, "The Evolution of Karl Rove," 1214. On the tasks and activities of Kenneth Mehlman, the first director of George W. Bush's political affairs office, see, for example, David Von Drehle, "The Detail Man behind Bush's Wins: Campaign 2004 Is Likely Next Charge," *Washington Post*, January 22, 2003, A13; Mike Allen and Dan Balz, "Bush's '04 Campaign Quietly Being Planned: Advisers See Raising Up to $250 Million," *Washington Post*, March 3, 2003, A1.

81. Andrew Kohut, quoted in Joshua Green, "The Other War Room: President Bush Doesn't Believe in Polling—Just Ask His Pollsters," *Washington Monthly*, 34 (April 2002): 11.

82. See, for example, Dana Milbank, "At the White House: 'The People' Have Spoken—Endlessly," *Washington Post*, June 4, 2002, A15; Kathryn Dunn Tenpas, "Words vs. Deeds: President George W. Bush and Polling," *Brookings Review* 21 (Summer 2003), 32–35.

83. Cook, "The Permanence of the 'Permanent Campaign," 753; Dana Milbank, "Bush by the Numbers, as Told by a Diligent Scorekeeper," *Washington Post*, September 3, 2002, A15. Cook draws attention, too, to the numerous Bush administration officials who moved from the campaign to the White House staff. Among those with public relations and outreach responsibilities were Hughes, Rove, Press Secretary Ari Fleischer, Director of Strategic Initiatives Barry Jackson, Director of Political Affairs Kenneth Mehlman, and Deputy Director of Communications Dan Bartlett (Carl M. Cannon, James A. Barnes, Alexis Simendinger, et al., "The White House Profiles," *National Journal*, June 2, 2001, 1881–97).

84. For example, Dana Milbank, "A Loyalist Calls the White House to Order," *Washington Post*, February 20, 2001, A1; Milbank, "Serious 'Strategery.'" The description of OSI was Karl Rove's, in Milbank, "Serious 'Strategery.'"

85. Dan Balz, "Bush's Political Guru Finds Himself on the Periphery: Rove Adapts Role to Post–September 11th Reality," *Washington Post*, October 31, 2001, A3.

86. D. T. Max, "The 2,988 Words That Changed a Presidency: An Etymology," *New York Times Magazine*, October 7, 2001, 32. Cf. Woodward, *Bush at War*.

87. Berke and Sanger, "Some in Administration Grumble as Aide's Role Seems to Expand."

88. Tenpas and Hess, "The Bush White House," 582.

89. Bumiller, "White House Letter: Still Advising, from Afar and Near"; Dana Milbank, "Hughes's New Role in Shaping Bush's Message Questioned," *Washington Post*, March 20, 2003, A12.

90. Thomas B. Edsall and Dana Milbank, "White House's Roving Eye for Politics: President's Most Powerful Adviser May Also Be the Best Connected," *Washington Post*, March 10, 2003, A1. On similar earlier predictions see, for example, Elisabeth Bumiller, "Minus One, Bush Inner Circle Is Open for Angling," *New York Times*, July 15, 2002, A12; Dana Milbank, "Karl Rove, Adding to His To-Do List"; Ron Suskind, "Mrs. [*sic*] Hughes Takes Her Leave," *Esquire*, July 2002, 110. On the fear of appearing to criticize Rove see, for example, Ron Suskind, "Why Are These Men Laughing?" *Esquire*, January 2003, 104.

91. The USA Freedom Corps Office was established by EO 13254; as in the case of the other cabinet councils, the White House unit serves as the staff to the USA Freedom Corps Council. See, for example, Tenpas and Hess, "The Bush White House," 581. The Office of Global Communications was formally created by EO 13283, signed on January 21, 2003; it is headed by Deputy Assistant to the President Tucker Eskew (former director of the Office of Media Affairs and of the Coalition Information Center). See Karen DeYoung, "Bush to Create Formal Office to Shape U.S. Image Abroad," *Washington Post*, July 30, 2002, A1; Alexis Simendinger, "Shepherding the Story," *National Journal*, March 22, 2003, 922–23.

92. John J. DiIulio, Jr., "The Future of Compassion: President Bush's Social Program Hasn't Yet Gotten a Chance," *Philadelphia Inquirer*, December 4, 2002, Commentary Section, K0361. See too "The DiIulio Letter" (DiIulio to Ron Suskind, October 24, 2002), *Esquire*, http://www.esquire.com/features/articles/2002/021202_mfe_diiulio_l (accessed December 5, 2002).

93. Jonathan Weisman and Dan Balz, "Bush Bids to Regain Economic Initiative," *Washington Post*, July 24, 2002, A1.

94. "Governing the Cabinet," *National Journal*, January 25, 2003, 237.

95. Associated Press, "Bush's Political Risk-Taker: Adviser Pushing Benefits Overhaul," *Richmond Times-Dispatch*, January 1, 2003, A1; Richard W. Stevenson, "Bush's Team Sensed Economic Slump Early," *New York Times*, April 22, 2001, A20.

Chapter 4: Bush's Budget Problem

1. As is customary, these ten-year totals are derived from the Congressional Budget Office's baseline methodology and include the debt service costs added by tax cuts.

2. When Bush became president, the Office of Management and Budget published ten-year projections of budget policy; it now limits these projections to five years.

3. I have characterized his father's presidency as failed solely because he did not win reelection. No other assessment is intended.

4. Office of Management and Budget, "A Blueprint for New Beginnings," February 28, 2001, 172.

5. David A. Stockman, *The Triumph of Politics: Why the Reagan Revolution Failed* (New York: Harper and Row, 1986).

6. Reagan's tax legislation is chronicled in C. Eugene Steuerle, *The Tax Decade* (Washington, D.C.: Urban Institute Press, 1992).

7. Ibid., Chap. 11.

8. These rules are detailed in Allen Schick, *The Federal Budget: Politics, Policy, Process,* revised edition (Washington, D.C.: Brookings Institution, 2000).

9. The Budget Enforcement Act (BEA) established distinct rules for discretionary and mandatory spending. Discretionary spending, defined as spending controlled by annual appropriations, was capped. These caps, which expire in 2003, were designed to limit the amount appropriated each year, but (as is explained in the text) actual appropriations exceeded the limits in 1999–2002. Mandatory spending was not capped, but it and revenue legislation were subject to PAYGO (pay-as-you-go) rules that required any increase in the deficit or reduction in surplus due to new mandatory spending or revenue legislation to be offset.

10. See Alan T. Peacock and Jack Wiseman, *The Growth of Public Expenditures in the United Kingdom* (Princeton, N.J.: Princeton University Press, 1961).

11. Before baselines came into vogue, spending changes were measured in nominal terms, with the previous year's "base" (rather than a projected baseline) used to calculate the dollar value of changes. Baselines are used to "score"— measure the budgetary impact—of a policy change and to enforce various budget rules. When the baseline is adjusted for inflation, the score does not include increases due to inflation, thereby making the spending increase smaller than if inflation were excluded.

12. Congressional Budget Office (CBO), "An Analysis of the President's Budgetary Proposals for Fiscal Year 2004," March 2003.

13. Richard Rose and Terrance Karran, *Taxation by Political Inertia* (London: Allen and Unwin, 1987), 1–2.

14. Martha Derthick, *Policymaking for Social Security* (Washington, D.C.: Brookings Institution), 1979.

15. For example, the federal estate tax would be phased out by 2010, but would reappear at 2001 rates in 2011.

16. Committee for Economic Development, "Exploding Deficits, Declining Growth: The Federal Budget and the Aging of America," March 2003.

17. See http://www.taxfoundation.org.

18. Bush proposed refundable tax credits for health insurance and education; he also proposed an expansion of the earned income tax credit. CBO has estimated that these proposals would add $23 billion to federal outlays during 2004–2010. CBO, "An Analysis of the President's Budgetary Proposals for Fiscal Year 2004," 13.

19. Council of Economic Advisers, "Economic Report of the President," February 2003, 52–58.
20. "With Tax Bill Passed, Republicans Call for More," *New York Times,* May 24, 2003.
21. *New York Times Magazine,* April 6, 2003, 51.

Chapter 5: Bush's Foreign Policy Revolution

1. Quoted in John Young, "Quick, Bush, Give Reporters Some Other Substance to Report," Cox News Service, August 26, 1999.
2. Robert Gallucci, dean of the School of Foreign Service at Georgetown University, quoted in James Traub, "W.'s World," *New York Times Magazine,* January 14, 2001, 31.
3. See Bush, *A Charge to Keep,* 97. For other discussions of Bush as CEO see James Bennett, "C.E.O., U.S.A.," *New York Times Magazine,* January 14, 2001, 24–28, and Donald F. Kettl, *Team Bush: Leadership Lessons from the Bush White House* (New York: McGraw-Hill, 2003).
4. Governor George W. Bush, "A Distinctly American Internationalism," speech made at the Ronald Reagan Library, Simi Valley, California, November 19, 1999, http://www.mtholyoke.edu/acad/intrel/bush/wspeech.htm (accessed May 2003).
5. Bush, *A Charge to Keep,* 123.
6. Ibid., 97.
7. "Transcript of President-elect Bush's News Conference Naming Donald Rumsfeld as His Nominee to Be Secretary of Defense," December 28, 2000, http://www.washingtonpost.com/wp-srv/onpolitics/elections/bush-text122800.htm (accessed May 2003).
8. Quoted in Maureen Dowd, "Freudian Face-Off," *New York Times,* June 16, 1999, 29.
9. "Bush's News Conference Naming Donald Rumsfeld."
10. "The First 2000 Gore-Bush Presidential Debate: October 3, 2000," http://www.debates.org/pages/trans2000a.html (accessed May 2003).
11. Bush, *A Charge to Keep,* 123.
12. Quoted in Bennet, "C.E.O., U.S.A.," 27.
13. See for example, Woodward, *Bush at War,* 137.
14. Bush, "A Distinctly American Internationalism."
15. "The Second 2000 Gore-Bush Presidential Debate." Bush also argued that nonintervention in Rwanda—even in hindsight—had been the right decision, and one he would make again. "Interview with George W. Bush," ABC News's *This Week with Sam Donaldson,* January 23, 2000.
16. Bush, "A Distinctly American Internationalism."
17. Ibid.

18. George W. Bush, "A Period of Consequences," speech made at The Citadel, South Carolina, September 23, 1999, http://www.citadel.edu/pao/addresses/ pres_bush.html (accessed May 2003).
19. Frank Bruni, "Bush Has Tough Words and Rough Enunciation for Iraqi Chief," *New York Times,* December 4, 1999, A12.
20. "The Second 2000 Gore-Bush Presidential Debate."
21. For a fuller description see Ivo H. Daalder and James M. Lindsay, "Power and Cooperation: American Foreign Policy in an Age of Global Politics," in *Agenda for the Nation,* ed. Henry E. Aaron, James M. Lindsay, and Pietro S. Nivola (Washington, D.C.: Brookings Institution, 2003).
22. Authorship of the 1992 defense planning document is commonly attributed to Wolfowitz. He says, however, that the paper was prepared by a member of his staff and leaked to the *Times* before he read it. "Eliminating the Threat to World Security Posed by the Iraqi Regime and Halting the Torture, Imprisonment and Execution of Innocents," Foreign Press Center Briefing, Washington, D.C., March 28, 2003, http://fpc.state.gov/19202.htm (accessed May 2003), and Lynn Sweet, "Why We Hit First in Iraq," *Chicago Sun-Times,* April 6, 2003, 16.
23. "Excerpts from Pentagon's Plan: 'Prevent the Re-emergence of a New Rival,'" *New York Times,* March 8, 1992, A14, and Patrick E. Tyler, "U.S. Strategy Plan Calls for Insuring No Rivals Develop," *New York Times,* March 8, 1992, A1. On the influence of this study on thinking in the younger Bush's administration see Nicolas Lemann, "The Next World Order," *New Yorker,* April 1, 2002, 41–44.
24. Bush, *A Charge to Keep,* 239.
25. See, for instance, Nicholas Lemann, "The Quiet Man," *New Yorker,* May 7, 2001, 56–71.
26. Condoleezza Rice, "Promoting a National Interest," *Foreign Affairs* 79 (January–February 2000): 62.
27. Bush, "A Period of Consequences."
28. Bush, "A Distinctly American Internationalism."
29. Paul Wolfowitz, "Remembering the Future," *National Interest* 59 (Spring 2000): 41.
30. Paul Wolfowitz, "Re-building the Anti-Saddam Coalition," *Wall Street Journal,* November 18, 1997, A22.
31. See Robert Kagan, "Multilateralism, American Style," *Washington Post,* September 13, 2002, 39. Richard Haass has called this approach "multilateralism à la carte." Quoted in Thom Shanker, "White House Says the U.S. Is Not a Loner, Just Choosy," *New York Times,* July 31, 2001, A1.
32. Richard N. Haass, *The Reluctant Sheriff: The United States after the Cold War* (New York: Council on Foreign Relations, 1997).
33. For unvarnished elaborations of this point of view see John Bolton, "Should We Take Global Governance Seriously?" *Chicago Journal of International Law*

1 (Fall 2000): 205–22, and Charles Krauthammer, "Arms Control: The End of an Illusion," *Weekly Standard,* November 1, 1999, 21–27.

34. Bush, "A Distinctly American Internationalism."

35. Powell's relationship with the younger President Bush continued to be distant as of mid-2002. See Woodward, *Bush at War,* 330.

36. Johanna McGeary, "Odd Man Out," *Time,* September 10, 2001, 28.

37. See Robert Kagan, "The Benevolent Empire," *Foreign Policy* 111 (Summer 1998): 28. Paul Wolfowitz expressed this sentiment thus: "The way we define our interest there's a sort of natural compatibility between the United States and most countries in the world." See "Deputy Secretary Wolfowitz Interview with the Los Angeles Times," April 29, 2002, http://www.defenselink.mil/news/May2002/t05092002_t0429la.html (accessed January 2003).

38. For a discussion of the divisions between democratic imperialists and assertive nationalists on the specific question of Iraq see Ivo H. Daalder and James M. Lindsay, "It's Hawk vs. Hawk in the Bush Administration," *Washington Post,* October 27, 2002, B3.

39. Quoted in "Excerpts from Pentagon's Plan."

40. See James M. Lindsay, "The New Apathy," *Foreign Affairs* 79 (September–October 2000): 2–8.

41. "Press Conference by President Bush and Russian Federation President Putin," June 16, 2001, http://www.whitehouse.gov/news/releases/2001/06/20010618.html (accessed May 2003).

42. David Sanger, "Bush Is Offering Taiwan Some Arms but Not the Best," *New York Times,* April 24, 2001, A1.

43. Quoted in Neil King, Jr., "Bush Leaves Taiwan Policy in Confusing Straits," *Wall Street Journal,* April 26, 2001, A3.

44. Quoted in Alan Sipress, "Powell Vows to Consult Allies on Key Issues," *Washington Post,* February 28, 2001, A22.

45. "Presidents Exchange Toasts at State Dinner," September 5, 2001, http://www.whitehouse.gov/news/releases/2001/09/20010906-1.html (accessed May 2003).

46. Bruce Stokes, "OK, Who's Got the Agenda," *National Journal,* May 12, 2001, 1433, and Bruce Stokes, "On 'Fast Track' Bill, Action Is Unlikely before Fall—If Then," *National Journal,* April 25, 2001, 13–14.

47. Quoted in Jeffrey Kluger, "A Climate of Despair," *Time,* April 9, 2001, 30.

48. David Frum, *The Right Man* (New York: Random House, 2003), 250.

49. Quoted in Alan Sipress, "Bush Retreats from U.S. Role as Peace Broker," *Washington Post,* March 17, 2001, A1.

50. "Remarks by the President and Prime Minister Blair in Joint Press Conference," February 23, 2001, http://www.whitehouse.gov/news/releases/2001/02/20010226-1.html (accessed May 2003).

51. Sipress, "Bush Retreats from U.S. Role as Peace Broker," A1.

52. "Remarks by the President and German Chancellor Schroeder in Photo Opportunity," March 29, 2001, http://www.whitehouse.gov/news/releases/2001/03/20010329-2.html (accessed May 2003).
53. David E. Sanger, "Leaving for Europe, Bush Draws on Hard Lessons of Diplomacy," *New York Times,* May 22, 2002, A1.
54. For a discussion of the various competing objectives the administration was trying to balance see Bruce Stokes, "Flip A Coin?" *National Journal,* March 24, 2001, 896.
55. "Remarks by President Bush and President Kim Dae-Jung of South Korea," March 7, 2001, http://www.whitehouse.gov/news/releases/2001/03/200103 07-6.html (accessed May 2003).
56. Frum, *The Right Man,* 240.
57. Quoted in "Old Friends and New," *Economist,* June 1, 2002, 28. See also Woodward, *Bush at War,* 281.
58. Quoted in John F. Harris and Dan Balz, "A Question of Capital," *Washington Post,* April 29, 2001, A1
59. Quoted in Peggy Noonan, "A Chat in the Oval Office," *Wall Street Journal,* June 25, 2001, A18.
60. Quoted in McGeary, "Odd Man Out," 30.
61. Quoted in Barton Gellman, "A Strategy's Curious Evolution," *Washington Post,* January 20, 2002, A16.
62. Quoted in Daniel Benjamin and Steven Simon, *Age of Sacred Terror* (New York: Random House, 2002), 328; Gellman, "A Strategy's Curious Evolution," A16.
63. Quoted in Woodward, *Bush at War,* 34.
64. Quoted in Benjamin and Simon, *Age of Sacred Terror,* 328, 334, 336.
65. Quoted in Gellman, "A Strategy's Curious Evolution," A16.
66. Quoted in Benjamin and Simon, *Age of Sacred Terror,* 335.
67. Adam Cohen, "Banking on Secrecy," *Time,* October 22, 2001, 73, and William F. Wechsler, "Follow the Money," *Foreign Affairs* 80 (July–August 2001): 40.
68. Quoted in Gellman, "A Strategy's Curious Evolution," A16. See also Judith Miller, Jeff Gerth, and Don Van Natta, Jr., "Planning for Terror but Failing to Act," *New York Times,* December 30, 2001, A1.
69. Woodward, *Bush at War,* 39.
70. "Statement by Chancellor Schröder to the German Bundestag on the Terrorist Acts Carried Out in the United States," *Plenarprotokoll* 14/186 (German Bundestag, September 12, 2001).
71. Quoted in Patrick Tyler and Jane Perlez, "World Leaders List Conditions on Cooperation," *New York Times,* September 19, 2001, A1.
72. UN Security Council Resolution 1368 (2001), adopted September 12, 2001.
73. George F. Will, "The End of Our Holiday from History," *Washington Post,* September 11, 2001, A27.

74. George W. Bush, "Address to a Joint Session of Congress and the American People," September 20, 2001, http://www.whitehouse.gov/news/releases/2001/09/20010920-8.html (accessed April 2003).
75. Vice President Dick Cheney on NBC News's *Meet the Press*, March 16, 2003. See also Marc Reuel Gerecht, "Crushing Al Qaeda Is Only a Start," *Wall Street Journal*, December 19, 2001, 18.
76. See Jonathan Chait, "9/10 President," *New Republic*, March 10, 2003, 18–23.
77. George W. Bush, "Address to the Nation," September 11, 2001, http://www.whitehouse.gov/news/releases/2001/09/20010911-16.html (accessed May 2003). Bush apparently decided to make this statement without consulting Cheney, Rumsfeld, or Powell. See Woodward, *Bush at War*, 30.
78. "DoD News Briefing—Deputy Secretary Wolfowitz," September 13, 2001, http://www.defenselink.mil/news/Sep2001/t09132001_t0913dsd.html (accessed May 2003).
79. Quoted in Nicholas Lemann, "After Iraq," *New Yorker*, February 17 and 24, 2003, 72.
80. Bush, "Address to a Joint Session of Congress and the American People."
81. Quoted in Woodward, *Bush at War*, 281.
82. George W. Bush, "Introduction," *The National Security Strategy of the United States* (Washington, D.C.: The White House, September 2002), ii, http://www.whitehouse.gov/nsc/nss.html (accessed May 2003).
83. Quoted in Woodward, *Bush at War*, 205.
84. Quoted in Frank Bruni, "For President, a Mission and a Role in History," *New York Times*, September 22, 2001, A1.
85. Quoted Michael Hirsh, "America's Mission," *Newsweek: Special Edition*, December 2002–February 2003, 10.
86. S.J. Res. 23, "Authorization for Use of Military Force," September 14, 2001, http://thomas.loc.gov/cgi-bin/query/D?c107:2:./temp/~c107sbZ4DL:: (accessed May 2003).
87. See James M. Lindsay, "Apathy, Interest, and the Politics of American Foreign Policy," in *The Uncertain Superpower: Domestic Dimensions of U.S. Foreign Policy after the Cold War*, ed. Bernhard May and Michaela Honicke Moore (Berlin: Leske and Budrich, 2003); James M. Lindsay, "Deference and Defiance: The Shifting Rhythms of Executive-Legislative Relations in Foreign Policy," *Presidential Studies Quarterly*, forthcoming; and James M. Lindsay, "From Deference to Activism and Back Again: Congress and the Politics of American Foreign Policy," in *The Domestic Sources of American Foreign Policy: Insights and Evidence*, ed. Eugene R. Wittkopf and James M. McCormick (Lanham, Md.: Rowman and Littlefield, 2003).
88. George W. Bush, "Remarks by the President at Anne Northup for Congress Luncheon," September 5, 2002, http://www.whitehouse.gov/news/releases/2002/09/20020905-5.html (accessed May 2003).

89. George W. Bush, "Remarks after Two Planes Crash into the World Trade Center," September 11, 2001, http://www.whitehouse.gov/news/releases/2001/09/20010911.html (accessed May 2003).

90. Glenn Kessler, "U.S. Decision on Iraq Has Puzzling Past," *Washington Post,* January 12, 2003, A1.

91. Barton Gellman, "Broad Effort Launched after '98 Attacks," *Washington Post,* December 19, 2001, A1.

92. Quoted in James Carney and John F. Dickerson, "Inside the War Room," *Time,* December 12, 2001, 117.

93. Woodward, *Bush at War,* 75–85.

94. Ibid., 98, 223.

95. Bush, "Address to a Joint Session of Congress and the American People."

96. See Michael E. O'Hanlon, "A Flawed Masterpiece," *Foreign Affairs* 81 (May–June 2002): 47–63, and Stephen Biddle, "Afghanistan and the Future of Warfare," *Foreign Affairs* 82 (March–April 2003): 31–46.

97. Quoted in Woodward, *Bush at War,* 81.

98. Donald Rumsfeld on CBS News's *Face the Nation,* September 23, 2001.

99. Michael R. Gordon, "Gains and Risks in New Low-Risk War," *New York Times,* December 29, 2001, A1.

100. Quoted in Gordon, "Gains and Risks in New Low-Risk War," B4.

101. George W. Bush, "Remarks to Employees at the Pentagon," September 17, 2001, http://www.whitehouse.gov/news/releases/2001/09/20010917-3.html (accessed April 2003), and Woodward, *Bush at War,* 254.

102. Bush, "State of the Union Address."

103. NBC News's *Meet the Press,* March 16, 2003.

104. *National Security Strategy of the United States of America,* 15.

105. "Press Conference with Prime Minister Tony Blair," January 31, 2003, http://www.whitehouse.gov/news/releases/2003/01/20030131-23.html (accessed May 2003).

106. Hubert Védrine, quoted in Suzanne Daley, "French Minister Calls U.S. Policy 'Simplistic,' *New York Times,* February 7, 2002, A14. Chris Patten, quoted in Jonathan Freedland, "Breaking the Silence," *Guardian* (London), February 9, 2002, 8.

107. U.S. Senate, Committee on the Budget, *Hearing with Secretary of State Colin Powell on the President's Fiscal Year 2003 Budget Proposal,* 107th Cong., 2d sess., February 12, 2002, http://www.fnsg.com (accessed May 2003).

108. For Wolfowitz's view see Michael Elliott and James Carney, "First Stop, Iraq," *Time,* March 31, 2003, 175. Cheney reportedly told friends after the 2000 elections that Bush had a historic opportunity to reverse the mistake of leaving Saddam in power. See Carla Anne Robbins and Jeanne Cummings, "How Bush Decided That Hussein Must Be Ousted from Atop Iraq," *Wall Street Journal,* June 14, 2002, A1.

109. "Press Conference with Prime Minister Tony Blair," January 31, 2003, http://www.whitehouse.gov/news/releases/2003/01/20030131-23.html (accessed May 2003).

110. "Press Conference with Prime Minister Tony Blair," January 31, 2003.

111. Bush repeated that sentiment on at least one other occasion. Woodward, *Bush at War,* 99, 167.

112. Elliott and Carney, "First Stop, Iraq," 177.

113. Quoted in Woodward, *Bush at War,* 99.

114. Kessler, "U.S. Decision on Iraq Has Puzzling Past," A1.

115. Robbins and Cummings, "How Bush Decided That Hussein Must Be Ousted," A1, and Susan Page, "Iraq Course Set from Tight White House Circle," *USA Today,* September 11, 2002, A1.

116. George W. Bush, "Address on the Future of Iraq," American Enterprise Institute, Washington, February 26, 2003, http://www.whitehouse.gov/news/releases/2003/02/20030226-11.html (accessed May 2003).

117. Elliott and Carney, "First Stop, Iraq," 173.

118. NBC News's *Meet the Press,* March 16, 2003.

119. CBS News's *Face the Nation,* March 16, 2003.

120. On these differences see Daalder and Lindsay, "It's Hawk vs. Hawk," B3.

121. See Nicholas Lemann, "How It Came to War," *New Yorker,* March 31, 2003, 39.

122. George W. Bush, "Address on New Palestinian Leadership," Washington, D.C., June 24, 2002, http://www.whitehouse.gov/news/releases/2002/06/20020624-3.html (accessed May 2003).

123. Richard Wolffe and Tamara Lipper, "Powell in the Bunker," *Newsweek,* March 24, 2003, 31.

124. Woodward, *Bush at War,* 332–34.

125. Dick Cheney, "Speech to the Veterans of Foreign Wars 103rd National Convention," August 26, 2002, http://www.whitehouse.gov/news/releases/2002/08/20020826.html (accessed May 2003).

126. George W. Bush, "Address to the UN General Assembly," New York, September 12, 2002, http://www.whitehouse.gov/news/releases/2002/09/20020912-1.html (accessed May 2003).

127. See Ivo H. Daalder and James M. Lindsay, "UN's Iraq Vote Sets Stage for More Friction," *San Jose Mercury News,* November 11, 2002, 1P, and William Kristol and Robert Kagan, "The U.N. Trap?" *Weekly Standard,* November 18, 2002, 9–12.

128. For one such proposal see Ivo H. Daalder and James M. Lindsay, "Iraq's Chances Are Slipping Away," *Newsday,* January 28, 2003, A27–28.

129. David E. Sanger, "North Korea Says It Has a Program on Nuclear Arms," *New York Times,* October 17, 2002, A1. See also Walter Pincus, "N. Korea's Nuclear Plans Were No Secret," *Washington Post,* February 2, 2003, A1.

130. Robert S. Norris, Hans M. Kristensen, and Joshua Handler, "NRDC Nuclear Notebook: North Korea's Nuclear Program, 2003," in *Bulletin of the Atomic Scientists* 59 (March–April 2003): 75.

131. See International Institute of Strategic Studies, "Iran's Nuclear Ambitions," *Strategic Comments* 9 (March 2003).

132. Ivo H. Daalder and James M. Lindsay, "Where Are the Hawks on North Korea?" *American Prospect,* February 2002, 27–28.

133. Quoted in David E. Sanger, "U.S. Sees Quick Start of North Korea Nuclear Site," *New York Times,* March 1, 2003, A9.

134. "Presidential News Conference," March 6, 2003, http://www.whitehouse .gov/news/releases/2003/03/20030306-8.html (accessed March 2003).

135. Quoted in James Dao, "Powell Seeks Asian Response for New U.S.-Backed Resolution," *New York Times,* February 23, 2003, 13. See also Colin L. Powell, "Interview on NBC's Meet the Press with Tim Russert," http://www.state .gov/secretary/rm/2002/16240.htm (accessed April 2003).

136. Quoted in Glenn Kessler, "U.S. Halts Overtures to Iran's Khatami," *Washington Post,* July 23, 2002, A1.

137. Quoted in Jackson Diehl, "The Accidental Imperialist," *Washington Post,* December 30, 2002, A17.

138. See Bush's comments on weak states in "Introduction," *National Security Strategy of the United States.*

139. See Ivo H. Daalder, "Bush's Coalition Doesn't Add Up Where It Counts," *Newsday,* March 24, 2003, A16.

140. "America's Image Further Erodes, Europeans Want Weaker Ties," Nine Country Survey by the Pew Center for the People and the Press, March 18, 2003, http://people-press.org/reports/pdf/175.pdf (accessed April 2003).

141. Mary McGrory, "Pit-Stop Presidency," *Washington Post,* October 27, 2002, B7.

Chapter 6: President Bush: Legislative Strategist

The authors are indebted to Caroline Rieger and Kimberly Spears for their diligent research.

1. Sam Howe Verhovek, "Texas Governor Succeeds, without the Flash," *New York Times,* June 7, 1995, A1.

2. See comments of *Austin American Statesman* reporter Jay Root, speaking at "How Would Bush Govern," a panel discussion at the American Enterprise Institute sponsored by the Transition to Governing Project. The transcript can be found at http://www.aei.org/events/eventID.282/transcript.asp. See also Fred I. Greenstein, "George W. Bush and the Ghosts of Presidents Past," *PS: Political Science and Politics* 34, no. 1 (2001): 77–80.

3. R. G. Ratcliffe, "President-elect Uses Texas as Unity Model," *Houston Chronicle,* December 14, 2000, 1.

4. "The Man Who, Finally, Will Be King," *The Economist,* December 16, 2000, 38.
5. Jackie Calmes, "Texas Tax Fight Yields Clues on How Bush Would Lead," *Wall Street Journal,* January 14, 1999, 24.
6. Ibid.
7. ABC News/*Washington Post* Poll, March 9–11, 2000: Which candidate [for president in 2000], [Al] Gore or [George] W. Bush, do you trust to do a better job on each of these issues? . . . Improving education and the schools?

RESULTS: Gore—44%; Bush—44%; Both (volunteered)—4%; Neither (volunteered)—5%; No opinion—3%.
POPULATION: National adult.
NUMBER OF PARTICIPANTS: 1,218.

Washington Post, Henry J. Kaiser Family Foundation, Harvard University Poll, May 11–22, 2000: Which [2000] presidential candidate, [Al] Gore or [George W.] Bush, do you trust to do a better job improving education and the schools?

RESULTS: Gore—40%; Bush—42%; Both (volunteered)—1%; Neither (volunteered)—7%; Don't know—6%.
POPULATION: National registered voters.
NUMBER OF PARTICIPANTS: 1,225.
SURVEY NOTES: Interview conducted by International Communications Research (ICR). Included in the sample was an oversample of 215 registered voters who said that education was an important issue in deciding whom to vote for in the 2000 presidential election.

8. Norman Ornstein and John Fortier, "Relations with Congress," *PS: Political Science and Politics* 35, no. 1 (2002): 47–50.
9. Daniel J. Parks, "Bush May Test Capitol Hill Clout Early with Expedited Tax-Cut Proposal," *Congressional Quarterly* 59, no. 1 (2001): 41.
10. Ibid., 42. See also Lori Nitschke, "Writing Size of Tax Cut into Budget Looms as an Early Turning Point," *Congressional Quarterly* 59, no. 4 (2001): 218.
11. Norman Ornstein, "Suitcase Full of Cash: There Will Be Many Stages of Bush Tax Cut," *Roll Call,* May 3, 2001, 8.
12. Andrew Taylor, "Tax Fight Energizes Democrats," *Congressional Quarterly* 59, no. 9 (2001): 465.
13. Lori Nitschke, "The Elusive Middle Ground," *Congressional Quarterly* 59, no. 9 (2001): 467.
14. Taylor, "Tax Fight Energizes," 466.
15. Ornstein and Fortier, "Relations with Congress," 50.
16. Lori Nitschke, "Big Breaks for Married Couples Offered in Latest House Tax Bill," *Congressional Quarterly* 59, no. 12 (2001): 653.

17. "For the Record," *Congressional Quarterly* 59, no. 13 (2001): 744.
18. Ibid.
19. Lori Nitschke, "House Presses Bush's Tax Agenda while Senate Talks of Stimulus" *Congressional Quarterly* 59, no. 13 (2001): 708.
20. Lori Nitschke, "Estate Tax Phaseout Passes House but May Be Scaled Back in Senate When Finance Panel Begins Work," *Congressional Quarterly* 59, no. 14 (2001): 775.
21. Lori Nitschke and Bill Swindell, "Grassley-Baucus Tax Blueprint Heads for Rough-and-Tumble Markup," *Congressional Quarterly* 59, no. 19 (2001): 1070.
22. Ibid., 1069.
23. Lori Nitschke, "Senate Tax Bill Trade-Offs Leave a Fragile Coalition" *Congressional Quarterly* 59, no. 20 (2001): 1145.
24. Ibid., 1148.
25. Andrew Taylor, "Shakeup in the Senate," *Congressional Quarterly* 59, no. 21 (2001): 1148.
26. David Nather, "Panel Easily Approves Education Bill, Deferring Rights on Vouchers and 'Charter States' to Senate Floor," *Congressional Quarterly* 59, no. 10 (2001): 540.
27. David Nather, "Bush's Education Plan Unveiled in House amid Muted Dissent," *Congressional Quarterly* 59, no. 2 (2001): 660.
28. David Nather, "Compromises on ESEA Bills May Imperil Republican Strategy," *Congressional Quarterly* 59, no. 18 (2001): 1010.
29. David Nather, "Democrats Leaving Their Stamp on Bush's Education Bill," *Congressional Quarterly* 59, no. 19 (2001): 1079.
30. James C Benton, "Senate-Passed Aviation Security Bill Declared a No-Go by House GOP," *Congressional Quarterly* 59, no. 39 (2001): 2402.
31. James C. Benton, "Bush's Appeal Gives GOP Victory on Airline Security Bill," *Congressional Quarterly* 59, no. 42 (2001): 2603.
32. "For the Record," *Congressional Quarterly* 59, no. 42 (2001): 2638.
33. Elizabeth A. Palmer, "Anti-Terrorism Bills Head for Floor Votes, but Tough Negotiations Lie Ahead," *Congressional Quarterly* 59, no. 38 (2001): 2327.
34. Julie Hirschfeld Davis, "Tough Talk Helps Move Jordanian Trade Bill but Clouds Prospects for 'Fast Track,'" *Congressional Quarterly* 59, no. 37 (2001): 2281.
35. Gebe Martinez, "After One-Vote Victory in House, Fast-Track Bill Lands in Senate," *Congressional Quarterly* 59, no. 47 (2001): 2919.
36. Adriel Bettelheim, "House Homeland Security Bill Bends Strongly Bush's Way," *Congressional Quarterly* 60, no. 29 (2002): 1927.
37. Adriel Bettelheim, "Homeland Security's Big Hurdle: Ceding Power to White House," *Congressional Quarterly* 60, no. 30 (2002): 2030.
38. Adriel Bettelheim, "Workers' Rights Issues Looming over Homeland Security Debate," *Congressional Quarterly* 60, no. 34 (2002): 2294.
39. Adriel Bettelheim and Mary Dalrymple, "Chafee Holds Key to Decision on

Union Rights for Homeland Staff," *Congressional Quarterly* 60, no. 36 (2002): 2442.

40. Ibid.

41. Adriel Bettelheim, "Personnel Issues Have Senate Stumbling on Homeland Security," *Congressional Quarterly* 60, no. 37 (2002): 2516.

42. Ibid.

Chapter 7: Capitalizing on Position in a Perfect Tie

1. Richard E. Neustadt, *Presidential Power and the Modern Presidents* (New York: Free Press, 1990).

2. Ibid., 150.

3. See Donald F. Kettl, *Team Bush* (New York: McGraw-Hill, 2003), Part 1.

4. The comparative data are based on percentage of the popular vote, percentage of the electoral vote, and job approval upon entering office for political standing and on percentage of the president's party in the House and the Senate, with bonus points for majority status, legislative standing. Author's calculations.

5. David Frum, *The Right Man: The Surprise Presidency of George W. Bush* (New York: Random House, 2003), 23.

6. Ibid., 20.

7. Ibid., 272.

8. Ibid., 275.

9. Woodward, *Bush at War*.

10. Quoted in Charles O. Jones, "The Presidential Transition into a Fifty-Fifty Government and Beyond," in *The State of American Politics,* ed. Byron E. Shafer (Lanham, Md.: Rowman and Littlefield, 2002), 104.

11. Charles O. Jones, *The Presidency in a Separated System* (Washington, D.C.: Brookings Institution, 1994), Chap. 1.

12. James W. Ceaser and Andrew Busch, *The Perfect Tie: The True Story of the 2000 Presidential Election* (Lanham, Md.: Rowman and Littlefield, 2001).

13. Quoted in Alan Murray, "White House Unveils Medicare Proposal That Lacks Punch," *Wall Street Journal,* March 4, 2003, A4.

14. Sarah A. Binder, "The Dynamics of Legislative Gridlock, 1947-96," *American Political Science Review* 92 (September 1999): 519-33.

15. Frum, *The Right Man,* 104.

16. Kenneth R. Mayer, *With the Stroke of a Pen: Executive Orders and Presidential Power* (Princeton, N.J.: Princeton University Press, 2001), 220-21.

17. David R. Mayhew, *Divided We Govern* (New Haven, Conn.: Yale University Press, 1991).

18. For details see ibid., 37-44 and Appendix A.

19. For details of Bush's travels and issues discussed see Corey Cook, "The Perma-

nence of the 'Permanent Campaign,'" *Presidential Studies Quarterly* 32 (Winter 2002): 753–64.

20. In a letter to the author dated June 2, 2003, Richard E. Neustadt observed that "Bush's switch from opposition to support of a Homeland Security Department was just in time to preempt the public relations of congressional performance for all summer in 2002, followed by the further preemption in the fall with his Iraq Resolution."

21. Quoted in Charles O. Jones, *Passages to the Presidency: From Campaigning to Governing* (Washington, D.C.: Brookings Institution, 1998), 84.

22. Both quoted in Helen Dewar, "Bush's Use of Clout Intensifies Senate Split," *Washington Post,* March 2, 2003, A4.

23. For example, David Firestone, "Democrats Pulling Together United Front against GOP," *New York Times,* March 3, 2003, A17, and Jim Vandehei, "Democrats on the Hill Split on the Agenda," *Washington Post,* March 4, 2003, A1.

24. Jones, *The Presidency in a Separated System,* 298.

Chapter 8: The Bush Presidency and the American Electorate

1. Only Dwight D. Eisenhower (president from 1953 to1961) enjoyed a longer stretch of approval ratings above 60 percent.

2. John Aldrich, *Why Parties? The Origin and Transformation of Party Politics in America* (Chicago: University of Chicago Press, 1995), Chap. 7; David W. Rohde, *Parties and Leaders in the Post-Reform House* (Chicago: University of Chicago Press, 1991), Chaps. 3 and 5; Barbara Sinclair, "Hostile Partners: The President, Congress, and Lawmaking in the Partisan 1990s," in *Polarized Politics: Congress and the President in a Partisan Era,* ed. Jon R. Bond and Richard Fleisher (Washington, D.C.: Congressional Quarterly Press, 2000), 137–40; Gary C. Jacobson, "Party Polarization in National Politics: The Electoral Connection," in *Polarized Politics,* ed. Bond and Fleisher, 9–15; Nolan McCarty, Keith T. Poole, and Howard Rosenthal, *Income Redistribution and the Realignment of American Politics* (Washington, D.C.: AEI, 1997), Chaps. 2 and 3; Richard Fleisher and Jon R. Bond, "The President in a More Partisan Arena," *Political Research Quarterly* 49 (December 1996): 729–48.

3. Gary C. Jacobson, "Public Opinion and the Impeachment of Bill Clinton," *British Elections and Parties Review,* Vol. 10, ed. Philip Cowley, David Denver, Andrew Russell, and Lisa Harrison (London: Frank Cass, 2000), 1–31.

4. Speech delivered at the Republican National Convention, August 3, 2000, accepting the nomination.

5. Gary C. Jacobson, "The Electoral Basis of Partisan Polarization in Congress," paper presented at the Annual Meeting of the American Political Science Association, Washington, D.C., August 21–September 3, 2000.

6. Gary C. Jacobson, "Partisan Polarization in Presidential Support: The Electoral Connection," *Congress and the Presidency* 30 (Spring 2003): 1–36; see also Figure 8.5 in this chapter.

7. Gary C. Jacobson, "A House and Senate Divided: The Clinton Legacy and the Congressional Elections of 2000," *Political Science Quarterly* 116 (Spring 2001): 13–18.

8. Ibid., 20; *Los Angeles Times* Poll, Study 450: National Post Election Survey, December 14–16, 2000.

9. In the March 2001 CBS News/*New York Times* Poll, 89 percent of Republicans, but only 25 percent of Democrats, said that Bush had won the election legitimately.

10. Although presidential honeymoons were already largely a thing of the past; see Jacobson, "Polarization in Presidential Support," Figure 23.

11. The average among independents was 50 percent.

12. "Bush and the Democratic Agenda," CBS News/*New York Times* Poll, June 14–18, 2001, available at http://www.cbsnews.com/htdocs/pdf/bushbac.pdf (accessed July 7, 2003).

13. Ibid.; CBS News/*New York Times* Monthly Poll, March 2001; *Los Angeles Times* Poll 455: Bush's Budget Speech to Congress, March 2001.

14. Most of the public did not notice any diminution; when an ABC News/*Washington Post* Poll conducted April 12–22, 2001, asked, "Do you think Bush has reduced the political partisanship in Washington, or not?" 54 percent said "No," 34 percent said "Yes," and 11 percent had no opinion.

15. Ordinary Democrats and Republicans were nearly 50 percentage points apart on the wisdom of Bush's tax-cut proposals (CBS News Poll, April 4–5, 2001; Gallup Poll Release, March 9, 2001).

16. Citizens were, characteristically, sharply divided along party lines over Jeffords's switch; according to the CNN/USA Today/Gallup Poll of May 24, 2001, Democrats thought it would be good for the country (75 percent said, "Good," 9 percent, "Bad"), while Republicans thought it would be bad for the country, (75 percent said "Bad," 14 percent "Good").

17. As usual, self-defined independents approximated the national figures, going from an average of 52 percent approving before September 11 to an average of 86 percent approving over the next month.

18. This was his rating in the final Gallup Poll taken prior to the election—the measure used in standard referendum models of midterm elections—and also the average of the thirteen polls taken during the month leading up to the election.

19. Democrats picked up five House seats in 1998; Reagan's Republicans lost only five seats in 1986, the best performance at the midterm for any Republican administration before 2002.

20. For a discussion of such models see Gary C. Jacobson, *The Politics of Congressional Elections*, 5th edition (New York: Longman, 2001), 143–45 and 158; for an application to 2002 see Gary C. Jacobson, "Terror, Terrain, and Turnout: Explaining the 2002 Midterm Election," *Political Science Quarterly* 118 (Spring 2003): 1–22, note 6.

21. Enron, once the nation's seventh-largest company, was a Houston-based energy conglomerate that collapsed into bankruptcy in late 2001 after the exposure of accounting schemes that had inflated its earnings by more than $1 billion. Enron's stockholders collectively lost billions of dollars, and thousands of former Enron employees had their pension savings wiped out. The head of Enron, Kenneth Lay, was a long-term supporter of fellow Texan George W. Bush and one of his leading campaign contributors. By one count Enron and its executives had contributed a total of $736,800 to Bush's various campaigns since 1993; see http://www.opensecrets.org/alerts/v6/enron_bush.asp.

22. Only 10.8 percent of Republican incumbents were opposed in 2002 by Democrats who had ever held elective public office, a figure 1.9 standard deviations below the postwar mean of 24.9 percent. The postwar low was 10.1 percent in 1990.

23. Jeffrey M. Jones, "Republicans Trail in Congressional Race Despite Advantage on Issues," Gallup News Service, September 26, 2002, available at http://www.gallup.com/poll/releases/pr020926.asp?Version=p; Lydia Said, "National Issues May Play Bigger-than-Usual Role in Congressional Elections," Gallup News Service, October 31, 2002, available at http://www.gallup.com/poll/releases/pr021031.asp?Version=p.

24. *Wag the Dog* is a 1997 film comedy in which a president's media adviser fakes a war in order to distract attention from the president's involvement in a sex scandal.

25. Richard A. Brody, *Assessing the President: The Media, Elite Opinion, and Public Support* (Stanford, Calif.: Stanford University Press, 1991), Chap. 5.

26. The model reported in Jacobson, "Terror, Terrain, and Turnout," note 6, would predict that Republicans would lose the House if Bush's overall approval rating were less than 50 percent.

27. In four Gallup Polls taken between September and the election, only about a quarter of poll respondents rated the economy "Excellent" or "Good," whereas nearly three-quarters found it only "Fair" or "Poor," the worst net rating of the economy since 1994 (see Figure 8.7). People who thought the economy was getting worse outnumbered those who though it was improving by 54 percent to 34 percent (http://pollingreport.com/consumer.htm, November 18, 2002). Consumer confidence was at its lowest level since 1993 (Consumer Research Center News Release, October 29, 2002, available at http://www.crc-conquest.org/consumer_confidence).

28. Jacobson, "Terror, Terrain, and Turnout," Table 2.
29. Al Gore had won six of the ten states losing seats, while Bush had won seven of the eight states gaining seats; Gore had won 54.1 percent of the total major-party vote in the former, compared with 48.3 percent in the latter.
30. Jacobson, "A House and Senate Divided," 5–13.
31. The classification is from Republican National Committee, "Redistricting Party Control," available at http://www.rnc.org/images/congonly.jpg, September 9, 2002.
32. The victories that defied this trend were those of conservative Democrats Lincoln Davis (Tennessee 4th district), who won a district where Bush's share of the 2000 vote was 50.5 percent, and Rodney Alexander, who won the December 7 runoff in Louisiana's 5th district, where Bush had won 58.0 percent.
33. The presidential vote for midterm years is taken from the immediately prior presidential election.
34. In the last Gallup Poll before the election (taken October 31–November 3), 93 percent of Republicans and 92 percent of Democrats planned to vote for their party's candidate; the same figures for the October 27–31 CBS News/*New York Times* Polls were 95 percent and 91 percent, respectively. See http://www.gallup.com.poll.releases/pr021104asp.?Version=p (November 4, 2002) and http://www.cbsnews.com/htdocs/c2k/election_back.pdf (November 20, 2002).
35. Diana Pollich, "A Divided Electorate,"cbsnews.com, November 6, 2002, available at http://www.cbsnews.com/stories/2002/11/06/politics/main528295.shtml.
36. CBS News/*New York Times* Poll, October 3–5, 2002, available at http://www.cbsnews.com/htdocs/sc2k/pol106.pdf.
37. The 2002 National Elections Study, Advance Release, February 28, 2003, available at http://www.umich.edu/~nes/studyres/nes2002/nes2002.htm; the comparison is among voters in contested House elections.
38. Jacobson, "Terror, Terrain, and Turnout."
39. Mary Clare Jalonick, "Senate Changes Hands Again," *CQ Weekly,* November 9, 2002, 2907–9; Rebecca Adams, "Georgia Republicans Energized by 'Friend to Friend' Campaign, *CQ Weekly,* November 9, 2002, 2892–93.
40. The average approval rating from opposition partisans at midterm is 34 percent; Bush's approval among independents, at 63 percent, was the third highest for postwar midterms.
41. *Los Angeles Times Poll Alert,* Study #480, December 18, 2002, 1.
42. "Six Tossups Muddy Forecast for the Senate," *CQ Weekly,* October 26, 2002, 2792–93; the exceptions were Minnesota, Arkansas, and South Dakota (lost by Republican challenger John Thune by 534 votes).
43. Jacobson, "A House and Senate Divided," 14–18.
44. The number of Democratic seats dropped from forty-six to thirty-seven in the

region, while the number of Republican seats grew from fifty to fifty-four; see Jacobson, "Terror, Terrain, and Turnout."

45. Jeffrey M. Jones, "Gender, Marriage Gaps Evident in Vote for Congress," Gallup News Service, October 11, 2002, available at http://www.gallup.com/poll/releases/pr021011.asp?Version=p; David W. Moore and Jeffrey M. Jones, "Higher Turnout among Republicans Key to Victory," Gallup News Service, November 7, 2002, available at http://www.gallup.com/poll/releases/pr021107.asp?Version=p.

46. Michael B. MacKuen, Robert S. Erikson, and James A. Stimson, "Macropartisanship," *American Political Science Review* 83 (December 1989): 1125–42; Robert S. Erikson, Michael B. MacKuen, and James A. Stimson, "What Moves Macropartisanship? A Response to Green, Palmquist, and Schickler," *American Political Science Review* 92 (December 1998): 901–12.

47. The Consumer Confidence Index is constructed from responses to five questions (regarding appraisal of current business and employment conditions, expectations regarding business conditions, employment, and total family income six months in the future) asked monthly of approximately five thousand households; see http://www.consumerresearchcenter.org/consumer_confidence/methodology.htm. The Index of Consumer Sentiment is based on a monthly survey of five hundred U.S. households conducted by the University of Michigan asking questions on personal finances and business and buying conditions; it is available at http://www.lim.com/newspage/michsent.htm.

48. Jeffrey M. Jones, "Poll Analyses: Americans Have Roughly Equal Views of Two Major Parties," The Gallup Organization, September 13, 2002, available at http://www.gallup.com/poll/releases/pr020913.asp.

49. See, for example, Donald Green, Bradley Palmquist, and Eric Schickler, *Partisan Hearts and Minds* (New Haven, Conn.: Yale University Press, 2002), 91

50. Among the 610 House voters in the panel component of the 2002 National Election Study, Democratic identification fell by 0.5 percentage points from 2000 (a net three respondents); Republican identification increased by 2.6 percentage points, mainly (thirteen of sixteen) via a net gain among respondents who had, in 2000, labeled themselves pure independents. These must be regarded as preliminary figures, because case weights were not included in the advance release of the study.

51. For the format of these questions see Table 8.2, section 4.

52. Compare the responses to issue questions in the CBS News/*New York Times* Polls conducted between February 2001 and January 2003.

53. CBS News/*New York Times* Poll, October 3–5, 2002, available at http://www.cbsnews.com/htdocs/c2k/pol106.pdf.

54. In the five CBS News/*New York Times* Polls taken between October 2001 and January 2002 that asked the relevant question, from 87 to 89 percent of re-

spondents approved of American military action in Afghanistan; it was approved by more than 80 percent of the Democrats as well as virtually all of the Republicans. Bush's approval ratings on his conduct of the Afghan campaign were equally high.

55. See the comprehensive selection of polling data on the issue at http://www.pollingreport.com/iraq.htm, January 28, 2003.

56. In late January 2003, in a question asking what the U.S. should do "now," 77 percent of Democrats favored finding a diplomatic solution, while 19 percent wanted to use military force; among Republicans, 44 percent favored diplomacy, 49 percent favored using force; CBS News/*New York Times* Poll, "Iraq and the U.N. Inspection Report," available at http://www.cbsnews.com/htdocs/CBSNews_polls/iraq_back0123.pdf.

57. The Gallup Organization, "Poll Analysis: Blacks Showing Decided Opposition to War," March 28, 2003, available at http://www.gallup.com/poll/releases/pr030328.asp.

58. CBS News.com, "Poll: Americans Say Use More Force," March 28, 2003, available at http://www.cbsnews.com/stories/2003/03/28/opinion/polls/main546585.shtml.

59. "*Washington Post*-ABC News Poll: War Support Widespread," April 7, 2003, available at http://www.washingtonpost.com/wp~srv/politics/polls/vault/stories/data040703.htm; CBS News Poll: Americans' Postwar Concerns, April 26–27, 2003, available at htttp://www.cbsnews.com/htdocs/CBSNews_polls/poll_iraq_0428.pdf.

60. The final preelection ratings of presidents since 1956 who have won reelection are as follows: Eisenhower, 67 (1956); Johnson, 74 (1964); Nixon, 56 (1972); Reagan, 58 (1984); and Clinton, 54 (1996). The losers have been Ford, 45 (1976); Carter, 37 (1980); and G. H. W. Bush, 35 (1992).

61. Five CBS News/*New York Times* Polls taken between April 2001 and November 2002 asked the question, "What do you think is more important—producing energy, protecting the environment?" The split among Democrats averaged 69 percent environment, 24 percent energy (the split among Republicans was 40 percent environment, 44 percent energy). The polls also asked what respondents thought Bush's priorities were; an average of 75 percent said energy, 11 percent environment.

62. Jacobson, "Terror, Terrain, and Turnout."

Chapter 9: President Bush and the Public

1. Data are drawn from the reports of ten media and commercial polling organizations that use the traditional Gallup Poll item, namely "Do you approve or disapprove of the way President Bush is handling his job as president?" to measure public support for President Bush. The charted coefficients are

averages—means—for those of the ten polls taken during a given week. These data are available at http://www.pollingreport.com.

2. Richard A. Brody, *Assessing the President: The Media, Elite Opinion, and Public Support* (Stanford, Calif.: Stanford University Press, 1991), Chap. 2.

3. James A. Stimson, "Public Support for American Presidents: A Cyclical Model," *Public Opinion Quarterly* 40 (1976): 1–21.

4. If we eliminate the first week's polls, the average for the next twenty-two weeks increases very slightly (55.46 percent to 55.8 percent), but the variance is substantially reduced, from $s2 = 9.1$ to $s2 = 6.77$. This difference approaches the commonly accepted standard of statistical significance ($t = 1.55$, $df = 31$; $.05 < p_t < .10$). If we eliminate the outlying value from the first week's polls, the difference between the averages for the remaining twenty-two weeks before June 30, 2001, and the following ten weeks (1.96 percentage points) is statistically significant ($t = 2.12$; $df = 30$; $p_t < .025$).

5. Nelson Polsby, *Congress and the Presidency* (Englewood Cliffs, N.J.: Prentice-Hall, 1964), 25.

6. John E. Mueller, *Presidents and Public Opinion* (New York: John Wiley, 1973).

7. Samuel H. Kernell, "Explaining Presidential Popularity," *American Political Science Review* 72 (1978): 506–22.

8. Richard A. Brody and Catherine R. Shapiro, "Policy Failure and Public Support: The Iran-Contra Affair and Public Assessments of President Reagan," *Political Behavior* 11 (1989): 353–69; see also Brody, *Assessing the President*, Chap. 3.

9. Brody and Shapiro, "Policy Failure and Public Support"; Brody, *Assessing the President*.

10. Richard A. Brody, "Crisis, War and Public Opinion: The Media and Public Support for the President," in *Taken By Storm: The Media, Public Opinion, and U.S. Foreign Policy in the Gulf War*, ed. W. Lance Bennett and David L. Paletz (Chicago: University of Chicago Press, 1994), 210–27.

11. Ibid., 220–21.

12. Brody, *Assessing the President*, Chap. 6.

13. The continuity may be a source of conceptual confusion, but the distinction is more than semantic. The consequences of policy success and failure are different in the rally and in the war/policy phases. Rallies boost support despite policy failure; indeed it is increased support in the face of policy failure that causes us to search for an explanation. In the war/policy phase we have no problem accounting for the movement of opinion.

14. Material in this section draws on my joint work with Simon Jackman. See Richard A. Brody and Simon Jackman, "President Bush, the Public and the 2002 Elections," *The Polling Report* 18, no. 17 (2002).

15. In Gallup data the mean level of approval for Republicans before September 11 was 89.1 percent; after September 11 it was 96.2 percent. For independents, be-

fore September 11 the mean was 52.8 September; after September 11 it was 76.1 percent. For Democrats, before September 11 the mean was 30.4 percent; after September 11 it was 64.2 percent.

16. Brody and Jackman, "President Bush, the Public and the 2002 Elections."
17. Figure 9.4 superimposes a regression line, in the form of an "expected approval value," on the data in Figure 9.1. Bush's approval level in the eighty-first week of his presidency—August 4–10, 2002—was 10 percentage points below the expected value.
18. Perhaps Grenada under the Reagan administration and Panama under the first President Bush provide examples. If they are precedents we would expect a rally in support when the Iraq War began. But Grenada and Panama came as a surprise to most Americans. By contrast, the public had a lot of time to consider our Iraq policy.

Chapter 10: A View from Within

1. Frum, *The Right Man.*
2. George E. Reedy, *The Twilight of the Presidency* (New York: Mentor, 1970), 88, 90.
3. John J. DiIulio, Jr., "Homeland Insecurity," *The Weekly Standard,* April 22, 2002, 15–16; "Mandate Mongering," *The Weekly Standard,* November 18, 2002, 18–20; "The Future of Compassion," *Philadelphia Inquirer,* December 1, 2002, C5; and "Why I Apologized to the Bush White House," *Philadelphia Daily News,* December 9, 2002, 19.
4. James Q. Wilson and John J. DiIulio, Jr., *American Government: Institutions and Policies,* 9th edition (Boston: Houghton-Mifflin, 2003), Chap. 12, and John J. DiIulio, Jr., "The Presidency and Political Science," *Polity,* Winter 1988, 427–38.
5. Gary King and Lyn Ragsdale, *The Elusive Executive: Discovering Statistical Patterns in the Presidency* (Washington, D.C.: Congressional Quarterly Press, 1988), 6.
6. James David Barber, *The Presidential Character: Predicting Performance in the White House* (Englewood Cliffs, N.J.: Prentice-Hall, 1972), 8, 11.
7. Ibid., 7, 8.
8. Ibid.
9. Tevi Troy, *Intellectuals and the American Presidency: Philosophers, Jesters, or Technicians?* (Lanham, Md.: Rowman and Littlefield, 2002).
10. George W. Bush, "The Future of Iraq," address delivered at the annual dinner of the American Enterprise Institute, Washington Hilton Hotel, Washington, D.C., February 26, 2003, 4.
11. John J. DiIulio, Jr., "What Is Compassionate Conservatism?" *The Weekly Standard,* June 12, 2000, and "Equal Protection Run Amok," *The Weekly Standard,* August 7, 2000, 25–26.

12. Joe Klein, "The Blinding Glare of His Certainty," *Time,* February 24, 2003, 19.
13. White House Office of Faith-Based and Community Initiatives, Unlevel Playing Field, August 2001.
14. Amy Goldstein, "On Medicare, Bush Left Details to Congress," *Washington Post,* April 20, A4.
15. Joe Klein, *The Natural: The Misunderstood Presidency of Bill Clinton* (New York: Doubleday, 2002), 156.
16. John W. Kingdon, *Agendas, Alternatives, and Public Policies,* 2nd edition (New York: Addison Wesley, 1995), 27.
17. Richard Rose, *The Postmodern President: The White House Meets the World* (Chatham, N.J.: Chatham House, 1988), 22.
18. Richard P. Nathan, *The Plot That Failed: Nixon and the Administrative Presidency* (New York: Wiley, 1975).
19. Stephen Hess, *Presidents and the Presidency* (Washington, D.C.: Brookings Institution, 1996), 102.
20. John J. DiIulio, Jr., Donald F. Kettl, and Gerald J. Garvey, *Improving Government Performance: An Owner's Manual* (Washington, D.C.: Brookings Institution, 1993).
21. Kingdon, *Agendas, Alternatives, and Public Policies,* 23–24
22. For a summary of Bush's initial public statements and directives on faith initiatives see John J. DiIulio, Jr., "Compassion in Truth and Action: How Sacred and Secular Places Serve Civic Purposes, and What Washington Should—and Should Not—Do to Help," address given at the annual meeting of the National Association of Evangelicals, Dallas, Texas, March 7, 2001, posted at the Web site of the Office of Faith-Based and Community Initiatives, www.whitehouse.gov, among the full roster of presidential public statements and speeches on the issue.
23. For a more detailed recitation of these principles see John J. DiIulio, Jr., "Government by Proxy: A Faithful Overview," *Harvard Law Review* 116, no. 5 (March 2003): 1271–84.
24. For an overview see Jo Renee Formicola and Mary Seegers, "The Bush Faith Initiative," *Journal of Church and State* 44 (Autumn 2002): 693–715.
25. DiIulio, "Homeland Insecurity."
26. Adriel Bettelheim and Jill Barshay, "Bush's Swift, Sweeping Plan Is Work Order for Congress," *Congressional Quarterly Weekly,* June 8, 2002, 1498–1504, and Bob Williams and David Nather, "Homeland Security Debate: Balancing Swift and Sure," *Congressional Quarterly Weekly,* June 22, 2002, 1642–47.
27. Bryan D. Jones, Tracy Sulkin, and Heather A. Larsen, "Policy Punctuations in American Political Institutions," *American Political Science Review* 97, no. 1 (February 2003): 159.
28. David Firestone, "Delay Rebuffs Move to Restore Lost Tax Credit," *New York Times,* June 4, 2003.

29. Donald E. Stokes and John J. DiIulio, Jr., "Valence Politics in Modern Elections," in *The 1992 Elections,* ed. Michael J. Nelson (Washington, D.C.: Congressional Quarterly Press, 1993), Chap. 1, and John J. DiIulio, Jr., "Valence Voters Are Not Fools," in *The 1996 Elections,* ed. Michael J. Nelson (Washington, D.C.: Congressional Quarterly Press, 1997), Chap. 10.
30. Howard Fineman, "How Bush Did It," *Newsweek,* November 18, 2002, 36.
31. Marc J, Hetherington and Michael J. Nelson, "Anatomy of a Rally Effect: George W. Bush and the War on Terrorism," *PS: Political Science and Politics* 36, no. 1 (January 2003): 40, 42.
32. "Terror War Tops Bush Re-election Agenda," Associated Press-General News, December 28, 2002.
33. Adam Clymer, "Democrats Seek Stronger Focus, and Money," *New York Times,* May 26, 2003.

About the Contributors

Richard A. Brody is emeritus professor of political science at Stanford University, where he taught from 1962 to 1994. His books include *Assessing the President: The Media, Elite Opinion, and Public Support* and *Political Persuasion and Attitude Change,* co-edited with Paul Sniderman and Diana Mutz. His *Reasoning and Choice: Explorations in Political Psychology,* co-authored with Paul Sniderman and Philip Tetlock, won the American Political Science Association's 1992 Woodrow Wilson award as the best political science book. He is a fellow of the American Academy of Arts and Sciences and the Center for Advanced Study in the Behavioral Sciences.

Ivo H. Daalder is a senior fellow in foreign policy studies at the Brookings Institution, where he also holds the Sydney Stein, Jr., Chair in International Security. A specialist in American foreign policy, European security, and national security affairs, Daalder is the author, co-author, and co-editor of nine books, including *Protecting the American Homeland, Winning Ugly: NATO's War to Save Kosovo, Getting to Dayton: The Making of America's Bosnia Policy, The United States and Europe in the Global Arena, Rethinking the Unthinkable: New Dimensions for Nuclear Arms Control, The Nature and Practice of Flexible Response: NATO Strategy and Theater Nuclear Forces since 1967,* and *Strategic Defenses in the 1990s: Criteria for Deployment.* Prior to joining Brookings, Daalder was associate professor at the University of

Maryland's School of Public Affairs, where he directed research at the Center for International and Security Studies. In 1995–96 he served as director for European affairs on President Clinton's National Security Council staff, where he was responsible for coordinating U.S. policy toward Bosnia. From 1998 to 2001 Daalder served as a member of the Study Group of the U.S. Commission on National Security/21st Century (the Hart-Rudman Commission), which engaged in a multiyear examination of U.S. national security requirements and institutions.

John J. DiIulio, Jr., is Frederic Fox Leadership Professor of Politics, Religion, and Civil Society and professor of political science at the University of Pennsylvania. At Penn he founded the Center for Research on Religion and Urban Civil Society and directs the Robert A. Fox Leadership Program. During his leave from Penn in academic year 2000–2001, he served as assistant to the president of the United States as the first director of the White House Office of Faith-Based and Community Initiatives. Professor DiIulio is a senior fellow at the Brookings Institution. From 1986 to 1999 he was professor of politics and public affairs at Princeton University. He is author, co-author, or editor of a dozen books, the most recent of which include *American Government: Institutions and Policies* (with James Q. Wilson, 8th edition); *What's God Got to Do with the American Experiment?* (with E. J. Dionne), and *Medicaid and Devolution* (with Frank Thompson).

John C. Fortier is a research associate at the American Enterprise Institute (AEI), where he is executive director of the Continuity of Government Commission and project manager of the Transition to Governing Project. He is also a regular participant in Election Watch, AEI's election analysis forum, and has provided radio and television commentary for British, Canadian, Dutch, and American networks. He has taught at Boston College, Harvard University, and the University of Delaware. Prior to going to AEI, he was a research associate at the Worcester Municipal Research Bureau in Massachusetts. Mr. Fortier was also the executive director of the Continuity of Government Commission (Cutler-Simpson Commission), which studied constitutional continuity of government institutions after a terrorist attack. He has published articles in the *Review of Politics, PS: Political Science and Politics, State Legislatures Magazine,* the *University of Michigan Journal of Law Reform,* and *Extensions* (a journal of the legislative studies section of the American Political Science Association).

Fred I. Greenstein is best known for his contributions to the systematic study of political psychology and its application to presidential decision making and leadership. After an initial appointment at Yale (1959–62), he taught at Wesleyan University (1962–73). In 1973 Greenstein joined Princeton University, where he directs the Program in Leadership Studies at the Woodrow Wilson School of Public and International Affairs. His early work included *Children and Politics and Personality and Politics: Problems of Evidence, Inference, and Conceptualization.* In the 1980s he applied political psychology to inquiries about American presidents and their advisers, which resulted in books such as *The Hidden-Hand Presidency: Eisenhower as Leader; How Presidents Test Reality: Decisions on Vietnam, 1954 and 1965* (with John P. Burke); *Leadership in the Modern Presidency;* and *The Presidential Difference: Leadership Style from FDR to Clinton.* Professor Greenstein is a fellow of the American Academy of Arts and Sciences.

Hugh Heclo is Clarence J. Robinson Professor at George Mason University and former professor of government at Harvard University. He teaches courses in American national politics, social welfare policy, and the philosophy of history, as well as religion and politics. His book *Modern Social Politics* received the 1974 Woodrow Wilson award from the American Political Science Association for the best book on government, politics, or international affairs. In 1976 his co-authored *Comparative Public Policy* received the Gladys Kammerer Award for the best book on national policy. His Brookings Institution volume *A Government of Strangers* won the National Academy of Public Administration's Louis Brownlow award for the best book in public administration. He was contributing senior editor of *Religion Reenters the Public Square.* Professor Heclo is a fellow of the American Academy of Arts and Sciences and the National Academy of Public Administration.

Karen M. Hult is professor of political science and adjunct faculty member at the Center for Public Administration and Policy at Virginia Polytechnic Institute and State University, where she teaches courses in U.S. politics and policy, organization theory, and research design. Previously she taught at Pomona College and the Claremont Graduate School; she also served as director of the Program in Public Policy Analysis at Pomona College in 1988–90. Professor Hult is the author of *Agency Merger and Bureaucratic Redesign* and the co-author, with Charles E. Walcott, of *Governing Public Organizations, Governing the White House: From Hoover through LBJ* (winner of the 1996 Richard E. Neustadt Award) and *Empowering the*

White House: Governance under Nixon, Ford, and Carter. Her articles have appeared in *Administration and Society;* the *American Journal of Political Science;* the *Policy Studies Journal; Polity, Congress & the Presidency;* the *Presidential Studies Quarterly;* and other scholarly journals.

Gary C. Jacobson is professor of political science at the University of California, San Diego, where he has taught since 1979. He has also taught at the University of California, Riverside; Yale University; and Stanford University. Professor Jacobson specializes in the study of U.S. elections, parties, interest groups, and Congress. He is the author of *Money in Congressional Elections, The Politics of Congressional Elections* (5th ed.), and *The Electoral Origins of Divided Government* and co-author of *Strategy and Choice in Congressional Elections* (2nd ed.) and *The Logic of American Politics* (2nd ed.). He is a fellow of the American Academy of Arts and Sciences.

Charles O. Jones is Hawkins Professor Emeritus of Political Science at the University of Wisconsin–Madison and a nonresident senior fellow in the Governmental Studies Program at the Brookings Institution. In 1994–95 he was the Douglas Dillon Visiting Fellow in Governmental Studies at Brookings. Previously he taught at Wellesley College and the Universities of Arizona, Pittsburgh, and Virginia. In 1998–99 he was the John M. Olin Professor of American Government at Nuffield College, Oxford University. Professor Jones's most recent books focus on the presidency and Congress: *The Trusteeship Presidency: Jimmy Carter and the United States Congress; The Reagan Legacy: Promise and Performance; The Presidency in a Separated System* (which won the Richard E. Neustadt Prize); *Separate but Equal Branches: Congress and the Presidency; Passages to the Presidency: From Campaigning to Governing; Clinton and Congress, 1993–1996: Risk, Restoration, and Reelection;* and *Preparing to Be President: The Memos of Richard E. Neustadt.* Between 1975 and 1981 he was editor of the *American Political Science Review;* he has also served as co-editor of the *Legislative Studies Quarterly.* He is a fellow of the American Academy of Arts and Sciences.

James M. Lindsay is deputy director and senior fellow in the Foreign Policy Studies Program at the Brookings Institution. His main research interests are the domestic politics of foreign policy, national missile defense, and globalization. Before joining Brookings, he was professor of political science at the University of Iowa. In 1996–97 he was director for global issues and multilateral affairs on the staff of the National Security Council. His responsibilities there included United Nations reform, State Department reorganization, and funding for international affairs. He has also served as a consultant to the United States Commission on National Security/21st Century (Hart-Rudman Commission). He has authored, co-authored, or edited thirteen books and more than fifty journal articles and book chapters on various aspects of American foreign policy and international relations. His books include *Defending America: The Case for Limited National Missile Defense* (with Michael E. O'Hanlon), *U.S. Foreign Policy after the Cold War* (with Randall B. Ripley), *Congress and the Politics of U.S. Foreign Policy, Congress Resurgent: Foreign and Defense Policy on Capitol Hill* (with Randall B. Ripley), and *Congress and Nuclear Weapons.*

Norman J. Ornstein is a resident scholar at the American Enterprise Institute in Washington, D.C., where he researches politics, Congress, and elections. He is the director of the Transition to Governing Project, founder of the Campaign Finance Reform Working Group, and a senior adviser for the Pew Research Center for the People and the Press. He is an elections analyst for CBS News, and his regular column, "Congress Inside Out," appears in *Roll Call.* Between 1971 and 1988 he was on the political science faculties of Catholic University of America and the Johns Hopkins University. His books include *Lessons and Legacies: Farewell Addresses from the Senate, Permanent Democratic Congress,* and *Campaign Finance* (with Jeremy Pope), and he was editor of *Permanent Campaign and Its Future* (with Thomas E. Mann).

Allen Schick is Distinguished University Professor of Public Policy at the University of Maryland and visiting fellow at the Brookings Institution. He previously served at the Congressional Research Service and taught at Tufts University. Professor Schick specializes in political institutions, public finance, and budget policy and politics. His most recent books include *The Federal Budget: Politics, Policy, and Process, A Contemporary Approach to Public Expenditure Management,* and *Modern Budgeting.* He has also served as chief consultant to the New Zealand government on its reform of the public sector.

Index

Page numbers for entries occurring in figures are followed by an *f*; those for entries occurring in notes are followed by an *n*; and those for entries occurring in tables are followed by a *t*.